The Cyberspace Handbook

D0222964

The Cyberspace Handbook is a comprehensive guide to all aspects of new media, information technologies and the Internet. It gives an overview of the economic, political, social and cultural contexts of cyberspace, and provides practical advice on using new technologies for research, communication and publication.

The Cyberspace Handbook explores how cyberspace has been constructed, as well as its functions, which range from providing us with immediate news to immersive games and virtual reality. *The Cyberspace Handbook* also addresses the challenges raised by computer and communications technologies in the areas of copyright and cybercrime, as well as key skills in employing the Internet for research or writing and designing for the Web.

The Cyberspace Handbook includes:

- A glossary of over 80 key terms
- A list of over 90 web resources for news and entertainment, new media and web development, education and reference, and Internet and web information
- Specialist chapters on web design and journalism and writing for the Web
- Over 30 illustrations of Internet material and software applications

Jason Whittaker teaches journalism and new media at Falmouth College of Arts, and has been a computer journalist for nearly a decade. His previous publications include *Web Production for Writers and Journalists* and *The Internet: The Basics*, also published by Routledge.

Media Practice

Edited by James Curran, Goldsmiths College, University of London

The *Media Practice* handbooks are comprehensive resource books for students of media and journalism, and for anyone planning a career as a media professional. Each handbook combines a clear introduction to understanding how the media work with practical information about the structure, processes and skills involved in working in today's media industries, providing not only a guide on 'how to do it' but also a critical reflection on contemporary media practice.

Also in this series:

To Sam

Contents

....

Illustrations

....

Figures

....

Tables

Preface

....

This book is intended as a course book for students of new media on the relatively recent expansion of IT and telecommunications-related phenomena which can be gathered together under the heading of cyberspace. That heading provides, in many respects, a flag of convenience, but one that also allows us to sail to many ports. As such, it is my hope that this book will provide resources for students and readers interested in the technologies, sociology, business and cultural study of cyberspace, the Internet and information technologies in general.

The book is arranged into four main parts. Part I, 'Introduction and contexts', begins by attempting to define what is meant by cyberspace, as well as to delineate in broad terms its main components. In Part II, 'Using cyberspace', the reader will find some information on gaining practical benefits from the Internet in particular, as well as more detailed explanations of the technologies that have driven cyberspace forward. Part III, 'Reading/writing cyberspace', concentrates on some of the features of new technologies that are particularly pertinent to students engaged in media research (in the widest sense), including new forms of journalism, researching the Internet itself and an introduction to Web design. Finally, in Part IV, 'Regulations, institutions and ethics', *The Cyberspace Handbook* concerns itself with some of the wider social and ethical implications of new technologies.

I first became involved with those new technologies on a professional level in the early 1990s, catching the crest of a wave that saw almost limitless potential in what – with hindsight – we can see was part of the dotcom bubble. While the hype of the late 1990s has often turned to gloom, however, it would be better to distinguish the dire effects of greed caused by dotcom mania as opposed to the more realistic potential offered by information technologies and telecommunications. I hope that this book will serve to provide readers with a stronger and more realistic base from which to appraise the effects and impact of cyberspace in all its forms.

Links to resources and sites mentioned in the text of this book may also be viewed at the companion website for this book at www.producing.routledge. com/cyberspace/default.htm

The Cyberspace Handbook

Jason Whittaker

Routledge
Taylor & Francis Group

LONDON AND NEW YORK

First published 2004
by Routledge
11 New Fetter Lane, London EC4P 4EE

Simultaneously published in the USA and Canada
by Routledge
29 West 35th Street, New York, NY 10001

Routledge is an imprint of the Taylor & Francis Group

Typeset in Times and DIN by Keystroke, Jacaranda Lodge, Wolverhampton
Printed and bound in Great Britain by MPG Books Ltd, Bodmin, Cornwall

British Library Cataloguing in Publication Data
A catalogue record for this book is available from the British Library

Library of Congress Cataloging in Publication Data
A catalog record for this book has been requested

ISBN 0–415–16835–X (hbk)
ISBN 0–415–16836–8 (pbk)

Acknowledgements

....

The authors would like to acknowledge friends and colleagues who helped in the production of this book, including Christopher Cudmore at Routledge, who initially mooted the idea, and Kate Ahl, who saw the final version through to completion. We would particularly like to thank Andrew Charlesworth, Emma Northam, Rosie Haworth, Ursula Seymour, Jim Hall, Denis Gartside, Mark Douglas, Clarissa Smith, Alex Goody and Catherine Spooner for their suggestions (or for suffering in silence when we insisted on working through our own ideas), as well as students who often provide the impetus for exploring new areas. Finally, but by no means least, this book could not have been written without the long-standing patience and support of my wife Sam.

Part I

Introduction and contexts

1 Cyberspace, digital media and the Internet

What is cyberspace?

When asked to define cyberspace, most people will probably envisage a personal computer connected to the Internet. Important as both these technologies are to our concept of cyberspace, it is clear that such elements constitute only a very small part of the wider political, social, economic, cultural and financial networks that constitute what we can call *cyberspace*. Cyberspace is not merely hardware, but a series of symbolic definitions, or 'tropes' as David Bell (2001) refers to them, that constitute a network of ideas as much as the communication of bits.

Imagine the following: a technologically savvy female student is speaking to a friend on her mobile phone while drawing money from a cash machine. Both the money and the conversation share a common purpose – visiting the cinema to watch a Hollywood blockbuster – but while the woman knows which film she wishes to watch (she has, after all, read a number of previews recommending the movie), she is not sure what time it is playing. Her friend has just checked listings for the nearby multiplex online and reminded her that she also needs to contact customer services for the company that made her MP3 player, which has developed a fault. She could send them an email, but as they have a 24-hour helpline it will probably be simpler to phone.

Cyberspace is one name for the technological glue that binds many of these elements together. Telephone masts and satellite connect the voice communication between the two friends, while similar networks link the woman to databases that hold details on her finances (including potential information on spending activities and personal financial ratings if she uses debit and credit cards to make purchases). Movie magic is not something particularly new to the age of cyberspace, but the film she wishes to see is of a kind that regularly uses digital effects to fill in details for the camera – special effects, furthermore, that often do not wish to draw attention to their own pyrotechnics but instead pass themselves off as reflections of the real world. As a young woman, she has grown up in a school environment where information and communication technology (ICT) is increasingly the norm for delivering many parts of education, and her music player will have probably been constructed in southeast Asia – probably China or Taiwan – while there is a good chance that the call centre which handles her request is based in India. Finally, while her friend could easily check the local newspaper for film times, this is the sort of information that indicates the commonplace, even banal, uses to which the Internet is put on a daily basis.

It is now possible to travel to more parts of the world than ever before, a world in which trade is increasingly globalised and, more than ever, dependent on services and information as much as on the trade of material goods. And while we tend to still think of books, films and photographs as *things*, information technology – in particular the Internet – is transforming our view of communications into texts and images that can be more easily downloaded as mutable bits rather than immutable atoms.

The term 'cyberspace' was invented by William Gibson in his cyberpunk novel, *Neuromancer*:

> The matrix has its roots in primitive arcade games . . . in early graphics programs and military experimentation with cranial jacks. . . . Cyberspace. A consensual hallucination experienced daily by billions of legitimate operators, in every nation, by children being taught mathematical concepts. . . . A graphic representation of data abstracted from the banks of every computer in the human system. Unthinkable complexity. Lines of light ranged in the nonspace of the mind, clusters and constellations of data. Like city lights, receding.
>
> (1984: 67)

Part of the success of Gibson's novel lay in the fact that he was able to provide expression to the emerging technologies (personal computers, the Internet, computer graphics and virtual reality) that were beginning to capture the popular imagination. Gibson, as poetic futurologist of cyberspace, provided a vision of the matrix that was much more than the bare technical bones of the putative Internet: for him, cyberspace is technical complexity – computer-generated graphical representations of data that are transferred across networks – but is also framed by psychology, epistemology, juridical and social systems. It is taught to children, a 'consensual hallucination' shared by users defined by their relation to legitimate (and also, the source of many of Gibson's plots, criminal) sources of power. Such power can be political, military and commercial, the huge transnational conglomerates that fill the backgrounds of his novels.

As Katherine Hayles (1996) points out, Gibson's vision of cyberspace did not spring out of nothing, but emerged from technical and social innovations that changed our worldview in the 1980s and 1990s, some of the consequences of which will be explored in this book. Outside science fiction, then, we encounter cyberspace most obviously when we use the Internet from a personal computer or, increasingly, a handheld device or our television sets. It integrates with older communication technologies, such as the telephone, and draws on theoretical conceptions of information and space that have enabled such things as communication and representation to be digitised and networked. We participate in cyberspace when we talk across a GSM phone network, change channels on a digital television set, or access our finances from an ATM. In its widest sense, then, cyberspace is space transformed by networks of information and communication. As Dodge and Kitchin (2001: 1) point out:

> At present, cyberspace does not consist of one homogeneous space; it is a myriad of rapidly expanding cyberspaces, each providing a different form of digital interaction and communication. In general, these spaces can be categorised into those existing within the technologies of the Internet, those within virtual reality, and conventional telecommunications such as the phone and the fax, although because there is a rapid convergence of technologies new hybrid spaces are emerging.

Margaret Wertheim, in *The Pearly Gates of Cyberspace* (1999), draws attention to the fact that the human conception of space has not been fixed throughout history. The world of the Middle Ages, at the centre of the universe and connected to higher spiritual spheres or planes, was transformed by a series of revolutions from the Renaissance on due to discoveries in the solar system as well as transformations of perception and perspective. From the sixteenth century, we have become used to changing discernments of our psychological, philosophical and scientific world, but, suggests Wertheim, perhaps the most significant change was from the perception of ourselves as embedded in spaces of both body and soul to a universe in which the material body alone was important. Some of the claims made for cyberspace revolve around the recognition that if not the soul then at least the perceiving psyche is integral to our conception of the technospaces in which we live.

The emergence of cyberspace

One way to envisage the changes made to the practice of everyday life by cyberspace in all its forms is to compare current technologies to those available immediately after the Second World War. This was the point when many information and computer technologies came into existence, the history of which has been explored by a number of commentators such as Flichy (2002) and Winston (1998).

Fundamental to cyberspace is telecommunications, literally communication over a distance. This itself is nothing new: telegraph, in the mid-nineteenth century, established a vital communications network across the British Empire, replacing or supplementing other long-distance systems already in place such as mail and

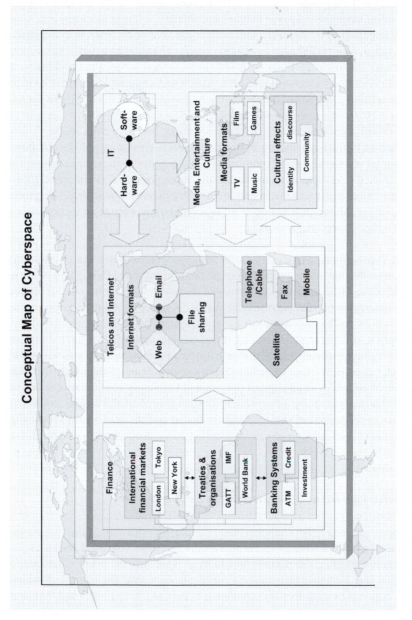

Conceptual Map of Cyberspace

Figure 1.1 A conceptual map of some of the elements of cyberspace.

semaphore, while the end of the nineteenth century saw the invention of the telephone. Until the 1960s, however, telephones even in the West were in short supply, extremely expensive, and – more importantly – connections still had to be made manually for anything other than local calls. Ironically, answering machines and even primitive faxes were available by the 1950s, but until automation of telephone exchanges was implemented fully, telecommunications faced a huge bottleneck. Transatlantic communication had long been possible, with Atlantic telegraph cables having been laid during the mid-nineteenth century, but the space race of the 1950s began the mobilisation of a geostationary satellite system that would provide comprehensive contact worldwide.

The post-war entertainment boom was, of course, only just beginning in certain areas such as television: transformations in printing during the inter-war period made colour reproduction of glossy magazines simpler than ever, although wartime rationing represented a retrograde movement. Television was only just starting to emerge as a popular mass medium in the West at this time: at the beginning of 1952, for example, there were only 600,000 television licences in the UK, although a similar number were sold in the months preceding the Queen's coronation that year, an event watched by an estimated 20 million people and which marked the emergence of TV as a popular medium. Radio, long favoured in the home, also shifted from valves to transistors after 1947: in the long term, this enabled more portable sets and reduced their price considerably, although the first to go on sale in 1954 were still extremely expensive.

Throughout the early 1950s, most electronic and communication equipment still used valves: the triode vacuum valve, invented by Lee de Forest in 1906, enabled a signal in one circuit to control the current in another circuit, giving rise to effective electronics. Manufacture was largely a manual process and miniaturisation was restricted, meaning that there was a limit to how cheaply these important components could be reproduced. In addition to being limited in terms of size and cost, each valve also consumed at least two watts on average, so the move from valves to transistors, coupled with the integrated circuit after 1959, meant that components and interconnections could be mass produced as single, relatively cheap items.

Technology is not the only component of cyberspace; indeed, of the three elements we have briefly considered here – computer, telecommunication and entertainment technologies – the latter is probably most important insofar as it represents a shift in social perceptions of ourselves as consumers. Post-war innovations, however, were important for the following, interrelated reasons: miniaturisation (particularly following the invention of the transistor and integrated circuit), coupled with increased automation of electronics and telecommunications, effected huge increases in production capacity coupled with rapidly falling costs. More and more electronics became *consumer* electronics, indicating the ways and means by which cyberspace technologies could infiltrate daily life to an ever-greater degree.

Imagining the future

Just as the term 'cyberspace' was coined by a science fiction writer, so SF in film and literature is often the best place to begin looking for blue-sky thinking on the way that cyberspace will exist in the future.

Future gazing has been a favourite activity of the twentieth century. Jules Verne and H.G. Wells outlined their visions of impending decades and centuries, and – particularly following the Second World War – the information technologies and telecommunication networks that constitute cyberspace have played an important role. Often the vision that is important to the development of narratives is far from the mark: not only was man not travelling to the further reaches of the solar system in 2001, but the superior AI of HAL also has yet to emerge in the near millennium. At the same time, many writers and film-makers have attempted to capture details of the present that may inform the future, such as the integrated computer and entertainment systems used in Ridley Scott's *Blade Runner*, or the miniature communication devices in various *Star Trek* television episodes of the 1960s that look surprisingly similar to the mobile phones and handheld computers of the 1990s and the new century.

Probably the most detailed recent vision, elements of which are more than possible in the next few decades, was the 2002 Steven Spielberg film *Minority Report*, adapted from a book by Philip K. Dick. The potential future shock realism of the film was due to the fact that the film's production designer, Alex McDowell, had consulted a wide range of experts from the worlds of computing, car design, robotics and even advertising (McIntosh and Schofield 2002). Thus, for example, when John Anderton is besieged by advertising screens appealing to him directly as he attempts to evade his former colleagues ('John Anderton: you could use a Guinness right now'), these ideas were drawn from technologies – such as retinal scanning and databases of consumers' preferences – that already exist. Likewise, when Anderton is on a subway train and a fellow passenger's newspaper is updated to show the face of the wanted fugitive, the technology that will make digital paper linked wirelessly to content providers widely available is already underway at Xerox PARC, where developers are working on a project called Gyricon, a flexible plastic containing millions of multi-coloured beads suspended in an oil-filled cavity that can be manipulated by electrical power.

Some elements of the film, such as hundreds of cars traversing buildings verti-cally, or fully autonomous spider robots, are, for the time being at least, purely the stuff of fantasy. Even technologies such as those listed above, while perfectly possible, do not operate in a social and psychological limbo: thus, for example, while it may be technically possible to provide personalised advertising in the very near future, concerns over privacy and even advertisers' fears that consumers will be repulsed by such tactics are larger obstacles to their widespread adoption. McIntosh and Schofield point to one example in the film where technical feasibility does not automatically lead to usability: Jetpacks, which had their original inspiration in the Buck Rogers comic books of the 1920s, have been designed and engineered, notably the Bell rocket belt designed by Wendell Moore at Bell Aircraft in the 1950s or, more recently, the SoloTek, created by the company Millennium Jet, but have all proved too dangerous or costly to be effective.

Cyberspace and cybernetics

The term 'cyberspace', invented by Gibson, obviously owes much to the term 'cybernetics', coined by Norbert Wiener in 1948. Cybernetics is the science of control theory applied to complex systems, and was defined by Wiener as 'the science of control or communication, in the animal and the machine', from *kubernetes*, the Greek for 'steersman' or 'pilot'. Cybernetics is a theory of machines and systems that treats not things but ways of behaving: any system that is not spiralling out of control or in a state of collapse must be self-regulating to some degree, and it is how such systems are controlled or regulated that is of interest to cybernetics. At its simplest, a cybernetic system works like a thermostat, turning heat on or off when a system falls or rises to a certain point.

Cybernetic theory has been applied far beyond its original application in systems science, for example, in the field of regulation and social phenomena (Dunsire 1993; Beer 1994). Dunsire, for example, has identified three main strategies of control that may be employed by governmental regulators: the first is simple steering, where policy-makers intervene on an ad hoc basis; more complex is homeostasis, where alterations are made to correct a system that deviates from a desired state or range of states; and finally the calibration, or balancing, of opposing forces such as requirements of equal access to information sources versus the demands of the free market. The more complex a system, the more complex the system of regulation is likely to be, so that single controllers are unlikely to be sufficient.

In 1991, Timothy Leary expounded an entertaining – if limited – theory of cyberpunks as 'reality pilots', guiding the rest of us to decentralised self-reliance (returning to the original meaning of the *kubernetes*, as opposed to the Latin *gubernare*, 'to govern'). Leary opposed his vision of cybernetics to refer to self-organisation and self-direction, as opposed to systems of control and governance. The opposition is not as clear as Leary supposes: Wiener's theory of cybernetic systems is that ultimately they are *self*-controlling. The important contribution of cybernetics to notions of cyberspace is that this is a complex system of fields or possibilities that will adapt and change, and redirect in order to continue functioning, the analogy being to a living organism or multifarious social system.

Cyberspace and ICT

While we have already seen that cyberspace is much more than simply information and communication technologies (ICT) – many of which will be examined in

greater detail in Chapter 5 – its relationship to technology is profound. As Sally
Munt (2001: 6) observes:

> Science and technology have had a profound effect on the way humans
> perceive space and time – think, for example, of the way information
> technologies such as the telephone have reduced our former perception of the
> world as inaccessible, unknowable and exotic to a sensibility of nearness,
> friendliness, fellowship and instantaneity (the so-called 'global village'). Think
> how the invention of the microchip opened up the 'inner worlds' of the body.

As Lovelock and Ure (2002) point out, the explosion of new media, the Internet
and thus cyberspace may be partly explained by three observed factors, popularly
labelled 'laws'; that is, Moore's law, Metcalfe's law and Gilder's law. Moore's
law, named after one of the co-founders of Intel, Gordon Moore, and first expressed
in 1964, stated that the number of transistors that could be etched on to a computer
chip would double every eighteen months; since then (and with some adjustments
to the time scale), this has commonly been interpreted to mean that computer power
doubles every year to a year and a half.

Significant as it is, Moore's law contributed to the computer boom of the 1980s
and 1990s but is perhaps less important overall than Metcalfe's law, so called after
Bob Metcalfe, the inventor of Ethernet. Metcalfe observed that the value of a
network is proportional to the square of the number of people using it; that is, the
rate of return from a network increases exponentially as more and more people
connect to it – doubling the number of users from two to four does not merely
double its value, but increases it eightfold. Known as the 'network effect', this is
often linked to Gilder's law, named after the futurologist George Gilder who has
predicted that total bandwidth will triple every year for the next twenty-five years.

These three laws are often treated as technological imperatives, deterministic
laws that must be obeyed in a similar manner to Newton's observation that every
action has an equal and opposite reaction. This is not so: a number of commentators
(Chapman 1994; Kroker and Kroker 1996; Wilson 1997) have warned of the
dangers of isolating technology from social and historical conditions. Machines –
at least for the moment – do not evolve without human interaction and the requirements of governments, business and other social groups. Munt also points out that
there is a much more complex philosophical relationship between the laws of
science and human beliefs, that 'the perspectives of science are thought-structures,
that is ideologies, which organize the world into sets of believable fictions' (2001:
7). Munt's ideas owe much to Michel Foucault and Thomas Kuhn, that scientific
knowledge relies on comprehensible models or 'paradigms' which are partial
in their representation of the world and hence ideological: such observations on
the nature of scientific knowledge have been criticised, particularly from within
the scientific community, but at the very least the discovery of scientific 'truth' is
frequently dependent on institutions and practices (universities, grants, a publishing
industry) that are demonstrably tied to less pure ideologies.

Cyberspace and society

In addition to technologies and media, any text dealing with cyberspace must devote attention to the effect of new technologies on society and culture, which will be the focus of the following two chapters. What Castells (1997, 2001) refers to as a 'network society' is important not merely because computers and communications networks have been introduced into the home and workplace, but because such commodities as email and ecommerce are also transforming working and living relations. As he observes in *The Internet Galaxy* (2001: 1):

> The Internet is the fabric of our lives. If information technology is the present-day equivalent of electricity in the industrial era, in our age the Internet could be likened to both the electrical grid and the electric engine because of its ability to distribute the power of information throughout the entire realm of human society. Furthermore, as new technologies of energy generation and distribution make possible the factory and the large corporation as the organisational foundations of industrial society, the Internet is the technological basis for the organisational form of the Information Age: the network.

MacKenzie and Wacjman (1999) point out that most assumptions about the relationship between technology and society are driven by 'technological determinism', the notion that contact between the two is one-way and that technology shapes – even causes – social interactions. This, as has already been suggested in this chapter, is extremely simplistic and contributes to a passive approach, that our choice as consumers at most consists of accepting or adapting to new technologies as they come online. Castells (2001: 36) agrees with this: 'Technological systems are socially produced. Social production is culturally informed. The Internet is no exception.'

One example of the intricacy of social, economic, political and technological relations centres on the powerhouse of the ICT revolution – the microchip. Invented by Intel in 1971, huge improvements in miniaturisation have resulted in vast leaps forward in processing power as more and more components can be built into each chip. The results of this have been a steady decline (in real terms) of the price of computers as their capacity has doubled every eighteen months or so. And yet, as Russell Cowburn of Durham University points out, the apparently technologically deterministic first Moore's law is accompanied by what has become known as Moore's second law: that the cost of a chip-manufacturing/fabrication plant, or fab, doubles every three years, so that the cost of constructing such a fab in a decade's time could cost up to $500 billion (cited in Akass 2003).

One of the consequences of this is that sales of one generation of processors finances research and production of the next. If research and development costs cannot be recouped, technology does not continue its inevitable progress. Something close to this has been seen in the shift from second-generation mobile phones to a third generation (3G): successful attempts by governments such as those in the UK to charge heavy fees for licences resulted in a stalled roll-out of 3G devices – particularly when it became clear that consumers did not wish to pay the excessive prices required of them. In such situations, new technology is affected by economics, government policy and consumer trends.

In their introductory essay to *The Handbook of New Media* (2002), Leah Lievrouw and Sonia Livingstone outline some of the main approaches to the study of new media that include sociology (such as Daniel Bell's arguments around 'post-industrial society'), social psychology, political economy, management and communication theory, and cultural studies as well as more traditional approaches based on systems engineering and analysis. They suggest two broad categories to the study of new media and ICT: researchers interested in technological, economic and behavioural issues have tended to concentrate on systems, industry structures and ownership, or the psychology of users, while researchers from a critical or cultural studies background focus more on new media content and its forms (2002: 5).

Cyberspace and cyberculture

We shall be exploring another important relationship – that between cyberspace and digital or new media – in the following section, but before doing so it is worth pausing for a moment to highlight the significance of cultural studies in this area, what is often referred to as 'cyberculture'. While not coterminous, cultural studies and the concerns of new media have often overlapped and, once the study of ICT moved outside specialist computing and engineering departments, it was often eagerly seized upon by those who had made a study – social, textual and psychological – of other media formats such as television, magazines and films.

Cybercultural concerns recur repeatedly throughout this book, complementing its interest in describing new technologies. Recent significant work in the area includes David Bell and Barbara Kennedy's *Cybercultures Reader* (2000), as well as Bell's *Introduction to Cybercultures* (2001), David Gauntlett's collection of essays on *Web.studies* (2000a), and Andrew Herman and Thomas Swift's *The Worldwide Web and Contemporary Cultural Theory* (2000). Some of the main contributions made by cultural theorists to the study of cyberculture deal with themes around configurations, representations and perceptions of bodies and identities, the significance of social formations such as virtual communities, and the discourses of cyberspace in popular culture and elsewhere.

Stories of cyberspace

One useful way of thinking about cyberspace and cyberculture, proposed by David Bell (2001), is as a series of stories. Bell distinguishes what he sees as three main types of narrative by means of which we attempt to understand cyberspace: material stories, symbolic stories and experiential stories.

Material stories include histories of technology – 'the story of *how it came to be what it is*' (2001: 8) – and in this category Bell includes the various histories of the Internet that have proliferated in recent years, as well as accounts of virtual reality and computing itself, of which Paul Edwards' *The Closed World* (1997) is an excellent example. Such histories tend to concentrate on the innovations implemented by scientists and engineers, often due to the intervention of the military. These stories tend to fall into Lievrouw and Livingstone's definitions of technological and economic research, dealing with political economies of technology and its social implications for labour and consumption, as well as counter-cultural aspects associated with the personal computer and Internet. In this chapter, we have seen material stories of cyberspace associated with its emergence, and will deal with a number of other material accounts related to the growth and development of the Internet and cyberspace more generally in Part I of this book.

Symbolic stories include literary and generic accounts, most notably in cyberpunk but also SF and other forms of speculative fiction. Such symbolic retellings are an important source of our myths of cyberspace (to such an extent, suggest some critics, that those myths have obscured the reality of cyberspace), though they are not the only source. Popular culture provides another reference point for our understanding of cyberspace, not merely insofar as the Internet provides the ultimate means for disseminating urban myths, but also because films, television and newspaper stories often provide us with the terminology and frameworks to discuss our shared experiences of new technologies.

This leads on to Bell's third category – experiential stories, where material and symbolic stories are folded into their everyday use. Such experiential descriptions and analyses have become one of the most fruitful areas of the cultural study of cyberspace at the end of the 1990s, concentrating on the more ordinary (but often more profound) aspects of ICT in daily life. Bell provides a fairly extensive account of his own relations with computers, as well as examples of how other users such as Sean Cubitt (1998) come into contact with the human–computer interface. Computer games, the ease with which we transform ourselves into mouse-wielding cyborgs, and our experiences with technologies in areas such as medicine – these and many other areas have important effects on our understanding of ourselves as citizens, consumers and subjects into the twenty-first century.

Digital media and communication

Contemporary notions of cyberspace have been tied up with the development of digital media and communication technologies, a means of quantifying information so that it can be transmitted as a series of bits. In contrast to analog information, which records a continuous stream or spectrum of data, digital descriptions of data store or transmit those data as a sequence of discrete symbols from a finite set. Analog data are best thought of as a wave, or rolling down a hill; digital data break down the wave into finite quantities, similar to walking down steps. Computers do not have to be digital – early computers were analog, measuring fluctuations in a current, and electronic equipment often still makes use of analog systems. Digitisation, however, samples signals and, if such sampling is accurate or closely spaced enough, can be used to re-create an apparently perfect replica of that signal: the virtue of digital over analog systems is that because the digit is a symbol of the signal it can be converted more easily into another format.

An important contribution to computing has been the use of binary code or, more specifically, the binary digit – the bit. This is conventionally represented by the numbers 1 and 0, which in turn represent a current passed through a transistor or circuit: if a charge is present, this is represented by 1, otherwise it is a 0. What is important here is how binary digits can then be used to quantify information, that numbers can be treated as symbols to be manipulated, after the work of George Boole, who used such symbols to define logical statements as true or false. The transition from number-cruncher to symbol-manipulator was recognised by Alan Turing in his essay 'On computable numbers' as the first step to building a general purpose computing machine. In the words of Nicholas Negroponte (1995: 14):

> A bit has no color, size, or weight, and it can travel at the speed of light. It is the smallest atomic element in the DNA of information. It is a state of being: on or off, true or false, up or down, in or out, black or white. For practical purposes we consider a bit to be a 1 or a 0. The meaning of the 1 or 0 is a separate matter.

Because certain problems, or algorithms (sets of rules for defining and solving problems in a finite number of steps) can be represented by such symbols, they can be converted into digital forms; this is, however, not true of all problems.

New media and ICT

Another important aspect of cyberspace is its relationship to media, both media forms, particularly those associated with the loose category, 'new media', and *the* media – the press, television, film and publications online that constitutes what is often referred to as the public sphere. The relationship with the latter is the focus of Chapter 14 on virtual communities and online public spheres, while we deal with a number of new media formats throughout this book – film, video and games as well as the obvious formats associated with the Internet.

Lievrouw and Livingstone (2002) indicate how the phrase 'new media' is used as shorthand for cultural and technological industries associated with multimedia, entertainment and ecommerce, all of which are predicated in some shape or fashion on digital technologies. As Wise points out, the closely associated term 'multimedia' was originally devised as a marketing concept for Apple's Multimedia Lab (Wise 2002: 46) before expanding into business, entertainment, training and consumer formats such as kiosks, CD-ROM and DVD. Is there anything distinctive about such new media? Since Wilbur Schramm's work in the 1970s, one attempt to classify difference between new media and old is in terms of those which may combine parallel human sensory perception, such as combining visuals and sound, or provide two-way (duplex) as opposed to one-way (simplex) transmission.

The combination of human sensory perception cannot be restricted to new media: while it is rare for inanimate media to combine such effects before the twentieth century (books may mix words and images, but they do not combine audio and visual perception), this was not the case with live performances such as theatre; the same is true of duplex versus simplex transmission. If we leave live performance outside the equation, however, it is extremely rare for truly multimedia media prior to the twentieth century, and the claim often made for computer-based or digital media is that they encourage user participation and interaction. Multimedia, then, may be a feature of twentieth-century phenomena such as cinema and television, but it is mainly with the digital media of the past two to three decades that such multiple sensory experiences have been combined with interactivity.

At the beginning of the twenty-first century, many of the concerns associated with new media appear to be slightly in the doldrums, but this is largely because the expansion of multimedia and new media enterprises was so rapid during the 1980s and 1990s. Key to this expansion, at least for the digital market, was the notion of convergence, that while the output of film, text and photography was very different, the software and hardware required to create them could all be run from the same box. In the early stages of ICT, specialist fields such as video editing required equally specialist hardware to ensure that performance was as effective as possible, but in recent years, as desktop PCs and Macs offer processing power equivalent to the supercomputers of the 1970s and early 1980s, this is no longer the case.

Dissemination and suppression of new technologies

In his history of technology from the telegraph to the Internet, Brian Winston proposes a model for the dissemination of new technologies in which suppression is as important as diffusion. Put simply, it is not enough for novel gadgets, techniques and devices simply to work well – they must also fulfil a social need and not threaten an overtly powerful way of doing things already in practice. 'The most obvious proof of the existence of a "law" of suppression of radical potential, then, is the continuation, despite the bombardments of technology, of all the institutions of our culture in forms subject to alternation but not revolutionary change' (Winston 1998: 13). If technologies were disseminated as soon as they were invented, it is unlikely that there could be social continuity.

Technology has always been important to the economic conditions of communication and media. Thus, for example, the ability to reproduce texts, music, images and films has contributed to the developments of each of these as a viable industry beginning with what McLuhan called the 'Gutenberg galaxy' of print. The first real boom for mass-media technology was in the period 1880 to 1930 which saw, among other developments, the growth of photography, cinema, radio and cheap printing, but which has also been surpassed by the post-Second World War boom, in particular during the 1980s. Combined with deregulation, eight new important technologies entered the mainstream in the 1980s and 1990s – video, CD, DVD, mobile communications, cable, satellite, teletext/videotext and online databases – of which only videotext (familiar to most in the UK via Teletext) did not enjoy widespread global support.

These technologies – in particular cable, satellite and online systems – have three main results in relation to distribution:

1 They reduce the time to diffuse communication of material between producer and distributor.
2 They raise the number of units in circulation massively despite initial high set-up costs.
3 They reduce the costs related to distribution.

Such technology often has contradictory results, resulting in wider decentralisation of information at the same time that ownership becomes more concentrated. Thus, in the 1980s, for example, local TV and radio stations in the USA broke the monopoly of the networks in providing news by using satellite for images and information – at the same time that more and more of these independent stations were being bought up by companies such as Rupert Murdoch's News Corporation. New technology can mean more efficient information gathering and distribution, opening it up to more and more groups, but also making it easier for larger, transnational companies to control their services.

Some of the ways in which new technologies have been adopted can be understood when considering the steps taken with older forms, in this case the first successful digital communications medium: Morse code.

When old technologies were new: Morse code and the telegraph

Morse code was used in maritime communication for over a hundred years, from 1897 when Marconi sent a series of messages between an Italian warship and a shore station until 1999. Morse code was the world's first successful digital communication system, invented by Samuel Morse, the son of a New England Congregationalist minister, in 1844, when he sent his first public message, 'What hath God wrought', across the telegraph line between Washington and Baltimore (Standage 1998; Winston 1998).

The telegraph had been in use for nearly a decade by that time, the claimants for its invention including Baron Pawel Schilling, Sir William Fothergill Cooke and Charles Wheatstone, as well as Edward Davy, who proposed telegraph lines as a means of preserving rail safety. Tom Standage, in his book *The Victorian Internet* (1998), has drawn parallels between the steam age and the electronic age, and certainly Morse code in particular served as a precedent for digitising information that would be useful for encoding cyberspace: operators have been communicating in bits for more than a century and a half.

The basic time interval for sending messages via Morse code is the duration of the dot, with dashes being the equivalent of three units. The letter E, the most common in the English language, is one dot in Morse, with less common letters such as Q or Y consisting of three dashes and one dot in different combinations. Despite its sophistication (evidenced by its long life), Morse code was difficult to automate, and so as electro-mechanical typewriters were developed in the early 1900s, users began to employ the Baudot code, so-named after its inventor, Emile Baudot, that used fixed character lengths, as did its successor, ASCII.

While Morse code per se was ultimately a dead-end for digital computers, the telegraph itself became 'the model of all electrical signalling systems which follow' (Winston 1998: 29). This was not limited to its technical innovations: investments that had been made in alternative communication systems, such as semaphore, meant that governments were often unwilling to adopt the new technology, while ambiguities over ownership slowed down dissemination of the telegraph. None the less, along with the invention of the telephone in the late nineteenth century, the foundations had been laid for the digitisation of telecommunications and the beginnings of cyberspace.

Policy and regulation

At the time that Morse code was finally phased out for official communication, more pressing matters concerned the distribution and dissemination of digital media technologies that had been introduced in the final decades of the twentieth century. As has been mentioned several times in this introduction, concentrating on new technologies at the expense of social, political and psychological consequences provides only a limited picture of the effects of such technology. In particular, many governments and commercial enterprises have been concerned about the implications of digital media while, at the same time, attempting to benefit as much as possible from them.

Issues around policy, regulation and ethics form the major part of the final section of this book, but it is also worth drawing attention to some of the main factors facing regulators of new media. For producers of content distributed across new media channels, a major concern is protecting intellectual property rights, as the ease with which information in the form of text, music and even video can be digitised and copied has placed copyright rules under considerable strain.

Another area of contention arises due to the friction – by no means unique to digital media – between individual rights and social responsibilities to society. This has become more important in the aftermath of various governments' crackdown on terrorism, as the spread of global telecommunications systems has provided both the means for new, widespread forms of communication (one thinks of satellite transmissions of videos made by Osama bin Laden) as well as tools to track and monitor individuals more closely than before. Some see this as a diminution of the individual's right to privacy and free speech, while others argue that policy makers have social responsibilities to police digital networks more thoroughly, not merely in terms of fighting terrorism but also against other crimes such as fraud and child abuse.

Most if not all media formats have brought with them considerable headaches for a political elite, and few have been as dramatic as the Reformation that was, in part, fuelled by developments in print media. In the twentieth century the dumbing effects of television, video nasties, a press often depicted as out of control have all been depicted as problematic, but few have so easily crossed national boundaries and mores as the Internet.

The Internet and the Web

Thus far, we have said relatively little about the most obvious current incarnation of cyberspace in everyday life: the Internet. The reason for this has been to emphasise that cyberspace and the Net are not synonymous terms; we prefer to use cyberspace to refer to a wider range of cultural, social and political networks in which a particular system of communications, in this case the Internet, can work.

At the same time, it is clear that the Internet in its manifold forms – including the World Wide Web – has provided a radical transformation of the way in which we communicate, work, consume, find information and entertainment and connect to other people around the world. The Internet is typically described as a 'network of networks', a system of hardware (computers, routers, cables or wireless transmitters and receivers) and software (the protocols that provide rules for connecting between different machines) that has resulted in huge changes in the post-war computer industry. If computers, particularly the personal computer, following its invention in the 1970s, made a significant difference to the way people worked with and processed information, it was clear that much of the information supplied to and from computers still needed to be turned from bits into atoms, or vice versa. If you wanted to view the output from a computer, such as a typed message or image, you would typically have to print it out. Transferring information between computers was difficult, extremely so if different machines used different operating systems.

The revolutionary effect of the Internet has been to provide an open system of rules that may be used to transfer information quickly and easily from machine to machine. It is for this reason that Metcalfe's so-called law, that the value of a network is proportional to the square of the number of people using it, will probably be more significant in the twenty-first century than Moore's law, that the number of transistors capable of being fitted onto a microchip will double every one to two years. Throughout large parts of this book, we will consider the impact and influence of Internet technology on cyberspace, but it is important to remember that as the Internet of today is very different to its predecessor from the late 1960s,

ARPANET, so the Matrix envisaged by Gibson, and the cyberspace of the future, will be very different to what we experience today.

The development of the Internet

The origins of the Internet lay with the Advanced Research Projects Agency (ARPA), which was founded following the launch of Sputnik to pursue scientific, military and academic research. Between 1963 and 1967, ARPA investigated the feasibility of building computer networks before selecting a number of computer hosts to join ARPANET, as the project was later known, in 1968. Work began in 1969, providing protocols that would connect computers at different sites and would also create a resilient network, capable of rerouting information in the event of failure on any part of the network (Hafner and Lyon 1996; Naughton 1999).

We shall examine the technologies that constitute the Internet in later chapters in this book: throughout the 1970s, however, the prototype of the Internet grew slowly as other networks around the world, such as ALOHAnet in Hawaii and University College London, connected to ARPANET. Alongside official development, other computer users were exploring ways of communicating online, most significantly through the work of Jim Ellis and others at Duke University who developed Usenet, the 'poor man's ARPANET'. At this stage, such computer networks remained the preserve largely of scientists and computer engineers, but the introduction of the personal computer in the late 1970s signalled the potential for those networks to form the backbone of a mass medium.

Throughout the early 1980s, ARPANET remained one network – though an important one – among many, with governments and institutions developing their own information systems, such as Minitel in France. Important work in the 1980s concentrated on the development of an architecture that could be connected to more easily, particularly via the introduction of the Domain Name System (which would eventually mean that every server attached to the Net would not need to carry the address of every other server – something that severely restricted growth). By the end of the decade, the infrastructure for a unified and universal system was in place, but the Net still remained a hostile environment for those who were not computer experts.

The 'killer app' that was eventually to make the Internet essential for many users was probably email, but the eye candy that first caught their attention – and also focused computer engineers' attention on ease of use – was the World Wide Web, developed by Tim Berners-Lee while he was working at the European Centre for Nuclear Research (CERN) in Geneva (Berners-Lee 1999). Berners-Lee developed the language for formatting pages and communicating between web servers (HTML and HTTP respectively) in 1990, and companies such as the National Center for Supercomputer Applications (NCSA) and later Netscape took up his work to popularise the Web for many more users. Equally significantly, Berners-Lee was committed to developing the Web as an open standard that would be adopted as widely as possible as a means for exchanging information, having realised that proprietary systems had severely affected the capabilities of computer-mediated communication until that point.

By the mid-1990s, aided in particular by the Web and email, Internet usage expanded rapidly, fulfilling the conditions of Metcalfe's law as individuals, governments and corporations began making available huge amounts of data in open and immediately accessible forms. The transformation between 1995, when Microsoft launched the Microsoft Network alongside Windows 95 as a superior alternative to the 'over-complicated' Internet, and 2000, when dotcom boom-and-bust stories dominated the media and Microsoft was under investigation for allegedly monopolising access to the Internet via its browser, was profound: the Internet was still a primary place of research and communication for scientists and computer engineers – only now they constituted a tiny fraction of the estimated 500 million users connected online.

The Grid

While the Web has often become synonymous with current configurations of cyberspace, new developments such as peer-to-peer networking serve as a warning that this is not always the case. As such, it is worth ending this chapter with a glance at some of the developments that could affect the way we use cyberspace in future years.

In the past decade we have become used to an international computing network, the roots of which were established in the late 1960s and early 1970s and which has expanded as part of a global telecommunications network. The current Internet effectively provides a planet-sized hard drive of constantly updated information, yet this may only be the first step to creating a planet-sized computer.

As we shall see later in this book, current technologies that have been following a variant of what is known as Moore's law cannot do so forever: the technical processes by means of which computers are manufactured are within sight of barriers of physics which means that such development will probably plateau in the first few decades of the twenty-first century. Different technologies (such as quantum computing) will probably have an enormous contribution to make, but there remains a limit to what can be done.

More powerful computers, however, do not merely rely on cramming more components into smaller spaces. Over the past ten years or so, the fastest machines have relied less and less on the sheer computing muscle of one or two processors; instead, supercomputers such as ASCII White work by connecting massively parallel processors, capable of achieving twelve teraflops (twelve trillion calculations per second), some 35,000 times faster than the speediest Athlon computer in 2001. Even IBM's supercomputer, however, was some six times slower than Seti@Home, the program that analyses astronomical data in search of extraterrestrial life by utilising spare processing cycles of volunteers' computers. Throughout 2001, Seti@Home averaged seventy-one teraflops (setiathome.ssl. Berkeley.edu), yet its constituency of 500,000 users represents only a small fraction of the potential computers that could be connected to the Internet. It has been estimated that were all those computers joined up to form a worldwide grid, a global super-processor, as it were, the computing power available would rise to more than 250 petaflops, 20,000 times faster than ASCII White.

Commercial grid-like products, that distribute tasks around networks, are already available from IBM and Sun, but a generic Grid is a long way off, particularly as companies such as Microsoft with .Net are not enthusiastic about an open source alternative. None the less, prototype grids such as the University of Wisconsin's Condor (www.cs.wisc.edu/condor/), DAS, based in the Netherlands (www.cs.vu.nl/~bal/das.html), and the EuroGrid (www.eurogrid.org) have demonstrated how such projects can work on a small scale. Much of the current research into grids is concerned with the economics of such a project, how resources can be pooled in order to encourage users and organisations to share spare processing power, and how data may be distributed across networks. If and when the Grid becomes a reality, the current wired world of cyberspace will appear extremely restricted by comparison.

Bodynets, personal webs and the future

Projects such as the Grid – and indeed the Web and Internet itself – are immense and ambitious, but cyberspace envelops us in ways that are also intensely personal. Theories that move towards a definition of us as a cyborg, particularly in the aftermath of Donna Haraway's (1991) influential essay, are often concerned less with the relationship of biology and invasive technology than with the ways in which we surround ourselves with instrumental extensions of ourselves – pens, watches, mobile phones, personal organisers. The social and psychological effects of such machinic extensions can be immense: Neil Postman (1990), for example, has remarked on the ways in which the invention of the clock, created by Dominican monks to regulate their worship, engineered a complete social transformation as part of the Industrial Revolution.

At present, cyberspace still tends to be something we plug into, an opaque boundary that we generally must make an effort to interface with, such as by sitting in front of a computer and dialling into the Internet. This is not always the case, however, even now: if we accept the wide-ranging definition of cyberspace with which we began this chapter, then withdrawing money from a cash machine or ATM links us to global financial systems where capital functions largely as pure data. Likewise, mobile phones form part of an extended telecommunications network that is measured not merely by its extent but also in terms of its saturation of our daily lives. One technological aim (which was, for example, hinted at in *Minority Report*) is to transform our individual spaces into clouds or nets of personal data that will be able to interface with global networks almost transparently.

2 Mapping cyberspace

Studying cyberspace

While the study of cyberspace is itself a recent discipline, the term not having existed before 1984, there are some obvious precursors that have contributed to the field. The rapid development of electronic and computer courses following the Second World War was concerned with the production of computer hardware and (at a later date) software that would power what was to become the new economy. At this early stage, government and university institutions such as Stanford, ARPA and MIT provided probably the most important hothouses for incubating new ideas, with significant contributions from commercial organisations such as IBM and the Xerox Palo Alto Research Center (PARC). During the 1950s, 1960s and 1970s, important theoretical innovations such as the transistor, Ethernet and the graphical computer interface were developed into commercial products that slowly transformed the post-war environment of the information society.

Such vital occurrences, which we will explore in detail in later chapters on the technology of cyberspace, were clearly significant in terms of the development of the science of cyberspace as well as its economics and, to a lesser degree, its politics. Computer science courses that sprang up throughout campuses worldwide, as well as associated degrees such as electrical and software engineering, were concerned with training the next generations of computer scientists who would, through their development of new computing techniques and processes, provide the key skills and technologies that would contribute to the growth of national and international economies.

It was perhaps after the dissemination of personal computers to a much wider public from the late 1970s onward that a wider interest developed in other theoretical conceptions of cyberspace outside the spheres of physics and engineering – important as these are. The identification of new technologies and the social and cultural condition of postmodernism was initiated by Jean-François Lyotard in 1979, and since that time it has become a commonplace to consider the role of ICT in relation to sociology and other aspects of media studies, approaches that have contributed greatly to many of the chapters in this book.

Following the publication of William Gibson's *Neuromancer* in 1984, the term 'cyberspace' itself began to gain ground, and an important text in the theorisation of the field was Michael Benedikt's *Cyberspace: First Steps*, published by MIT Press in 1991. Although it obviously missed out on some of the important developments of cyberspace that were to form its popular conception during the 1990s – most obviously the World Wide Web that was only just beginning to emerge at that time – *Cyberspace* was an important text in establishing some of the paradigms for the discussion of cyberspace that have continued till this day. David Silver (2000) provides a good summary of cyberspace studies from 1990 to 2000, indicating three main phases in the field, from an initial popularising phase to a move to a more theoretical (but still enthusiastic) stage and, finally, much more critical discussions of the impact of cyberspace which indicate that the field is finally beginning to mature. It is perhaps noteworthy that the saturation of (largely abstract or ultimately uncritical) 'postmodern' studies of cyberspace that were published in abundance in the mid-1990s have given way to a wider variety of social, political and economic studies of which Castells' series *The Information Age* (1996–98) and Lievrouw and Livingstone's *The Handbook of New Media* (2002) are good examples.

Maps of cyberspace

It is important to recognise the fact that cyberspace deals with notions of space in ways that are not strictly metaphorical. By this, as we have already seen in Chapter 1 with reference to commentators such as Benedikt (1991) and Wertheim (1999), we mean that cyberspace does not only represent space but also reconstructs certain notions of space: cyberspace, then, does not merely stand in for the real world, but also forms relationships between agents and participants in that real world. This is something that is missed in 'common-sense' or mundane comparisons of the 'virtual' and the 'real', which assumes that the latter is more substantial than the former. Consider the following example. I have to do business with a colleague in another country that requires me to speak to her on the phone and via email on an almost daily basis, and though I have never met her we exchange birthday and Christmas cards; I bump into my next-door neighbour probably once a month, and though we exchange pleasantries, I know no more about her than her name. Which relationship is more substantial? For most people, despite the physical proximity of the neighbour, they may be more intimate with other people who exist for them in information rather than physical space. Of course, the neighbour still has an impact on our lives in a number of ways: where they shop, if they drive a car, whether they send their children to a local school – all these decisions will in turn affect the locality where we live, but intimacy (by which I mean a sense of understanding and connection with another) is created through information about, or knowledge of, another person as much as by physical contact.

The distinction between the virtual and the real, if it does not privilege the latter, often tends to idolise the former: the virtual is superior to the physical, transcends it. As we shall see in this chapter, while mental maps are important to the construction of cyberspace, it also very much shares a connection with the real world – with geographical servers and governments as well as the material effects of global finances and economics. Another way of mapping cyberspace is via the informational or symbolic, which in turn may be divided into the mathematical and cultural. Mathematics, as the basis of much computer science, is important, as it is a way of manipulating abstract symbols. Most significant for this chapter, as we shall see below, are the ways in which such symbolic manipulation is regularly employed by new technologies to provide a visual or geometrical representation of cyberspace.

Notions of the cultural mapping of cyberculture, as Slack and Wise (2002) point out, have tended to owe a great deal to the theories of Giles Deleuze and Félix Guattari and, behind those, Michel Foucault's linkage of mental and physical spaces and structures of power. For Deleuze and Guattari, the social and cultural existence of capitalism *territorialises* the human subject and the mental and physical spaces in which he or she lives: it fills and gives (restricted) meaning to the rituals and activities of our daily lives in the same way that lines on a map mark out nations, regions and localities. There are ways in which this rigidly structured space, argue Deleuze and Guattari, can be *de*-territorialised; for example, via the practices of nomadic cultures or the activities of schizophrenia (a term they use very differently to its conventional employment). For theory, the importance of analysis is to articulate contexts of phenomena, to describe, or trace, connections between the structures of everyday life, and to draw, redraw and thus map out those connections in potentially liberating ways.

Mapping cyberspace

The process of creating conceptual and visual maps of cyberspace, then, has dominated the activity of a number of commentators. In addition to those discussed above, for example, Castells (2001), drawing on the work of Matthew Zook, distinguishes three types of cyberspace geography: a technical geography, which focuses on such things as nodes of information and bandwidth; a spatial geography of users, their position globally or within social and physical networks; and finally an economic geography of production, that concentrates on areas such as Silicon Valley or the manufacturing base of southeast Asia.

A more complex schema of mapping is provided by Martin Dodge and Rob Kitchin in their books *Mapping Cyberspace* (2001a) and *Atlas of Cyberspace* (2001b). They distinguish 'geographies of the information society' from those associated with cyberspace. The former include: cultural and social geographies, such as McLuhan's notion of the global village or E. Soja's critique of Los Angeles as a pastiche of other locales; geographies of power, whether the sites of main-stream surveillance or participation, or sites of resistance, such as those created by the Zapatistas; and economic geographies, what they refer to as urban, regional and global restructuring, the back-office systems that power businesses, tele-commuters and financial markets.

Geographies of cyberspace, the authors remark, are slightly different, often more complex for us to grasp because they involve differences in our cognition of that fundamental frame of reference: space. Such geographies, then, can involve notions of identity and community, notions of geometry, space and form that are often (but not always) architectural, and ideas of the 'docuverse', the series of connected files and retrieval procedures that exist in cyberspace. In answer to the question: Why map cyberspace? Dodge and Kitchin (2001a: 69) reply:

> In the case of information that has a geographic referent and spatial attributes (e.g. ICTs), constructing a map or spatialisation provides a means by which to visualise and describe that form. It also reveals important insights into who controls the infrastructure, who has access to cyberspace, how the system can be surveyed, and how and from where cyberspace is being used.

Of the actual practice of producing maps of cyberspace, Dodge and Kitchin outline the following in *Mapping Cyberspace* and *Atlas of Cyberspace*: first of all there are maps of infrastructure, often literal geographies of where equipment is located as well as economic and financial charts; another way to map cyberspace is through traffic, demonstrating the use of technologies such as the Internet; we can map topologies of networks that show their technical organisation and layout; finally – and most complex of all – we can map information, such as email usage, chat conversations or social data of users. In these areas, the authors probably push their metaphor of the map a little far, but their maps lie behind the organisation of many of the chapters in this book. What is more, mapping cyberspace can draw upon centuries of practice cognising physical space to help us cognise cyberspace:

> It is clear that space and geography continue to matter, and in some senses they have taken on more importance. Cyberspace is inherently spatial. Its adoption and utility are founded on its spatial qualities . . . Moreover, its form and modes of operation are largely built on foundations that often depend on spatial metaphors and spatialisations.
>
> (Dodge and Kitchin 2001a: 219)

Depth and virtual space

One way of considering the effect of cyberspace is to ponder, for a moment, how we perceive *depth*. Depth is something that we take for granted, and yet its theorisation can be incredibly subtle and sophisticated. As Wertheim (1999) and

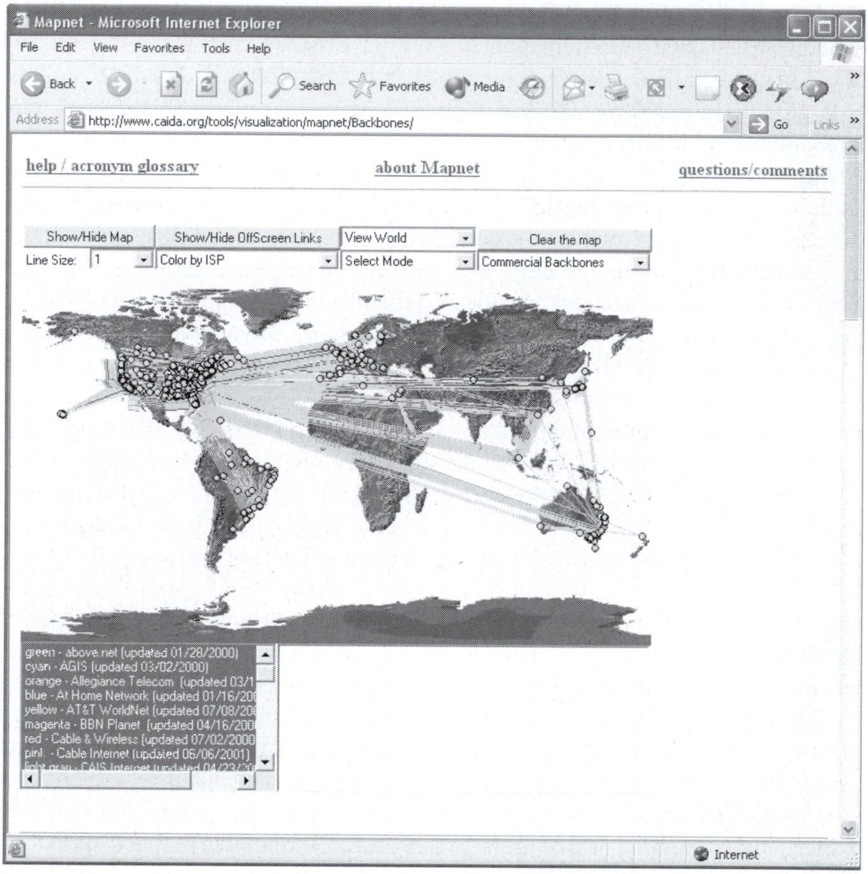

Figure 2.1 The Mapnet interactive mapping tool showing international IP links at www.caida.org/tools/visualization/mapnet/

Roof (2001) observe, contemporary senses of depth owe much to the rediscovery of perspective during the Renaissance, and the 'pairing of perception/rendition is the necessary condition of our understandings of what depth might be' (Roof 2001: 27). The conceptualisation after Galileo and Descartes of the body as matter in three-dimensional space was an important stepping stone in the development of Western scientific knowledge. In addition, depth functions as a cultural metaphor – something to be valued as opposed to the superficial. It is ironic, therefore, that it is precisely our ability to simulate depth from the Renaissance onward that enables the construction of cyberspace.

Perception of depth operates at its most basic via monocular and binocular cues, such as two overlapping squares which, when interpreted by us (and this is a cultural as well as a biological process, argues Roof after Myron Braunstein and others) indicates one square as lying 'behind' the other. Likewise, as most evident in optical

Figure 2.2 Walrus, created by Young Hyun, offers an interactive exploration of complex Internet structures at www.caida.org/tools/visualization/walrus/

illusions, size can also serve as a cue not merely of two-dimensional but also three-dimensional space: if two objects are the same in all factors other than size, we may read the smaller one as further away. Two other important cues are lines of perspective, so that converging lines indicate distance, and shadow, so that an unshaded circle appears to be flat whereas a shaded circle is read by us as a globe.

The important point is that these cues can all be simulated in two-dimensional space, which in turn means that they are capable of being depicted on the flat screen of a monitor – still our most important means of interfacing with the virtual reality of cyberspace. William Gibson's definition of cyberspace, recounted in Chapter 1, places an important emphasis on the visual representation of the Matrix, as a three-dimensional space that we perceive in an almost monosensual fashion – through

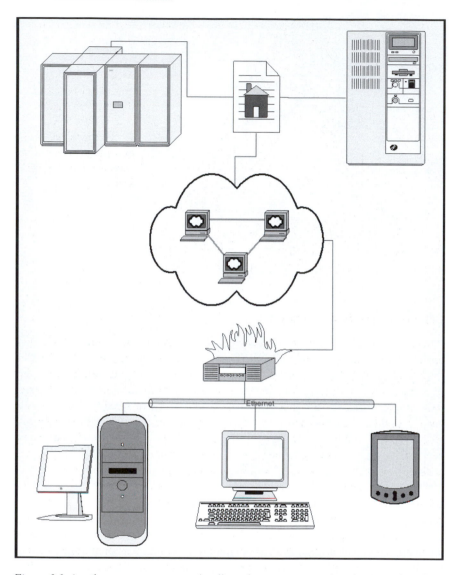

Figure 2.3 Another common way to visualise cyberspace connections is as a series of network topologies, linking together different hardware, content and users.

the eyes. This is perhaps the biggest distinction at present between physical and geographical space and cyberspace: while we often encounter the former by the physical movement of our bodies through it, the latter is almost always experienced through our eyes – at its simplest, as opening windows, overlapping them and resizing their contents, in more complex forms as the virtual motion of a character in a 3D game.

Figure 2.4 Common optical illusions, such as this Penrose Triangle, demonstrate how we interpret three-dimensional information from two-dimensional surfaces.

Chaos, fractals and maps

The implications of complexity have long been realised in the natural world. Such things as ferns and conch shells demonstrate curves that are perfectly formed mathematically, but these apparently simple shapes can disguise intricate results, as, for example, in Benoit Mandelbrot's question, 'How long is the coastline of Britain?' If the coast were measured with a metre ruler, it would miss the twists and turns that are smaller than a metre; reducing the size of the ruler to a centimetre would increase the length of the coastline, but still miss variations smaller than a centimetre, and so on down to measurements the size of an atom. As the measuring stick decreases, the coastline of Britain expands, approaching infinity.

Theories of chaos and complexity frequently include fractals, objects that are self-similar at a range of scales as demonstrated by the best-known fractal, the Mandelbrot set: no matter how many times one zooms in on the shape generated according to principles established by Mandelbrot, one will see the shape repeated again and again. Most fractals involve 'iteration', or repeated operations, such as the Sierpenski triangle, created by drawing a triangle and then drawing another triangle inside it. The example of the coastline discussed above does not provide exact iterations along the lines of Sierpenski's triangle, but the degree and type of twisting and turning along the coast is statistically the same at all levels (Gleick 1987).

The term 'fractal' comes from Mandelbrot's definition of the 'fractional dimension' of a line, the ratio of the log of its length and the log of the zoom factors between 1 and 2. The practical applications of fractals are to be found in a wide range of digital media, from compression of images to the generation of realistic-looking 3D scenery. More than this, however, principles of self-similarity and

Figure 2.5 An example of the Mandelbrot set: zooming in on this complex image reveals self-similarity.

Figure 2.6 Sierpenski's Triangle demonstrates how even simple objects when iterated become increasingly difficult to quantify.

complexity arising from even the simplest expressions have provided a theoretical model for describing cyberspace itself.

Space and place

One of the important functions of cyberspace has been to force a re-evaluation of our conceptions of space: as we have already seen, since the Enlightenment the reification of physical, geometric space via Descartes, Newton and Leibniz has been an important contribution to our sense of the real world as operating in three dimensions. Although critiques of three-dimensional space do not belong to virtual reality alone, cyberspace has none the less played an important part in helping to configure other symbolic formations of space.

Classical conceptions of space have been problematised by a number of cyberspace theorists (Benedikt 1991; Heim 1991; Oswald 1997; Wertheim 1999), drawing on post-structuralist or postmodern theorists such as Foucault who have sought to explore space as not merely the geometricisation of symbolic mathe-matics, but also as territorialisations of power by dominant social and economic groups. Put simply, for many writers and thinkers space is not only that void through which we move but also the *place* in which we live and experience. Benedikt, drawing on Karl Popper, discriminates three types of space – the physical, the subjective and the structural – and sees cyberspace as the third type of world, the structural spaces that provide 'patterns' for our experiences.

> For Popper, in short, temples, cathedrals, marketplaces, courts, libraries, theatres or amphitheatres, letters, book pages, movie reels, videotapes, CDs, newspapers, hard discs, performances, art shows . . . [are] the physical components of – objects that exist more wholly in *World 3*. They are 'objects', that is, which are patterns of ideas, images, sounds, stories, data . . . patterns of pure information. And cyberspace, we might now see, is nothing more, or less, than the latest stage in the evolution of *World 3*, with the ballast of materiality cast away – cast away again, and perhaps finally.
>
> (Benedikt 1991: 4)

The information society

It is frequently claimed that we live in an information society. For example, in the mid-1990s then US Vice-President Al Gore, claiming to coin the term 'information superhighway', wrote in an article for the *Financial Times*, 'the information infrastructure is to the US economy of the 1990s what transport infrastructure was to the economy of the mid-twentieth century.'

Tadao Umesao, a professor at Kyoto University, was one of the first to predict the coming of an information industry in 1963 in his book *Industry Theory: Dawn of the Coming Era of the Ectodermal Industry*. Umesao was followed by a small but growing number of visionaries, such as Daniel Bell and Marshall McLuhan, who believed that the industrial age was to be replaced by an age of information. Many of the more outlandish comments made by these thinkers in the 1960s are now taken for granted. The explosion of computers means that students and pupils at most schools in the Western world are familiar with the capabilities of the PC – and an even higher percentage are *au fait* with a console at home.

Not that it is easy to define what an information society would consist of: we shall look at some of the economic measures of cyberspace in the next chapter, but even before that there is a fundamental problem with determining what information is. According to the French philosopher, Jean Baudrillard, information in our new, wired-up world is no longer knowledge but 'ersatz transcendence'. We live on a planet where virtually any region, any culture is accessible, but at the same time we rely increasingly on places such as Disney World to convince us that the rapidly transforming globe outside is real – just as more and more information beamed into our homes, workplaces and heads turns our view of what is real upside down and inside out. Certainly attempts to segue seamlessly between an *information* economy and a *knowledge* economy are extremely difficult.

This problem was addressed by a Fritz Machlup (1962), at Princeton University, at the same time that Umesao was predicting that an information industry would dominate the global market of the future. Machlup attempted to measure the apparently immeasurable: knowledge. The production of knowledge, argued Machlup, is the process whereby someone learns something they did not know before, and he applied the measurement of such production to five areas – education, research and development, media and communication, information machines, and information services. Machlup was able to show that an increasingly important percentage of the US GNP was accounted for by knowledge-production workers and that this in turn contributes to the 'informatisation' of the economy, as more and more people depended for their income on producing information and distributing it via TV, radio, newspapers, fax, telephone – and the Internet.

It is not always clear where the distinction is drawn between the contribution of pure 'knowledge' to an information society and other forms of production, such as manufacturing. None the less, while we should remain sceptical of simple assertions that we now operate in a knowledge – or even an information – economy, none the less 'informatisation', whatever its value, has been particularly important to the growth of cyberspace. A report commissioned by the French media and advertising group Havas in 1991, for example, at the moment when the World Wide Web was just coming into existence, established that the average European spent just over three hours per day watching TV and over two hours listening to the radio, with approximately forty minutes spent reading a newspaper. For Europeans born after 1990, the amount of time spent pursuing these particular activities will change – for example, as more and more people use the Internet – but the basic fact remains that for nearly all of us our time is dominated by three things: sleep, work and the media.

James Slevin (2000) offers a social theory of cyberspace, drawing on ideas from John B. Thompson, Manuel Castells, Jürgen Habermas and Pierre Bourdieu, that combines theories of mass communication and mass community. Thus the elements important to mass communication, which incorporates institutionalised production and diffusion of symbolic forms across an extended audience, operate within a public sphere where users may not simply be passive but also interactive within 'repertoires of possibilities': we do not simply consume what is offered to us, but also select and participate in the formats we appreciate most.

The global village

The growth of the Internet is but an extreme example of one of the key areas where technology is changing our lives – the globalisation of information. We fully expect to see, hear and read about events anywhere in the world, increasingly at any hour of any day, with more people able to travel with greater ease in a twenty-four-hour society. In Marshall McLuhan's (1964) oft-misquoted phrase, we are seen to be living in a 'global village'. McLuhan's prescience had more to do with television, but his comments regarding electronic media in general seem more accurate in the digital age:

> After three thousand years of specialist explosion and of increasing specialism and alienation in the technological expansions of our bodies, our world has become compressional by dramatic reversal. As electrically contracted, the globe is no more than a village.
>
> (1964:5)

Globalisation is not a complete novelty – news companies such as Reuters and Havas were established by colonial powers (Britain and France respectively) in the nineteenth century to report on events in the far reaches of the empire, in particular with the invention of the first real high-speed telecommunications link, the telegraph. None the less, the ability to share information still remained limited until the mid-twentieth century by the crudity of much of the technology as well as economic and political factors. Reporting an event anywhere in the world still depended on one's country having influence in that region, and it was not really until the fall of the Berlin Wall in 1989 that the actual prospect of a global village envisaged by McLuhan began to be realised. As Glen Renfrew, a former MD of Reuters, observed, 'it's becoming increasingly difficult to divorce the concept of information from the concept of telecommunications. . . . The faster and further you move information, the more valuable it becomes' (cited in Tunstall and Palmer 1991: 61).

Language and communication

With the explosion of computer-mediated communication in the 1990s, email, newsgroups and, above all, the Web have demonstrated one of the major difficulties for a globalised, networked economy: language. In 1999, half the users of the

Internet were based in America, but this proportion has been declining steadily since the turn of the century. Surprisingly, given its dominance of the international market, English is not even the largest linguistic group on the planet, at least in terms of native speakers: that position is held by Mandarin, with 835 million speakers in 2000, followed by English (470 million), Spanish (330 million) and Hindi (300 million).

While American English has dominated the Internet, considerable work has also been done to transform the Babel of cyberspace into a multilingual communications network. Difficulties with translation, however, may ultimately be beyond the capacity of computers, at least in the short term: in addition to complexities of semantics (the meanings of individual words or parts of words), translation software must also deal with pragmatics (the arrangements of words into sentences and their contexts) as well as local and regional idioms. Thus, for example, 'bank' may refer to a river or a financial institution, and the meaning of the cliché 'don't bank on it' may not always be clear to speakers of different languages.

One of the problems for computer translation, then, is that deciding the meaning of words or phrases does not always lend itself to recursion: computers work best when they are able to check all possible solutions to a problem and move through them quickly, checking off inferior ones until they find the best one, one of the reasons why computers are so good at chess, for example (Kurzweil 1999; Whittaker 2002). None the less, the history of machine translation is surprisingly old: Petr Smirnov-Troyanskii patented a device for translating the roots of words back in 1933, but machine translation (MT) really began in 1952 when Yehoshua Bar-Hillel at MIT organised the first MT conference. The first public demo of computer translation took place at Georgetown University in 1954, when forty-nine Russian sentences were translated into English using a 250-word dictionary, but at the end of the 1950s Bar-Hillel published a report arguing that fully automatic and accurate translation was impossible (Demos [*Wired* 8.05, 'Talking to Strangers']).

From the vantage point of the 1960s, machine translation was simply too difficult. While basic sentences obeying uncomplicated grammatical rules could be transferred into another language, those grammatical rules frequently did not correspond across languages. While federal funding was halted for MT, however, Peter Toma at Georgetown continued to work on projects and set up one of the first MT companies, Latsec (Language Automated Translation Systems and Electronic Communications) in 1968. As MT developed, so it contributed to and received support from other growth areas such as speech recognition and automated speech generation; outside the USA, where compatibility with English was a problem, countries such as Japan devoted funds to studying multilingual translation and the German-funded Verb-mobil project began in 1993. It was not until the mid-1990s that the first off-the-shelf translation packages began to appear, quickly followed by online services such as that offered by Systran. Similarly, researchers at the University of Southern California Information Sciences Institute (USCISI) have been working on a project called Gazelle that can self-learn by analysing large online collections of texts to learn translation rules. USCISI has produced what it calls a Controlled Skip Parser to improve translation by skipping some words in a sentence.

In the meantime, sites such as Altavista's Babel (babelfish.altavista.com/tr) and FreeTranslation (www.freetranslation.com) rely on the fact that in most situations we tend to rely on a fairly restricted range of sentences and well-established conventions. Thus 'Dear John' is likely to begin a letter, while 'Fine, how are you?' is probably a reply to the question about health. These are the sorts of tricks we tend to use when learning a second language, and ones that can also be programmed into software.

3 ICT, telecommunications and cyberspace

....

The new economy
....

Thus far, we have concentrated on some of the social and cultural implications of cyberspace, but underpinning these developments are economic factors that, in turn, contribute to political decisions and influence socio-cultural representations and production.

In the final years of the decade leading up to the new century, claims were constantly made for a 'new economy' that would not merely transform old notions of economic activity but revolutionise them. With the bursting of the dotcom bubble – dramatically in the cases of the collapse of WorldCom, or the crash in value of AOL Time Warner – the worst excesses (and fantasies) of this new economy have been trashed. As Lovelock and Ure (2002: 350) observe, however:

> Yet something important survives – something that is a new permanent feature of the political economy landscape. Whether it constitutes a 'new paradigm' or just an evolving feature of the rapid developments in communications, computers and the media content sector – all of which in fact have a longer history than the commercialisation of the Internet – is subject to debate. . . . What does seem to be obvious is that a larger absolute number of people are more mobile across boundaries – geography, skill, language, industry and so on – than ever before, that new (IT) skills are in high demand, that the idea of lifetime employment with one organisation is dying out, and that this idea of economic and demographic flux advantages and disadvantages different sets of people and communities.

We have already considered some of the implications of this 'economic and demographic flux' in relation to ideas around a network society. What is important from Lovelock and Ure's summary is that – at least in the Western world – if a new economy exists it is marked by a decline in the importance of manufacturing productivity and an increase in information management and skills, combined with enhanced mobility and an increased significance attributed to the media, in such areas as advertising and promotion as well as other forms of news and information distribution. It is worth sounding a note of scepticism at this point: many factors involved in new ICT industries are precisely that – industries. While Western consumers are less likely to be involved in the process of manufacturing the electronics that they buy in increasing amounts, part of the ICT boom has consisted of expanding the productivity of fabrication plants and factory outlets around the world, especially in southeast Asia and, increasingly, in the former Eastern European bloc.

Definitions of the new economy are themselves in flux at present, but the OECD (2000) indicates that the underlying factors include higher rates of non-inflationary growth and lower rates of unemployment compared to traditional manufacturing cycles, combined with new sources of growth in networking, IT and telecommunications. In this chapter, we shall concentrate on two of Lovelock and Ure's primary contributors to the new economy: the computer industry and telecommunications. The dotcom boom – which may have been no more than economic flotsam and jetsam – is the subject of later chapters: even if the excitement of Internet mania was exaggerated, however, the two areas of computing and communication have been dramatically transformed since the 1970s and, in the process, have changed the ways in which we live and work.

ICT and the economy

Some estimates of the information industry placed it at over 45 per cent of the US gross national product (GNP), with a worldwide industry worth $875 billion by 2003 according to IDC (though this was a decrease of 3 per cent on the previous year). Not that it is always easy to determine exactly what constitutes such an information industry. Despite some of the grander statements about how such a society is constructed, if we look at one area where communications seems to make an important contribution to our society, the media, the reasons for this contribution seem hard to justify in purely economic terms. According to research by the Institute of Media Economics (Pilati and Libbey 1993), by the beginning of the 1990s only about 2.7 per cent of European gross domestic product (GDP) was generated by media industries, with approximately 3.7 per cent in the USA – a far cry from the 50 per cent predicted by some analysts in the 1970s and early 1980s. The contribution of computing and ICT would, on the face of it, appear to be much more self-evident. However, this equation is not so clear when the cost of the IT revolution is factored in against its effects.

In his book, *The Trouble with Computers* (1995), Thomas Landauer amassed a considerable amount of information relating specifically to the use of IT and productivity. The highest periods of productivity growth in the USA had been in the period between 1913 and 1973, as with Western Europe, while since 1973 growth in output per hour had achieved less than 1.5 per cent, diminishing as the cost per IT/white-collar worker doubled between 1979 and 1992. This paradox, according to Landauer, is not due to the fact that computers do not provide real and tangible benefits – for example, in the field of telecommunications. Rather, it is due to the fact that companies have not been clear about the uses to which they put computers and do not distinguish between information which is essential and productive and that which is sought out for inefficient aims. In addition, Landauer points to errors in computer design and the lack of user-centred development, which has too often meant that computer companies follow their own design and engineering agendas, rather than concentrating on the needs of users and their specific tasks.

One strong area where ICT has demonstrably contributed to the economy has been in terms of computer sales. In contrast to many other areas, sales of personal computers increased annually in the twenty years following their introduction. However, increased sales disguised the profitability of that industry, with declining costs forcing many manufacturers to cut corners. During 1999, PC sales grew by 23 per cent and led some commentators to predict a 'PC-plus' rather than 'post-PC' era established on a higher take-up of broadband services supported by faster processor speeds and more services available online (Bajarin 2001). This was, however, the high point of the 1990s bull market, so that by 2001 the IT market began to suffer the effects of dotcom fallout as PC sales declined by over 6 per cent in the second quarter of 2001. This led to unprecedented layoffs in Japan, Toshiba, for example, shedding 17,000 jobs, while the PC manufacturer Gateway pulled out of Europe and smaller – but still substantial – companies such as Tiny folded. Probably the biggest shockwave at the end of 2001 was the merger of Hewlett-Packard and Compaq into the world's biggest IT company, worth $18 billion. Compaq, once the most important of the IBM clones that emerged in the 1980s, was absorbed into HP with job losses estimated at 15,000.

IBM

In the mid-twentieth century, IBM *was* the computer market, a position which seems somewhat anomalous to readers whose entire experience of ICT has been formed in a post-Microsoft (and increasingly post-Internet) era. Significantly, the mega-corporation that formed from companies set up to provide technology for early US censuses has reformed itself as one of the major powers in the Internet age, although at the height of dotcom mania it was often held up as one of the dinosaurs that would be circumvented by smaller, leaner, networked agencies.

Following the war, IBM dominated the mainframe industry and, when the company released the PC in 1981, primitive desktop computers had been available for half a decade: computing, which had been regarded as a specialist realm for technical experts, was starting to be more widely disseminated due to companies such as Apple, Atari, Commodore and Digital Research, which had released an operating system CP/M (Control Program/for Microprocessors). An IBM team in Florida, led by Bill Lowe, was charged to produce a desktop computer within a year: to reach this deadline, the team used readily available components such as the Intel 8088 processor.

While the IBM PC was not particularly spectacular in terms of performance (the 8088 processor was a cut down version of the much faster 8086), its importance was in terms of providing a standard. Until the early 1980s, computer manufacturers had made their systems as different as possible in order to sell proprietary software. Within months, however, the IBM PC had more programs created for it than any other computer and achieved its five-year target of a quarter of a million sales in one month. Within a year IBM clones had appeared, and although IBM attempted to prevent sales of such machines, the open architecture of its original PC made that task impossible. What was more, products from rivals such as Compaq were not only cheaper than 'official' PCs but often offered superior performance: Compaq, for example, launched a PC based on Intel's 386 chip long before Big Blue. When IBM attempted to reassert its control over the market with a new, proprietary architecture, Micro Channel Architecture (MCA), in 1987, clone rivals teamed up to produce the Extended Industry Standard Architecture (EISA) that was quickly snapped up by consumers.

In the late 1980s, IBM saw its dominance of the IT market collapse as mainframe-based computing gave way to cheaper networked PCs, a field that it had lost to clone manufacturers. In 1991 the company that was once twice the size of the rest of the computer industry posted a $2.8 billion loss followed by an even larger deficit, $4.96 billion, in 1992; the decline of its monopoly position, however, forced IBM to adapt to a very different environment so that, by the end of the century, it was richer and more powerful than ever with revenues three times the size of those for Microsoft (Akass 2001).

At the time of the launch of the PC in 1981, IBM held a near monopoly over the computer market and was feared and respected by its competitors, its maxim 'nobody ever got sacked for buying IBM'. It had, however, become sclerotic, generally incapable of adapting to the rapid changes that were driving forward PCs (the creation of the IBM PC in a year was – and still is – seen as a heroic feat for the company). Its huge losses in the 1990s forced massive restructuring, with various divisions being hived off and given more autonomy, making it a more successful company by the end of the decade. One consequence of the success of the original PC was that, in presenting the industry with a standard, the burgeoning and diverse computer market that had begun to emerge in Europe as well as the USA became fixated once more on Big Blue so that, a decade later, the European computer industry as an originating force in desktop computers had all but disappeared.

Intel and its competitors

One of the foundation stones of cyberspace has been the microprocessor, invented by Intel (from Integrated Electronics) in 1971. Essentially a computer on a chip, the microprocessor combined many key components that, until the 1970s, had to be constructed on separate integrated circuits; following its introduction, miniaturi-sation and thus the extension of computing into smaller devices such as the PC and handheld computer became possible.

Intel was founded in 1968 by Robert Noyce and Gordon Moore, who had already been involved in two startups: Shockley Laboratories (named after William Shockley, who led the team at Bell Labs that developed the transistor) in 1956 and Fairchild Semiconductor a year later (Jackson 1997). Intel began life manufacturing memory circuits, and even until the end of the 1990s many engineers at the company argued that the chip which made Intel famous (and which Moore called 'one of the most revolutionary products in the history of mankind') was a diversion from its core business. This changed after the launch of the IBM PC, which used an Intel processor (the 8088).

For nearly twenty years after the launch of the PC, Intel clearly dominated the microchip market, with revenues of $7 billion for the year 2002. In the early and mid-1990s, the company had engaged in costly lawsuits against competitors – principally AMD – to prevent them from launching chips compatible with its x86 architecture and, more importantly, to slow down research and development. In 2000, however, Intel seemed to falter: it was AMD that reached the psycho-logically important number of one gigahertz (a thousand megahertz) with its Athlon processors, and Intel was hit by a chip shortage in the early months of that year.

While Intel quickly pulled ahead in terms of processor speed, as well as providing other innovations that established the superiority of its microchips in certain areas, its dominance had been slightly shaken by the emergence of com-petition that had not really existed for nearly a decade. In 2001, Intel's profits dropped 94 per cent in the second quarter and 77 per cent in the third quarter, its business hit badly by the downturn in PC sales and losses in the dotcom market which Intel Capital had invested in heavily. None the less, despite recession the company invested in manufacturing capacity and new technologies, determined to be in a good position when the IT market recovered (Magee 2002).

Microsoft

While companies such as IBM and Intel may have larger revenues than Microsoft, they have attracted nothing like the attention that the Redmond-based software giant has seen. Throughout 1999 and 2000, Microsoft's woes filled business pages as one of the greatest success stories of American industry appeared on the verge of breakup, accused of abusing a monopoly position that had made it a worldwide brand as recognisable as Nike and Coca-Cola. The small operation, founded in 1975 in Albuquerque, New Mexico, had grown to outstrip commercial leviathans such as US Steel and General Electric in a mere twenty-five years. During the boom years of dotcom mania, part of the reason for such huge investments in unproven companies was the simple, greedy hope that one of them would become the next Microsoft, providing astronomic returns on investment.

Much of Microsoft's later success was built on the operating system it produced for the original IBM PC in 1981. This was by no means a given: at the time, Microsoft was seen principally as a producer of computer languages, with the most widely used operating system, CP/M, having been produced by Gary Kildall at Digital Research. Kildall, however, was becoming increasingly complacent: he had not, for example, provided CP/M support for Intel's 8086 and 8088 processors, leading a motherboard manufacturer, Tom Patterson, to write a quick and dirty operating system named, appropriately, Q-DOS. When Kildall and his wife refused to sign a deal with IBM, the company turned to Microsoft, which in turn bought Patterson's Q-DOS for $50,000 and renamed it MS-DOS (Cringeley 1996; Gates 1995).

Microsoft became a convert to cyberspace at a relatively late stage. Its huge successes on the desktop meant that it took a relatively complacent view of the Internet. In his 1995 book *The Road Ahead*, Gates did indeed argue for a telecommunications network that would transform the way users lived and worked, but it was clear that he envisaged a proprietary system similar to the services such as AOL, CompuServe and Prodigy that dominated online access at the time. For Gates, the universal network would be the Microsoft Network. What proved him wrong was the rapid growth of Netscape in the mid-1990s, the progress of which appeared to demonstrate Microsoft as a sclerotic casualty of the old economy and espoused the values of the new. Valued at over $2 billion shortly after its initial public offering (yet with revenues of only $100 million), the biggest danger for Microsoft was that the company did not quickly fold but indeed went on to set its sites on the Internet as a universal operating system that would replace MS Windows. Late in 1995, Gates bet the company on the Internet and devoted massive resources in developing technologies that would defeat the competition: initial responses to Internet Explorer were desultory – by 2002, it was the software that users employed automatically to access the Internet.

For Microsoft at the turn of the twenty-first century the outcome of the browser wars with Netscape was an ambivalent one. In 2000, Bill Gates stepped down as CEO, to be replaced by president Steve Ballmer, though he remained as chairman of the company. While this was announced as a major structural change, in reality the move was an evolutionary one: the proposed breakup of Microsoft had not taken place by 2002; in any case, as some commentators observed, the division of Microsoft into two companies for applications and operating system could create two monopolies where only one existed before. Ultimately, Microsoft emerged relatively unscathed by the anti-trust incident with its core markets more or less intact, although it was notably more cautious throughout 2002.

AOL Time Warner

For many people connected to cyberspace, 'AOL *is* the Internet' (Bayers 1999: 114). Founded by Steve Case in 1985 as Quantum Computer Services, the company that was to become America Online, later AOL and then AOL Time Warner, began as a small, proprietary online service provider that aimed to provide simpler means of connecting computer users to servers and each other. Compared to the dotcom players of the late 1990s, AOL's growth was modest, but this slow growth enabled it to adapt and develop, from just over 180,000 subscribers at the beginning of the 1990s to nearly 18 million by the decade's end. In addition, AOL experienced many of the problems that affected later competitors, such as difficulties over quality of service and converting free users into paying subscribers, but had a much longer period in which to address such problems while facing much lower expectations.

For the final quarter of 1999, AOL posted a net income of $224 million on revenues of $1.6 billion, an increase of 41 per cent in a year, and it was such successes that led to the acquisition of Time Warner in a $350 billion merger agreement. Two years later, however, and AOL's astronomic achievements were beginning to look more suspect. AOL admitted that its 'synergy' dividends were vastly inflated and it posted a $54 billion loss after re-evaluating its assets.

Having lost more than $200 billion on its over-inflated valuation of $290 billion, the balance of power within the company has been reversed as old Time Warner executives replaced the new media power players. According to commentators such as Douglas Rushkoff (2002), AOL had understood that the 'pyramid scheme' on which its fortunes had been based was coming to an end and so used a temporarily inflated stock price to acquire something more tangible, changing the corporate culture at Time Warner to such an extent that former chairman Gerald Levin left in disgust. By the end of 2002, the company was left hoping that AOL Time Warner would 'become as good and real a conglomerate as Time Warner was in the first place' (Rushkoff 2002: 6), but even worse news was to follow: in January 2003, the company posted the largest ever US corporate loss, at $98.7 billion for the year 2002.

Most of the loss came from the fact that the company had written down the value of its AOL Internet division by $35 billion, with another $10 billion loss due to its cable division. The heady promises made in preparation for the merger of AOL and Time Warner at the end of the 1990s had quickly unravelled, and from a height of $71 per share after the announcement of the merger in January 2000 the company fell to its lowest value of $8.70 in July 2002. After news of the huge losses, shares fell by 14 per cent to $12 and investors in AOL Time Warner were concerned that its Internet division did not simply become a source of losses. Another casualty was Ted Turner, one of the strongest critics of the original merger, who stood down as vice-chairman. The Internet losses, as well as concern at how many of AOL's 27 million customers were converting to broadband subscriptions, led to predictions that AOL could once more be spun off.

Empires of the sun

Thus far, we have concentrated on the brand-name players of the IT market, to which could be added a number of important players, such as Hewlett-Packard and

Dell, which have become household names in their own right. It is no accident that all these companies are based in the USA, the birthplace of most (though by no means all) significant developments in ICT from the microprocessor to the Internet.

The real home of the computer and electronics industry in terms of production, however, is the complex web of Asian suppliers, largely unknown, which supply the dominant, US-based brand names discussed in this chapter. The most important centre is Taiwan, the electronics and computer exports of which amounted to $5 billion in 2001 according to its Ministry of Economic Affairs. Concentrating on producing computer components and peripherals, many of the factories that were previously in Taiwan have been moved to China, attracted largely by low wage costs: typical wages for Chinese workers are $30 a month, while Taiwanese labour costs now rival those in Western Europe or the USA (Magee 2001).

Taiwanese companies such as Asus, Mitac, Abit and Gibabyte provide components (for example, motherboards and notebooks) to Western suppliers who then rebrand them for a particular market. Larger manufacturers such as IBM and Dell engage such companies to produce equipment to a certain specification, and many producers in the Far East were family companies prior to the IT boom of the 1990s.

The growth of the IT sector in southeast Asia has been one indicator of the growth of multinational and globalised markets during the 1990s. While it has undoubtedly contributed to a massive increase in such international markets during that period, however, it has also brought other problems as the Taiwan computer industry suffered along with US and European customers during the recession of 2001.

Open source

A very different approach taken to the commercial IT companies considered thus far in this chapter, but one that has been fundamental to the development of cyberspace itself, has been the development of free, or open-source, software. Free software does not necessarily mean that no money is paid for it, but rather that source code is freely available for further modification. In an essay posted to the web in 1997 and issued later in book form as *The Cathedral and the Bazaar*, Eric Raymond contrasted the formal enterprise of the cathedral builder (and traditional IT) with the free trade of a bazaar, arguing that the latter was more efficient than traditional processes because it encouraged faster sharing of developments (Raymond 2001).

The driving force behind open-source software is GNU (for GNU's Not Unix), associated most strongly with Richard Stallman and the Free Software Foundation. As the name implies, GNU is based on Unix, which developed out of a project at AT&T's Bell Labs, Multics. Multics was a bloated, ambitious OS that ran over time and over budget in the late 1950s. When the plug was pulled, two engineers, Ken Thompson and Dennis Ritchie, devised their own OS, originally known as Unics (in reaction to Multics).

Unix is probably the most important OS ever created – a powerful multitasking OS originally written in 11,000 lines of code (compared to 5.6 million for Windows NT 4.0 and an estimated 29 million for Windows 2000). After testing and development, Bell began to distribute Unix. Because the US government had filed an anti-trust suit against AT&T in 1949, AT&T had agreed in 1956 to restrict itself to the telephone network and government work – which meant it was barred from the computer industry. As such, Bell distributed Unix at low cost ($150) and with the source code, which could be altered according to its licence.

With such a boost, Unix spread very quickly through many professional, governmental and academic organisations. By 1982, the Bell operating companies had been hived off from AT&T in return for the restrictions of 1956 being lifted. AT&T decided to capitalise on the increasingly popular Unix system by copyrighting the source code and charging considerably more for its product. Enter stage left Richard Stallman.

Stallman had joined the Artificial Intelligence Laboratory at MIT in 1971, and has been described as 'somewhere between Superman and Moses' (Naughton 1999: 195). In 1984 Stallman set up the Free Software Foundation, which operates on the assumption that software development works at its best when programmers are free to adapt and redistribute code: the idea is more 'free speech' than 'free beer' (Stallman 1985). During the remainder of the 1980s, Stallman and a group of hackers had created many of the programs that would comprise GNU, but not the kernel – the heart of the operating system that would communicate between software and hardware. This was provided by a student at the University of Helsinki, Linus Torvalds, who had enrolled on a Unix course in 1990 and set about creating a series of device drivers that was eventually released as Linux in 1991.

While the most commonly encountered form of open software, there are other variants of Unix to Linux, including FreeBSD (named after the Berkeley System's Distribution of Unix developed in the 1970s). The ethos of open source development, particularly insofar as it could be tied to a structure verifying standards rather than a proliferation of interesting but incompatible software, has also been fundamental to the expansion of cyberspace, enabling systems such as TCP/IP and the Web. In addition, Linux has attracted increased interest as the main competitor to Microsoft Windows, particularly as figures such as Raymond compare the cost for each Windows licence as a 'tax' on PCs with rapidly falling hardware prices.

Telecommunications

Along with computers, the other twin pillar in terms of technology on which cyberspace is constructed is the telecommunications industry. We have already traced briefly the development of telecoms that led to the invention of the Internet, and here we will be more concerned with the technical and economic structures that enable cyberspace to operate.

Telecoms structures and the Internet

At its simplest, the telecommunications industry provides the means for communication that, from its origins in the nineteenth century with the invention of the telegraph, has been almost global since its inception. In this chapter, we will concentrate on the data services provided by modern telcos, although obviously the voice services on which they built their wealth in the mid-twentieth century remain vitally important. One important feature in the early extension of the Internet past the networks that linked major research institutions was the ability to piggy-back computer networks across national POTS (plain old telephone service) networks, with users connecting to cyberspace via a telephone exchange. In turn, remote computers and servers relay their information across telephone exchanges or cable hubs, so that data may be passed between local and national access points.

To connect to the Internet via POTS, a user requires a modem (modulator/demodulator) that converts digital signals into analog audio signals that can be transmitted along copper telephone wires. As we shall see in relation to broadband, however, while this method of connection has now proved itself fairly reliable for decades, it is also extremely slow, leading to developments in cable and digital subscriber line (DSL) technologies. Equally important is satellite broadcasting, which has long served voice and broadcasting traffic but, with operations such as Eutelsat's Open Sky streaming service launched in 2001, now offers multimedia data. In the UK, BT began testing a wholesale satellite service that other ISPs would be able to offer in 2002, one which would be much cheaper than previous offerings but restricted to download speeds of 256Kbits per second and upload speeds of 33.5Kbits.

Another major change in the way we connect to cyberspace is the physical medium of connecting. With the exception of satellite, common means for linking to the Net all involve cables of some sort, which tends to physically restrict connections and has, for example, restricted what devices can connect to cyberspace. This is likely to change as wireless technologies become much more widely used. BT, for example, announced in 2002 that it was testing a new wireless LAN system that could cover much of the country, whereby users would be able to connect via a laptop or personal digital assistant (PDA) to the Internet via one of 400 'points of presence' in the UK. Initial locations proposed included railway stations, airports, hotels and bars, with BT estimating 4,000 such access points being available to subscribers by 2005. Elsewhere around the world, other people are campaigning for similar wireless zones to be available in cities, ideally free of charge and providing instant wireless access courtesy of the municipal authority itself.

While telecommunication technologies such as cable and satellite enable cyberspace, Internet technologies such as Voice-over-IP (VoIP) are slowly changing the way people use a relatively old technology, the telephone, to communicate. Rather than employing expensive public branch exchanges (PBX) for phone communications, many companies are starting to employ VoIP to connect users

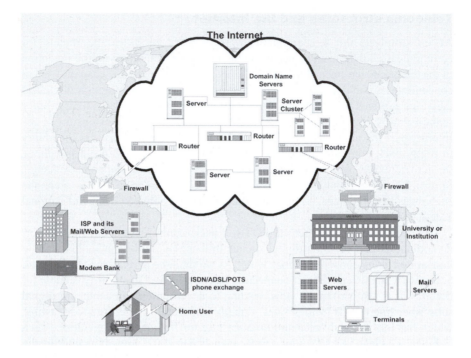

Figure 3.1 Users connecting to the Internet to receive messages or download files from a remote server will usually dial into an ISP, which itself is part of a network of computers routing and caching information across the Internet.

and pay only standard web charges, even for international calls. Such a system is not perfect, however, as it suffers from latency (gaps or pauses in speech) and poor-quality end-to-end service.

US and European telecommunications

The American ISP market is huge, although it has shrunk significantly since 2000 when more than 7,400 companies competed for business. As an ISP, AOL dominates the field with 33 million subscribers at the end of 2001, but that domination has been countered by a number of rival companies. In the USA, national telecommunications are supplied primarily by AT&T, which also extended into the ISP market with AT&T WorldNet, while Sprint Communications had purchased a large share of the major US ISP's Earthlink and MindSpring after they merged early in 2000. Other megamergers included that which took place in the same year between Pacific Bell, Southwestern Bell and Prodigy, resulting in a slimmed down market. One effect of this means that whereas in the mid-1990s half the number of Internet users would connect via a local provider, by 2000 this had fallen to less than a quarter (Keizer 2000).

America has, not surprisingly, dominated cyberspace since the introduction of the Internet at the end of the 1960s. According to industry monitor Nua.com (www.nua.com), however, Europe overtook the USA and Canada in 2002 in terms of numbers of Internet users: 186 million in the former, compared to 182 million in the latter. European users now account for 32 per cent of the global Internet population (Johnson 2002).

The largest Internet players in Europe are Germany's T-Online (Deutsche Telekom), France's Wanadoo (France Telecom) and Italy's Tiscali, with 25 million subscribers between them in mid-2002. Each of these three has been very keen to expand as quickly by purchasing smaller businesses although rapid acquisition could result in similar problems that affected dotcoms at the end of the 1990s. In late 2002, for example, Wanadoo announced losses worth billions of euros, while Tiscali has spent huge amounts of money to come from nowhere in three years, leading to persistent rumours that it will be forced eventually to sell to one of its competitors. None the less, while Internet penetration is probably close to saturation in the USA, there is still considerable room for growth in Europe, particularly in broadband; here, T-Online leads the way, with 50 per cent of German customers linked up by high-speed connections.

The problems affecting WorldCom in 2002 led some commentators to question whether the Internet could survive such a disaster (see Wray 2002). At its peak, WorldCom's fibre optic network carried half the world's emails and 70 per cent of those sent in the USA. Important as this was, it was not a problem restricted to America as WorldCom had also purchased the major European backbone UUNet. While the Internet was unlikely to collapse, having been designed precisely to withstand such shortages, many were concerned that traffic would slow down as large sections of the network were removed. The reason why this did not happen was probably as much due to the fact that the 1990s saw massive over-investment in telecommunications networks, with it being estimated that less than 10 per cent of Europe's fibre optic network was in use by the beginning of the twenty-first century.

The UK market

Unlike its market for Internet access, British Telecom still overwhelmingly dominates the general UK telecommunications market, despite the fact that it was much slower to capitalise on its massive user base than its French and German equivalents. As such, in the ISP market it has been overtaken by two other competitors, AOL and Freeserve, while certain aspects of its operations have been competed for by cable companies such as Telewest and NTL. As we have already seen, AOL is the largest (though also troubled) Internet service provider worldwide, but Freeserve has rapidly emerged as its strongest competitor in the UK: founded in 1998 by the Dixons Group and sold to Wanadoo in 2000, Freeserve was extremely influential in opening up toll-free Internet access, helping to prompt the UK dotcom boom at the end of the 1990s. With AOL and BT Openworld,

Freeserve shares the sometime title of largest ISP in the UK, but many observers feel that BT's failure to lead the domestic market means that it has lost its chance to be a major player in Europe (Johnson 2002).

An important link in UK Internet provision is the London Internet Exchange (LINX), which processes up to 96 per cent of Britain's Internet traffic. Founded in 1994 as a co-operative venture to offer connectivity between five ISPs, by the beginning of 2002 it was servicing the 120 largest UK service providers via its eight London hubs. The concentration of so much traffic in one place did lead to concern that LINX's central offices Telehouse, in Docklands, would provide an easy target to terrorists keen on damaging the UK network, but even before 11 September Telehouse proclaimed itself one of the most secure buildings in Europe (Akass and Middelton 2002).

While Telehouse has come to monopolise the physical transfer of data into and out of the UK, for most telecommunication customers in the country the company most likely to dominate their business – despite attempts by previous Conservative governments to shake up competition – remained BT. Following the privatisation of British Telecom in 1984, Oftel was established to regulate the UK telco giant. For many of BT's competitors and customers, Oftel rarely appeared to perform well and, within a decade, was clearly becoming archaic: companies such as BSkyB, the BBC and NTL had interests that spread across the entire spectrum, making it difficult to justify splitting the communications industry into several sectors. As such, in December 2000, the government published plans to bring together Oftel, TV regulators and the Radio Authority into one independent watchdog, Ofcom, by the end of 2003.

From the late 1990s until early 2002, attempts to make the UK telecom market more competitive concentrated on BT's monopoly of the copper network that covers more or less the entire country. Following the purchase of G3 licences that helped push BT's debt to £30 billion by 2001, the company looked vulnerable to attempts to force it to unbundle the local loop, the final few miles of copper that connects homes to telephone exchanges, and the German bank WestLB led a consortium that put forward a reported £25 billion for the entire local-loop network, including BT's exchanges. BT refused the deal (as well as a smaller bid of £8 billion from Earthlease) when it halved its debt in 2002, but pressure remains on the UK giant to engage in a future deal.

Broadband

The growing dependency on digital media, the Internet and other aspects of cyber-space to drive the so-called information economy led many experts and the UK government to insist on the importance of broadband connections. Broadband, a general term for a variety of connections such as cable, ADSL (asymmetric digital subscriber line) and satellite, is a means of communicating online at much faster speeds than are possible using conventional modems. Large businesses and organisations may already have dedicated leased lines, also known as T-Carriers, that range in speeds from 64Kbits per second to nearly 275Mbits. For a successful online economy to function, so the argument runs, it is essential that large parts of the country – if not all households and businesses – are connected via broadband technologies in order to facilitate such things as ecommerce, teleworking and online entertainment.

Difficulties in rolling out broadband technologies such as ADSL, however, meant that the UK was near the bottom of the league of European broadband-enabled countries in 2002. BT had announced trials in 1997, but by the beginning of 2002 there were only an estimated 150,000 subscribers using ADSL, with a further 100,000 for Telewest's Blueyonder cable service. Problems included high prices, not enough engineers to set up home access, and accusations against BT that its failure to unbundle the local loop (the final few miles from exchanges to customers' homes and businesses) was stifling competition.

BT (which was often held responsible for the slow rollout of faster access) announced a number of changes at the time to improve subscription rates, cutting the price of its ADSL service in the face of competitive offers from cable companies and moving to faster DIY installations using a plug-in filter, meaning that subscribers could go online without the need for connection by an engineer. The company also reported that exchanges capable of supporting ADSL covered 13 million households, half of all schools and nearly three-quarters of all Internet users at the time, but it was also clear that many rural areas were unlikely to be covered. While ADSL could cover the majority of the population in the UK, it covered only a small area of the country – though the ACT NOW project launched in the first half of 2002 demonstrated how BT could operate in more remote areas such as Cornwall (though this was only possible with a £5.25 million subsidy).

While the adoption of cable broadband was much quicker in the period between 2000 and 2001, this was at considerable cost to operators such as NTL and Telewest, which accumulated large debts when creating a cable infrastructure. By 2002, the broadband revolution that had been heralded as imminent for nearly a decade was improving only slowly, with most Internet users still connected by narrowband modems.

Table 3.1 Broadband and narrowband connection speeds

Type	Speeds (Kilobits or Megabits per second)
Modem (V.90/V.92)	56Kb download, 33.6Kb/48Kb upload
ISDN	65–128Kb
ADSL	512Kb–8Mb download, 256Kb upload
Cable	512Kb–55.2Mbits
T1	64Kb–3.152Mb
T2	6.312Mb
T3	44.736Mb
T4	89.472Mb–274.176

ADSL

DSL (digital subscriber line) is an overarching term for a number of connection standards, the most famous of which is ADSL. The A stands for asymmetric, indicating that download speeds are faster than those for uploads, so that the subscriber can receive data more quickly than he or she can send it.

Like the older standard ISDN (integrated services digital network), ADSL is an always-on service that also allows users to surf the Internet without disturbing voice calls. Unlike ISDN, ADSL does not require a second phone line for voice calls; also, whereas ISDN operates at a maximum speed of 128Kbits per second with two lines in use, ADSL has the potential for connections up to 8Mbits per second, although no service currently available in the UK offers speeds faster than 2Mbits. ADSL works by making full use of the 1.1MHz bandwidth available in copper wires that run from a local exchange to most properties in the UK, of which less than 4KHz is typically used by voice and fax data.

Because it can make use of the existing copper line infrastructure, ADSL would seem to be the most obvious upgrade route for broadband users in the UK. The technology does require the use of a splitter to separate voice and data signals, and the requirement for technicians to install this equipment did slow down progress for several years; with the appearance of DIY kits, however, it would seem that the only thing holding back users would be price. There is another technical difficulty, however: just because ADSL works over standard phone lines does not mean it is available everywhere, as local exchanges have to be fully digital. In addition, a customer had to be within 3.5 kilometres of such an exchange to access ADSL, although the launch of RADSL (rate-adaptive DSL) in 2001 extended this range to 5.5 kilometres.

While the adoption of ADSL has been slow in the UK, BT has none the less begun to trial a related technology, SDSL (or symmetric DSL), that will enable businesses to transfer data at up to 2Mbits per second, making it potentially a much cheaper alternative to T1 leased line connections.

Mobile

Any overview of telecommunications in the twenty-first century cannot ignore mobile phones, the use of which exploded in certain parts of the world in the final decade of the twentieth century. On New Year's Day, 2001, for example, there were enough mobile phones in circulation in the UK for more than 65 per cent of the population and 290 million users in Europe. Worldwide, that number was expected to reach a billion by 2003, not 2005 as originally predicted.

Mobile phone technologies first began to emerge in the early 1980s, growing from experiments in cellular-based communication that had taken place at Bell Labs in the 1970s. In 1982, the Conference of European Posts and Telegraphs (CEPT) set up a working group to develop standards for the Groupe Spécial Mobile (GSM), followed a year later by Bell's Advanced Mobile Phone System (AMPS), which looked similar to field radios then in use by the military.

By 1985, an analog mobile network was in place in the UK, followed by the first GSM (now known as the Global System for Mobile comms) system in 1991, marking a shift from analog to digital networks that would be able to carry data other than voice more easily. While GSM enjoyed enormous success in Europe and other parts of the world, particularly Asia, Japan and the USA developed their own standards some of which, notably i-mode, the Japanese alternative to WAP, could be even more successful.

Due to the massive takeup of mobile technologies during the 1990s, as well as expectations that improved access would fuel further growth, telecommunication companies appeared more than willing to put their money where their mouths were. At the height of telecommunications mania in 2000, the UK Labour government, aware of the unpopularity of direct taxation, auctioned off licences to major players for £22.4 billion: the Montreal-based operator TIW UMTS paid £4.4 billion, Vodafone £5.9 billion, Orange and BT 3G £4.1 billion each, and One2One £4 billion. By mid-2002, however, technical difficulties in integrating 2.5G and 3G networks – alongside problems in applying for masts – led some commentators to question the feasibility of 3G phones before 2005, requiring some operators to write off the massive fees they had paid for their licences only two years previously. Companies such as the BT spin-off, mm0$_2$, increasingly believed that 3G use would not become significant until 2004, and only then in certain urban hot spots.

Third generation

The willingness of companies to spend huge amounts for 3G licences indicated an inflated value of the significance of 3G, yet this still represents a step forward in mobile technology that will be at least as big as the cross-over from analog to GSM systems. Cellular phone systems are so named because an area is divided into cells, each containing one or more transceivers: these transceivers are not too powerful, enabling precious frequency resources to be reused, with more powerful transceivers being used in more sparsely populated areas.

The first GSM networks operated at 9,000MHz, while later 1,800MHz and 1,900MHz used different parts of the radio spectrum to allow more data to be communicated. GSM was originally designed to be compatible with ISDN, but was never capable of achieving similar connection speeds of 64Kbits/sec. Most GSM sets today are capable of receiving and transmitting data at between 9.6Kbits/sec and 14.4Kbits/sec. It is partly the slowness of such connections that limited the overhyped Wireless Application Protocol (WAP), a service capable of browsing specially designed web pages over a mobile phone.

GSM has proved remarkably robust, and current improvements to the system such as the General Packet Radio Service (GPRS) and High Speed Circuit Switched Data (HSCSD), often referred to as 2.5 generation systems, promise more reliable connections and faster speeds. Full third-generation (3G) systems offer a theoretical maximum data transfer of 2Mbits/sec, although this would be possible only in optimum conditions; speeds of 400Kbits/sec are still possible, however, and work has already begun on 4G networks that could provide connections of 100Mbits/sec by the end of the decade.

While demand for mobile phones has barely slowed, however, this is not the same as suggesting that there is a particular hunger for 3G services. At present, most mobile users seem content to rely on phones for voice data, making even 400Kbit connections (and UK companies' £22.4 billion investment) relatively unimportant.

Free or FRIACO

Despite current difficulties, mobile technology is almost certainly the future of cyberspace connectivity: for the time being, however, connection is still most likely to occur via a computer and landline. There were many reasons for the early takeup of the Internet in the USA, including such factors as its initial development in US institutions and the ubiquity of English as the language of communication and certain North American mores and customs. In addition, US telecom customers are used to paying slightly more for line rental in return for unmetered local calls; as these same customers connected to the Internet via a local phone call, such connections were effectively free after their fixed subscription to an ISP.

This situation contrasted greatly to that in the UK, and fear of the costs of going online was cited widely as one of the issues hindering the development of the new economy on that side of the Atlantic. As part of general dotcom mania in 1999, AltaVista mooted freephone access to the Net in return for a £30 startup fee, while the cable company NTL offered completely free access to users who spent £10 per month on voice calls.

Problems soon set in for the various companies that jumped on the bandwagon: fixed fees from subscribers could not be squared with rapidly rising costs from suppliers (principally BT), and companies such as Screaming.net quickly imposed time limits on freephone numbers, while others such as RedHotAnt went into liquidation. BT, which was criticised increasingly by large players in the ISP market such as AOL and Freeserve, launched a series of subscription services where users would pay a fixed rate in return for unmetered Internet access. When MCI WorldCom sought a flat-rate connection agreement with BT, the first response was BT SurfTime, which was seen by many as an attempt by BT to maintain its monopoly. When WorldCom complained, Oftel ordered the UK company to offer a more transparent connection agreement; BT responded with FRIACO (flat-rate internet access call origination) in 2001, a system whereby a flat fee of £425 was charged per 64Kb line that could then be used to provide access for six to twelve customers.

One of the consequences of FRIACO was that by the end of the year UK Internet users, while less likely to be connected online via a broadband connection, were leading the way in terms of Net access. A report by the EU estimated that almost 40 per cent of the 10 million UK homes with Internet access were using unmetered packages by the end of 2001, and encouraged other member states to follow suit.

Taxing ISPs

While unmetered services demonstrated the cut-throat nature of Internet provision in the late 1990s, another row that blew up at the end of 2001 demonstrated some of the other problems for competitors operating in a global market. Freeserve, the UK's largest ISP, complained to Customs and Excise that one of its main competitors, AOL, was taking advantage of tax rulings that allowed non-EU ISPs to operate in the EU without paying VAT. Telecoms services have had to pay VAT since 1997, but AOL escaped this by presenting itself as a content provider. A Merrill Lynch report in 2001 suggested that the levy of VAT on its customers, who number more than a million, would cost AOL more than £30 million a year.

Freeserve argued that changes in legislation made the exemption for AOL obsolete, and Customs and Excise were engaged in talks with the US-based company. Changes, however, were unlikely to arrive quickly – the Internet Service Provider Association (ISPA) did not expect to receive clarification until the end of 2002 – but Freeserve swiftly lost patience, its parent company, Wanadoo, threatening to move the business outside the UK unless the tax anomaly was rectified: when this did not happen, Freeserve was moved to Madeira in August 2002, thus depriving the UK government of an estimated £17 million tax a year.

Part II

Using cyberspace

4 Using the Internet

The first step to becoming a cyberspace practitioner is to understand how to use the Internet, how to collect and transmit information via email, browsers, newsgroups and so on. Experienced users will probably wish to skip this chapter, although it covers the most important elements of connecting to the Internet and using various technologies outside the obvious browser and email combination employed by most people, such as videoconferencing and instant messaging.

Connecting to cyberspace

In order to use cyberspace, one must have an Internet connection. For students, Internet access is usually provided via a university or similar institution, but only the largest organisations have this kind of direct access. Most users will need to join an Internet Service Provider (ISP).

Selecting an ISP

One of the biggest changes to ISPs since the end of the 1990s has been the widespread adoption of subscription services, following the rapid success of Wanadoo's Freeserve (www.freeserve.com, formerly owned by the Dixon group). As we saw in Chapter 3, the end of the 1990s saw a rush of ostensibly free ISPs that would charge nothing after an initial setup fee: with the introduction of FRIACO, however, and the possibility for ISPs to fix costs to users, many of these free companies disappeared. At present, the main choice for most users is some version of subscription, no-toll-charge connection, or one that charges per minute for time spent online but does not demand a fixed subscription fee.

While all ISPs provide the same essential service – connection to the Internet – not all are equal in terms of their service. Until the end of the 1990s, a common problem with ISPs was that most were too small and a few were too large: very small businesses were unlikely to be able to provide the infrastructure required to connect their users unless they charged considerably more to guarantee quality of service; however, even the largest companies could then become victims of their own success, with too many users attempting to connect at the same time. In the mid-1990s, the computer press in particular was full of complaints about poor quality of service, although post-2000 this appears to be less of an issue for most users. It is, however, worth checking sites such as ISP Watch (www.voicendata. com/content/ispwatch/default.asp) before selecting an ISP.

Going global

One potential problem facing many users is that while the Internet is a global phenomenon, ISPs are usually national entities that can be difficult to connect to when abroad. This difficulty is one reason for the (relative) success of Internet cafés, at least in large cities, as well as web-based email services: a user who subscribes to a service such as Hotmail or Yahoo! can simply log on to their account anywhere in the world and send or receive messages.

For more complex tasks, AOL (and formerly CompuServe) has been a good choice for global connectivity, offering local numbers in many countries. An alternative for many users, however, is the GRIC Alliance Network (www.gric. net), an association of some 300 top-tier ISPs from more than 150 countries. The GRIC network offers some 15,000 local call-rate locations around the globe, making it simpler to connect to an ISP worldwide.

Making the connection

Once an ISP is chosen, the next step is how to link to the Net, which can be as simple as a modem hooked up to a single PC or as comprehensive as a leased line connected to a local area network (see Table 4.1).

- **Analog**: The most common type of link to the Internet, at least in terms of numbers of individuals, remains dial-up. While a 56Kb (kilobytes) per second modem may be more than sufficient for a home user, speed and reliability can become a real issue for more demanding users.
- **ISDN**: ISDN (integrated services digital network) is effectively a leased line on demand, offering a theoretical dial-up connection of 64Kb, or even 128Kb, per second. ISDN connects more quickly than analog modems, but other bottlenecks such as slow servers or busy lines may affect data transfer.
- **Cable/ADSL**: Fast alternatives to ISDN, including ADSL (asymmetric digital subscriber line) and cable modems, offer connections theoretically measured in Mb not Kb. ADSL offers a potential 2Mb per second link across a standard copper wire, and is increasingly available to users. Cable has made greater inroads in the UK, with a theoretical data transfer rate of 20Mb per second. In practice, cable modems are much slower because users share

bandwidth with other users on a line. It is, however, considerably cheaper, with prices comparable to ISDN.

- **Leased line**: All the above services are dial-up in one form or another, the alternative being a permanent connection best suited for businesses or institutions. Although one of the most expensive options, a flat fee of approximately £500 per month provides multiple-user access to a 64K voice and data line: larger bandwidth lines cost more. Another advantage of being connected via a leased line is that a web server can be set up much more easily.

Table 4.1 Options for connecting to the Web

Connection type	Pros	Cons
Analog modem	Low cost; supported by every ISP.	Slow; less reliable connection rates.
ISDN	Effectively a dial-up leased line; instant and more reliable connection.	Adapters and lines more expensive than modems; once online, may not be fast enough to justify the expense.
ADSL	Faster than ISDN.	Availability limited in rural areas.
Cable	High speed with faster connection.	Availability limited; speeds may decrease as more users come online.
Leased line	Permanent connection; best way to connect to an in-house server.	Very expensive.

Other ways to connect

At present, the most convenient way to connect to the Internet is via computer. While a billion personal computers have been sold in the past three decades, however, it is estimated that at most half of these are in use and, since many will be used in businesses or homes where more than one computer is available, this restricts considerably the number of people who are able (or willing) to go online. As such, while the PC currently dominates cyberspace, and will continue to dominate it for some time, other methods of linking up to the Internet will need to be pursued to provide the next great leap forward.

Web-enabled television

Nearly thirty years of the personal computer has made it a much more ubiquitous device, but it is still nowhere near as prevalent in households as television. This is why the late 1990s saw a number of projects to enable TV sets to connect to the Internet, including Tivo and WebTV. The combination of television and Internet access is potentially a good idea: many broadband users, for example, link to cyberspace via cable, and millions more users employ their television sets as the monitor for console games. However, for most users Web-enabled television generally represents too many compromises: screen resolutions for televisions are dramatically different to those for computer monitors, and navigation via a remote or (in some cases) a keyboard is much more difficult than with a mouse. As such, while the potential for home entertainment centres incorporating Internet access is considerable, convergence has been slow for a number of reasons.

WAP, i-mode and 3G

While the growth of the PC and Internet has been considerable, the explosion of mobile phones in two decades has been little short of astonishing. Because of this, mobile technology has often contributed to visions of more personalised conceptions of cyberspace, where users will carry data around with them and interface with other networks via a small device. Like televisions, mobile phones are generally much easier to use than computers (although ones that combine PDA elements perhaps push this notion of ease of use as far as it will go): although the screens of such phones are worse even than television resolutions, they do have the advantage of built-in connectivity.

Indeed, if mobile technologies are used more extensively to connect to the Internet, they will almost certainly transform some of our perceptions of cyberspace. At present, cyberspace (particularly the Web) tends to be conceived of in primarily *visual* terms, which do not transfer especially well to small mobile devices designed for voice use. Yet text-to-speech and voice-recognition technologies have made huge improvements in recent years, and it is increasingly likely that the way we will connect to certain parts of cyberspace in future years will be through an *audio* interface. In particular, such interfaces would make it easier to use small devices for navigation – speaking instructions rather than attempting to use a small keyboard or trackball.

While mobile technologies may be seen as having extended cyberspace per se over the past decade in particular, creating a communication network that lies alongside and permeates the Internet, combining the two has generally been less auspicious than initially anticipated. WAP (wireless application protocol) phones at the end of the 1990s were over-hyped and under-powered: while 3G services could suffer the same level of advertising propaganda, they do offer better potential for connecting to the Internet, particularly as companies such as BT have begun to install wireless 'hot spots' that would offer high-speed access in public places to subscribers. In addition, as the experience with i-mode (an alternative connection to WAP) demonstrated in Japan, when the expectations of more limited demands can be met, users are more than happy to employ mobile technologies for a wider range of communication than just voice messages.

The cyberspace toolkit

As the Internet has exploded over the past decade, so the tools required for its use have become increasingly sophisticated. This sophistication has developed both in terms of enabling users to perform more tasks than ever before but also, due to the increased power of computer hardware and greater maturity in user interfaces, most of those tasks are simpler than ever to perform.

This simplicity often conceals its own problems: as users require less technical knowledge to participate in cyberspace, so they are often more exposed to dangers such as hackers. Likewise, while a graphical user interface (GUI) makes it easier to explore the Internet, experienced users may still be able to find out more about elements of their connection through powerful command line tools, where simply typing a batch command can perform a multitude of mouse clicks. None the less, for cyberspace to succeed as a sphere of human endeavour rather than as the private club of a minority of technology enthusiasts, computers and the Internet must continue to develop simpler interfaces that can be understood as easily as possible. One comparison which is sometimes made is that between the complex interface of present-day computers and the simple interface of the telephone dial tone: international in nature, a series of sounds (or their absence) can convey a wealth of information to the user. The telephone is, of course, much more limited in its capabilities than the variety of digital technologies available even today, but developments such as HTML and HTTP have been extremely important in making the use of those technologies as transparent as possible.

Until the late 1990s, anyone attempting to connect to the Internet would need to access a wide range of separate programs to perform a number of tasks. Email would require a separate application to that used for browsing the web, while looking at newsgroups or downloading files would, in turn, require additional programs. Gradually, however, these applications became more closely integrated; this has never happened in such a way that one program covers all possible tasks online, something that is not necessarily desirable, as an email client performs a very different task to a web browser. Rather, the motif of office suite software gradually came to dominate the way users and producers looked at their Internet applications: just as Microsoft Office or Lotus SmartSuite provided a range of programs for dealing with common computer tasks, so Internet Explorer or Netscape came to offer a suite of applications that would perform most operations online. Such suites, centred on a browser, are still unlikely to do everything a user may require, but they are the most common starting place for using and communicating in cyberspace. For more information on the concepts behind these applications, consult *The Internet: The Basics* (Whittaker 2002).

Browsers

Browsers provide the essential tool for viewing the World Wide Web, a collection of files stored on thousands of servers worldwide. We have examined the basic concepts of the Web in Chapter 1, most importantly the distinction between those servers that store information and the clients who access them remotely. The browser is the most important piece of software on a client computer for accessing web servers, using the language of HTML and HTTP protocols to follow links between files and view them on the screen of a computer, television, or even a mobile phone.

At its very minimum, a browser must understand HTML, or, for some mobile phones, the Wireless version, WML. The protocols and languages of the Web are dealt with in much greater detail in Chapter 5, but the main versions used online today are Microsoft's Internet Explorer and Netscape (referred to in previous versions as Netscape Navigator or Communicator). Other, less popular browsers include Opera, Lynx and Mosaic. The simplest of these can display text files, but the changes made to the Web in the past decade have put pressure on such browsers to provide a complete multimedia environment that will cope with images, video and even 3D.

The most significant change browsers made to accessing cyberspace stemmed from the fact that they were developed almost from the beginning to provide a graphical user interface to the Web. Whereas other systems often worked by typing commands at a prompt, HTML files were designed to include links that could be followed by a mouse: rather than having to learn complex instructions, users would simply open a file in a browser and then use the mouse to navigate between documents online. As such, since graphical browsers were first introduced in the early 1990s they have steadily provided an increasingly sophisticated navigation system. Central to this is the window where files and pages are displayed, but this is surrounded by a cornucopia of tools to aid web browsing, such as the toolbar at the top of a browser (where you will find home, back and refresh buttons), menu options for opening, saving and printing files, an address bar where website locations may be entered manually, link buttons and status bars that indicate information about a site (such as where a link will lead, or the progress of a file download). In addition, the experience of viewing websites has been – depending on your point of view – enriched or slowed by the proliferation of plug-ins for such things as animation, interaction and the manipulation of objects in a virtual 3D environment. Finally, the most recent browsers also provide the ability to divide the main viewing window into a series of navigation tools that provide quick access to search tools online, or favourites and bookmarks.

One increasingly important feature of the browser, particularly after Microsoft launched Windows 98 with an improved version of Internet Explorer, is that it provides a unified interface for accessing local information on a hard drive and remote information on servers elsewhere in the world. It is this convergence that has been such a cause of concern for Microsoft's competitors, who fear that the company's domination of one market, the desktop operating system, could provide it with leverage to monopolise another: the Internet itself.

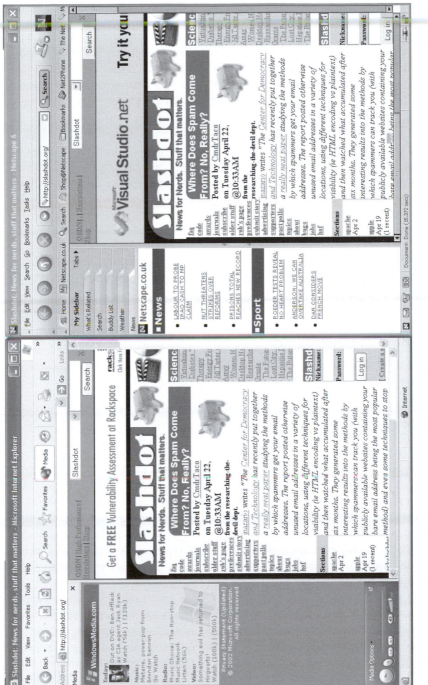

Figure 4.1 The most commonly used browsers are Internet Explorer and Netscape, the latest versions of which are more likely to display content similarly.

Web addresses

While web documents may be stored on servers around the world – indeed, with different elements of a single page such as images, adverts or multimedia components scattered across different servers and domains – the web address that is typed into the address bar of the browser provides what is known as a single uniform resource locator (URL), such as http://www.addamsfamily.net/gomez/ knifethrowing.htm. The first part of the URL specifies the transfer protocol, such as the hypertext transfer protocol (HTTP, discussed in more detail in the next chapter) or file transfer protocol (FTP). The next part of the address – www. routledge.com in the above example – indicates the host name of the Web server, and may sometimes include the name of a computer on that domain, such as http://fester.addamsfamily.net. The final part of a URL after the host name includes links to directories and individual files on the web server.

Plug-ins

Browsers are designed to display documents formatted by HTML commands, and extensions of the HTML language such as XHTML and XML. Contemporary browsers, however, are not restricted to files laid out with these languages, but can also display other multimedia elements by the use of plug-ins, applications that integrate seamlessly with the browser and are launched when particular files are downloaded. Common plug-ins include those for Flash and Shockwave documents that use Macromedia file formats, as well as video and 3D.

Email

While browsers form the basis of Internet communication suites, the most common application that most people use will be an email client. Email is, for most people, the killer app of cyberspace, the one program they will be unwilling to do without. Like a browser, an email program requires a server to store and relay messages across the Net and a client that can read those files, and the process for transmitting and receiving messages is divided into two protocols: simple mail transfer protocol (SMTP) for sending mail, and post office protocol (POP) or Internet message access protocol (IMAP) for receiving mail, mail servers using this protocol to store messages in mailboxes until a user dials into that server.

The earliest email clients provided a simple command line, where typing commands would display messages, retrieve them or perform other actions such as deleting old mail. Modern clients, such as Eudora or Outlook, provide a graphical user interface that makes it much simpler to compose and organise email. As it is still rare for users to be connected to the Net permanently, most clients work by dialling into a mail server to upload outgoing messages and download incoming ones.

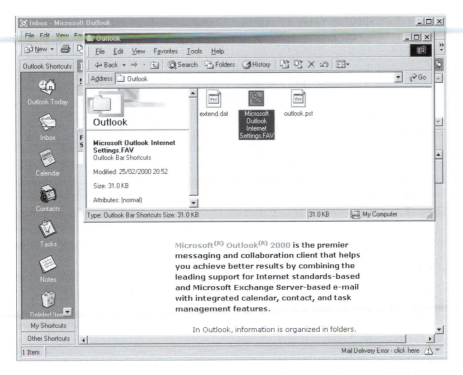

Figure 4.2 Due to its inclusion as part of Microsoft Office, Outlook is one of the most common email packages in use today.

Email addresses

Email addresses have two main parts joined by the @ (at) sign. The first part before @ is the user name, while that following the sign is the host name. Thus, for example, an email address such as morticia@addammsfamily.net would be the address for the user morticia at the domain addamsfamily.net. The part of the address following the @ sign may also include a computer name, so that morticia@ lurch.addamsfamily.net would address the mailbox of the user morticia on the computer lurch in the addamsfamily.net domain.

Every email also includes a header, namely text that provides users – and, more importantly, email servers – with information about the message. The header serves as an envelope, including details about the sender and recipient, when the message was sent and received, and other information such as the type of content (for example, ASCII text or HTML) and a message Id.

Chat and instant messaging

Online chat is a generic term that refers to the process of real-time communication, a more immediate form of exchange than email. The origins of chat lie in the invention of Internet Relay Chat (IRC) in 1988, the popularity of which grew during the Gulf War as people gathered on IRC to hear reports from the war (Young 1999). IRC networks employ servers that function as switchboards, enabling users to connect with appropriate client software and meet other IRC users in channels or chat rooms. Generally, IRC clients such as mIRC are more complicated and less popular than web-based chat rooms, which can be called in a browser.

The next step beyond IRC is instant messaging (IM), taking a similar approach to real-time chat but providing a simpler interface. Within a short period of time by the end of the 1990s, AOL, Microsoft (initially via MSN, but then as part of Windows XP), Yahoo! and several other companies had released clients to enable people to communicate quickly and simply, the most sophisticated of these also offering features for file transfer. The main producers of IM clients, however, realised that they had access to a potential treasure chest in terms of controlling messages, and a proprietary format war ensued, AOL, for example, suing Microsoft when the latter attempted to make its software compatible with the AOL instant messaging (AIM) service.

The outcome of this, at the time of writing, is that anyone interested in chatting via IM across multiple networks has to run several clients, with a complete failure to implement the standards – open or otherwise – that has characterised other elements of cyberspace such as web software and email. Of the attempts to standardise IM, only Jabber has had any real success (www.jabbercentral.org), using 'transports', software drivers that allow users to connect to proprietary systems – although early in 2002 AOL attempted to obstruct Jabber users from connecting to its servers.

Videoconferencing

Online chat is largely text-based (though users may exchange images and other files), but voice- and videoconferencing allow more sophisticated forms of real-time communication. Because of the demands that can be made on hardware and network infrastructures, such forms of conferencing (particularly for video) have only recently begun to become generally available, previously being restricted to specialised – and expensive – suites.

The advantages of conferencing are that it allows people to communicate at the same time in larger groups than is typically available via phone conversations (although phones with speakers provide a basic form of voiceconferencing) and, when connecting via an ISP, provides cheaper connections than long-range calls. However, many users simply do not have suitable hardware or – more pertinent here – network connections for data-intensive videoconferencing. There are also issues of security and reliability: while the Internet is generally resilient for sending files and emails, dial-up connections in particular are notoriously poor for online conferencing, with dropped data packets resulting in choppy voice or video streams. Unprotected connections also mean that personal and private messages may be accessed across the multiple networks that constitute the Internet, although the ability to create virtual private networks (VPN), simulating a private LAN (local area network) by 'tunnelling' across the public Internet, improves security.

Videoconferencing really began with a product called CU-SeeMe (www.fvc. com) in the 1990s, although many more users will now employ products such as Microsoft's NetMeeting or Instant Messaging software.

Media players

Media players are commonly used applications to play audio-visual material such as videos or MP3 sound files. The most commonly used media player is Microsoft's Windows Media Player, which has steadily progressed since its inclusion in Windows 3.1 to become an extremely comprehensive application (despite a few stability issues with the early releases of version 7). With appropriate codecs (instructions that compress and decompress audio and video), the Windows Media Player can deal with just about every file format encountered on the Net and, in its latest incarnation, may be used as a one-stop entertainment centre for everything from web radio to DVDs.

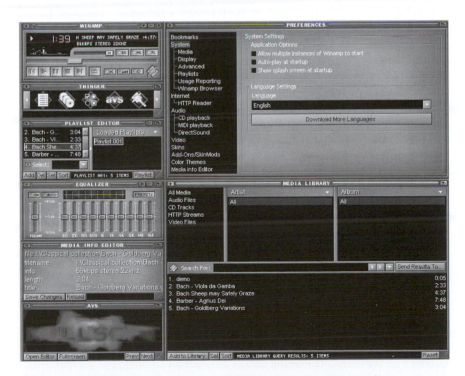

Figure 4.3 Modern media players such as WinAmp are designed as complete entertainment centres handling a vast array of files.

While Microsoft's Player may be the most commonly encountered application, however, it is not the only one, nor indeed the best for every situation. The trend towards webcasting was kickstarted by RealPlayer from Real Networks (www.real.com), which can play audio and video formatted with that company's highly compressed software and which has proved itself particularly suited for Net radio. Other popular media players include Apple's QuickTime player (www.apple.com/quicktime) and WinAmp (www.winamp.com), the latter designed specifically for playing music.

Media players were amongst the first sets of applications to become highly customisable in terms of appearance. By downloading graphics known as skins, the default look of a player can be radically transformed, something encouraged by most players in an attempt to persuade users to personalise them and thus use them instead of a competitor's products.

FTP/file sharing

Although files are transferred between applications such as web browsers and email clients, the types of files and transfer that can be performed are limited in each case. Browsers, using HTTP, request files from a web server, but the kinds of files that can be displayed are limited to the formatting language supported by the browser and any plug-ins that it uses. In addition, file transfer is one-way – a request is made from the browser to the server that then sends the file to the client machine. Email allows more or less any file type to be sent as an attachment, but many mail servers restrict the size of file that can be sent this way and, even if they do not, are not especially efficient for this kind of file sharing.

The file transfer protocol (FTP) is designed to allow two-way transfer, to a server as well as from it, and also does not necessarily restrict the number of recipients of a file. Once a file is stored on a server, theoretically any number of users can connect to that server for downloads: this may be restricted to users connecting with a particular password, or FTP may be anonymous, open to anyone with the proper software. Increasingly, FTP is incorporated into browsers, with the latest versions of Internet Explorer and Netscape offering facilities to upload as well as download files. However, there is a lively market for stand-alone FTP clients such as WS_FTP (www.ipswitch.com) that perform additional tasks, such as allowing downloads to be picked up again even if the connection is broken. There are also dedicated FTP engines such as www.filesearching.com that can be useful for finding particular files.

FTP uses a client server model: even if a file is shared between only two users, the connection between those users is not a direct one as a server stands between them. By the end of the 1990s, however, more and more users were employing peer-to-peer (P2P) systems by means of which each computer would function as both a server to remote users as well as a client that could download files across that connection. Peer-to-peer sharing attracted attention early on as a means of transferring music files (although the most popular piece of software, Napster, was not a true P2P system, in that information on users' files was stored on a central server, although not those files themselves). P2P is increasingly being built into instant messaging clients, as well as dedicated applications such as Morpheus and Kazaa.

Newsgroups

A popular means of communicating outside the Web is Usenet, a distributed series of messages that work like bulletin boards. While a bulletin board system (BBS) is not restricted to Usenet, and may be set up on websites or (very popular until the mid-1990s) on a direct-dial number that users may connect to in order to download and upload messages, Usenet has become the most widely used system offering a simply astonishing range of topics for discussion.

Usenet groups are arranged in a hierarchical system of categories, the first word of which indicates the overarching category. The following are the most commonly used hierarchies:

- **alt**   alternative topics (that is, outside the range of the following seven categories)
- **comp**   computer-related topics
- **misc**   miscellaneous topics
- **news**   information on Usenet itself
- **rec**   recreational topics
- **sci**   scientific topics
- **soc**   social topics
- **talk**   general discussion

Each of these top-level categories is followed by further subdivisions, separated by dots, so that, for example, alt.gothic refers to the family of newsgroups that deals with gothic topics, divided further into groups such as alt.gothic.music and alt.gothic.culture.

There are two ways to read a newsgroup: either via a website such as groups. google.com that links to discussion topics, or a dedicated newsreader client that connects to a news server. Email clients such as Outlook Express or Netscape Messenger have a newsreader built in, so it is becoming increasingly rare to use stand-alone applications. To read and post messages online with a newsreader, it is necessary to subscribe to particular groups that you are interested in, and some groups are moderated; that is, messages are reviewed by a human or computer-based moderator who filters out inappropriate messages or spam.

Telnet

Although less commonly used than other applications considered so far in this chapter, telnet is one of the oldest Internet services that remains useful because it allows users to log into a remote computer and run (usually limited) commands on that machine. Telnet is employed most commonly for managing websites, but it is also frequently employed by users who need to check email accounts remotely.

To log into a remote computer, users must have a telnet client running on the local machine; having connected to the Internet, this client is run and instructed to connect to the host computer, which then provides a text shell from which commands (usually UNIX) may be run, navigating to different directories on the host and performing actions such as deleting or moving files, or running applications on the remote computer.

Personal security

The fundamentals for computer protection in cyberspace consist of anti-virus software and a firewall. The term 'firewall' comes from building and architecture, referring to a brick wall that divides parts of a structure and is designed to prevent a fire from spreading. In the computing world, the metaphor has been adopted to refer to preventing Internet dangers from spreading to your PC or local area network (LAN).

Firewalls come in two main forms: hardware and software. While hardware firewalls are probably more reliable and are gradually becoming widely available,

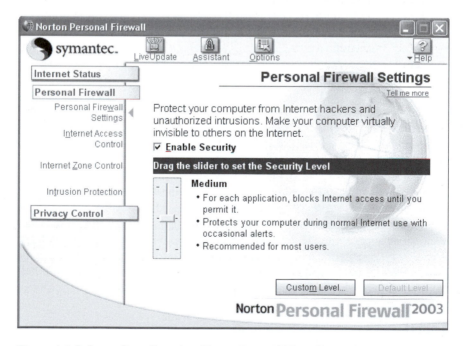

Figure 4.4 Software firewalls such as Norton Personal Firewall provide an extra layer of defence against intruders using the Internet to access your machine.

particularly for households that are connected to the Net by a broadband medium such as cable or ADSL, they generally represent overkill for the average user. At their simplest, such firewalls work by using two network cards, one connected to the Internet, the other to the local network, filtering data from the former to ensure that it is as safe as possible.

Even with a hardware solution, software is required to do one of two things: filter information, or set up a proxy server that controls outbound traffic. Packet filtering is so-called because it analyses selected 'packets' of network data to check their type, source address, destination address and port information. Suspicious packets are then blocked. Proxy servers, on the other hand, cache the requested data: generally these are used to relieve the strain on Internet servers, but they may also be used as firewalls because, once stored on a cache, data can be checked before they are transmitted elsewhere across the network.

Viruses or Trojans (computer programs that pretend to be something more innocuous than they really are) can be particularly useful to a hacker seeking to own a system, which is why regularly updated anti-virus software is so important. While the chances of one computer being deliberately singled out from the millions online is miniscule, scripts and software can automatically scan ports, or sockets, into software, looking for known insecurities in browsers and operating systems to gain information about a target system. One of the key functions of a firewall is to close down ports that are not currently in use, effectively helping to hide the computer from remote users. Before scanning for an open port, a hacker may simply ping through thousands of IP addresses (the unique address provided to every machine connected to the Internet) to determine whether there is a computer at that address. Good firewalls also protect your privacy by preventing your PC from responding to a ping request.

Setting up your cyberspace toolkit

To make the most of your cyberspace toolkit, this section will outline the sites you need to visit for the latest versions of software.

Browser

The two most popular browsers, Internet Explorer and Netscape, may be downloaded from the Microsoft (www.microsoft.com/windows/ie/) and Netscape (www.netscape.com) websites respectively. There are alternatives, however, most notably Opera (www.opera.com/download/), while Mac users may wish to consider Apple's fast new browser Safari (www.apple.com/safari/).

Email

Email is often handled as part of the browser if you use Internet Explorer or Netscape, using Outlook Express or Netscape Mail. Another common application is Outlook, part of the Microsoft Office suite, but free alternatives include Pegasus Mail (www.pmail.com) and Eudora (www.eudora.com).

Media player

There are a number of free media players online, but probably the top four are the Windows Media Player (now up to version 9 at www.microsoft.com/downloads/), Apple's Quicktime (www.apple.com/quicktime), RealPlayer (a free version is available at www.real.com, but be prepared to dig around on the site for the link to the free player), and WinAmp (www.winamp.com).

Instant messenger

The two most commonly used IM applications, Windows Messenger and AOL's Instant Messenger (AIM) are included as part of Windows or AOL. One IM application worth considering, however, is Jabber (www.jabber.org), which connects to a variety of different services.

Security

Most firewall packages, such as Norton Firewall (www.symantec.com) and McAfee Firewall (www.mcafee-at-home.com), are relatively expensive compared to other elements of the cyberspace toolkit. However, ZoneLabs (www.zonelabs.com) does offer a free version of its ZoneAlarm firewall that is also one of the better packages around.

5 Cyberspace technologies

....

Computer technologies
....

While the technology of cyberspace is probably associated most often with the Internet, a more fundamental substratum that enables the conception of cyberspace is computer hardware and software used to create, analyse and communicate multimedia, database stores and other types of files that form a fundamental part of our network society.

Defining a computer is not always as simple as one would expect. Most people today, when they think of computers, conceive of a desktop personal computer or notebook, sometimes smaller devices such as a PDA (personal digital assistant) or a much larger mainframe computer. The term 'computer' once defined any machine that handled data, including manual calculators and even the people who operated them or performed calculations, as with, for example, Jonathan Swift's reference to 'a very skilful computer' in *A Tale of a Tub*. Early in the twentieth century, Alan Turing, the Cambridge mathematician who was part of the team at Bletchley Park which deciphered German war transmissions, established a working theoretical principle for a mechanical computer in his paper, 'On Computable Numbers'. In it, Turing argued that for any problem that could be solved by an algorithm, this could be converted into a series of numbers that could be analysed and the output of that analysis recorded.

Computers may consist of general all-purpose machines, such as desktop PCs, mainframes or certain handheld devices, or they may be single-purpose pieces of equipment that control one process. Many of the latter, no larger than the computer chips they lie upon, are often placed inside other machines such as car engines or washing machines; with the possibility that future circuits may be printed on paper or plastic it has been mooted that even the most basic foodstuffs and goods we buy could be computerised in the near future, super-smart barcodes that will create consumer data clouds which track what we buy and when goods will need to be restocked.

Binary computing

At the start of the twenty-first century, computers may accept analog or digital data, the latter much more familiar to most people from the PC. At its most basic, binary computing relies on a series of on-and-off switches, using two digits (1 and 0) to represent these states as data. Digital computing does not have to be binary – the decimal system used by the majority of currencies in the West and based on counting our fingers is a digital numerical system – but binary numbers, where 10 is equivalent to the decimal 2 and 100 is equivalent to 4, have the advantage of enabling electronic devices to calculate and regulate data types simply by diverting current through a transistor. In contemporary, electronic computers, each bit is represented by electrons transmitted along wires.

This combination of bits transmitted as electrons down ever smaller circuit wires has served the computer industry well over the past three decades, but it is estimated that sometime between 2010 and 2020 the physical limit will be reached. No matter what materials are used, as wires become smaller so their resistance increases. One way to improve performance that is being investigated by IBM and others is to use qubits, or the quantum bit. Whether employing transistors or vacuum tubes, computers in the second half of the twentieth century have relied on components that exist in two states: quantum particles such as electrons also exist in two states according to their 'spin', which can be up or down, 0 or 1. More than this, however, such particles can also be in what is known as a state of superposition, representing both 0 and 1 and everything in between. Multiple particles can also be 'entangled', wired together to produce results in parallel, potentially performing billions of computations in a single step.

In 2000, an IBM team led by Isaac Chuang created a basic quantum computer using radio pulses to alter the spin of Fluorine atoms and thus program the computer. The computer was indeed able to answer a classic problem in a single step, compared to conventional computers which would require multiple steps to reach the same solution.

Computer hardware

As has already been mentioned, computers may come in many shapes and sizes, but one of the most important advances in their development came with the distinction between computer hardware and software. In the early days of analog and even digital computers, processing required information routes to be hardwired: at best, this meant that operators had to plug in different circuits or wires to perform a simple calculation, but it also meant that most computers could perform only a simple range of tasks. Once software was separated from hardware, computers could become truly versatile, all-purpose machines of the type envisaged by Alan Turing in the 1930s.

Early computers

Claims for the first computer frequently date back to the abacus, which at the latest was known to the Egyptians by 500 BC but may have been invented by the Babylonians around 3000 BC. Abaci could be employed by experienced users to add, subtract, multiply and divide at speed.

Later mechanical computing devices included a set of rods known as Napier's Bones after their inventor, the seventeenth-century Scottish mathematician John Napier, and a mechanical calculator that could add and subtract invented by Blaise Pascal in 1642 (Moschovitis *et al.* 1999). Mechanical multiplication and division was added by Gottfried Wilhelm von Leibniz in 1671, and in 1745 Jacques de Vaucanson used drums punched with metal holes to control textile looms, something developed further by Joseph-Marie Jacquard in 1801.

With the exception of the ambitious but doomed Difference Engine of Charles Babbage, which was planned but never completed in the 1820s and 1830s, the next major step was the device invented by Herman Hollerith in 1889 to aid the 1890 US census. Hollerith's company was one of those that amalgamated with IBM in 1924, becoming the dominant force in computing for much of the twentieth century.

Enter the mainframe

Devices built before the twentieth century were mechanical rather than electronic, and consequently limited in speed. The discovery of electricity in 1780 had paved the way for huge advances in electronics, but these did not begin to emerge in computing until the invention of the first electronic calculator in 1936, built by Konrad Zuse (who was also responsible for the first binary electronic calculating machine, the Z2, in 1939, the same time that Bell Laboratories was constructing a relay computer).

Early electronic computers built during the Second World War and the 1950s were huge, immensely heavy devices, with relays operated by vacuum tubes: ENIAC (electronic numerical integrator and computer), for example, consisted of 18,000 vacuum tubes, measured 8 × 100 feet and weighed 80 tonnes (Brewer and Alveranga 2002). The invention of the transistor in 1948, followed by magnetic storage in 1949, meant that computers would eventually be able to rely on faster, more reliable solid-state components for the second half of the twentieth century.

As the computer industry slowly developed through the 1950s, witnessing, among other things, the invention of the integrated circuit in 1958 and the sale of the first packaged computer program in 1959, mainframe machines became commercially available. The first was UNIVAC I, built by Remington-Rand in 1951, and this was followed in 1952 by IBM's 701 mainframe computer. Throughout the 1960s and most of the 1970s, it was such mainframes that controlled the immediate prehistory of cyberspace.

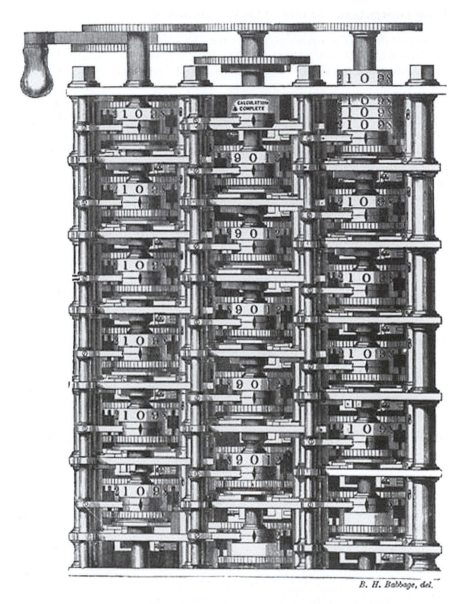

B. H. Babbage, del.

Figure 5.1 The Difference Engine, as envisaged by Charles Babbage in 1827.

Impression from a woodcut of a small portion of Mr. Babbage's Difference Engine No. 1, the property of Government, at present deposited in the Museum at South Kensington.

The microprocessor and personal computer

During the early 1950s, John Bardeen, Walter Brittain and William Shockley at Bell Telephone Labs invented the first transistor amplifier and, in 1957, Sherman Mills Fairchild founded the Fairchild Semiconductor Company to produce electronic transistors, at the same time that Jack Kilby at Texas Instruments was also working on the problem. Both teams at Fairchild and Kilby applied for patents in 1959: up until this point, computing had relied on power-hungry and fragile vacuum tubes, but the invention of the transistor enabled more switches to be combined on an integrated chip. In 1968, Robert Noyce and Gordon Moore left Fairchild to set up Integrated Electronics, later shortening the name to Intel. Originally established to produce memory, the company moved into processor design when it was called up to provide chips for Japanese calculators.

The invention of the microprocessor, the 4004, launched by Intel in 1971, marked a huge transformation in the development of digital computing. Initially, the microprocessor, effectively a computer on a chip, was intended for use only in personal calculators, but within a few years this invention had kickstarted the microcomputer market. Microsoft was founded in 1975 to develop software for the MITS Altair 8800 (Gates 1995; Wallace and Erikson 1994), and Apple followed two years later.

Apple provided the first pre-assembled computer to a potential mass market, the Apple II, in 1977, and thus began the long boom for personal computers (which has only showed signs of slowing since 2001). By 1980, IBM, the giant of mainframe computing, had recognised that computers such as the Apple II were gaining ground and, as a possible means of raising revenue, introduced its own PC in 1981. Because it had needed to bring its product to market quickly, IBM used readily available hardware and an operating system bought from Microsoft, with the result that the first 'clone' computer from Compaq was introduced a year later, compatible with the software used on the IBM PC.

Over the next two years, the development of the PC seemed to follow to the letter an announcement made by Gordon Moore in *Electronics* in 1965, that the number and complexity of transistors on a circuit would double every year. Known as Moore's law, the competition between companies such as Intel, IBM, Motorola (which constructed chips for Apple) and later AMD pushed forward the original 4004 microprocessor through a number of generations, from 8086 to 286, 386, 486 and, when Intel finally realised that it could not trademark a number, the Pentium processor and its various descendants (Jackson 1997).

By the end of the millennium, Intel had dominated the microprocessor market for almost a quarter of a century, yet found itself in an embarrassing position when AMD beat it to market with a 1GHz processor in 2000. While AMD's technical coup was not enough to topple Intel from market dominance, it indicated the sharpness of competition in the PC market.

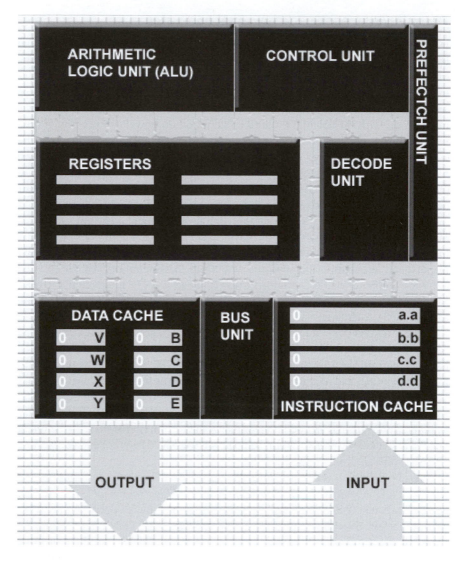

Figure 5.2 When a processor is told to fetch data or an instruction, it first checks the cache (a fast memory store) for each of these. If these are not stored, new data/instructions are input to the CPU from slower system memory. The prefetch unit places data in the decode unit, which converts code into a string of binary digits that are sent to the control unit. This binary code is either stored in the data/instruction caches until all the required information is available, or passed to the arithmetic logic unit (ALU). The ALU uses registers to store and complete the instructions sent to it by the control unit. Once these instructions are completed, the results are output to system memory.

Other devices and the future of the PC

For twenty years, the PC has been the predominant model of computing, but in 2001 and 2002 sales for such computers declined for the first time. This has led some to argue that the demise of the PC will not be too far off, to be replaced by myriad universal computers, self-aware networks that are not attached to one box but operate through mobile phones, personal items such as PDAs, or even items of clothing (as in the MIT MIThril project, www.media.mit.edu/wearables/mithril) and biological implants.

As Brewer and Alveranga point out (2002), the PC is unlikely to die in the immediate future, but its fundamental design – which had changed little between 1981 and 2001 – is undergoing major changes. In the PC itself, this means the abandonment of legacy devices such as the ISA (industry standard architecture) bus that communicates between processor and other devices, and an interest in concept PCs. Elsewhere, processing power is becoming more important in communication and personal devices such as handheld computers, mobile phones and wireless tablets that may be used in a wider range of settings than the desktop or notebook PC.

The microprocessor, key to the computer, is itself in a state of constant evolution and even revolution. Work at the University of Cambridge, for example, on magnetic microchips increased the maximum density of transistors per square centimetre from 6.6 million to 250,000 million (Swift 2000). Similarly, Hewlett-Packard filed two patents in late 2001 for advances that would enable molecular-scale computing based on the work of HP scientists Phil Kuekes and Stan Williams (www.hpl.hp.com/news/molecules_that_compute.html).

Yet it is unclear how much further technological progression will proceed. For the past twenty-five years, computing has been dominated by Moore's law, typically interpreted as the doubling of computing power every eighteen months. It had been assumed that this pattern would persist until the second decade of the twenty-first century at least, but according to Paul Packan (1999), companies such as Intel are reaching the limits of miniaturisation. As the thickness of transistor components becomes measured in terms of atoms, so problems such as tunnelling emerge, where electrons move between insulating layers, occurring when such layers reach the depth of about five atoms.

Biometrics

Until recently the stuff of science fiction (and still a favourite of films such as *Minority Report* and, more gruesomely, *Demolition Man*), biometric security techniques have slowly begun to appear in everyday applications. Biometrics, or the measurement of bodily characteristics such as a fingerprint or iris pattern, was given a boost when Microsoft incorporated a biometric API (application program interface) into Windows 2000.

Biometric methods work by comparing a scan of a particular part of the body – typically the end of a finger or an eye – against a pre-recorded map of that part.

Very popular (in that it promises greater security) is iris recognition, mapping the trabecular meshwork that gives the iris its corona-like appearance. While other biometric techniques tend to compare between ten and sixty unique points, the iris is said to have 266 such points.

By 2001, over 200 companies such as Compaq, NEC and Siemens were producing biometric devices. At the same time, while such devices offer virtues over other security techniques such as passwords and PIN numbers, which can be forgotten or more easily misused, biometric techniques are not perfect. Depending on their position, commentators have viewed developments to integrate neurological and computer systems as exciting or the stuff of Huxley's dystopian *Brave New World*. In 1997, the Emory University in Atlanta developed implants that enabled a physically disabled man to communicate with the external world by growing neurons on to an electrode that was then implanted in the brain's motor cortex. When the patient thought about moving part of his body, the electrode triggered a system that was amplified and transmitted to a computer. In the UK, Professor Kevin Warwick at the Department of Cybernetics, Reading, had a chip implanted in his arm that meant computers at the university would recognise him.

Networking

While computer hardware in the form of mainframes and PCs is the most visible aspect of technology that has made cyberspace possible, the most important development in the growth of that virtual space has been networking. Without connections between computers, it would be impossible for the Internet to exist: the precursor to the Internet, ARPANET, was devised to enable research scientists to share data, while proprietary network systems were being implemented before the 1990s to effect easier communication in areas such as commerce, banking and academia.

One of the earliest networking solutions was provided by Norm Abramson, a surfer and computer scientist who moved to Hawaii in 1969 and was responsible for connecting users on the island campuses that formed the University of Hawaii. AlohaNET used radio channels to connect users, and Abramson took advantage of a meeting to develop ARPANET later that year to add AlohaNET to the burgeoning network.

Radio connections had the advantage of being cheap, but the disadvantage of being in short supply. When relatively few users typed in messages at a terminal, there was little danger of radio channels being fully used. As the number of users and machines grew, however, so such connections would restrict expansion. The alternative developed for ARPANET, to connect computers directly, would also work only with a very small network. As such, another computer scientist working at Xerox, Bob Metcalfe, developed Ethernet in 1977. In a paper published with the aid of David Boggs, his assistant, Metcalfe described how two computers at Xerox PARC could be connected in a way that provided much greater possibilities for expansion. Those two computers were called Michelson and Morley after the two nineteenth-century physicists who had measured the speed of light and proved that the 'luminiferous ether' did not exist. As such, Metcalfe and Boggs called their network Ethernet.

Ethernet

There are various alternatives to Ethernet for connecting computers on a network, such as the token ring network developed by Cambridge University and promoted to businesses via IBM. Ethernet, however, which Metcalfe made into an industry-wide standard after he left Xerox to form 3Com in 1979, had the advantage of simplifying connections between computers across a single wire.

The method by which Ethernet works is often referred to as the 'cocktail party' strategy: a person at a party will wait for silence to speak, and if more than one person talks at once they will usually fall silent to wait for a gap. Similarly, Ethernet originally involved a physical connection of a single wire: should more than one computer attempt to communicate simultaneously this would lead to data collision and nothing would get through. As such, Ethernet connections listen to the network for a quiet time to begin transmitting information, what is known as 'carrier sense', before transmitting packets – or short bursts – of data. If a collision is detected, all computers wait a random time before re-transmitting data.

Today, TCP/IP packets that carry information across the Internet (see p. 86) are usually 'wrapped' by Ethernet data packets that ensure they are transmitted across networks between computers. As networks have increased exponentially, so the original Ethernet specification, initially promoted by Digital Equipment, Intel and Xerox and then by the Institute of Electrical and Electronics Engineers (IEEE), has changed to allow higher speed connections from 10 megabits to 10 gigabits and faster.

Wireless

While Ethernet has become the de facto networking standard, the most exciting developments in recent years have been in terms of wireless, originally developed as short-range radio networks that have since overlapped with developments in mobile technology. Wireless networks communicate within a certain frequency, enabling devices to be connected often even when they are not in line of sight. The two most common forms of WiFi are the 802.11 and 802.11b standards, the first of which was ratified in 1997, operating at 2Mbits/sec, upgraded to 11Mbits with 802.11b. Most alternatives, such as Bluetooth or HomeRF, operate in the same unregulated 2.4GHz band as WiFi (also used by microwave ovens), typically at speeds of 1–2Mbits/sec, although HiperLAN, ratified in 1996, works in the 5GHz range and offers connection speeds starting at 23Mbits/sec. In addition, at the end of 2001, companies such as Intel launched 802.11a wireless kits offering up to 54Mbits/sec and operating in the same 5GHz range as HiperLAN.

Some of the promises of wireless have not been fulfilled, however. One potentially interesting technology, Bluetooth, has been about to break for the past half decade but has never quite made it into the mainstream. While Bluetooth should enable devices to communicate with each other over short distances, its lack of bandwidth – particularly over any reasonable distance – means that it has quickly been overtaken by WiFi as the preferred means of wireless networking. The main use of Bluetooth at present appears to be for communicating between mobile phones and headsets.

WiFi has itself been hindered by regulatory problems: its use of radio bands means that, like Ethernet, all connected devices attempt to communicate at once. While Ethernet is restricted to physical cables, however, WiFi networks can potentially interfere with other devices, and this has led to demands for the regulation of 802.11a networks as they use the 5GHz radio band.

Client server and Peer-to-peer

An important distinction in networks is between those that operate on a peer-to-peer basis and those that use a client server model. In the case of the former, computers share data and services without any central 'hub'. This is the simplest type of network to set up, and all computers are treated as more or less equivalent on the network. Strictly speaking, all such computers are capable of being clients *and* servers in such a model, playing the role of server when they offer resources and clients when they access those resources.

In the client server model, the distinction between the different types of access and delivery is more marked. The server, as its name implies, offers a range of more centralised services (whether on one machine or across a farm of servers) to a remote client that dials into those resources or connects to them across the network. The client server model is more typical of the Internet as it is commonly used today, with the vast majority of users connecting online via their ISP's servers; at the same time, the end of the 1990s saw an increase in peer-to-peer, or pseudo-peer-to-peer systems such as Kazaa and Morpheus, that enabled users to share files without loading them on to a central server.

Software

While hardware often appears to be the most important part of computing (and is certainly the most visible), as we have begun to see with reference to networking, software is where the most important work is done. The ability to separate hardware from software is the most important principle when generating a multi-purpose computer, a principle that was first understood by Babbage.

We shall discuss the differences between various programming languages and codes below, but the feature shared by nearly every one of these languages is that a computer, which works only with machine code, does not understand relatively human-friendly instructions. Binary bit code makes the computer perform a particular task, and its instruction set is part of its internal architecture. As such, instructions from a high-level language such as C or Basic must ultimately be translated to machine code that corresponds to this instruction set.

In the early years of computers, programmers knew intimately how the machine worked at this most basic level and machine code was crafted to maximise results with the minimum of time and memory. Such programming, however, while capable of producing the most efficient results, is time-consuming and error-prone. As such, programmers developed assemblers, a series of mnemonics (such as ADD or MOV) that correlated directly to a computer's instruction set but included more user-friendly words. Important work was done by the IBM team brought together under John Backus in the mid-1950s to produce a compiler that would translate arithmetic expressions into machine code. By 1957, they had invented a means to parse programming languages and generate (compile) the appropriate assembly code, providing the means for a whole software industry to be formed.

Operating systems

While the separation of hardware and software enables computers to be more general-purpose machines than devices such as calculators (where instructions are hardwired), the operating system (OS) provides the means for different software applications to communicate with hardware. For very different reasons, probably the two most important operating systems ever devised have been UNIX, the backbone of the Internet, and Windows, the most ubiquitous OS on desktop computers.

The development of an OS for personal computers began in earnest with Gary Kildall's CP/M (Control Program/for Microprocessors), originally written for the Intel 4004 and then developed for subsequent processors. CP/M, rewritten for the 8086 and 8088 processors eventually used in IBM's PC as Q-DOS (Quick and Dirty Operating System), was bought by Microsoft and renamed MS-DOS. By the end of the 1980s the limitations of DOS were clear, and Microsoft and IBM collaborated on a new operating system, OS/2; at the same time, Microsoft was working on a graphical user interface for DOS that would work in the same way as the GUI for the Apple Macintosh, released in 1984. This finally appeared as a workable add-on with version 3.0 in 1990 and, in 1995, with the release of Windows 95 and Windows NT 4.0, established Microsoft's domination of the desktop market.

Unix, developed at AT&T's bell labs in the 1960s, achieved widespread use on mainframe machines because it was initially distributed at very low cost. Since 1991, when Linus Torvalds wrote a UNIX clone, Linux, the OS has become vital to the development and growth of the Internet. Linux is typically used to refer to the complete operating system and applications that are bundled on CD or down-loaded from the Internet. In fact, most of these components, such as text editors, disk utilities and tools for connecting across networks and the Net, stem from the Free Software Foundation's GNU project. Strictly speaking, Linux is the kernel of the OS, the device drivers that enable hardware to communicate with software applications. These applications are bundled with the kernel and distributed by companies such as Red Hat or SuSE, and while Linux is typically much more

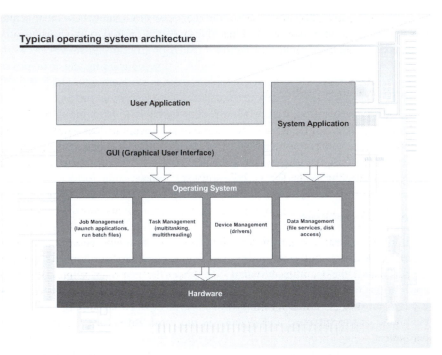

Figure 5.3 An abstracted diagram of the operating system shows how the OS works as 'layers' accepting instructions from the user and passes data input and output to and from hardware.

difficult to use than Windows, it has developed a reputation for stability and superior performance in terms of networking.

Graphical user interfaces

Very few computer operators today delve into the command line of a computer, typing instructions that are interpreted by the operating system to achieve set tasks. The success of the graphic user interface (GUI) is due to the release of the Apple Macintosh in 1984, although the basic elements of the MacOS were established much earlier.

Current 2D GUIs make use of windows, icons, menus and pointers (WIMP). The latter, the pointer used to select items on screen, was the first element to be developed when Tom Cranston, a radar engineer, developed a trackball to select positions on screen in 1952. Eleven years later, the basic idea of the trackball was converted into the mouse by Douglas Engelbart. Over the next twenty years, work continued on primitive graphical interfaces, most importantly at Xerox's Palo Alto Research Centre (PARC). Xerox had not patented its GUI and, when Steve Jobs was shown the mouse and graphics interface, he quickly adapted it for the

Mac. It was because Jobs used research originally carried out at PARC that Apple was later unsuccessful in its legal action against Microsoft Windows, which clearly owed a great deal to MacOS.

Programming languages

As we have already seen, a general-purpose computer can be made to perform a wide number of tasks because of the division between hardware and software. Although many instructions such as addition and logical commands are common to most processors, how they are implemented differs between microprocessors: the specific machine code differs from processor to processor.

At a very early stage, computer programming languages were one of the first elements of computer technology to be standardised, so that programmers would not necessarily have to learn every particular instruction set depending on which processor they were using. Low-level languages talk to the processor in terms of the machine code that sends it direct instructions, but high-level languages approximate linguistic instructions that can be understood by humans, compiling commands such as *if* x happens, *then* perform y into a set of low-level instructions that can run on a particular processor.

Fortran, developed in the 1950s at IBM, was the first high-level language to gain widespread acceptance; by the early 1960s, however, forty variants of the language were reported, so this was standardised as Fortran-66, 66 referring to the year in which the standard was formally accepted (subsequent standards, operating on the same principle, include Fortran-77, Fortran-95 and Fortran-2000). Fortran was devised for scientific and mathematical programming, and other early languages that have survived into the twenty-first century include ALGOL and Cobol. BASIC was developed to provide a simple-to-use programming language, gaining widespread acceptance when it was ported to early microcomputers.

The Web and Internet

The reason for beginning with a more general discussion of computer technology is to draw attention to the fact that cyberspace is not the same as the Internet: at the same time, the Internet serves as a giant computer nervous system connecting millions of devices around the world. As such, it is the most important development ever in the transformation of cyberspace from an idea into a practical reality.

The basic model for the Internet, which we have already encountered in relation to other, smaller networks, is a client/server model: although the Internet has no central node per se, distributed centralised servers store information and services that can be accessed by multiple clients, usually less powerful devices. Some degree of sharing data enables the easier administration of the Net, so that it is easier to find information, for example, but this is not the only way in which the Internet can operate. Recent developments in peer-to-peer sharing mean that individual computers can bypass servers, or rather applications running on a client act as a mini-server.

Over the following pages, we shall briefly consider the main technologies behind the Internet. Readers interested in exploring this subject in more detail should consult *The Internet: The Basics* (Whittaker 2002) or manuals such as *The Complete Reference Internet* (Young 1999).

Protocols

This chapter has already considered one of the fundamental divisions important to cyberspace as it currently exists, between hardware and software. While the Internet would certainly not exist without hardware, the computers and communi- cations links that store and transfer data, in many respects these are less important than the protocols, or software rules that govern the exchange of that data. The development of open-source protocols has been one of the great advantages of the Internet, providing a clear framework into which very different types of machinery and applications could plug.

TCP/IP

The most important rules for exchanging information across the Internet have been collected together as TCP/IP (transfer control protocol/internet protocol). Work by Paul Baran early in the life of ARPANET established a means of transferring data in small chunks, or packets, that made the network more resilient: if part of a message was not received (because a section of the network had gone down, for example), only the relevant packets would have to be re-transmitted, not the entire communication. TCP/IP, then, controls the ways in which machines are addressed, so that messages can reach the correct destination, as well as the ways in which those messages are broken down into packets and reassembled at the other end, operating on four levels: network access that facilitates transmission and routing of packets; network protocols that govern the delivery service; transfer protocols which ensure the machines are capable of receiving and sending packets; and application protocols, either applications themselves, or providing service to applications running across the Internet.

As well as creating and reassembling packets, another important function of these protocols is to ensure that computers are clearly identified, a function of IP addressing. Currently, IP addresses identify each individual machine connected to the network by means of a 4-byte number, each part of which ranges from 0 to 255 (for example, 123.14.252.7, or 65.255.7.132). This system provides a potential 4 billion addresses, but because the smallest unit of allocation is 256 numbers, as well as the fact that more and more machines are connecting to the Internet (including household items not originally envisaged by the designers of IP), and because each client connected to the Net must have its own, unique address, the current system of IP addressing is in danger of breaking down, particularly as countries such as China or India begin to use the Internet more extensively. As such, a new generation IPv6 (or version 6) is being introduced that will extend IP addressing beyond the 4,294,967,296 addresses currently available.

IPv6, or IPNG (next generation, as it is sometimes known), works by increasing the 4-byte IP address currently in use to 16 bytes, providing 10^{38} potential addresses, or more than 1,000 addresses for every square metre of the earth's surface. While IPv6 has been in development for some time, improvements in current IP addressing (version 4) to allocate addresses dynamically, and particularly classless inter-domain routing (CIDR) which, since 1993, has enabled the Internet to keep pace by treating it as a collection of networks: each network (a sub-network of the Internet) has only a few IP addresses allocated but then provides individual addresses to machines connected to the sub-network.

The domain name system

IP addresses identified by computers as a series of numbers is perfectly adequate for communication networks transferring information automatically, but is less suitable for mere humans looking for the right person. The domain name system (DNS) introduced in the 1980s compares an IP address to a domain name (ending in a suffix such as .com or .co.uk), so that the end user does not need to remember the correct four-octet number but can enter a more easily memorable name. DNS also serves another important function: before its introduction, each computer had to maintain an up-to-date list of all servers connected to the Internet so that it could transfer information correctly. As the Net grew, so this approach rapidly became unfeasible. DNS, by contrast, means that when a message is sent to a server, the server quickly checks its own network, so that an email from user1@ myisp.com does not have to be transferred to another network if it is addressed to user2@myisp.com; if the message is directed to another network, then the DNS query is transferred up the ladder until it can be matched against the correct network.

HTTP

While TCP/IP offers a series of rules for connecting different machines across the Internet to a range of servers, a much more specific protocol, the hypertext transfer protocol (HTTP) was developed alongside HTML to establish the basic rules for connecting documents via hypertext. As such, HTTP defines such things as how a uniform resource locator (URL) works to locate a specific document, as well as operations to be performed by a browser, or applications to be launched, when it downloads different types of files.

HTML

Fundamental to the Web is HTML, or hypertext markup language. Devised by Tim Berners-Lee at CERN at the beginning of the 1990s, HTML was intended to be an open formatting language that would display pages in any browser capable of recognising that language. As the Web became more successful, so the World Wide Web Consortium (W3C) was established to oversee future developments of the standard: each new version is designed to downgrade as elegantly as possible; that is, when used well, older browsers ignore elements that they cannot interpret (see also Powell 2001; Whittaker 2002b).

Fundamental to HTLM is the element; that is, a tag indicated by angular brackets <> that may include a number of attributes, or modifiers affecting how an element is formatted. Typically at present, most but not all elements have an opening and closing tag (something that has been addressed by XHTML): for example, a web page usually begins and ends with the tags <html> . . . </html>, the closing tag indicated by the use of a forward slash.

The first version of HTML was intended only to display text with some basic formatting elements such as headers and paragraphs, as well as the ability to link to other documents. The demand quickly arose for images, and HTML 2.0 outlined the basic standards for formatting text, linking and adding images to pages. The next important standard, HTML 3.0 (modified shortly afterwards as 3.2), added the ability to format pages using tables, as well as the first steps towards the use of cascading style sheets (see below), developments that were taken further by HTML 4.0, which also included layers, absolute positioning and some dynamic effects.

HTML is relatively simple to learn although web pages soon become very complex, particularly when designing with modern web editors such as Dreamweaver or GoLive. Pages are typically divided into two parts: a header (indicated by the element <head> . . . </head>) that includes meta-information about the page – its title, tags describing content and so on – and the body (defined by the element <body> . . . </body>) that holds information displayed in the main window of the browser. A simple web page, therefore, would look something like the following in its original code:

```
<html>

    <head>
    <title>A Simple Web Page</title>
    </head>

    <body>
        Any text included here outside a tag will be displayed in
        the main window of a browser.
    </body>

</html>
```

XHTML, XML and other advances to HTML

Although HTML has served the Web well, providing a simple and resilient language to format pages and connect documents, it has been pushed in a number of ways that its original inventor Berners-Lee could not have foreseen. The successor to ENQUIRE was intended for text only, or primarily text-based documents, but it is being used increasingly to handle multimedia sites and powerful databases. At the same time, the personal computer, which Berners-Lee reasonably saw as the main, indeed, the only, client of the Web in the early 1990s, has been joined by a multitude of devices, including personal digital assistants (PDAs), web-ready television sets and even mobile phones, all of which access the Web in different ways.

XHTML

Early in 2000, the W3C, the body responsible for Web standards, recommended XHTML (or eXtended HTML) to be used on websites. The main difference made by XHTML is that rules now matter: whereas previously browsers would ignore poor markup (for example, missing tags), this will not be the case with browsers that comply with strict XHTML standards. Because there are so many websites, many of them with mistakes that require a forgiving browser, it is likely that for the foreseeable future versions of Netscape or Internet Explorer will remain backwards compatible. None the less, implementing rules is important to the future of HTML: mobile phone or web-TV browsers, for example, display web pages very differently from those designed for PCs, and establishing how a page will display in various browsers will become increasingly important.

As such, XHTML pages must have what is known as a 'doctype indicator', an instruction at the beginning of the page which tells the browser what version of HTML it will use, and all relevant elements indicating the markup type (such as <html> . . . </html>). For the moment, HTML is the main formatting language on the Web, but this may not be the case in the future. More information on XHTML is available at www.w3c.org/MarkUp/.

Style sheets

As web designers have sought more eye-popping sites, so HTML has been pushed to extremes as a tool for layout and design. Another problem for site designers is that it is unusual for a single individual to combine the talents required to create content for pages *and* present them on a page in an appealing fashion. In other media, content creation and layout are often separated, so why not on the Web?

One solution to this problem has emerged in the form of cascading style sheets (CSS), markup rules for text and positioning that offer more control over layout. Because such style sheets may be nested one inside another, they are referred to as 'cascading', and CSS creates a presentation style for a particular HTML element using a selector (the element) followed by a rule (information about the style) within curly brackets, for example:

    h1 {font-family: arial,helvetica;
        font-size: 14pt;
        color:blue;}

A comprehensive reference to CSS is available at www.w3c.org/Style/CSS.

XML

As well as distinguishing design from content, current developments within web technology are concerned to distinguish different types of data within a document, and an important development in this regard is XML (eXtensible markup language). HTML itself was developed as a simplified subset of an older technology, SGML, or standard generalised markup language, but one of the problems with this simplification – elegant though it is – is that it is incapable of defining data types. XML, by contrast, although another restricted form of SGML, is a data-structuring language, one that allows documents to describe the type of information that they contain, and in this respect is much more like SGML (which is, in fact, a metalanguage used to define other languages).

XML, then, is an attempt to define a subset of SGML specifically for use in a Web context. XML provides elements that identify the *structure* of a document, for example, in an address:

```
<?xml version="1.0" encoding="UTF-8" standalone="yes">
<addressfile>
        <name>
                <first name>John</first name>
                <last name>Doe</last name>
        </name>

        <address>
                <street>1 The street</street>
                <town>Newtown</town>
                <country>UK</country>
                </address>
        </addressfile>
```

The XML elements in the above example do not define the format of the entries for an address, how it is laid out on a web page. Rather they define different types of data that can be searched for (for example, when looking for a particular last name or town). The layout of an XML document is determined according to the use of eXtensible style language (XSL), style sheets that transform XML elements into HTML. For more information on XML and XSL, consult the W3C website at www.w3c.org/XML/ and www.w3c.org/Style/XSL/.

XML promises huge flexibility for the web, but to be meaningful information must be parsed; that is, the contents of a file read and reformatted or presented in a usable way. This has led to the development of parsing tools such as SAX, or the Simple API for XML, which run through an XML document and strip out information that can be re-presented in different formats on different applications. More information on SAX is available at www.megginson.com/SAX.

WML and other standards

As has been mentioned already in this chapter, the spectacular growth of the Web by the end of the 1990s led to an increasing number of applications that could not be accounted for in its initial development. The use of mobile phones and other WAP (wireless application protocol) devices, for example, to display web pages required a new wireless markup language (WML), developed by the WAP forum (www.wapforum.org) and based on an earlier handheld device markup language (HDML). WML replaces pages with a deck, a document that is called up by the WAP device but displays only sections of information, or cards, at a time on the much smaller screens of clients such as mobile phones.

Other developments in recent years have included generally available languages such as SMIL (Synchronized Multimedia Integration Language), for multimedia presentations and streaming audio-video, and more specialised variants of SGML such as NewsML, an XML-based format for news production.

Scripting and dynamic HTML

Soon after its development, web designers were keen to add increased interactivity to sites. One way to achieve this is by adding server-side components, which will be dealt with later in this chapter. An alternative is to use client-side scripting languages, the most popular of which is JavaScript, instructions embedded in a web page that are interpreted by the browser.

While most scripting functions at a very low level (powering rollover buttons or pop-up boxes), the development of dynamic HTML (DHTML) and what is known as the document object model (DOM) indicates ways in which web pages can become intrinsically less static: rather than downloading a set arrangement of text, images and links, the browser downloads a series of components, or objects, that can be rearranged according to whichever script is executed.

JavaScript

JavaScript, originally ECMAScript (after the European Computer Manufacturers Association, which validated the language in 1997), is the most commonly used scripting language at present, with a syntax similar to C or Java. Although not a true object-oriented programming language, it does include some OOP features and is capable of addressing objects such as forms, images and links.

As with other scripting languages, JavaScript is denoted by the <script> . . . </script> element. Statements are followed by brackets that contain possible variables, such as alert ('Hello World') to display a pop-up box with the text 'Hello World', and end with a semicolon or new line. The language can use programming syntax such as if-else, while, for, repeat, break and continue, and employs only a few basic commands and variable types: numbers, strings, and the Boolean values true or false.

A simple JavaScript would look something like the following:

```
<script language="JavaScript">
        document.write ("Hello World");
</script>
```

VBScript

VBScript, as its name suggests, is a version of the widely used visual basic language. VBScript has been gaining in popularity, particularly as it is used with active server pages, but still remains less widely employed than JavaScript because it is only fully supported in later versions of Internet Explorer.

Although a subset of Visual Basic, VBScript provides considerable functionality and is also popular with developers who have already devoted time to Microsoft's programming language.

The document object model

Browsers have been capable of treating the various components of the browser and web pages as objects since Netscape 2. As such, the browser itself, including the window, its buttons, status bars and document contents such as images, forms and links, are treated as collections of objects, or the document object model (DOM). Each object has a set of properties associated with it, such as alignment or colour, and events that are triggered by the mouse or key strokes.

DOM indicates a structure to HTML elements: a typical window contains a document or a collection of other windows (frames), each of which in turns holds a document; in turn, this document is a collection of HTML objects, some of which, such as forms, contain other objects. Despite its benefits (DOM may be used to script page elements), the document object model has been adopted only slowly because it was applied very differently in earlier versions of Netscape and Internet Explorer.

DHTML

The introduction of 4.x versions of these two browsers saw the implementation of dynamic HTML, a means of dynamically changing HTML elements to modify a web page's structure in significant ways. For example, different layers containing text could be displayed or hidden or the formatting of buttons and paragraphs changed according to mouse events.

DHTML combines advances in HTML 4 with JavaScript and CSS to access elements of a web page using DOM. Pages may thus be created that control JavaScripts and cascading style sheets on the fly, adding dynamic interactivity to pages.

CGI and server-side technologies

While scripting and the document object model offers some degree of interactivity, more complex forms of processing, of payments or of information included in a form, require server-side technologies. At the most basic, these comprise the common gateway interface (CGI), a protocol built into HTTP that enables web pages to transfer instructions to an application on a web server. During the 1990s, more complex server-side programming environments such as JSP or ColdFusion were developed to enable websites to cope with a much larger number of tasks such as querying databases and processing information created on the fly.

CGI

As already mentioned, CGI proper is a specification for transferring data between a web page in the browser and an application on a server rather than any specific programming language. While scripting can transform a page and make it appear more dynamic, a file is still relatively static insofar as alterations to the page depend on the scripts embedded within the file. Truly dynamic websites will create pages based on variables entered by the user. For example, when visiting a site that uses CGI, logging on with a particular password will load a very specific page, perhaps containing personalised links and news. This is not simply a DHTML page that hides and reveals some information but is always, ultimately, the same page; rather it is a unique page created for that user.

When a browser requests a page from a server, it typically knows very little about the page, simply submitting a URL and displaying information or opening another application depending on the multipurpose Internet email extensions (MIME), such as a compression program for a zip file or a graphics program for an image. CGI, by contrast, allows the browser to write data to the hard drive, which in turn means that it can be read again in the future: thus a variable, such as a user name or a password, may be used to create or load different files depending on what is contained within that variable.

Perl

If CGI governs the means for transmitting data between a browser and application on the server, that application must employ a programming language to execute instructions based on those data. One of the most commonly used languages is Perl (Practical extraction and reporting language). Perl is an interpreted rather than compiled language (that is, code is not compiled into a stand-alone executable, but converted to machine on the fly each time the program runs); this makes it slower than other languages such as C or C++, but its strength lies in the fact that it can locate strings of information quickly and easily (such as words, phrases or sentences) that makes it particularly useful for the Internet. The official sites covering Perl syntax and development are www.perl.org and www.perl.com.

Python and PHP

Python is another, increasingly popular interpreted language, but one that is object-oriented. The language is considered particularly appealing because it has an elegant syntax, but is not over-simplified. Because of its object-oriented nature, Python may be extended by adding new modules compiled in a language such as C or C++, allowing the programmer to define new functions and object types. For more information on Python, visit www.python.org.

PHP is a recursive acronym, that is, its first letter refers to the acronym, as in 'PHP: hypertext preprocessor'. It is another widely used scripting language developed by the Apache Software Foundation (also responsible for the popular Apache web server), that parses, or preprocesses, files before creating an HTML page. The official site for PHP is www.php.net.

ASP

While CGI has become widespread across the Internet, it is not without its problems. First of all, the common gateway interface must launch an application for each request it receives, and even on the most powerful web servers this can place an incredible overhead on system resources. To cope with this, a number of server environments were created that would not need to launch applications separately, one such example being Microsoft's active server pages (ASP).

ASP, which is an extension to the company's Internet Information Services (IIS) bundled with Windows NT and 2000, can be used for routine tasks such as storing variables and tracking users to a site, but is employed most often to provide an interface between web pages and databases. For more information on ASP, as well as Microsoft's updated version, ASP.NET, see www.microsoft.com/asp and www.asp.net.

JSP

JavaServer pages (JSP), based on Sun Microsystem's Java technology (java.sun. com), is another common technology used by developers to provide dynamic sites. The technology is an extension of Sun's Servlets, platform-independent, Java modules that reside on a server and can execute instructions regardless of the operating system the server uses.

ColdFusion

Originally developed by Allaire, but now owned by the multimedia company Macromedia (www.macromedia.com), ColdFusion uses its own tagged language – ColdFusion metalanguage (CFM) – to provide active servers, particularly useful for dealing with database-driven sites.

Java and .NET

Two of the most exciting technologies currently in development are Java and Microsoft's new programming environment, .NET. Java, which is the more established language, has been most appealing because it is platform-neutral, offering the promise (if not always the realisation) that applications developed on one operating system may be used again on very different computer systems. Microsoft's .NET, on the other hand, is an audacious attempt to integrate the desktop (almost completely dominated by Microsoft) with network services to provide a next generation Windows.

Java

Java, initially known as Oak, was developed in the early 1990s as a programming language for consumer electronic items, but was adapted by Sun Microsystems in 1994 for the Internet and renamed Java in 1995.

Java (java.sun.com) is an object-oriented language like C++ but offers a number of unusual features. Because it is platform-independent, Java does not execute directly within the operating system but instead employs what is known as the Java virtual machine (JVM). Small Java programs, or applets, are compiled to machine-independent code that may be downloaded to very different computer platforms and executed by the JVM. This can be time-intensive, particularly as Java applets are generally not persistent (that is, they do not remain on the client system), and has led to the development of just-in-time (JIT) compilers that have speeded up Java performance considerably, although this can still be a slow technology.

Another area taken seriously by Sun was security: as programs may be downloaded and run automatically, this is an easy way for malicious code to execute without a user even being aware that anything has happened. Initially, the Java specification used a 'sandbox' to prevent applets from writing to the hard drive or performing other, potentially harmful functions. This has since developed to allow limited disk access in later releases.

.NET

With the launch of Windows 2000, Microsoft indicated that future thinking around its operating systems was going to be very different. Throughout the late 1990s, computing had increasingly moved away from the discrete, isolated desktop to networked computing. With the launch of .NET in February 2002, Microsoft indicated that it would pour all its resources into this new system of software technologies, one founded on XML web-based services that will enable roaming users to access their data and profiles from any client on a suitably configured network (including, potentially, the Internet at large).

Because XML, as we have already seen, defines the data structures of documents, it means that there is an open standard for transferring such data between applications. Previously, data types were often proprietary and very different, so that a file created in one program could not be read by another. XML offers the possibility for a universal language of data exchange, and Microsoft refers to this as a 'third generation of computing' that will involve a shift from individual sites or devices to distributed 'clouds' or 'constellations' of information (www.microsoft.com/net/).

Microsoft's aim with .NET is to provide the ability for users to move information and profiles simply between different sites and devices. Ultimately, the company envisages a system whereby users will be able to access personal details across a network regardless of whether they are using a personal computer or mobile phone, with sites able to plug into that information and share it more easily than before. The greatest dangers, for many sceptics, lie in the fact that Microsoft could monopolise the Internet as it has monopolised the desktop, and that personal and valuable information may become an even more tempting prospect for hackers.

Multimedia

One of the promises held out by cyberspace is that it is (or has the potential to be) a fully multimedia environment, offering not only texts and images, but also sound, animation, interactivity, even tactile experiences through much-touted (but rarely felt) virtual reality.

If one considers multimedia (quite reasonably) as the combination of more than one medium, then this has been a feature of media life at least since the days of illustrated books (or, perhaps, illuminated manuscripts). Film, live performances, television and other media provide countless instances of combinations of different formats, but the multimedia of cyberspace is often held as something intrinsically different. A key element of such difference is interactivity, that unlike television or radio, for example, the person in front of a computer is not simply a passive spectator or listener but is, rather, expected to *do* something to access video, audio, text and images. That is why we so often refer to a computer *user* rather than any other term. More than pressing buttons and following links, however, as Hall (2001) observes, true interactivity privileges the active reader, the engaged participant who does not simply consume texts but gleans and combines them into his or her own narrative.

Of course, the differences between computer multimedia and other forms of multimedia can be overstated, particularly by interested parties who are more concerned with hyping up the role of this or that technology. A visit to the Natural History Museum in London offers a good example of a multimedia sensorium that computers may probably never come close to – although, like Napoleon, I admit that nothing is impossible. Wandering through various rooms (in which IT has an important part to play), reading posters, touching those exhibits that are not off-limits or playing with interactive displays, the immersive quality of such an event involves all the senses in ways that cyberspace can only currently approximate.

At the same time, I have never had the opportunity to visit the Smithsonian and experience it in the same way as the Natural History Museum, but its online exhibition at www.nhm.ac.uk/interactive/index.html does allow the virtual visitor to lose him- or herself to some degree. A completely immersive version of cyberspace remains in the future, but it also offers remarkable potential even now.

Digital imaging

A practical definition of multimedia would probably consist of text, images, audio and video, 3D and interactivity, with the possible inclusion of some form of virtual reality (VR). After text, the most common component consists of digital imaging.

The art of photography, which has its origins in the experiments made by Henry Fox Talbot at the end of the 1830s, was supplemented by digital techniques in the 1950s when Russell A. Kirch and a team of colleagues at the National Bureau of Standards succeeded in constructing a mechanical drum that could trace variations in intensity from a photograph which were then fed into a SEAC computer (Mitchell 1992). Throughout the 1960s and 1970s, digital imaging was used primarily in institutions such as NASA, which employed computer image processing to enhance pictures sent back from spacecraft.

Following the introduction of the personal computer, however, particularly the launch of the Mac and its graphical interface in 1984, image editing gradually became cheaper and simpler to use. Initially, digitising pictures required a photograph to be scanned into a computer, but the introduction of digital cameras in the 1990s provided an alternative means to capturing photos without film.

Image sampling

A scanner or digital camera uses a CCD (charge couple device) to convert light into an electrical charge. Darker or lighter objects or coloured areas on a photograph reflect light in different intensities, something that can be measured by a scanner or camera and converted into digital information, a process known as filtering.

The amount of information recorded by this filtering process depends on several factors: the size of the sampled image, its bit rate (how many bits of information are used to record each colour), dots per inch, and other issues such as whether compression is used. Computer screens, like most printed media, do not consist of continuous tones of colour but produce colours from arrays of pixels, one each for red, green and blue. While computer screens display a fixed number of pixels, or dots, per inch (typically 72 or 96), to print out a clear copy of an image usually requires a resolution of between 300 and 1,200 dots per inch (depending on such things as the quality of the paper used for printing).

The 'bit rate' or 'bit depth' of an image refers to how much information is stored for each pixel. Pixels for each primary colour – red, green or blue – are arranged in grids of four (with an extra green pixel, because this is the colour to which the eye is most responsive). If only one bit of information is stored for each pixel – on or off – an image appears as black or white. Grey images require eight bits, offering 256 monochrome shades, and eight bit images are also common on the Web as GIFs (graphic interchange formats), which are likewise restricted to 256 colours. Most monitors today are capable of displaying 24 bits per pixel, eight bits for red,

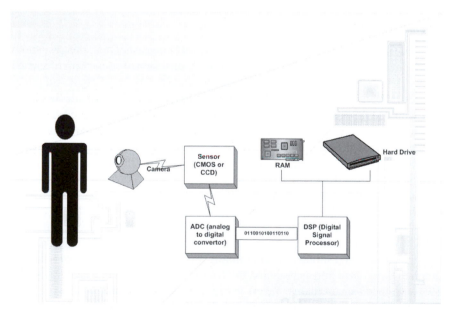

Figure 5.4 When taking a photograph with a digital camera, the sensor captures light wavelengths for red, green and blue pixels, then passes this information to the ADC, which converts that analog information into digital bits. This digital information can then be processed and passed to a hard drive or flash memory for storage.

green and blue information, enabling a potential 16.7 million shades of colour. It is also common to read of 36- or 48-bit scanners and displays, the additional information being used to record mask, or 'alpha', channels.

Colour models

Colour models indicate methods of displaying and measuring colour, which the eye perceives differently depending on the wavelength of light it receives. Light from the full colour spectrum is perceived as white, while the complete absence of light is perceived as black. Light is also perceived differently according to whether it is viewed from a source such as a monitor or television screen (which projects light), or from a printed page or surface of an object (which reflects light). The former is usually represented by the RGB colour model (after the primary colours red, green and blue), while the latter – at least in print – is represented by the secondary colours cyan, magenta and yellow. Mixing red, green and blue in equal amounts produces white; mixing cyan, magenta and yellow produces black – or rather, a muddy grey-brown. For this reason, true black is added to colour prints, making what is known as the CMYK model. RGB is an additive model, while CMYK is subtractive; that is, a surface absorbs light and reflects back only part of it.

The range of a colour model is referred to as its gamut. The RGB gamut is smaller than the natural colour gamut (that is, it can display fewer colours), while the gamut for CMYK is smaller still.

Vector and raster images

One important distinction between types of images that can be produced digitally is that of vector and raster, or bitmap, images. The comments in image sampling relate to the latter type of image, where each pixel is mapped to a raster 'grid'. This is particularly effective for capturing photographic images, but is not always the most efficient way of producing images. Pixels on a grid become blocky when the viewer zooms too far into the picture.

Vector graphics, by contrast, use formulae to describe lines and colour (after a vector, a point moving in a certain direction). Vector graphics typically appear most similar to line drawings and scale up or down with no loss of quality.

Compression

Storing images with a high bit rate results in extremely large file sizes, something that is extremely problematic when transmitting images across the Internet. As such, most images viewed on screen tend to use some form of compression, of which the two most common types are GIF and JPEG. GIFs, although restricted to 256 colours, are still used because they offer certain advantages over other formats, including animation and the ability to set one colour as transparent; also significant, however, is the fact that the compression employed by GIFs (LZW, or Lempel Ziv and Welch) is lossless; that is, information is not discarded but rather mapped on to a colour palette. For images with large blocks of colour, such as logos, this means that the image will still retain its sharpness.

JPEGs (joint photographic experts groups), by contrast, employ a lossy compression algorithm, discarding information to produce much smaller images with a wider range of 24-bit colours. A new format, PNG (portable network graphics), combines some of the best features of GIF and JPEG formats, enabling much smaller files to be produced with lossy compression while also supporting transparency and animation.

Audio and video

Two important elements of multimedia are sound and moving images – so important, in fact, that Chapter 8 is devoted to the complexities of digital audio-visual technologies. At present, it is worth noting the key features of multimedia AV.

While audio and video can be treated as separate entities, video is much less likely to be encountered on its own. The similarities of both are that they are time-based media, and as such they have converged more quickly than other elements such as digital imaging and hypertext. A stand-alone video editor, for example, is almost certain to include tools for editing sound as well (although the reverse is less likely to be true).

Analog music on vinyl, developed in the early part of the twentieth century but perfected in the period after the Second World War, made use of a single groove pressed into plastic. Digital technologies transfer these variations into bits, represented on compact disc, for example, as fixed length indentations in the surface of the disc: when a CD laser encounters an indentation it reads a 1, and a 0 where there is no indentation.

Video proved more time-consuming to transfer to digital formats, mainly because the quantities of information stored in film required huge amounts of storage space and processing power to manipulate. It is literally only in the past couple of years that such power and storage has become widely available to the average computer user. The process of creating moving images, at its simplest, transferred the technique of photography to reels of celluloid film: twenty-four frames per second would, because of the optical phenomenon of persistence of vision (where an image is retained by the optic nerve for a fraction of a second), create the illusion of fluid movement.

Digital video, unlike celluloid film, rarely presents simple frame-based motion, because uncompressed flames flashing on to a screen in quick succession increase the demands made on computer hardware. As such – and the same has become increasingly true of digital audio, particularly for transfer across the Internet – an important part of creating AV files consists of compression: as we shall see in the next chapter, unlike image compression that for AV not only operates within a

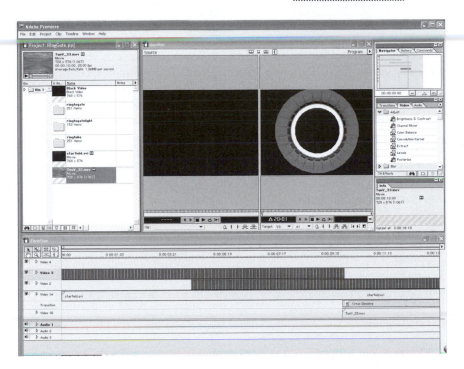

Figure 5.5 Popular editing applications such as Adobe Premiere have made digital video editing simpler than ever before.

single frame, locating similar colours and patterns, but also across frames, so that the same image or part of an image (such as a background) can be compressed to a greater degree than one which changes rapidly.

3D

Alongside digital imaging and audio-visual materials, 3D is an important area in multimedia. The development of digital special effects in the movie industry, for example, has been greatly influenced by advances in 3D software. The principles of 3D originate with the discovery of perspective, first by ancient Greeks such as the architect Agtharcos in the fifth century BC and then again during the Renaissance. The understanding that there is a single vanishing point for all objects within a scene, and that such objects grow or decrease in size as they move nearer to the eye of the spectator, is essential to the creation of an illusion of depth in three-dimensional space on a flat, two-dimensional surface.

Although important work began on the principles of computer 3D in the 1960s (for example, the concept of ray tracing developed by Arthur Appel in 1969), it was only during the 1970s that computers became powerful enough to put these theories into practice. Henri Gouraud, for example, worked on a means of providing smooth-shaded images, a technique that was improved to provide more realistic reflections in 1975 by Bui-Tuong Phong (Fearon 2002: 135). Another important figure was Ed Catmull, who invented techniques such as texture mapping and tweening during the 1970s before becoming one of the co-founders of Pixar after Lucasfilm's computer graphics division was sold to Steve Jobs in 1986.

It was during the 1980s and 1990s that 3D graphics became an increasingly common part of a wide range of entertainment and communications industries such as film and gaming. David Brabant's *Elite* was one of the first computer games to immerse players in a virtual 3D (if wireframe) world, with more impressive graphics finally appearing with *Doom* in 1993. Disney's *Tron* (1982) contained about half an hour of CGI, but the first entirely computer-generated film was Pixar's *Toy Story*, released in 1995.

Modelling

The starting point for all 3D work is to create a model or object mesh, a wire frame that describes the outline of a shape without colour or texture. An object is defined as a set of co-ordinates in the 'world space' of three dimensions represented by the axes X, Y and Z. Polygon meshes are often described as primitives, and 3D applications such as 3ds max or Maya offer a range of basic primitives such as spheres, cubes, pyramids and cones.

One problem with polygon meshes is that creating a curved surface can be difficult: such objects actually consist of flat facets, and though these can be sub-divided to produce the illusion of curved space, creating an object with thousands of facets slows down modelling greatly. One alternative is to use a NURBS (non-uniform rational b spline) mesh, a framework with fewer points that serve as guides for the rendered surface, rather like the fabric of a tent stretched over its frame.

Rendering

While objects are essential to creating 3D scenes, basic wire frame meshes do not provide any sense of verisimilitude. Rendering simulates the lighting of a scene to produce a more realistic image. The most basic form of render consists of flat shading, where the angle between a ray of light and the surface of an image is calculated. Flat shading displays the facets of an object, while Gouraud and Phong shading calculates the effect of lighting on an object as a whole rather than each individual facet.

The next step in rendering techniques, developed in the 1980s, used ray tracing to produce images that not only computed the way light reflected from an object, but could also trace light that had already been reflected from other surfaces, producing more realistic simulations of surfaces such as glass or marble. To calculate the interaction of multiple reflections requires considerable processing power, but even more is required in the case of radiosity: while ray tracing only calculates light reflected in one direction, radiosity rendering can take into account the diffuse scattering of ambient light.

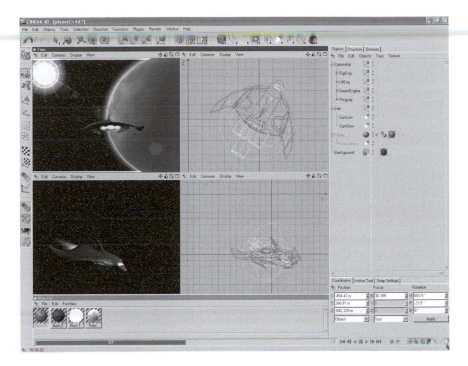

Figure 5.6 Modern 3D applications such as Cinema 4D provide tools for all elements of modelling, rendering and animation.

Finally, another important aspect of 3D simulation aimed at producing more realistic images is texture mapping, providing more complex surfaces to an object. At its simplest, this consists of simply mapping a flat image on to the surface of a mesh, but more complex techniques use displacement or bump maps to simulate the rougher surfaces of objects such as wood or cloth.

Animation

Pixar's first short film, *Luxo Jr*, in which two anglepoise lamps played with a ball, was nominated for an Academy Award in 1985. Nearly a decade later, Pixar had produced the first CGI feature film, *Toy Story*, and such films have since become an established part of Hollywood.

Computer animation relies on key framing: unlike traditional animation, where every frame has to be drawn or moved by hand using stop-motion techniques, key frames such as the beginning, middle and end of a movement are marked out with the computer completing the in-between frames, a process known as tweening. To provide more realistic motion, animators frequently employ motion capture and inverse kinematics (IK), the latter consisting of a jointed skeleton that replicates the effects of gravity and the movement of limbs more accurately.

VR

While multimedia formats that combine text, image, audio-video and 3D animation are the most common ways in which we experience cyberspace, the elusive grail for cyberspace technologies is virtual reality (VR). At the beginning of the 1990s, over-enthusiastic prophets such as Jaron Lanier and Howard Rheingold predicted that VR was imminent, yet as the technological capabilities of computers increased throughout that decade, their wilder prognostications appeared further away than ever before.

This is not to say, however, that there have been no advances whatsoever. In various forms of entertainment, particularly computer games, developments such as surround sound and pseudo-3D environments have contributed to the rapid expansion of the gaming industry. Yet while most encounters with VR, in however limited a form, tend to take the shape of explorations of fantasy worlds, much VR research has been motivated by the need to verify human perception, a requirement that dates back to Galileo's telescope and other developments of the Renaissance which Francis Bacon referred to as 'augmentative machines', and what Rheingold (1991: 5) has since called 'mind amplifiers'.

Rheingold traces the history of virtual reality back to Morton Heilig's 'Sensorama', invented in the 1950s as part of a stereophonic craze that took hold of the industry at the time. Other breakthroughs took place in the 1970s, for example, in the work of Nicholas Negroponte and Ivan Sutherland at MIT, or Myron Kreuger's computer art shows VIDEOPLACE and CRITTER. Most of the important developments that still determine many of our ideas about VR came out of NASA's Ames Research Center in the 1980s, including the head-mounted VIVED (visual environment display) and data glove, which also involved Jaron Lanier, the CEO of VPL Research, who is widely held to have invented the term 'virtual reality' (Rheingold 1991; Sherman and Judkins 1992).

To be effective, VR depends on a range of techniques to provide successful 'affordances', or tokens of a fully immersive environment. Most important (because it covers the clues we rely on most in daily life) is the visual environment, but as well as stereoscopic vision VR concentrates on 3D sound and interactive tactile – or 'haptic' – environments, through some sort of data glove or data suit.

6 Webcasting and digital broadcasting

If one of the holy grails of cyberspace is to produce as completely immersive an environment of 'rich content' as possible, then it must move beyond the static textual- and image-based format that dominated its early years. Fantasies of virtual reality will probably remain just that – fantasies – for the foreseeable future, but huge leaps have already been taken in terms of online and digital broadcasting: indeed, the important medium that led McLuhan (1964) to talk of a global village was television (even if the process of creating global media began with the 'Gutenberg Galaxy' of the printing press), so it is hardly surprising that online environments such as the web should be complemented by new forms of broadcasting.

Throughout this chapter, we will examine some of the ways in which two different but related forms of broadcasting – digital television and radio and online audio-visual webcasting – are being implemented and will transform cyberspace in coming years. There is considerable cross-over between both technologies (particularly in terms of encoding and compressing signals that are received by computers or television sets), but when discussing digital broadcasting this chapter will generally refer to digital-to-air or digital-to-cable transmissions that are typically viewed or listened to on television or radio; webcasting, by contrast, uses technologies based on sending data packets across satellite, cable and phone networks that are received and interpreted by computers, usually PCs but sometimes other devices such as mobile PDAs (personal digital assistants). There has been considerable talk of the convergence of these technologies, but at present they remain separate with only a slow adoption of devices such as web TVs.

It is also worth bearing in mind that, despite the massive advances made in terms of digital broadcasting of all sorts, the reality of mass markets for these technologies remains relatively small at present. While technically possible (unlike many of the promised blue-sky projects predicted as part of VR research), considerable economic obstacles have prevented widespread takeup of many features. Content-rich webcasting can be a frustrating experience for users with a narrowband connection to cyberspace, while the meltdown of ITV Digital in 2002 demonstrated that simply throwing huge amounts of money at a new technology would not necessarily make it popular. The moral is not a new one. Negroponte (1995) explained how something very similar happened in the early 1990s: media companies and technology manufacturers sought to push forward HDTV (high-definition television) that would transform the 'viewing experience'; most viewers, however, were perfectly happy with their experience, and this major trunk road of the information highway, which had received large amounts of investment, was a disaster, while a neglected side alley – the Internet – grew exponentially.

Casting the Net

Webcasting consists of sending audio and video across the Internet and is related to a wide variety of technologies: digital audio, video and television, the Internet itself and the World Wide Web, and the rapid growth of faster and more powerful computer platforms. As such, although webcasting itself is only a recent phenomenon (having emerged in the mid-1990s), it plugs into technologies and systems that have been developing since the 1960s and 1970s.

The term 'webcasting' is intended to draw attention to its similarity to broadcasting. When the Internet was first developed, and especially the web at the beginning of the 1990s, it was designed as a fairly static system in which documents would be stored on a server and 'pulled' to a client browser when a user wished to view them. A fairly close analogy is with a library, in which books reside on a shelf until a visitor takes them from their filed system. Broadcasts, on the other hand, are 'push' systems, in which (typically) radio and television waves are streamed through space until someone with a relevant receiver tunes into them.

There are some ways in which webcasting is very close to this broadcasting experience. Tuning into a live online radio station, for example, is not dissimilar to tuning in via a regular radio set: anyone listening at that moment will hear the same music or conversation at the same time. Yet there are subtle differences between webcasting and broadcasting: popular sites such as the BBC and CNN provide not only live feeds but archived material that can be viewed asynchronously; that is, at a time to suit the visitor.

Asynchronous broadcasts, the discrepancy between transmission and reception, is not entirely new. At least since the advent of tape cassettes and, more particularly, video, we have been used to capturing broadcasts on tape in order to watch or listen to them at a more convenient moment. Innovations such as webcasting, however, as well as digital broadcasting, mean that we are becoming more and more used to systems that are closer to video-on-demand rather than true broadcasting. These digital systems bring with them important consequences, social and political as well as technological, foremost of which is an increasing fragmentation of audiences: it is increasingly difficult to assume, as with large television and radio audiences of the mid-twentieth century, that most households will be settling down to watch or listen to a specific programme at a precise time.

Webcasting, multicasting, pointcasting

While webcasting is not quite the same as broadcasting, it can in turn be distin-guished in several ways. Multicasting is a common term to describe the process whereby some TCP/IP networks allow packets of information to be broadcast across a certain range of addresses on the network (see Chapter 7 for more infor-mation on TCP/IP); users 'tune in' to receive these packets, rather than having each one sent individually from the server to the client, the closest webcasting comes to true broadcasting.

Multicasting requires special server protocols to be effective (see 'How webcasting and digital broadcasting work' on page 111), but many sites stream content across a network to a browser only when the client requests data. It is not uncommon for sites to use a combination of push-and-pull technologies, waiting for a client to request data and then streaming a range of content to the browser or hard drive, a process sometimes referred to as pointcasting.

Another important distinction is between streaming and pseudo-streaming. When a user requests content from a website, usually the file downloads and begins playing as soon as enough information is stored on the hard drive. This is pseudo-streaming. For webcasters, this has two disadvantages. First of all, files usually pause or 'stutter' when they need to download the next chunk of information; second, the transmitted file can be saved on the remote computer. RealPlayer streaming buffers information to minimise pauses and decodes a transmission in real time that does not need to be stored on the client's hard drive.

A brief history of digital broadcasting

Obviously a complete account of the origins of webcasting and digital broadcasting would have to include detailed information regarding the history of the Internet and computing technologies, some of which may be found elsewhere in this book (for example, in Chapter 1). What is most significant at this point, however, is the digitisation of audio-visual signals, which lie at the heart of webcasting as it is typically understood.

The UK Post Office and others had experimented with transmitting digital audio signals down phone lines by the 1960s (Winston 1998), but the quality of sending a 64Kb/sec stream across such lines made for very poor quality. It is not entirely surprising that innovators of the time had looked to the phone network to broad-cast music: as Winston (1998) observes, a primary use for telephones at the turn of the twentieth century had been not to provide point-to-point communication, but rather access to live musical events. Even if these early experimenters had been given access to faster fibre optic networks, however, we would not have seen a digital broadcasting revolution at this point. To decode even the paltry 64Kb of information that could be transmitted each second was the maximum that could be processed in real time, requiring equipment far outside the reach of the vast majority of people.

As such, any form of digital broadcasting would have to wait until much greater processing power became widely available during the 1980s and 1990s. Before this, however, work was begun by the end of the 1970s with digital audio recording on to vinyl LPs, preparing the way for the digital revolution of the 1980s. We shall consider the specifics of digitisation of music in more detail in the next chapter, but its early significance for digital broadcasting was that it indicated the ways in which entertainment media could be converted into electronic formats for easy distribution.

The MBone's connected to the backbone

Big changes to the potential use of the Internet as a broadcast medium were made in the mid-1990s with the implementation of MBone, or multicast backbone. While the transfer protocols governing most online technologies such as the web and email required specific connections to servers in order to access information, MBone made use of a special section of the TCP/IP protocol (specifically addresses beginning 224–239) reserved for multicasting. The original aim of the MBone network was to experiment with live media and meetings online, using tools such as shared whiteboards for researchers. To publicise the possibilities of such multicasting, however, and as a sign of its potential future uses, MBone came to the attention of a wider public when it was used to webcast the Internet's first concert, the Rolling Stones, in 1994. A more dramatic example of a similar event was the web broadcast of Madonna's 2000 concert by MSN, though by this time MBone had been superseded.

By this time, the various technologies (processor power, bandwidth, compression techniques) had come together to make webcasting a real possibility. In 1995, Progressive Networks (which later changed its name to Real Networks) released a product called Realaudio, with which it was possible to produce usable – if low-quality streaming audio. This was quickly followed by Realvideo, and the following year the protocols RTP/RTSP (real-time protocol/real-time streaming protocol) were defined, providing a common standard for the delivery of streaming content across the Internet. Alongside this, other innovations such as SMIL (synchronised multimedia integration language) provided rules by which multimedia could be integrated into browsers so that webcasting would be as transparent an activity as possible to the end user.

Digital broadcasting

While broadband webcasting attracted considerable attention during the dotcom boom of the 1990s, digital broadcasting is more likely to attract early returns on investment in the fields of television and radio. The introduction of NTSC (national television system committee) in colour television in the USA in 1953 and PAL (phase alternate line) across most of Europe in the early 1960s began the process of bringing analog television to the masses. By the 1970s (as with music), techniques were emerging that could digitise video signals in the form of digital time base correctors (TBCs), meaning that cheaper videotape could be used to record shows.

Digital techniques slowly started to creep into special effects and, in the early 1980s, D1 and D2 videotape formats were developed that allowed signals to be recorded digitally. Further development was held back by the high bit rate of digital video, making distribution costs over cable or satellite prohibitive, and the fact that television sets and VHS recorders would in any case only downgrade the final quality of the transmission.

Serious work on digital television in the USA began in 1982 with the creation of the Advanced Television Systems Committee (ATSC), and received a boost in 1987 when the FCC (Federal Communications Commission) was requested by fifty-eight broadcast organisations to investigate advanced services. This led to the formation of the Advanced Television Test Center (ATTC) in 1988 (Brice 2002). Around the same time, work began on digital audio broadcasting (DAB) by organisations such as the European Broadcast Union (EBU).

By 1990, General Instruments' work on the first all-digital high-definition television system (HDTV) led many pundits to predict that the technology's time had come. As Negroponte (1995) and others noted, however, the fact that HDTV was of a demonstrably higher quality than NTSC was not compelling enough a reason for consumers to upgrade. At the same time, it was essential that there was no disruption to consumers of services during a transition period. In contrast to the global oligopoly maintained by a few music companies who were able to push through adoption of CD, digital broadcasting had to contend not only with public provision (particularly in Europe), but also with the fact that this was a much more fractured market.

Throughout the 1990s, however, the ATSC continued to refine digital television standards, and in 1996 these were adopted by the FCC. Under the FCC's subsequent aggressive timetable, stations in the largest US cities would go digital first, followed by smaller metropolitan centres, with the first digital services being launched in November 1998. A year later, 50 per cent of the population had access to DTV signals (with an appropriate receiver), and by May 2001 there were 195 American DTV stations on air. It was assumed that analog broadcasts would cease nine years after the first steps had been taken, assuming that enough of the population had embraced digital broadcasts.

In Europe, by 2001 2.5 million households had switched to digital in the UK, with 1.8 million in Germany and 1.3 million in Italy, with digital radio up and running in Germany, Portugal, Sweden and the UK. The British government set a deadline for the adoption of digital services that was as aggressive as the FCC's, committed to switch over between 2006 and 2010. At the same time, the Secretary of State for Culture, Media and Sport, Tessa Jowell, recognised that this was 'a mountain we have to climb' which could, if mishandled, deepen the divide between the digital haves and have-nots (Martin 2001), leading critics to complain that the government was wavering in its commitment (Bulkeley 2002). More significant was the cool response of consumers: by March 2002, ITV Digital, which had swallowed £800 million since 1998, was placed in administration, jeopardising government targets (Cassy and Wells 2002).

Other difficulties have included the attempt to lock-down choice by using proprietary networks, as well as simple inertia: in a speech delivered on his first working day as Director General, Greg Dyke remarked to MEPs at the Bibliotheque Solvay that 'one of the regular complaints about public service broadcasters like the BBC is that we want yesterday all over again' (Dyke 2000). At the same time, Dyke was also staking out a major role for the corporation by indicating how competing proprietary standards (such as ITV Digital and Sky) lock out consumer choice and so would slow down the takeup of digital. Committing his corporation to investment in digital services, Dyke called for greater inter-operability between network operators and broadcasters – enforced by the European Commission if necessary.

The promise of convergence

In the early 1990s, audiences were largely unwilling to pay for what digital services existed, while alternative transmission systems such as cable and satellite were only beginning to take off in Europe. Between the beginning and the end of the decade, the broadcasting landscape had been transformed by a more popular acceptance of DVD and, more importantly, the Internet.

Cable (and to a lesser extent, satellite) systems offered a means not only of transmitting broadcasts to the public, but also access to increasingly popular Internet services. While these could obviously be accessed by the plain old telephone system, many of the apparently most enticing and attractive features of the web in particular, such as video on demand, needed broadband connections. This has led a number of commentators to predict a moment in the near future when various broadcast and telecommunication operations will converge to provide convenient entertainment and information portals, the Internet and television being accessed from the same point. This in turn led to investments in companies such as Tivo and Pace that would provide the hardware for these services.

The promise of convergence, however, can easily lead to the sort of overhyping that the Internet experienced in the late 1990s. As well as the slow rollout of broadband services (such as cable and ADSL), a key term used by those involved with webcasting and digital broadcasts is quality of service (QOS). To make it more reliable, the Internet was devised to privilege resilience over speedy delivery: a packet was split so that it would make it to its destination (being requested several times if necessary), but there would not necessarily be a guarantee of when or by what route. Alternative multicasting protocols do not necessarily ensure the arrival of data packets to a particular client, so QOS for such things as video on demand across the Internet cannot be assured as multimedia requires what is known as an 'isochronous stream', namely that it arrives at its destination in line with how it left its source. The new generation of IP protocols, Ipv6, may improve matters by privileging video information, but as sceptical commentators such as Akass (2002) have remarked, the near future of digital broadcasting is unlikely to impress the millions of potential consumers required to make it a commercial success.

In the late 1990s, it was often assumed that new digital technologies would sweep away traditional media in an avalanche. As Cornford and Robins (1999) observe, however, nothing could be further from the truth: the highest ranking media properties are dominated by major media corporations, so that the web is not a break with conventional companies but rather 'the refinement, extension and embellishment of traditional media' (p. 124; see also Naylor *et al*. 2000).

How webcasting and digital broadcasting work

While online webcasting still has a long way to go before it becomes a really viable form to other forms of broadcasting, it is becoming simpler to use each year as more and more innovations are incorporated into the browser. The process is still not always transparent, however. What happens when a visitor to a site clicks on an audio or video file depends on what type of file it is (such as MP3, QuickTime or RealVideo), as well as the plug-ins installed on the client and how the server is configured to respond. Some file formats will launch an external application, such as the QuickTime or Windows Media Player, while others will play within the browser and, to effect as fast transfer times as possible across the Net, nearly every single file format encountered uses some form of compression. Some of these compression rates are extremely high, such as that used by Qualcomm's Purevoice (www.eudora.com/purevoice) for attaching voice files to emails, and of relatively low quality; others, such as MPEG-2, used for DVD, are high quality but much lower compression rates.

The vast majority of audio-visual material currently available online is of the pseudo-streaming variety: it begins to download to a computer and, when a large enough chunk of data has been retrieved, begins to play. Live broadcasts work very differently, requesting a file that in turn connects to a streaming media server.

One of the main problems with webcasting has been the growth of proprietary formats, RealVideo and RealAudio, Microsoft's Windows Media Format or Apple's QuickTime and MPEG-4 being the main options. Each of these requires server software specific to the format in order to stream live video or audio properly. Because of this difficulty, RealNetworks, one of the innovators in web streaming, released a software platform, Helix (details available from www.helix community.org and www.realnetworks.com), in mid-2002 that should rationalise requirements for streaming audio and video to any platform.

Codecs

For webcasting to be achievable, the very high data rates required to capture sound and video must be compressed so that files can be transmitted more easily across the Internet. A codec, or COmpressor/DECompressor, is a series of software instructions used to reduce the size of AV files and then expand them so that they can be played. A second of VHS-quality digital video will take up over 7Mb of hard disk space: a frame with a resolution of 320 [x] 240 pixels, in true colour, requires 300Kb, with 25 frames per second for TV. None the less, it is possible to achieve nearly the same, full-screen quality for a minute in a file the same size or smaller using compression.

We shall see in the next chapter how codecs may work with respect to certain audio formats such as MP3. Perceptual encoding discards those parts of a sound wave that the human ear either cannot physically hear, or which the user typically ignores. Similar effects are achieved with video codecs, which can operate spatially and temporally. Spatial compression, or run-length encoding, looks for repeated patterns in a frame (such as the same colour), while temporal compression looks for repetition across frames. For example, spatial compression may be employed to describe a frame in which two cars are the same colour; when those cars are at a standstill, with little movement onscreen, temporal compression will also be much higher (fewer changes from frame to frame) than when they are involved in a high-speed chase across a rapidly changing environment.

There are many different codecs available, many of which perform slightly better or worse depending on the type of video or sound to be compressed. Ones already encountered include MPEG and MP3, as well as QuickTime, WMA and RealAudio and RealVideo; other commonly used codecs are Cinepak, Indeo and Sorenson Video. MPEG, probably the most important, relies on three types of frame: I, P and B. I, or intermediate, is a still image used as a reference point for compression. Between each I frame are P, or predictive frames, that describe the difference from each preceding frame. I and P frames or their equivalents are also found in other codecs, such as QuickTime, but MPEG also adds B, bi-directional frames, that look both backward and forward to the nearest I frame, enabling even greater compression.

Clients and servers

Encoding audio and video material is the first step to producing digital broadcasts, but such material must still be transmitted to an audience. Across the Web, this may be as simple as sending a file via email or uploading it to a web server: the latter in particular has become very popular as pseudo-streaming, but although TCP guarantees delivery even across congested networks, viewing such files live on busy servers can result in a lot of stops and starts as requests are sent out for data to be retransmitted.

As with other elements of online connectivity, webcasting relies on a client/ server model: files and data are stored on one or more central computers, servers, with software that can handle multiple requests simultaneously from remote computers, clients. Of the various procedures that govern connections between clients and servers, TCP (transfer control protocol) is a high-level protocol that makes a direct link from one computer to another and also provides error correction: if a packet of data does not make it to the client, it is requested again until it arrives. For real streaming, UDP (user datagram protocol) is used instead: this does not establish a connection between two computers; rather the server sends out information without the same error-checking information found in TCP. It is then left to the client to work out what to do should a datagram not arrive, usually to miss a few frames of video before continuing the transmission as normal.

Developments to UDP, such as RTSP, also provide some feedback from the client to let the server know whether it should keep on pumping out data or not and helping to prevent a network from becoming overloaded. RTSP is a new standard that is not necessarily understood by all browsers: those that do request the file at the end of a link, usually a short text file that tells the client which application to use to read it and connect to a streaming media server. The server then transmits information to the application, which decodes it and plays back video or audio in real time.

Digital broadcasting basics

Digital broadcasting is a means of allowing more channels to be transmitted on fewer frequencies. For analog television, for example, a camera takes a picture of a scene at the rate of 30 (NTSC) or 25 (PAL) frames per second before rasterising that image, converting it into a series of pixels complete with horizontal and vertical sync commands (the composite video signal) that tells a TV set how to display those pixels. This signal, along with the sound signal, is broadcast as a radio wave or cable signal, a system that has proved extremely reliable in the fifty years or so since it was first developed as a mass medium.

Analog broadcast signals are restricted in terms of their resolution – when the system was first developed, lines on a television screen were displayed alternately; that is, they were interlaced, making the image more indistinct compared to a computer monitor. (Television screens do have one advantage over most computer monitors: their pixels are large, which, while it may make an image less definite, also makes it brighter.) Another major problem for producers is that a signal broadcast as a radio wave must make use of one of the 6MHz frequency bands allocated to it: if it wishes to broadcast other content simultaneously, typically it must purchase another frequency.

For digital broadcasting, a company will again have a single digital channel (allowing it to send 19.39 megabits per second in the US), but this channel can be divided into separate streams or sub-channels, for example, four streams at 4.85Mbits per second each. The reason for this is that digital television allows for the broadcasting of multiple formats, from 704×480 pixels on NTSC to 1920×1080 pixels for HDTV. In addition to these different formats, broadcasters can select alternative bit rates; that is, higher or lower levels of compression. It is very probable that many companies will broadcast highly compressed sub-channels during the day, reserving most or even all of a digital channel for high-quality, mass audience shows during the evening.

From analog to digital: case studies

The US television market has traditionally been much more fragmented than that for Europe, which has tended to be split between public broadcasting services and a few terrestrial channels – although, following deregulation at the end of the 1980s, this began to change dramatically. In the USA, network channels such as CBS (bought out by Viacom in 1999), ABC and Fox competed with various cable and satellite channels such as MTV and CNN. The huge market in the USA, however, has also meant that even segmentation of that market was seen as a profitable target for digital players, although all the main players were hit hard in the aftermath of the 11 September attacks (Phillips 2001).

In the UK, the major digital player is BSkyB, with 5.7 million subscribers by 2002 – nearly twice as many as its main competitors (NTL, Telewest and ITV Digital) combined. Sky's success has not simply been due to aggressive marketing but the promise of hundreds of additional channels and superior interactivity. ITV Digital struggled to keep up with mounting debts, and while digital channels such as BBC4 attracted critical acclaim, government plans to switch off the analog signal at the earliest possible stage have begun to appear very shaky. At the same time, Britain has the 'highest level of digital TV coverage in the world' (Cassy and Wells 2002: 4), with 40 per cent of homes connected to a digital service by March 2002.

The BBC and digital broadcasting

Elements of BBC Internet activity are dealt with elsewhere in this book, but the company is also probably at the forefront of combining content for digital broadcasting and online, not merely in the UK but worldwide. Greg Dyke's inaugural speech as Director-General of the corporation used the opportunity to espouse the fact that viewers around the world, despite having grown used to the 'grammar and techniques' of American television, prefer indigenous programming, but that with the fragmentation of the broadcasting market fewer companies could afford such programming (Dyke 2000). In such a climate, remarked Dyke, public service broadcasters form the 'backbone of our strong indigenous audio-visual industry and they must remain so'.

More than this, however, broadband services (combining BBC Online and digital broadcasting) have also been much more ambitious in terms of expanding content and services elsewhere around the world. In some senses this is a continuation of the BBC's long-standing role via provisions such as the World Service (Briggs 1985; Curran and Seaton 1997; Scannell and Cardiff 1982), taking a global perspective into new markets. The first steps online were taken in 1994, when the BBC established its first web server, followed by beeb.com, a joint venture with ICL in 1996 (Naylor *et al.* 2000). By the beginning of 2001, BBC Online was the most visited website in Europe with 124 million hits every month, and while Dyke believed that this had helped to drive forward Internet takeup in the UK the corporation was looking for similar compelling content for its other broadband services.

One such service, launched in November 2001, was BBC News Interactive, initially available to 5.5 million digital satellite viewers before being extended to cable viewers. Building on digital text services (described by the BBC as 'Ceefax for the digital age'), News Interactive aims to provided value-added content by integrating links to extended services such as forums and discussion groups with the news. Mike Smartt, Editor-in-Chief of New Media at the BBC, has argued that this 'is the start of a whole new way of receiving and consuming news, sport and

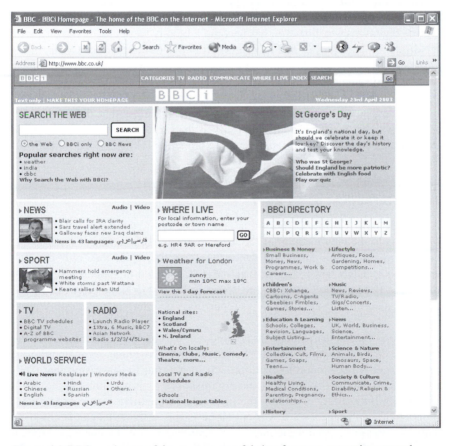

Figure 6.1 BBC.co.uk, one of the most successful sites for news, entertainment and education worldwide.

other information and entering into a two-way relationship with the broadcasters'. This has been followed by BBC3 (previously BBC Choice), aimed at the youth market, and BBC4 in March 2002 that was, in part, intended to make amends for 'recent lapses' in arts programming on BBC1 and BBC2 (Wells 2002).

Currently, BBC Interactive TV (BBCi) is available via satellite, aerial and digital cable. During 2001 one of the ways in which the BBC attempted to push forward these services was through providing enhanced coverage of sporting events, such as Wimbledon and the Open Golf Championship, becoming much more combative in an area where it had lost ground to terrestrial and satellite commercial channels. In addition, by the start of 2002 the BBC was ready to begin trials of a local, interactive broadband service, BBC Hull Interactive, working with Kingston Communications to offer 10,000 web pages for TV, 35 hours of additional video, and other discussion forums and chat groups to link to popular broadcasts such as *Eastenders* and David Attenborough's *The Blue Planet*.

The combination of online and digital broadcasting services indicates some of the ways that the BBC may make a success of its broadband strategy. Staking out the digital market, however, has become a bloody battlefield in the UK, with ONdigital losing millions and its original identity in the process. Competitors, while emphasising options such as a wider range of movies or more sport, have also taken to complaining that the BBC's role as a public broadcasting service has provided it with an unfair advantage: at the same time, the BBC's role as a digital broadcaster has been placed in a parlous position by the fact that, once the analog television signal is switched off, its means of distribution will be in the hands of third parties – NTL, Telewest and, a main competitor, BSkyB (Cassy and Wells 2002).

CNN Interactive: news 24–7

Alongside BBC Online, CNN.com is one of the most successful transitions of old media to the new medium of the Web, particularly in terms of repurposing content produced for television for webcasting. Not that the 'old' medium employed by CNN was particularly antiquated: founded in 1980 as a subsidiary of Turner Broadcasting Systems Inc, the role for Cable News Network was to concentrate on round-the-clock news reporting, becoming part of Time-Warner in 1996.

As Küng-Shankleman (2000) has pointed out, the core inspiration for CNN was to concentrate on news and provide twenty-four-hour coverage. As an unorthodox organisation with an unorthodox approach, it was hardly surprising that CNN would be one of the first major media organisations to move online in the 1990s with CNN Interactive, extending the intensely competitive nature of US news broadcasting on to the web. It was not alone in this venture: its parent company Time-Warner introduced the umbrella-site Pathfinder, BBC Online was in development, and Microsoft had teamed up with NBC to provide MSNBC, a multimedia news venture combining cable and Internet services. MSNBC deserves credit for being probably the first service to recognise the possibilities of convergence between TV and PC, but has been less successful worldwide than CNN.

Part of the secret of CNN Interactive's success is, as has already been suggested, 'repurposing'. Material produced for CNN, CNN International, CNN All News Radio and other parts of the corporation may be redeployed online and, particularly as Ted Turner 'made it his personal mission to cultivate world leaders and heads of state' (Küng-Shankleman 2000: 124), such material has become essential viewing for those involved in government worldwide. On a practical level, digitisation of broadcast-editing has also made it easier to reuse video and audio in a variety of formats. New technologies were used from the start of CNN's existence to make it a lean organisation, and its 'network organisation' structure means that components such as CNN Interactive are more easily bolted on to the information flow of 24–7 news.

Figure 6.2 Despite recent difficulties at AOL Time Warner, CNN Interactive remains one of the leading sites for convergence between Web and cable television technologies.

As well as repurposing, however, CNN also realised the significance of the Internet as an adjunct to its core news services. In the case of another American cable/online service, C-NET, which recognised the value of broadcasting and Internet convergence at an early stage, websites can be invaluable in providing added value to television programmes, incorporating contextual and background material that is too expensive to produce for traditional broadcasting: television programming can drive viewers to the Web for more information and expose them to additional advertising (Reid 1997). Users who search for information online can be directed to the broadcasting schedule, but are also likely to use the website at times when they cannot view cable television (particularly at work). Finally, CNN.com has been very important in terms of extending the brand into new markets.

The point at which CNN's cable operations became essential viewing (at least for international subscribers) was during the Gulf War. As Hall (2001) has observed, conflict in the Balkans stimulated unprecedented levels of visitors to CNN.com (as well as other online news services) in the late 1990s, while the terrorist attack of 11 September also resulted in vastly increased site hits. At the same time, this massive increase in consumption indicated the shortcomings of current webcasting, sites slowing to a crawl making video downloads impossible: most people turned to television for pictures of the tragedy and used the web to contact friends and relatives or find information.

Like a (webcasting) Virgin

Following the Rolling Stones' webcast in 1994 which announced the arrival of MBone, a number of artists, including Radiohead, David Bowie and Paul McCartney, began to wise up to the possibilities of the Internet as a performance medium in its own right. The largest such event (at least in terms of hype that it generated) was the Madonna webcast of songs from her album, *Music*, hosted by MSN with cameras trained on her and 2,800 fans crammed into London's Brixton Academy on 28 November 2000. While the live event was select, the webcast was watched by an estimated nine million viewers, three times larger than the previous record-setting event, McCartney's webcast from The Cavern in Liverpool, which attracted three million viewers.

Reviews of this technological feat were mixed: fans who had queued for the live event heard only six songs over twenty-nine minutes, and MSN had to pay $45 million for computer time, equipment and promotion (Kieren McCarthy of The Register impishly noted that Madonna was paid $0 million by MSN for her performance). For John Hand at the BBC, the exercise was a lesson in broadband frustration as the high-performance link crashed repeatedly, while Gwendolyn Mariano of C-NET remarked tersely that the webcast demonstrated that the Internet is not TV: 'Update Live by the stream, die by the stream' (2000).

Although it may have been a triumph of style over substance, however, the concert was a dramatic example of the ways in which online entertainment is developing. The Talking Point section of the BBC website appended to news stories of the webcast led many commentators to suggest that such broadcasts were here to stay (regardless of their opinion of the gig itself). Microsoft also considered the event a success, despite the costs, marking its presence as a webcast player capable of competing with RealNetworks and AOL (which is also part of the parent company that owns Madonna's label, Warner Music).

The Madonna webcast exposed limitations to the Web as a mass entertainment medium other than technological difficulties. As *New Media Age* reported six months later, there was no agreed way to audit MSN's claims for audience figures at the time of the gig (meaning that the company could have counted as multiple viewers users such as John Hand who logged on multiple times after their browser crashed), something that was addressed by ABC Electronic in April 2001. Finally, spending $45 million on the event did not help one organiser, MediaWave, which despite also organising webcasts for Robbie Williams and Elton John then faced liquidation.

7 Games and entertainment

While the original inventors of cyberspace probably envisaged the tools they created as being useful primarily for business, government and communication, as with all technologies the success and diffusion of cyberspace into everyday life owes a great deal to the ease with which it may be linked to different forms of entertainment.

Most forms of ICT entertainment may be seen as extending technologies and forms, such as film, video and music, that pre-existed computers and the Internet. Video and computer games, however, probably constitute a special exception: obviously humans have played games for centuries, and there are plenty of computer games that take a pre-existing format, such as the board game, and convert it into an electronic version. However, many other types of games, such as the simulator or first person shooter, while they have certainly existed in children's imaginations for centuries (envisaging themselves in aerial dogfights or playing cops and robbers), computers have transformed the means by which a visual environment may be created for such games – growing into a billion-dollar industry in the process. For many players, judging by the amounts spent on PlayStation, PC, Gamecube and Xbox titles, this is no bad thing, even though many commentators may lament the apparent decline in imagination that has transpired as a result.

Entertainment forms such as games and video have also been important in pushing the limits of technology. Many business users, for example, would have been more than happy with the perfectly functional 286 processor that powered most computers throughout the 1980s: those who wished to use their PCs to play games, however, pushed different elements of the hardware – particularly in terms of graphics – to new heights. Likewise, storage formats such as CD-ROM and DVD have gained widespread acceptance as a medium for distributing games and videos, while it is even possible to argue that the requirement for ever larger hard drives is to store such things as MP3s and digital videos. Economically, technically and socially, games and entertainment form an important part of the development of cyberspace.

Game On: a brief history of the computer game

Gaming technology, according to David Nasaw (1993), came to the fore at the turn of the twentieth century when slot-coin phonograph arcades and kinetoscope parlours provided a means for the masses to become acclimatised to the products of industrialisation as well as earning a pretty penny for their manufacturers. Listening to cylinder music and recordings of popular speeches, or watching trapeze artists and circus performers, gave way to pinball machines, more likely to be encountered at the end of the twentieth century standing next to a videogame cabinet.

The beginning of actual computer games is usually traced to the invention of *Spacewar* for the Digital Equipment Corporation PDP-1 in 1962 (Herz 1997; Le Diberder and Le Diberder 1998). As Herman (1998) and Poole (2000) note, however, the world's first videogame actually came into existence in 1958 at the Brookhaven National Laboratory, a nuclear research facility in the USA. Here, William A. Higinbotham designed a rudimentary tennis game for visitors to Brookhaven: what would later take worldwide markets by storm as *Pong* never left the research centre, and Higinbotham remarked wryly that he had not considered applying for the patent that would have made him a rich man (Poole 2000: 30).

Spacewar

Not that the inventors of *Spacewar*, the first computer game to be disseminated successfully, considered themselves on the brink of an entertainment boom that would bring them immense financial rewards. A PDP-1 from DEC, a 'mini-computer' the size of three refrigerators, was delivered to MIT in 1961 and, during the following year, Steve Russell (helped by Dan Edwards, Martin Graetz and others) wrote a game in which two spaceships fired torpedoes at each other (Herz 1997: 6–7).

DEC licensed copies of *Spacewar* in order to demonstrate the capabilities of the PDP-1 to interested parties. Other early mainframe and mini-computer games of the 1960s included *Lunar Lander*, which did not even use a screen, but printed lines indicating descent and thrust and awaited the next instruction to simulate moon landings, and *Hammurabai*, a precursor to *SimCity* and *Civilization*, where players controlled a feudal kingdom.

Until the 1970s, however, the vast majority of consumers had no opportunity to play videogames since they had no access to computers. This changed with the introduction of Atari's arcade tennis game, *Pong*, in 1972, hot on the heels of the Magnavox Odyssey, another tennis game (Atari was forced to pay a licence fee to Magnavox) and the first home console. *Pong* was not quite the first arcade game: its inventor, Nolan Bushnell, had developed the unsuccessful *Computer Space* a year before going on to found Atari.

With the success of *Pong*, however, particularly for the home console market, Atari had created a monster. By the mid-1970s every videogame manufacturer in the world had released a *Pong* clone so that the glut of hardware led to the first crash in 1977. As quickly as they had arrived, computer games appeared to be on the edge of extinction, but the arcade market was really only on the verge of a golden age. The renaissance came with Taito's release of *Space Invaders* in 1978.

Arcade fever

The late 1970s and early 1980s saw an explosion of videogames, so that by 1981 arcades had become a $5-billion fixture of American urban and suburban life (Herz 1997: 50). It was at this time that the foundation stones of the action genre were laid, with games such as *Asteroids* (1979), *Battlezone*, *Defender* and *Pac-Man* (all 1980) and *Donkey Kong* (1981). The latter marked an important moment in the evolution of games, being Nintendo's first hit; while Taito, a pachinko manufacturer, had kick-started the videogame revolution with *Space Invaders*, most successful games were being manufactured in the USA at this point. From the mid-1980s, however, arcade games and then consoles were dominated for a decade by the Japanese company Nintendo and its rival Sega. Even when these were deposed, the console crown passed not to an American firm but to Sony. By 1985, the US home videogame industry was moribund.

As Steven Poole remarks, videogames such as *Donkey Kong* (in which Mario was first introduced, although he was known as Jumpman at that time) and *Pac-Man* represented the emergence of a new and surreal aesthetic. Reliant on brightly lit, crude graphics and audio beeps at first, practical considerations and limitations were approached with a brio that resulted in 'the most purely fantastical sort of gameworlds' (Poole 2000: 43). Restrictions such as the limited number of pixels used to paint Jumpman, for example, resulted in a hat and oversized head – which also made it easier to animate basic responses. While game designers since have reasonably pursued the goal of ever-more realistic graphics, one of the reasons for Japanese domination of the game market has been the realisation that the world-space occupied by videogames is not that of the 'real' world; it is, rather, an iconic empire of signs that may be translated easily from one market to another.

An important stepping-stone in the development of videogames was the separation of hardware and software. With *Pong* and its many imitators, buying a console meant that the consumer purchased a single game: cartridges, such as that for the Atari VCS, released in 1978, meant that henceforth buying a console was the first step in unlocking a whole range of games – at least until the manufacturing company went under.

This golden age was not without its dark underbelly, however. The bright, flashing schemes of games such as *Tempest* and *Zaxxon* seemed to appeal primarily to teenage boys who would presumably become hooligans. *Time* and other opinion-formers led the battle-cry against this latest contribution to delinquency, one which persisted in popular imagination for another decade despite the work of Desmond

Ellis and others (Ellis 1984; Greenfield 1984) proving these opinions to be baseless, persisted, in fact, until these would-be hooligans grew up into the main, 20-plus market for Sony's PlayStation. While many boys (and an increasing number of girls) proved that they could hold down a day job *as well as* get their fix of *Sonic the Hedgehog* or *Gran Turismo*, concerns about the effects of computer games continue to be raised, particularly after grisly episodes such as the Columbine High School massacre of 1999 that was blamed on, among other things, the young murderers' fascination with the violent computer game *Doom*. Arguments continue as to whether such games increase the aggression of children or provide a cathartic outlet for such violence, even contributing to cognitive development (Griffiths 1997; Haddon 1999; Kinder 1991; Poole 2000).

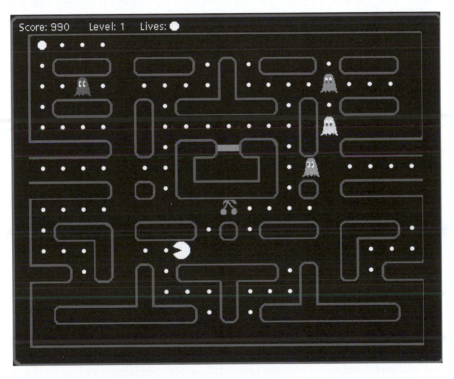

Figure 7.1 Arcade games such as *Space Invaders* and *Pac-Man* were early examples of technological moral panics.

Consoling passions

While groups of teenagers gathered in malls and arcades provided a focus for social fears, games were stealthily introducing a generation to the dubious pleasures of computer technology. Consoles for the home began with the mass of *Pong* boxes that became a plague in 1977, only to be relieved by the introduction of the Atari

VCS the following year. For nearly ten years, home game systems plodded along with a multitude of devices such as the Magnavox Odyssey2 and Commodore 64 (actually an all-purpose computer, but also an excellent games machine). When Nintendo released its Nintendo Entertainment System (NES) in the USA in 1985, retailers were so sceptical that the company agreed to buy back unsold inventory; in fact, as David Sheff (1993) pointed out, Nintendo was on the brink of a decade-long monopoly of home gaming.

After the NES was rolled out across the rest of the USA and international markets in 1986, Sega released its own contender, the Sega Master System (SMS). Until the release of *Sonic the Hedgehog* in 1991, however, Sega trailed far behind Nintendo (with Atari a distant third): in 1990, *Super Mario Bros. 3* became the best-selling game of all time, grossing $500 million, and the following year the 16-bit Super-NES was released. Over the next five years, Sega and Nintendo battled for market domination with a number of casualties along the way, including the Atari Jaguar and 3DO platforms. The years 1995 and 1996, however, marked another revolution as hardware advanced to a new level with the Sega Saturn, Nintendo 64 and a new player – the Sony PlayStation.

Sony had originally been approached by Nintendo to provide CD hardware to the game giant, which then pulled out of the deal (Poole 2000; Sheff 1993). Sony, deciding to go it alone, targeted the PlayStation at adult gamers and stole the show, selling five million consoles in Britain alone by 2000. Children who had played *Donkey Kong* and *Pac-Man* grew into super-attenuated adolescents revelling in *Tomb Raider* and *Gran Turismo*. The adult market was also helped along by rapid improvements to PC hardware so that games such as *Doom*, released in 1993, were huge hits on the PC before being ported to consoles.

By 2001, the US and UK games industry was worth £5 billion (Williams 2002) and the spread of computer games to the PC had not gone unnoticed by the dominant force in personal computing: Microsoft had been involved in the game market for a decade, producing titles such as *Flight Simulator* and *Age of Empires* and, wanting more than dominance of the desktop, Bill Gates announced in March 2000 the development of Microsoft's own console, the Xbox. As new devices such as PlayStation2 and Nintendo GameCube would come online, offering additional features such as DVD playback, Microsoft was very aware that the rapid growth in PC sales that had taken place during the late 1990s was sure to decline during the new millennium. As with the Internet, consoles threatened its core business and the company acted in typical fashion, announcing that it would be a major player. After its launch in 2001, the Xbox performed poorly outside the USA, and Microsoft was forced within six months to cut the price of its console by £100 in the UK. While Microsoft still dominates huge swathes of cyberspace, it cannot control every market it targets.

Immersive worlds

The release of *Doom* did not merely mark out an interest in games on the PC, but also pointed to future development of computer games. While single-player mode was frightening enough, the title's longevity was also due to the fact that it could be networked across multiple computers including, because of its support for TCP/IP, those connected by the Internet. Subsequent releases by Id and competitors, such as *Quake* and *Unreal*, were supported by dedicated online servers, and interest in online gaming spread to the console market, including Sega's ill-fated Dreamcast and the Xbox.

The online market for games has often been overstated (Poole 2001), and additional connectivity did not lead to the massive sales Sega had hoped for the Dreamcast. At the same time, the Internet has provided a niche for many different types of interactive play. Online gambling, for example, has boomed since the end of the 1990s, particularly as it offers opportunities to evade strict gaming laws in different countries. At the same time, the growth of 'persistent worlds' has become especially popular for MMORPGs (massively multiplayer online role-playing games) such as *Ultima Online*, *EverQuest* and *Asheron's Call*. By extending player interaction beyond the usual videogame hack and slay, such online worlds combine features more akin to chat rooms with the more traditional assumption of fantastical

Figure 7.2 Games such as id's *Quake* marked a new departure for 3D technology on the home computer or console.

roles or avatars, returning these games to the social forum they occupied as paper, pen and dice games in the 1970s and 1980s.

Emulating success

Throughout their short history, videogames and computer games – particularly consoles – have operated on a simple economic model: hardware is sold relatively cheaply, often subsidised, with profits made on game titles. As such, game formats are usually tied to one proprietary format unless the designer chooses to port them to another platform. As such, many games made for 'classic' machines such as the Atari or Amiga become literally unplayable: the hardware on which they run is no longer available, and changes in technology and gaming styles mean it is uneconomic to try to update such titles.

One consequence of this tendency is the market for emulators, applications that create a virtual environment providing a simulated operating system so that games created for a particular console may be run on a PC or Mac. Sites such as Game Revolution (www.game-revolution.com) and MegaGames (www.megagames. com) offer a number of emulators for old titles – but emulation has not been restricted to defunct gaming platforms.

In 1998, programmer Randy Linden created a PlayStation emulator called Bleem that could run PS titles on a personal computer. Realising that Sony would be unlikely to appreciate such competition, Linden first advertised Bleem as emulating not the circuitry of the PlayStation but merely its functionality; when that particular piece of sophistry did not emolliate the gaming giant, Bleem was positioned as a PS accessory that would increase sales for Sony. Sony attempted to prevent sales of Bleem (and another emulator, Connectix) but its temporary restraining order was rejected. Bleem counter-sued Sony as a monopoly conspiring to restrain trade, only to fold in 2001.

As with music, images and, increasingly, video, emulators such as Bleem indicate some of the difficulties facing games companies as they make use of new forms of digital entertainment. Unlike music and video, technological developments for which run in much longer cycles, without emulation computer games face extinction much more quickly.

Genres and players

Games can be surprisingly complex to define: game theory can cover economics, mathematics, the social and life sciences (particularly as a theory to explain evolution), and military strategies. These are not always far removed from the process of providing entertainment. Mathematics is always present in terms of computer game design, sometimes hidden from the designer – as when he or she creates a visual environment using software applications such as 3D and digital imaging packages – but sometimes very much at the forefront, as when designing

AI opponents. Military operations often provide the raw economic impetus to design new technologies that end up in computer games, typical examples being flight simulators that were first developed for training armed forces.

Johannes Huizinga (1930: 47) defined a game as:

> A voluntary activity or occupation executed within certain fixed limits of time and place, according to rules freely accepted but absolutely binding, having its aim in itself and accompanied by a feeling of tension, joy, and the consciousness that it is different from ordinary life.

While Huizinga's definition does not necessarily cover all aspects of gaming (indeed, one criticism is that it is difficult – if not impossible – to have a single definition of games), it has the advantage of providing a concise but wide-ranging account of the important elements most game players would recognise: that the activity is not compulsory, and involves sensations of pleasure or tension (not necessarily incompatible) which feel different to ordinary activities. Such sensations can be so intense that many players would probably argue that they are almost compulsory, as when we speak of games being addictive, but the fact is that most players – for all that they may indulge obsessively in one more level, another go – take up video and computer games only at certain times of the day or week as an alternative to the other tasks of daily life.

Games and playing

Before turning to discuss the theories of computer games as entertainment, it is worth exploring some of the ways in which game theory has influenced other areas such as mathematics and economics. Classical game theory, such as that used in the mid-twentieth century to account for economic activities or military strategies, was typically non-co-operative and based on what was known as 'complete information'; that is, the outcomes of a game would be known to all players. Such theory treats a game as a strategic and limited set of rules in which the aim of the player is simply to win – or at least, not to lose, which often amounts to the same thing: games of this type are frequently referred to as 'zero-sum', or 'Nash equilibria', games, after John Nash (Jones 2000).

One simple example of a zero-sum game is as follows: two players must announce to a referee one of two decisions – that the referee give the other player £3 (co-operate) or give me £1 (defect). If both players co-operate, each will make £3, but if one defects, one will make £4, the other nothing, while if both defect each will gain £1. Co-operation brings the greatest rewards for the largest number of players, but the tendency to view such games purely on the grounds of immediate self-interest tends to lead to defection (I cannot trust the other player and at least I will make £1).

Such game theory has tended to assume that all rules and constraints are known, whereas people live in a world of imperfect information. As such, their actions cannot always be assumed to be rational: players are more likely to make more money if everyone co-operates, but lack of information tends to make players more selfish. This has led to an 'evolutionary' theory of games, one which assumes not complete rationality and information, but bounded rationality, in essence trial and learning by playing games repeatedly. This enables a more dynamic approach to games, making it more suitable for studying situations where players are not necessarily entirely rational.

Game theory of the type described above is concerned largely with outcomes, which it attempts to predict on the basis of probability. Yet although winning games is important for many players, this rarely explains completely the reason for playing games as a form of entertainment (as opposed to a form of economics or military strategy). Psychologists following Jean Piaget, for example, have tended to consider the role of play – rather than game theory – in human development. Piaget (cited in Frasca 2001) distinguished three main types of games: exercise, symbolic and rules games. Exercise games develop senses and co-ordination; symbolic games, which involve the imagination (for example, making a box into a 'car'), develop a child's understanding of its environment; rule-based games, such as football, stimulate socialisation.

Piaget believed that the earliest games played by children have no rules at all, something contradicted by Daniel Vidart who suggests that even the simplest activity, such as pretending to be a plane, involves some form of rule (that extending arms will create wings). The important point for Piaget, however, is that before socialisation play does not involve winning and losing – it is this that distinguishes it from classical game theory. Both games and play may have rules, but the former also involves an aim.

Games, representation and narrative

In recent years, theories of computer games have drawn on discussions of hypertext, for example, in the work of George Landow (1992, 1997) and Jay Bolter (1991) that combines computer-mediated communication with literary theory. Brenda Laurel, for example, in *Computers as Theater* (1993), has attempted to explain a poetics of software design that takes into account user performance (something traditionally missing from narrative theory). Similarly, Janet Murray, in *Hamlet on the Holodeck* (1997), discusses how computers provided a new medium for story-telling. Computer games, along with other forms of computer-mediated communication such as chat rooms and hypertext, are significant in that they allow the development of new forms of what she calls 'cyberdrama'. This cyberdrama is effective insofar as it encourages immersion (not simply the suspension of disbelief, but the construction of new beliefs), agency (whereby performing actions have an effect on representations in the game), both of which lead to transformation.

The Le Diberder brothers (1998) have argued that computer games have developed their own particular narratives of representation, for example, in simulations.

Such simulations, which clearly developed from mathematical and scientific models, create computer 'worlds' that pay great attention to details but have no clear goals. As such, these are games that come close to play rather than classical game theory, but this is not to say that there are no rules: obviously games such as *SimCity* have a host of rules (often very complex), and in addition the player can set him or herself a set of tasks – to create the largest city possible, to build a small but perfectly functioning city, to raze their creation to the ground by means of a natural disaster – but it is not clear-cut how each game should end. The narrative of the game can only be established during performance. To use a term from Espen Aarseth (1997), such narratives are 'ergodic cybertexts'; that is, texts where 'nontrivial effort is required to allow the reader to traverse the text' (p. 1). Put more simply, such texts are interactive, but this is not an interactivity that involves selecting one choice from a set predetermined and limited by the producer or author: rather each selection in an ergodic text calls into range a further set of possible performances.

Different types of games implement different narratives and simulations in very different ways. Some of the most common genres of videogames and computer games are listed below.

Arcade/action

The most extensive of game genres (if it can be called a genre), action games have comprised most arcade and console products since *Space Invaders* (1978) and *Frogger* (1979) until *Incoming* (1998) and *Alien vs. Predator* (1999). Action games offer constant progression, such as increasing levels of difficulty, but must also provide instant gratification: the best of the breed are learnt in moments but only mastered after months of practice. The following four genres are subcategories of action games.

Shoot 'em ups

Spacewar (1962) was probably the first shoot 'em up, a genre that quickly established itself in arcades following the advent of *Space Invaders* because its rules were so simple: kill anything that moves. Cabinets for *Asteroids* (1979), *Defender* and *Battlezone* (both 1980) appeared worldwide, the latter initiating the first-person shooter (FPS) that was made more popular with Id's *Wolfenstein* (1992) and *Doom* (1993). So-called after the perspective of the character, whose line of sight is meant to match the player's, this has become one of the most ubiquitous genres around with follow-ups such as *Quake* (1996), *Half-Life* (1998) and *Return to Castle Wolfenstein* (2002). Another subcategory of the shoot 'em up is the beat 'em up, examples of which include *Mortal Combat* (1992) and *Virtua Fighter 2* (1995), which marked the entry of this type into 3D.

Platform

Defender, which assaulted the player with battalions of ships against a side-scrolling landscape, was perhaps the *ur*-platform game, but the genre was really established with Nintendo's *Donkey Kong* (1981), the lead character of which, Jumpman, evolved into Mario in *Mario Bros.* (1983) and *Super Mario Bros.* (1985). In such games, a central figure (usually extremely cartoon-like) must navigate pitfalls and ledges, avoid enemy fire and collect power-ups to progress to the next level, other popular examples including *Sonic the Hedgehog* (1991) and *Crash Bandicoot* (1995).

Driving and flying

Many games revolving around driving and flying involve some level of simulation, but ever since *Pole Position* appeared in 1982 plenty of action gamers have simply wanted to make their way around a racetrack as quickly as possible, without worrying about how suspension or tyre pressure will affect performance. Racing games may follow the layout of a road (if not its rules), such as *World Rally Championship* (2002), but they may equally operate in the air, as with *WipeOut* (1995).

Sports

Sports games often represent a cross-over between pure action and strategy, operating across a spectrum where titles such as *Championship Manager* (1993) and its successors deal solely with managing teams as sets of statistics, to fast and furious action events that are the descendants of *Pong*. Trend-setters have included Konami's *Track and Field* (1983) or *NBA Jam* (1993).

Strategy

When manufacturers began to make games for personal computers in the late 1980s, a new field of entertainment opened up that did not depend so much on the visceral appeal of arcade action. The origins of strategy games lie in chess and tabletop wargames, where players would re-enact famous battles. Computer versions, however, also quickly developed into 'god' games such as *Populous* (1989), *SimCity* (1989) and *Civilization* (1990). Most strategy games were turn-based, each player taking it in turns to make a move, but following the introduction of *Command and Conquer* in 1995 the real-time strategy (RTS) game has become the most popular example of this genre.

Simulations

Many simulations, whether set on the road, in the air or in outer space, share superficial similarities with arcade driving and flying games. However, whereas a player could pick up a gamepad and seconds later be flinging their vehicle around the track in *WipeOut*, they would probably fail to manage take-off in *Flight Simulator* without reading the manual. *Flight Simulator* set the tone for future attempts to re-create the experience of flying or driving as realistically as possible, but simulation games also cross over with strategy games, as in *SimCity* and its various descendants.

Role-playing

Role-playing games (RPGs) for the computer developed out of paper-based games such as *Dungeons & Dragons* and *Traveller* that were popular in the 1970s and 1980s, where players assumed a character for the duration of the game. Arcade games such as *Dragon's Lair* (1983) or *Gauntlet* (1986) included rudimentary role-playing elements, but the earliest examples were text-based, such as *The Hobbit* (1982). Such RPGs became more visually sophisticated with the introduction of *Final Fantasy* (1987), while the long-running *Ultima* series was one of the first to take game-playing online.

Figure 7.3 Massively multiplayer online role-playing games (MMORPGs) such as *Everquest* have become persistent virtual worlds that continue long after individual players depart.

Puzzle

An often-neglected genre, puzzle games rarely push the limits of computer hard-ware but are actually the most popular, particularly if one takes into account the related genre of quiz games, including titles such as *Who Wants to be a Millionaire*. In such games, a simple logical task – assemble a picture, match different coloured blocks, locate the hidden mines – can become fiendishly difficult, especially when playing against the clock. The exemplary game in this category is *Tetris* (1989), designed by a Soviet mathematician, Alexi Pajitnov, in which descending coloured/shaped blocks must be matched together to delete them at ever-increasing speeds. So popular was this game that it caused an international copyright war (Sheff 1993).

Adventure

Whereas the logical task is the *raison d'être* for puzzle games, puzzles frequently feature in adventure games as a means to an end: opening a door, defeating an opponent, releasing a tool required for a further stage of the game. Adventure games often share similarities with RPGs, and the earliest versions were usually text-based, as with *ADVENT* (1972) and *Zork* (1977), but have become visually richer, particularly in the series that began with *Myst* and stylish titles such as *Grim Fandango*.

The inner life of videogames

The varied genres and huge successes of certain game platforms indicate not merely clever marketing and a technological-economic imperative to shift large numbers of boxes each year (though these have an important part to play in the game business), but also the immense pleasure that videogames provide.

Stephen Poole, in *Trigger Happy: The Inner Life of Videogames* (2000), argues that games are finally becoming accepted as a mature medium for entertainment, one that will eventually compete with films, books and music in terms of providing emotional fulfilment as well as simply testing hand–eye co-ordination. Part of this is due to demographics, the fact that arcade-players of the 1980s became the console-owners of the 1990s, but also because technological developments have been matched by investments in scripting, and thematic and visual design. Ironically, one area where technology has not necessarily provided improvements per se is the mysterious element of 'gameplay', the combination of feedback and pleasurable stress that comes when a game is neither too easy nor too difficult, extending the player's abilities just enough so that he or she will return for one more go.

What computing advances have done is to offer a broader canvas to map out a fantasy life, providing more sophisticated 'coherence' within a game world. Manufacturers often refer to a game's 'realism', but many of the most successful releases are not in any sense realistic, drawing more on the surrealist world of cartoon imagery (such as Japanese *manga* or Tex Avery). Coherence, suggests Poole, is the key to our immersion in videogames, inculcating the sense that we can explore a complete virtual environment through projection into avatars such as Lara Croft or Crash Bandicoot.

Games do not necessarily compete with film (itself a despised medium at the beginning of the twentieth century), though quasi-cinematic titles such as *Outcast* draw upon some of the conventions of film narratives: 'We like stories in general' remarks Poole, 'because they're *not* interactive' (2001: 122). Narratives in games can drive forward gameplay, but not at the expense of interactivity: full motion video (FMV) clips may be stunning the first time they are witnessed, but soon pall after the tenth viewing. Rather, the narrative, thematic and semiotic structures of games work best when they enable us to invest in the signs that comprise their characters in much more interactive ways.

Game control

As has been noted previously in the brief history of computer games that began this chapter, at different times such games have been at the centre of moral or regulatory dilemmas. Initially, such concerns largely dealt with the role of these games as they affected the leisure time of players, particularly young males. As computer and videogame technologies have progressed, however, and the scenes they are capable of depicting become more realistic, so anxieties have shifted more to the content of games rather than simply their contexts.

Since the release of *Doom* in the mid-1990s, games with extremely violent (and, less frequently, sexual) content have attracted potentially censorious attention, similar to that aroused by so-called 'video nasties' in the 1980s. As an attempt to counter the imposition of external controls, a number of European manufacturers formed the European Leisure Software Publishers Association (ELSPA), providing a collective identity for the European games industry and also setting up its own age-based rating system (www.elspa.com).

Most games now sold in countries such as the UK carry the ELSPA rating, indicating the preferred age range – though this rating is voluntary and does not necessarily deal with all possible conflicts over game content. In 2001, for example, some members of ELSPA issued a press release announcing that they did not want to be associated with the game *Hooligans*, a title developed by the Dutch company Darxabre in which players recruited, trained and led gangs of football hooligans. Likewise, the publishers of the gory game *Carmageddon* agreed to tone down the cartoon violence of their first title after consultation with ELSPA, replacing human victims with zombies.

Sony

Established in Tokyo in 1945, Sony quickly became associated with electric and white goods, but its involvement with videogames began in the early 1990s (initiated by Nintendo, much to that company's cost). Since then, its games enterprise has become part of an important electronics and entertainment empire that includes Sony Music Entertainment Inc, Sony Pictures Entertainment, Sony Electronics and its entertainment division, Metreon.

At the time of the launch of the PlayStation in 1995, the console market dominated by Nintendo trailed by Sega. Within a year, Sony was announcing bull-ishly on its PlayStation news site (www.scea.com/news/) that it was the 'next generation' system of choice: it was the first platform to break the one-million unit barrier with sales of 900,000 consoles in the US in December 1996 alone, bringing the user base up to 3.2 million players spending $13 million per day by January 1997 in an industry that was then worth $5.2 billion. The secret of Sony's success, as well as keen marketing aimed at older users, was to ensure a vast range of titles (300 within the first year): while competitors argued about the technological bene-fits of their system over the PlayStation, Sony developed strong links with game developers. By the end of 1997, Sony was outselling competitors by a ratio of two to one, having shifted 8.7 million consoles in the USA in two years.

Demand for the PS1 (as it came to be known) increased as Sony dropped its prices in 1999, but the videogame industry was also gearing up for new hardware to replace ageing consoles. Sega appeared to gain a potential upper hand in 2000 with the launch of a new Dreamcast system, but the announcement of PlayStation 2 in March 1999 led many consumers to await the release of a system that would be compatible with their own games (an important lesson Sony had learned from Microsoft). Promising far superior graphics capability via its much-touted 'Emotion Engine' and support for DVD, the PS2 represented Sony's Trojan horse to capture the home leisure market. The release of the PS2 in Japan in March 2000 resulted in phenomenal demand for 980,000 units in one weekend as well as a fourfold boost for DVD sales.

Ironically, considering the success of the PlayStation, commentators such as Marc Gunther (2001) remarked that the rise of Sony during the 1990s was marked by caution. Stung by earlier failures in Hollywood, Sony resisted the temptation to invest large amounts of money in dotcoms with far-reaching business plans. None the less, Nobuyuki Idei, Chairman and CEO, has described a 'Sony Dream World' of a vast array of content available across networked devices, providing 'new forms of entertainment lifestyles for the broadband age' (cited in Gunther 2001), while the CEO of Sony Corporation of America, Howard Stringer, argues that the company is 'one of the grand ringmasters in the convergence of computers, consumer electronics, telecommunications, music, movies, television, and new forms of digital entertainment' (SEL 2001).

From silver screen to computer scene

Videogames are, for better or worse, frequently compared to the movies. Some games attempt to emulate a cinematic feel, while movies such as *The Mummy*

Returns (2001) forgo normal conventions of film such as plot and characterisation for a white-knuckle ride that owes much more to *Tomb Raider*. The previous chapter paid special attention to webcasting and digital broadcasting: while much of the technology that lies behind digital video is obviously the same for movies online and broadcasting (with the possible exception of DVD, touched on briefly in that chapter), the way such video is consumed and experienced as entertainment is often substantially different.

Persistence of vision

The first movement towards film was Eadweard Muybridge's work between 1872 and 1877, which captured the movements of horses and human figures using a series of still photographs. During the 1890s, William Dickson began to make short movies using George Eastman's celluloid film and Edison's 'Kinetograph', employing to his advantage the phenomenon of persistence of vision whereby still images appear in motion when changed quickly enough. In Europe, the Lumiere brothers invented a portable Cinematographe, similar to Edison's machine, and began the history of cinema with a series of short motion pictures presented in a Paris café in 1895.

The remarkable social, economic and even political effects of cinema are beyond the scope of this book, although the destruction of the European film industry during the First World War and the rise of Hollywood were to have immense consequences for CGI (computer-generated imagery) at the end of the twentieth century, as it has affected almost every area of the movies. More significant to notions of cyberspace, film developed a rich vocabulary of seeing and constructing the subject in new ways, often taking its cue from modernist art movements such as Surrealism in the 1920s and 1930s. At the same time, technical innovations such as sound (1927–28) and colour in the 1950s were important contributors to the success of cinema as a spectacle (although other novelties such as 3D did not thrive).

Special effects and CGI

Films have employed optical special effects since the first reels of moving vehicles were spliced together to create spectacular crashes on screen, and in 1902 George Méliès used the silver screen to paint phantasies from the pages of Jules Verne with *A Trip to the Moon*.

The real break in computer special effects, however, began with *Star Wars* in 1977 – not so much the film itself, which relied largely on more traditional techniques of matte painting and optical trickery, but the establishment of Industrial Light and Magic (ILM). According to Steve Silberman, the development of ILM throughout the 1980s and 1990s was aimed at providing 'filmmakers absolute control over the image' (1999: 133). Important points in the development of f/x could occur outside ILM, for example in Disney's *Tron* (1982), but Lucas' company virtually brought the CGI industry into existence with work on movies such as *Star Trek: The Wrath of Khan*, *Terminator 2* and *The Abyss*. In 1994, ILM made an agreement with SGI that enabled it to test the most powerful new computer hardware available for each new movie.

By 1999 and the release of *The Phantom Menace*, digital f/x had come to entirely dominate the process of filming (indeed, Lucas intends talk of 'film' itself to become a technological anachronism). Mark Hamill had remarked previously that 'if there were a way to make movies without actors, George would do it' (Silberman 1999: 135). Unfortunately, Lucas' first attempt at a completely digital 'synthespian' was the almost universally loathed Jar-Jar Binks. Indeed, the obsession with digital f/x among a certain class of Hollywood blockbuster has led to accusations of the infantilisation of the medium, with acting and scripts being left far behind, allegations not much helped by the follow-up *Attack of the Clones*.

A happier union of special effects and story-telling emerged with the first episode of Tolkien's *Lord of the Rings*, directed by Peter Jackson and released at the end of 2001. Ironically, Jackson's post-production digital effects (which also had the serendipitous effect of enabling him to fashion virtually every step of the film in his native New Zealand) were employed with the express intention of making the film appear more 'realistic' and 'historical', building on the rich – indeed, obsessive – detail of Tolkien's original story. As Erik Davis remarks (2001: 127), the text itself has become a remarkable example of an interactive virtual space in which fans have immersed themselves: 'Like Eden or Dante's *Inferno*, Middle-earth has become a collective map of a moral universe, a fabulous landscape that, in its depth and detail, floats just beyond the fields we know.' In addition, Jackson's film indicates some of the ways in which film entertainment increasingly crosses over with Internet technologies to promote movies but also offer alternative forums for audience participation. The official movie site, www.lordoftherings.net, offered merchandise and information, but Tolkien's book has also spawned a number of compendia and fanzines, including www.lordoftherings.com, www.glyphweb. com/arda and www.eds.ed.ac.uk/misc/local/TolkLang. The Internet was also an important rumour mill for the movie, from semi-official sites such as Ian McKellen's personal website, www.mckellen.com, to unofficial ones such as www.xenite.org/faqs/lotr_movie.

Probably the most successful CGI company, one that combines new technologies with strong narratives and characterisation, has been Pixar, established by Steve Jobs following his separation from Apple. Although it had achieved some recognition with shorts such as *Luxo Jr* that were generated digitally, its breakthrough came following an agreement made with Disney in 1991 to produce three full-length, computer-generated movies. *Toy Story*, the first film to be produced under this deal, was released in 1995, followed by *A Bug's Life* (1998) and *Toy Story 2* (1999). With each film, as well as productions by competitors such as Dreamworks (responsible for the 1998 film *Antz* and 2001's *Shrek*) and Square (producers of the *Final Fantasy* games and movie of the same title), technological limits have been rolled further back. Chris Lee, producer of *Final Fantasy*, sees the real possibility of hyper-real synthespians in forthcoming movies, but he also sees their roles as limited to blockbuster movies rather than more intimate dramas (Laing 2001).

Synthetic actors and agents

Final Fantasy has demonstrated the most realistic CGI characters on screen to date, but synthetic actors, or synthespians, have been slowly closing the divide between computer games and movies for almost a decade. As games began to include longer cut scenes to develop plot or atmosphere, and as 3D technologies became ever more sophisticated, so the techniques to create in-game characters, including motion capture and 3D modelling, gradually grew closer to film.

The first virtual pop star, Kyoto Date, was created by HoriPro in 1995, a virtual idoru keshu, or idol singer. In William Gibson's novel *Idoru*, he describes such a synthetic actor as 'Entirely *process*; infinitely more than the combined sum of her various selves. The platforms sink beneath her, one after another, as she grows denser and more complex' (1996: 202).

While fully functioning synthespians are rarely popular on the silver screen, the trend for these agents or avatars has slowly been gaining ground on the Web. Agents take various forms: at their simplest (and, perhaps, most useful), agents consist of bots that can collect and collate information for users. Nor are agents restricted to entertainment: the Press Association became a subject of the news (rather than reporting it) in 2000 when it launched a cyber-presenter created by Digital Animations, Ananova (www.ananova.com), who used sophisticated text-to-speech technology to read news items (though the presenter was later reduced in role). Digital Animations also created a virtual pop star the following year, TMmy (www.tmmy.co.uk), with her own invented biography.

It is significant that most of the virtual agents created thus far, certainly those that have attracted widespread attention from the media, have been female. This certainly reflects the bias towards male programmers and designers in the CGI industry, and in the case of at least one computer game avatar, Lara Croft, some critics have seen her as fulfilling a fantasy of male control over a strong-willed female.

Versatile entertainment

Digital special effects are transforming what we see on film and television screens, but digitisation is also affecting the ways in which we access such material. As with music and audio CDs, arguments made for DVD (digital versatile disc) include the potential for much higher quality and more perfect copies of information – the latter something that has not been ignored by the film industry. DVD is certainly much higher quality than VHS tape at twice the resolution, although connoisseurs argue (as with CD and vinyl) over the relative merits of digital versus an analog medium such as celluloid.

Ten companies, including Sony, Philips and Time Warner, founded the DVD Consortium in 1995 to develop the technical format of DVD and promote it as a medium for video, audio and data storage. Based in Tokyo and now known as the DVD Forum (www.dvdforum.org), this group is responsible for defining DVD specifications, licensing, verifying and promoting the format.

Although some Hollywood companies had initially resisted the new medium during the late 1990s, an estimated forty-six million DVD players had been sold by 2000, mainly in the USA, Europe and Japan. Physically, the medium appears very similar to CD, comprising a plastic disc some five inches across with a microscopic groove running in a spiral around the disc. DVDs, however, use much smaller tracks, 0.74 microns in width compared to 1.6 microns on CDs; this enables them to store seven times as much data as a CD. What is more, DVDs can be dual-layered (with information on both sides) and also joined together, providing potential storage of up to 17 gigabytes.

DVD also, like CD, offers the potential for recording, although this has been held back by a number of different and often incompatible formats: DVD-R, DVD-RAM, DVD-RW and DVD+RW.

Coding and encryption

In the late 1990s, it was frequently predicted that DVD sales would be slow to take off due to incompatible (and extremely expensive) DVD recording formats. In fact, as with audiotape and CD, people seem likely to keep VHS players for recording information for the next few years while using DVD to watch high-quality movies. A greater difficulty for the format in its early years was the initial truculence of Hollywood, which did not want to see high-quality material available in a format that was easy to pirate.

The response to this was CSS (content scrambling system), which made it more difficult to copy digital information. More difficult, but not impossible: in 1999, software called DeCSS was made available so that users of the Linux operating system would be able to play DVDs. The Motion Pictures Association of America (MPAA) and DVD Copy Control Association (DVD CCA) brought court actions against the software distributors, arguing that it violated trade secrets, and Norwegian police arrested 16-year-old Jan Johansen, accusing him of helping to code DeCSS. In response, various organisations such as the Electronic Frontier Foundation (EFF) and OpenDVD.org (www.opendvd.org) appealed against the decision to ban independent development of DVD players, contending that such decisions violated consumer rights to fair use, including the ability to watch DVDs on a platform of choice.

While fear of piracy (particularly in the wake of Napster) aroused considerable sympathy for producers with regard to DeCSS, it was hard for all but the most loyal commentators to justify region coding. Typically, Hollywood releases films in the USA several months before Europe and elsewhere in the world; with video, different technical specifications (PAL and NTSC) meant that tapes released in America were useless elsewhere, but a common DVD platform, as well as the emerging potential of the Internet to open up international trade, meant that studios were concerned to maximise profits.

The resulting fix was the concept of region codes, with the world divided into the following regions:

- Region 0: all regions
- Region 1: North America (including United States and Canada)
- Region 2: Western Europe and Japan
- Region 3: southeast Asia
- Region 4: South America and Australia
- Region 5: Africa, Eastern Europe and Russia
- Region 6: China

Region codes for DVDs are encoded into their digital data, and most (though controversially for movie studios) DVD players are region locked, so that Region 2 players work with discs produced for the Western European and Japanese markets, or multi-region discs, but not those made for consumption in the USA. More than measures to protect against piracy, region coding has been one of the most controversial aspects of DVD.

Movies online

As David Gauntlett (2000b: 82) has remarked, 'cinema is perhaps the popular medium *least* similar to the Internet'; certainly online movies have been much slower to take off than DVD. While broadband access, principally for large corporations and institutions such as universities, has encouraged some growth in movie distribution (and pirating) online, for users connected by a 56K modem the experience is more likely to be one that is frustrating rather than enthralling.

And yet, as Gauntlett continues, the movie industry quickly embraced the Net as a medium for publicity, notably via *The Blair Witch Project* (www.blairwitch. com) and *The Matrix* (www.whatisthematrix.com), and it has boomed in terms of audience and expert reviews as at the Internet Movie Database (www.imdb. com). Films such as *Star Wars* and *The Lord of the Rings* were not harmed in terms of hype by releasing trailers on their websites. At the same time, the notion of video on demand has been a somewhat illusory grail for network suppliers as diverse as BT and Worldcom, while online movies have also offered opportunities for independent film-makers (Kenner 1999).

Of sites promoting original material, good examples include Atom Films (www.atomfilms.com) and iFilm (www.ifilm.com), which, according to *Hollywood Reporter* in May 2001, were among the top twenty most visited sites (cited in Evans 2001). Here low-budget film-makers can find an outlet for short films that tend to be neglected elsewhere, and cater for specialist tastes. Urban Entertainment (www.urbanentertainment.com), for example, is a black culture site mainly for

US-based producers, while Hypnotic (www.hypnotic.com) showcases experimental movies that are unlikely to appear on a TV or cinema screen near you: often this is for a good reason, but as David Lynch demonstrated with *Mulholland Drive*, experts in a field such as television do not always know best.

The Net, then, is at present incapable of supporting full-length features but has already provided an alternative venue for some remarkable shorts. Probably the most well known has been Kevin Rubio's *Troops* (www.theforce.net/troops), a ten-minute mockumentary about the daily life of storm-troopers that was made for $2,000 and attracted millions of viewers after its release in 1998 (Gauntlett 2000b: 84).

Music machine

As with many other areas of entertainment, digital technologies have had a huge impact on the production of music – yet in few other fields has that impact been so unsettling. The twentieth century saw the mass production of music for the first time, with inventions such as the phonograph and audiotape, with fortunes being built on a genuinely popular form of entertainment. Technology, which was key to this explosion, has also emerged in the final decade of that century as the main threat to the profits accumulated by the six main music companies which dominated some 90 per cent of the industry. As John Perry Barlow, former songwriter for The Grateful Dead and occasional contributor to *Wired* magazine remarked, 'the great cultural war has broken out at last' (2000: 240).

For libertarians such as Barlow, peer-to-peer networks would restore a balance between consumer, producer and distributor that had gone too far towards the latter part of this triangle, although some observations, such as 'the free proliferation of expression does not decrease commercial value. Free access *increases* it' (Barlow 2000: 241), appear with hindsight to be part of the general wish-fulfilment that marked the height of dotcom mania.

None the less, it is equally obvious that cyberspace is having a remarkable impact on music distribution, just as digital media in general transformed its production. From the drive to improve recording techniques in the 1970s and 1980s, music hardware and software has become increasingly sophisticated, to such an extent that leading lights such as Brian Eno have prophesied autonomous, self-generated music (and even tried to make that prophesy a reality in the mid-1990s with a piece of software, Sseyo Koan). Music is one area where human autonomy is most easily called into question: as Erik Davis (2002: 98) asks of Japanese electronica artist Keiko Uenishi (or O.blaat), 'Who exactly is responsible for the music? . . . Who's in control? The machine or the musician?' Ultimately, the distinction between the two is becoming less relevant.

Digital music

As we saw in the previous chapter, digital recording on to vinyl was subtly transforming consumers' listening experience by the end of the 1970s. The major change that occurred in the production of such music, however, was the launch of digital audio for the masses in 1983 in the form of the compact disc, launched jointly by Sony and Philips. The initial public response to audio CDs was fairly cool, and as Brian Winston (1998) and others have pointed out, the massive transformation in listening and buying habits was effected principally by music companies rather than by consumer demand. CD audio is recorded in 16 bits with a transfer rate of 150Kb/sec, which was more than adequate for most listeners and proved that good-quality music could be produced digitally.

Computers, however, were still generally incapable of processing such information, so work began in the 1980s to find more efficient ways to compress data for digital transmission. Most important was the work undertaken in 1987 at the Fraunhofer Institute in Germany on perceptual audio encoding, which eventually led to the popular MP3 format. Put simply, the range of sounds the human ear can hear is limited, so that doubling the amplitude of a sound does not double its loudness. MP3 uses a 'psychoacoustic model' to determine which parts of a wavelength can be removed without degrading the quality of a sound. Around the same time, the Motion Picture Experts Group (MPEG) was formed to work on ways of compressing pictures digitally, again hiding parts of video that the user would be unlikely to notice (www.mpeg.org).

MP3 is, at the time of writing, the most popular audio file format for transmission across the Internet, although MPEG2 Advanced Audio Coding (AAC) has provided two alternative formats in the shape of MP4 and Microsoft's Windows Media Audio (WMA). Each of these claim to provide higher quality sound at the same time as greater compression, but the fact that they are both proprietary formats means that they have been adopted more slowly than MP3.

File sharing and peer-to-peer

At the end of the 1990s, music, more than any other format, sparked the fascination and irritation of users and opponents of the Internet. While almost any information format from text to video can be digitised and used in a multimedia environment such as the Internet, it was music that caught the attention of the press most spectacularly.

The reasons for this occurring at a particular time are manifold. First, while words and images were the media first translated successfully to the Web (and, indeed, are themselves the cause of considerable anxiety for copyright holders around the world when transferred to digital media), the industries for print and graphics in all their forms are not controlled by such clearly defined oligopolies as the music industry. Second, while film is perhaps closest to the market for music in terms of its production and distribution, even at its highest form of compression digitised video is not suitable for distribution across networks for most users: once broadband is widely available, this will probably change (and certainly movie studios are gearing themselves up for video piracy on a scale similar to that for music), but at present audio remains more suitable for peer-to-peer (P2P) file sharing in cyberspace.

With the rise of peer-to-peer file sharing and piracy, particularly in the case of Napster, most of the music industry was up in arms. However, there were a few professionals who saw file sharing as something potentially beneficial. Thom Yorke of Radiohead, for example, went on record as saying that Napster actually encouraged enthusiasm for music 'in a way that the music industry has long forgotten to do', while other figures such as Moby, U2's The Edge and Courtney Love disagreed with record companies that wished to close down Napster (although, equally, there were plenty of artists such as Eminem, Dr Dre and Metallica who wanted the online service buried as quickly as possible). Supporters of file sharing have indicated that home audio or videotaping did not kill the music and film industries, and may even have helped to expand them, while companies such as EMI and Sony began trials of their own proprietary distribution systems in 2002 via services such as MusicNet (www.musicnet.com) and PressPlay (www.pressplay.com) in an attempt to control the market for bits as they had controlled that for atoms. As Chuck D of Public Enemy has remarked, however:

> Soon you'll see a marketplace with 500,000 independent labels – the majors can co-opt all they want, but it's not going to stop the average person from getting into the game. Today a major record label makes a CD for as little as 80 cents, then sells it wholesale for $10.50 so retailers can charge $14 – that's highway robbery. They were able to pimp that technology. Well, MP3 is a technology they can't pimp.
>
> (Freund 1999: 139)

Napster and the killer app

If the big six of the music industry were not able to pimp MP3, however, they worked hard to protect their intellectual property being used for free by the average person in the form of downloads from Napster, most infamous of the music-sharing sites that sprang up at the end of the 1990s.

Napster is probably destined to become a footnote in the history of online music, having descended from notoriety to obscurity in less than a year. None the less, even after it had closed down in 2002 it occupied an important position in the transformation of music provision for a number of reasons, not least of which was the fact that it was the first service to become a household name. Established in 1999 by Shawn Fanning, who gave it his school nickname, Napster occupied an almost unique position: software enabled users to share files stored on their hard drives without needing to upload them to a central server, but unlike subsequent peer-to-peer services such as Kazaa, Napster maintained a centralised list of files available on remote computers, and at its peek attracted sixty million users. This made it easier both to search for music and to sue as an obvious target for potentially copyrighted music. By September 2002, the company released its remaining staff and filed for bankruptcy (English 2002).

The closure of Napster, however, did not mean the end of P2P: as Kuptz (2000: 236) observed when the RIAA first moved against what it saw as public enemy number one, alternative P2P systems such as Gnutella are 'unstoppable by design'. They do not require a central server to connect to for information, but rather send handshake messages to identify any other peers connected to the Internet at that time: once connection is made, a search can be made for files across what is known as a *radius* of peers (anything up to 10,000 connections simultaneously). Files may be downloaded from those peers, even across firewalls in many cases. While true P2P may be unstoppable (whether legally, because there is no one to sue, or technically, because peers do not rely on central servers at all), this also brings its own problems, namely inefficiency in terms of maintaining connections between peers, and also no way of telling if a search is complete. As such, for other distributed projects Napster provided a potentially superior model, keeping customer files in-house but farming out infrastructure to a captive audience.

Part III

Reading/writing cyberspace

8 Sources, resources and research

....

While cyberspace has begun to affect a huge range of activities and interactions, in the spheres of commerce, entertainment and publishing, by emphasising the importance of data to such activities, locating information has become more important than ever. As we saw in Chapter 2, notions of an information society can be extremely problematic: at the same time, it is probably true to say that tools such as the Internet have had their most dramatic impact in terms of the dissemination of data, making readily available material that has often been difficult to access previously, whether because of limitations of geography, expense or membership of relevant bodies.

In this chapter, we will concentrate on using the Internet to locate information, as this is fast becoming the main way in which electronic data can be accessed. Networked data is not synonymous with the Internet, even though most databases are being made available online. As Sherman and Price (2001) remark, while the sort of sophisticated techniques associated with database searches date back to the 1960s and even the late 1950s, it was assumed for a long time that these could not be employed on the Internet because traditional information-retrieval techniques would not work well in an open, unstructured environment. Although this has been demonstrated to be untrue, some databanks are still in the process of conversion, while others may never be made available on the Internet because of issues of security or policy.

Internet research

....

Later in this chapter, we will explore the different ways of researching the Internet, some of the questions and methodologies that you will need to consider when taking the Internet as the object of your study. More frequently, however, students and general Internet users use search engines and online databases as a tool to locate data for such things as essay projects, work reports, the best price for a book or car, government information . . . the list is almost as extensive as the number of users logged on at any one time.

Whereas Internet search tools essentially consisted of requests to a system administrator for help, this began to change with Archie, a system created in 1990 to locate files on FTP servers. In the early 1990s, a number of Internet search technologies were devised, including WAIS (wide area information servers) and Gopher (Deutsch 2000). While such technologies represented a massive advance over previous access technologies, they were still limited in that they were often confined to particular locations (the user still had to know the server on which to search for files) and were unable to connect between different types of data.

The virtue of the Web, developed from Berners-Lee's original concept ENQUIRE, was that it provided a single, uniform interface for different types of information contained on different servers. This ease of use gradually brought with it greater demand for simplicity in finding information. The first important web tool was not really a search engine at all, but a directory of interesting sites, Yahoo! (for Yet another hierarchical officious oracle); devised and maintained in 1994 by two Ph.D. students at Stanford University, David Filo and Jerry Yang, Yahoo! became a popular tool for locating material from 1995 onward when it was hosted on Netscape's servers (Whittaker 2002).

Directories – typically categorised listings of links to sites – have an important place even today, offering a level of editorial control that comes from the fact that such lists are compiled by human agents. According to a report in 2000 by Cyveil-lance (www.cyveillance.com), however, more than 7.3 million new web pages were being added every day, with a potential 1 per cent, or 21 million, being up-dated. This meant on average that 6Mb of information was being uploaded on to the web every minute, far more than could be processed by even the most dedicated team of researchers. Enter the search engine.

Search engines

Because of the lack of centralised structure on the Internet, the only way to find pages and files is to follow links to other pages and files that can then be indexed. To do this effectively would require automation, and in 1993 a physics student at MIT, Mathew Gray, created the first recognised Web 'robot', an autonomous agent that would follow links (Sherman and Price 2001). This first robot, the 'World Wide Web Wanderer', was limited to measuring the growth of the Web, simply reporting on the existence of links and pages without indexing them.

The following year, Brian Pinkerton at the University of Washington created a robot called WebCrawler, which did index its findings and was made available by Pinkerton as the first publicly accessible search engine. Throughout 1994 and 1995, other search engines such as Lycos, Altavista, Excite and, of course, Yahoo!, came online, refining the process of locating and indexing files (Lycos, for example, was the first site to provide abstracts of documents so that a user could evaluate the suitability of a link before clicking through).

Search engines, therefore, have three important components: the web crawler (after Pinkerton's original robot, also often known as a web spider), which is used to locate pages; an indexing tool to compile a database of search terms based on files located by the crawler; and a query processor, used to match terms entered by a visitor against the database stored on the server. Because of the potential difficulties at each stage – trawling the Web for files is an expensive process, requiring fast computers capable of keeping track of a vastly expanding net, crawlers rely on links to find pages (meaning that they frequently miss pages that are not linked to), and users have different expectations and experience of using such engines – no single search engine can ever hope to cover every search. For this reason, metasearch engines have started to become popular; these are sites that send queries to multiple search engines and directories simultaneously.

For a more extensive list of search engines, see the Search Engine Colossus (www.searchenginecolossus.com) and Search Engine Watch (searchenginewatch. com).

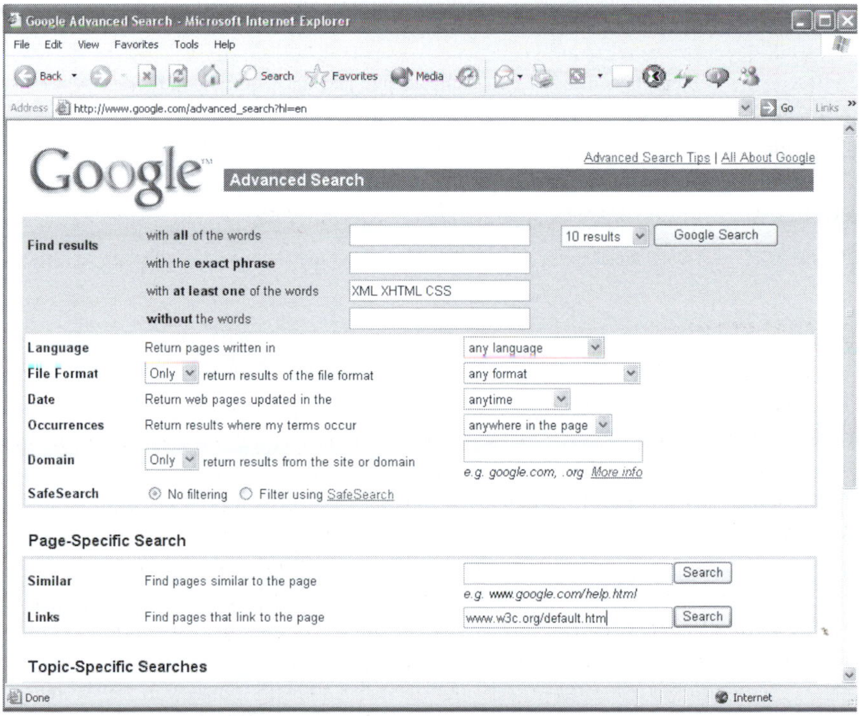

Figure 8.1 The advanced search features of the Google search engine allow you to refine your searches considerably.

Table 8.1 Some of the most commonly used search engines

Name	URL	Comments
AltaVista	www.altavista.com	A fast search engine with multiple advanced search options, although it does not always return the most relevant results.
Ask Jeeves	www.ask.com	A natural language directory: useful for some searches, but with fewer direct links than other search engines.
Dogpile	www.dogpile.com	A metasearch site that searches through other search engines.
Excite	www.excite.com	Average directory and search engine.
Fast	www.altheweb.com	Generally lives up to its name: fast with very good results.
Google	www.google.com www.google.co.uk	Probably the best search engine, which uses an innovative page-ranking system to improve relevance.
HotBot	www.hotbot.com	Metasearch site that is best used for business and technology.
LookSmart	www.looksmart.com	Directory that uses a pay-for-placement model.
Lycos	www.lycos.com	Directory that uses Fast as its search engine.
MetaCrawler	www.metacrawler.com	The first of the metasearch sites, although no longer the best.
MSN Search	search.msn.com	A mixture of directory entries prepared by editors and a wide-ranging automatic search engine.
Northern Light	www.northernlight.com	Excellent for research, particularly as it includes links to reports and articles.
Open Directory	dmoz.org	Directory that uses volunteers to compile a database of websites.
Teoma	www.teoma.com	Not the most comprehensive of search engines, but worth considering in that its results are often more relevant.
Yahoo!	www.yahoo.com	Directory that also uses Google as its search engine. Although the directory is not the most comprehensive, it often provides more relevant results.

Searching, browsing, and directories

While search engines are an important starting point for many types of research, they are not the only tools available. According to WebSideStory (www.webside story. com), a service that measures Internet audiences, 52 per cent of users in early 2002 arrived at sites via direct navigation or bookmarks, indicating that once many people have decided on sites that appear of interest these are the ones to which they return on a regular basis.

Similarly, rather than relying on general-purpose search engines, many on-line users may prefer to use targeted directories that restrict their searches to particular topics. Examples include LawCrawler (lawcrawler.lp.findlaw.com) and SearchEdu.com (www.searchedu.com) that, as their names suggest, trawl through legal and education sites respectively. Such tools may miss some of the rich detail of the wider Web, but they can be very useful when specific information is required.

Invisible cyberspace

One of the difficulties of locating information online is due to the nature of the hypertext protocol and markup language that binds it together. When Berners-Lee and others involved in the creation of the World Wide Web devised HTML and HTTP, they provided an elegant solution to two of the three main problems affecting the transfer of data across networks, hardware and software incompatibilities. More or less any computer capable of running a browser can display a document designed for that browser.

The third problem, however, stems from incompatibilities between data stored on computers, which can range from simple text files to complex and highly structured relational databases. Indeed, developments in database design from the 1960s onward had led many experts to believe that it was extremely difficult – if not impossible – to share such data across open networks.

In one respect, the critics were right. The assumption behind HTML was that links would be made between text files, but any attempt to structure the format of information using HTML is extremely difficult. Consider the following example. You may keep some form of electronic address book on your computer. At its simplest, this may be no more than a text file listing names, addresses, phone numbers and emails. If you wish to search for names only, however, or for post or Zip codes, you will need to use some form of database that tags different types of information.

What a database does, then, is to provide 'metadata', or data about data. The trend towards XML (eXtensible markup language) is aimed at providing metadata which can be used to format not merely the way a document appears in a browser but the structure of its data, so that information may be displayed in different ways depending on what is requested from the page (a search for names, for example). Our address book as a web document could resemble the following:

```
<name>Joe Bloggs</name>
<address>
<road>1, The Street</road>
<town>Newtown</town>
<postcode>NT1 12N</postcode>
</address>
```

Information entered in these tags for each element of a document does not necessarily have any effect on the way the file is displayed in a browser, but may be used as metadata to be used with search queries (such as when looking for a post code or everyone you know who lives in a particular town).

The applications of XML promise to be enormous (Microsoft, for example, has begun to use XML in its Office applications as a means of exchanging information between programs as well as the Internet). In the meantime, there are large chunks of the Internet that do not divulge their secrets easily. Sherman and Price (2001) speak of an 'invisible web', information or 'dark matter' that is not accessible to search engines. Due to technical limitations, search engines cannot search Acrobat PDF files (Google excepted), Flash or Shockwave applets, most program executables or databases, and compressed zip files.

While the various formats listed here generally do not form a particularly large or authoritative part of the Web, databases are very different. These have developed over decades in libraries, government departments, universities and businesses, and within each one is locked extremely valuable data. Unfortunately, many databases are unique in terms of the design of their data structures; some are connected to the Web, but to use them you must employ the query tools provided by the database itself.

Disguised adverts and other search scams

With the reverse in dotcom fortunes in the early twenty-first century, search engines were forced to find sources of funding in order to keep functioning. By the end of the 1990s, the most popular sites such as AltaVista and Yahoo! were busily turning themselves into portals, offering a portfolio of added-value services such as news, share information and email, that would attract millions of users. During the boom years, large numbers of users were easily converted into capital, as simply building up brand awareness on the web was considered sufficient to send share prices rocketing. Once the recession began, however, the costs of those users and the services they consumed for free began to bite.

In mid-2001, Ralph Nader's Consumer Alert group asked US trade officials to investigate eight major search engines, including AltaVista, LookSmart and HotBot. Consumer Alert's argument was that these sites had broken the law against deceptive advertising in that they included such adverts inconspicuously in their listings, a charge denied by AltaVista.

It is partly because it clearly marks out which links are advertisements or 'sponsored' that Google does so well. The important (if obvious) point about disguised adverts, however, is that users should not necessarily trust what they find on a search engine.

Prime materials

It is beyond the remit of this book to provide a fully comprehensive listing of resources available on the Internet for finding information: there are plenty of web directories available on the market, of which the best is probably *The Mini Rough Guide Website Directory* (Angus Kennedy and Peter Shapiro); certainly it is the most up to date, indicating the main difficulty for books in keeping abreast of changing sites. You will find a catalogue of links in the Appendices particularly relevant to the topics discussed in *The Cyberspace Handbook*, but the following also outlines some of the important gateways to online resources in a number of significant areas.

Arts and humanities

- Academic Info (www.academicinfo.net): a gateway for general academic information, including arts and humanities as well as the sciences.
- ADAM (Art, Design, Architecture and Media Information Gateway, adam. ac.uk): a searchable catalogue of higher education resources for the arts and media.
- Art Atlas (www.art-atlas.net): a search engine for international art collections worldwide.
- Art Library Directory (iberia.vassar.edu/ifla-edu): the directory of 3,000 specialist databases provided by IFLA (International Federation of Library Associations and Institutions).
- Britannica (www.Britannica.com): no longer free, none the less this offers one of the world's best encyclopedias online as well as links to magazines and books.
- Literature Classics (www.literatureclassics.com): part of the classics network of websites that offers information on literary texts.
- Project Gutenberg (promo.net/pg/): the Internet's oldest producer of free electronic texts that began in 1971.

Government and public records

- Archisplus (europa.eu.int/comm/secretariat_general/sg1/archives/home-en. htm): the database of historical archives for the European Commission.
- Fedstats (www.fedstats.gov): official US statistical information.
- Labour Statistics (www.bls.gov/flshome.htm): basic statistics on international labour provided by the US Bureau of Labor Statistics.
- Public Records Office (www.pro.gov.uk/default.htm): a catalogue of all records placed at the Public Record Office, along with links to other relevant databases.
- THOMAS (thomas.loc.gov): a Library of Congress service that provides access to US government legislation.

- United Nations News (www.un.org/News/): information on UN press briefings.
- Unesco Archives Portal (www.unesco.org/webworld/portal_archives): collection of UN educational resources.
- US Government Publications (www.access.gpo.gov): a catalogue of US publications.

Health and medical

- CHID (Combined Health Information Database, chid.nih.gov): US database of health information.
- CRISP (Computer Retrieval of Information on Scientific Projects, www-commons.cit.nih.gov): database of research projects maintained by the National Institutes of Health.
- International Digest of Health Information (www.who.int): texts on international health legislation.
- National Research Register (www.update-software.com/National/nrr-frame.html): database of research projects of interest to the NHS.
- NHS services (www.nhs.uk): the starting point for a range of information on the National Health Service, including organisations, services and medical information.

Libraries

- Archon (www.hmc.gov.uk/archon/archon.htm): gateway to manuscripts related to British history.
- British Library Public Catalogue (blpc.bl.uk): information about the major collections at the British Library.
- COPAC (Consortium of University Research Libraries, copac.ac.uk): a central search engine for some of the largest university libraries in the UK.
- Internet Archive (www.archive.org): archive of more than ten billion web pages from 1996.
- Librarians' Index to the Internet (www.lii.org): a searchable directory of over 7,200 online resources.
- Library of Congress (www.loc.gov/catalog): an online catalogue with a database of approximately twelve million records.
- New York Public Library (digilib.nypl.org): provides online guides to using archival and manuscript collections.
- Public Records Office (www.pro.gov.uk): information on births, deaths and marriages of UK citizens.
- The Smithsonian (www.si.edu): the main access point to the Smithsonian collections that are gradually being digitised.

News and current affairs

- BBC.co.uk (www.bbc.co.uk): huge resource for education and entertainment as well as news and current affairs.
- Google News (news.google.com): a convenient point for reading articles from over 4,000 sources worldwide.
- MediaInfo (www.mediainfo.com): online media from around the world.
- Moreover (www.moreover.com): access to more than 1,800 web-based news services.
- Newslibrary.Com (www.newslibrary.com): archives from a number of US papers.
- Profound (address): news search engine for more than 5,000 magazines, newspapers and journals.

Science and technical

- AGRICOLA (www.nal.usda.gov): database of agricultural-based research.
- CORA (cora.whizbang.com): a special-purpose search engine for computer science research papers.
- GEOLEX (ngmsvr.wr.usgs.gov): search engine for earth sciences.
- Microsoft Knowledge Base (www.microsoft.com): technical support and information for Microsoft software.
- Plants Database (plants.usda.gov): botanical database maintained by the US Department of Research.
- PubSCIENCE (pubsci.osti.gov): scientific journal search engine.
- ResearchIndex (www.researchindex.com): a comprehensive search engine for scientific and technical information.
- SciBASE (www.thescientificworld.com): database of over twelve million articles published since 1993.
- Webopedia (www.webopedia.com/quick_ref): a quick reference section for computer terminology.

These links are intended merely as a starting point for research into specific areas. For more details, check the Appendices at the end of this book and also www.routledge.com/cyberspace/resources.htm.

Look beyond the obvious

Most of the comments here have concentrated on the Web, but when looking for information online always consider less obvious sources. One important place to look is in newsgroups, or Usenet posts: until recently, this meant subscribing to a particular group that interested you and waiting until someone replied to a post you made or began a thread that was of interest to you. DejaNews had begun to provide searchable access to Usenet postings and this was extended greatly when Google took over DejaNews (groups.google.com).

Another source of frequently transitory but useful data are email lists, whereby a posting made to the list is passed on to all subscribers. The main email lists are maintained at CataList (www.lsoft.com/lists/listref.html).

Verifying data

Search engines and robots can automate the process of finding information, but notions that the 'intelligence' of these operations can extend to verifying that information are misguided. Because of its open nature, anyone with access to the Internet may publish online, whether in reply to a posting in a newsgroup or a fully-fledged website. I really do believe that there is something remarkable in this process that has a positive effect in terms of breaking down traditional forms of gatekeeping that can stultify the dissemination of information.

That granted, however, there are plenty of times when gatekeeping seems to be a very good idea. As many sites are created by enthusiasts, so the value of information may be doubtful and, even worse, online authors may have something to hide. The same, of course, is very true of the professional media, the effects of which can be even more pernicious in that consumers of such media expect practitioners to act without bias and with regard to accuracy and the truth.

A simple trick for verifying any data online is to triangulate it, at the very least to discover whether it is available elsewhere online but (a better approach) to follow up any possible references to books, newspapers or broadcasts. There are then a series of questions that may be asked of any content:

- *What is the site address?* This is similar to asking who publishes the information. If it is hosted on an ISP's free web space it is unlikely to be an official resource. This is not infallible, however, particularly as it is relatively easy to register official-sounding domain names.
- *Who maintains the site?* Do the authors of a site provide any credentials or information about themselves? What is the authority of the individual or institution responsible for the site?
- *How current is information?* This can be particularly important in that out-of-date information can be especially misleading.
- *Is there bias?* The notion that any information provider can offer entirely unbiased material is probably misleading (in that all publication requires some level of selection), but some sites are more obviously biased than others. Indeed, obvious bias may be less of a problem – because more easily recognised – than sites which attempt to hide a particular angle by apparently presenting both sides of an argument. Bias should always be considered, even with professional and authoritative sites.

Copyright and Rights in Databases Regulations

When using online research materials, it is worth paying attention to the fact that these often represent substantial examples of labour and skill in terms of collecting material and that, in turn, they may be protected by intellectual property laws. The 1997 Copyright and Rights in Databases Regulations, for example, protects UK databases, although it amended previous legislation that had simply considered databases as subject to copyright protection. Databases that are felt to lack human intellectual creativity, and are thus inappropriate for protection by copyright, may none the less be commercially valuable.

A database-maker, therefore – that is, anyone who obtains, verifies and presents material which may be accessed by electronic or other means – may claim a database right to restrict temporary or permanent reproduction of any part of the database, as well as distribution or display of material contained in that database. As such, the copyright section of the Regulations protects the author's creative selection or arrangement of the contents included in a database, while database rights cover the investment of compiling and maintaining such records.

Research methods

Thus far we have been concerned with methods for finding information in cyberspace; increasingly, however, cyberspace is becoming an object of study in its own right for media students and professionals. Internet research has taken much from other areas of media research, particularly in terms of methodology: drawing upon other disciplines that have evolved in the twentieth century such as sociology and linguistics, media and communication studies have been keen to emphasise the explicit method that is used to locate, evaluate and organise information, rather than relying on an implicit (and frequently vague) 'competence' that has traditionally been inherent in some other disciplines such as the arts and humanities.

Much of *The Cyberspace Handbook* is concerned with different methodological approaches to studying cyberspace, but here we will be concerned with outlining explicitly some of those modes of analysis.

Researching cyberspace vs. research via cyberspace

In an extremely useful essay on web research, 'New Media, New Methodologies: Studying the Web', Nina Wakeford outlines some of the 'eclectic' and 'scattered' approaches that currently exist with regard to the Web. These various techniques include quantitative data collection (of the sort popular with market researchers, but which can also pay dividends in other areas of research), semiotic and discursive analyses, and behavioural studies. As Wakeford remarks, 'some of the methodological challenges of researching the Web resemble those involved in studying other systems of mass communication, but there *are* distinctive technical features of the Web which allow the collection of particular kinds of data' (2000: 33).

Thus, for example, it is possible to track certain relationships between individuals or groups by following hyperlinks from one site to another. Most servers also accumulate a considerable amount of data regarding site statistics, such as how many people visit a site, how long they remain, where they browse to and from. Such 'access statistics' may be useful for broad views of the location and behaviour of those accessing a site but, as Wakeford points out, are less useful for assessing the cultural importance of the Web.

Cyberspace, then, may provide almost unparalleled access to technical information, but the use of such information is never unproblematic: it does not automatically validate different types of research. In addition, as Wakeford remarks with reference to Denzin (1997), Fielding and Lee (1998), Oelson (1994) and others, during the 1990s, traditional methodologies were called into question by such issues as the rise of computer-assisted analysis, the reflexive nature of the subject involved in research, and ethical or political issues involved with selecting material for research.

Steve Jones, in his introductory essay to *Doing Internet Research* (1999a: 1–2), offers a complementary warning: despite the apparent novelty of cyberspace and the Internet, 'the narrative surrounding it is quite predictable', following the hype that has accompanied the introduction of many other technologies previously. Jones advises students engaged in cyberspace research not only to be explicit regarding their methodology (and his collection of essays is an admirable guide to this field), but also to study it 'within the context of the particular combination of late twentieth-century history and projections of twenty first-century existence' (ibid.: 23).

Quantitative vs. qualitative research

The peculiar nature of cyberspace and particularly the Internet for communication research has raised some important issues for researchers engaged in quantitative research. With the explosion of networked technologies at the end of the twentieth century it is apparently easier than ever to accumulate data; likewise, advances in computing have placed in our hands processing power that would have been unimaginable a decade ago.

Traditionally, research in areas such as communications studies and sociology has operated on a dichotomy that separates quantitative and qualitative analysis: research proceeds by collecting data that is directly measurable or can feed into a simulation, leading to hypotheses concerning the nature of the data collected (quantitative), or researchers concentrate on the form of the content through a description or observation of the objects of research (qualitative). Put simply, the purpose of quantitative research is to explain observed phenomena, while qualitative research seeks to understand phenomena that may be more loosely or incompletely observed: the former begins with a formulated theory or set of hypotheses that may be proved or disproved by research, while the latter begins with a question from which a theory may emerge.

The easy separation of these two methods has been critiqued more recently, for example, by Sudweeks and Simoff (1999), who offer a useful outline for integrated research as shown in Table 8.2.

Table 8.2 Sudweeks' and Simoff's outline for integrated research

	Quantitative methods	*Qualitative methods*
Purpose of inquiry	To test a hypothesis	Typically case research
Role of investigator	Objective	Participatory and personal
Acquisition of knowledge	Data analysis designed to verify or falsify a model that may then be *generalised* into a theory	Discovering knowledge that may be *extrapolated* to the wider population
Presentation of research	Typically simplification to display general trends	May need to include a great deal of raw data

For Sudweeks and Simoff, the problem with a majority of Internet research is that it is conducted as quantitative analysis under laboratory, or controlled experimental, conditions. Study groups tend to be small and unrepresentative, and generally fail to deal with heterogeneous cultures, and this is where qualitative analysis can be useful in terms of exploring the make-up and interaction of virtual communities, online learning, virtual organisations and business information systems.

A detailed example is that provided by Garton *et al.* (1999) for studying online social networks and drawing on a methodology developed in journals such as *Social Networks* and *Connections*. Networks, then, can be studied as 'whole' or 'egos', concentrating on a formal criterion such as membership, or on a specific individual and the relations of others to him or her within that network. Analysis then builds up a picture of the composition of the network in terms of its relations (how strong they are, or in which direction they operate) that build up into ties (for example, frequent contact or self-disclosure); the more relations or strands in a tie, the more complex the network.

When studying social networks, Garton *et al.* recommend collecting data through questionnaires, interviews, diaries, observations and even computer monitoring, with some combination of these techniques providing the best results. The important point of such research is to recognise that 'computer networks often are social networks' (ibid.: 100), so that understanding the structure of cyberspace frequently requires an understanding of social structures that may be explored and analysed via a combination of quantitative and qualitative techniques.

Other modes of analysis

As Nina Wakeford has remarked, while quantitative and qualitative data may be immensely important with regard to researching cyberspace, these are not the only approaches open to investigators. In particular, textual or rhetorical studies of the documents that constitute cyberspace (or what Ted Nelson pertinently termed the 'docuverse' of networked files and communication) have yielded considerable insights into computer-mediated communication (CMC) and virtual communities. Likewise, as web pages participate in cultural systems, so they benefit from the types of semiotic and socio-political models applied to other media forms.

Sociological studies in particular benefit from the type of quantitative and qualitative approaches outlined above, but other techniques (as well as some useful guides) include:

- *Rhetorical/textual analysis*: The largely textual nature of cyberspace, particularly the Internet, means that accounts of online rhetoric have been particularly fruitful in terms of explaining the nature of groups and identities constituting virtual communities. James Sosnoski (1999) offers a good description of how far traditional literary models can be used to explain CMC, as well as the value of less text-oriented versions, such as the work of Edward Tufte (1997), that explore how individuals are configured by a complex range of phenomena. Examples of the intricacies that can be revealed by careful attention to the rhetorical nuances of online communication include Connery's (1997) study of egalitarian exchanges in newsgroups and Zickmund's (1997) analysis of the often vicious baiting that occurs on race hate sites.
- *Semiotic models*: While rhetorical analysis serves a useful function, it is immediately obvious to even the most casual visitor to cyberspace that networked communities and communication are relying on sign systems other than the textual to communicate. Related to the sort of textual analysis outlined above is the use of semiotic models to explore the cultural contexts of cyberspace. A particularly useful example of this is Daniel Chandler's work (1997, 1998) on personal homepages as constructs of sign systems, providing a methodological approach to the study of such sites. Leigh Star (1999) also provides some useful work on the ways in which the infrastructure of cyberspace affects our perception of sign systems on an ethnographic level; for example, how the skills required to construct sites are distributed through the population.

The place of Internet research

The Internet has created a marvellous resource for locating information, but the tendency to treat it as a one-stop solution for research is a dangerous one. There are plenty of data that are not available on the Net, some of which will probably never make it there, and other sources that are available but in proprietary form (that is, expect to pay).

Proprietary databases and networked information services, such as LexisNexis and the Dow Jones, may be accessed online but restrict information to paying subscribers. Likewise, research conducted for scholarly journals may be available across the Internet but also requires subscription to a service such as Ingenta (www.ingenta.com); as these resources often provide the fruits of extensive research, they can be invaluable, but you may have to resort to paper copies in a library that subscribes to each journal. One alternative is the Northern Light's Special Collection (www.northernlight.com), which offers some content from journals for a reasonable price.

Newspapers are another source of important information, and the Web in particular has become a source of mixed blessings. Anyone who has conducted research into newspaper archives realises that this can be a laborious and time-consuming task: the ability to search online databases suddenly makes yesterday's news a valuable source of information. At the same time, very few newspapers offer complete archives, and of those that do, few extend even to ten or twenty years back. At the same time, reprinting material from a period before the Internet even existed creates problems for publishers who may have to pay additional fees to authors, and not many archives include images. A news search site such as NewsBank (infoweb.newsbank.com) demonstrates the best features as well as the limitations of using the Internet for such research: over 5,000 newspapers, magazines and journals worldwide can be searched for full-text articles, but the service extends back only to the late 1990s.

Finally, while governments such as those in the USA and Britain are committed to placing a great deal of data online, and businesses and corporations have seen the value of making available information that is useful to customers, millions of documents will never be placed on the Internet. Likewise, attempts to convert print culture into digital formats such as Project Gutenberg (promo.net/pg) have barely begun to digitise the huge number of books that have been created in the past half millennium. As such, the Internet is not, and never can be, a universal remedy for those engaged in research: libraries or firsthand sources with physical access to printed information remain as important as ever.

Practical research

While the Internet is a constantly changing collection of resources, the following exercises are intended to provide a basis for using the Internet for common research tasks.

Investigating biographical information

Incorporating information on an important figure is a common task for students undertaking academic essays, and will serve to illustrate how this type of general academic research can take place on the Internet.

The first starting point for the vast majority of cases (unless you already have specific addresses) is to use a search engine. This typically demonstrates both the value and uselessness of the Internet, in that usually too many results will be returned, so that sorting the information provided becomes extremely difficult. Some tips are to try to narrow your search by common techniques such as including speech marks around specific quotations, or adding logical operators such as + or AND before/between entries.

When using the Internet as a research tool, do not simply latch on to the first results you stumble across: Google includes a link entitled 'I feel lucky', which takes you to a random link, but while luck may play a part in research it is foolish to rely on luck alone. Follow all substantial links that you think will be relevant and query how authoritative you consider each source to be.

Nor should you rely on a search engine (or even the Web) alone. Newsgroups provide a wealth of information, though much of it may be spurious. These are easier to search than ever now that DejaNews has been bought up by Google. Finally, consider email lists as a valuable source of potential information where you may also post your own queries.

Researching institutional information

Students engaged in some form of media research will often need to contact or investigate a company or institution, and everyday users of the Internet may wish to contact a particular organisation. The most obvious starting point is to check whether or not the company has a website. If it does, check for links to 'About us' or something similar, which will begin to provide basic information about that organisation, as well as any contact links.

Limited companies in the UK are required to register with Companies House (www.companies-house.gov.uk), an excellent site for some financial and corporate information on such bodies. Such information varies on a state-by-state basis in the USA (some states require more information than others), but the Federal US Business Advisor (www.business.gov) provides related sites.

Triangulating information

This chapter has already reiterated the importance of checking information, and the superior researcher will always, at least, triangulate his or her information; that is, check it against multiple sources. At a minimum, this should consist of three separate websites; this is easy enough to check in a search engine – though be aware that many sites simply repeat information found elsewhere. As such, information should also ideally be checked against a non-Internet-based resource, such as a newspaper or book.

Investigating or participating in a subculture/social grouping

Some of the most valuable and rewarding research involves itself in sociological studies of different social groups or subcultures. There is only space here to direct the reader to the types of resources that he or she should consider when investigating such a social formation. Websites are obvious targets, but although they may provide information about a subculture they are rarely the most engaged sites for social interaction. As such, as well as performing web searches, remember to pay particular attention to newsgroups, whether on Usenet (most easily accessible via Google) or sites such as Yahoo! and Tripod. Simply logging on to such sites and asking questions is a sure-fire way to annoy regular participants, so be prepared to contribute over a period of time.

9 Online news and journalism

One area of publishing and broadcasting that has taken the Internet to heart is news production and journalism. The promise of interactive media, updated not merely by the hour but minute by minute as information breaks, has proved too great a temptation for countless journalists and news providers: as Andrew Anker of *Hotwired* remarked in 1997, 'newspaper publishers embraced the web more than any other group' (Reid 1997: 310).

This embrace has not necessarily been a force for unalloyed good: as Anker also notes, many newspapers in the mid-1990s were particularly unimaginative in their use of cyberspace, simply spraying 'shovelware' online that would remain largely unread other than by researchers searching through these 'wonderful archives'. Furthermore, the tendency towards reporting breaking news has had potentially negative effects on the nature of journalism: if a story must be reported from the field as it happens, so the traditional press virtues of objectivity and impartiality tend to suffer. At the same time, as Hartley (1982) and Hall (2001) observe, the intrinsic merits of these particular qualities are not as self-evident as the press has often depicted them: certainly the proprietors and journalists of the nineteenth-century press viewed themselves as partial in their fight for particular social and political perspectives, and, as Hall notes, objectivity was a useful tool for the professionalisation of the press that would enable it to present its views as inherently better. What is more, as Hartley points out, the ways in which news stories are constructed tend to be too neatly antagonistic, ironing out confusion and difficulties to present two opposing sides, each of which can be reported 'objectively' so that the self-evidently superior viewpoint will win.

Yet, while objectivity and impartiality may be ideologically suspect (tools that make it easier for the journalist to pass off his or her views – as well as those of proprietors, advertisers and the state – as closer to the truth than the unprofessional audience that passively consumes the news), their passing may still be mourned. At its best, cyberspace increases our own journalistic engagement with the day's news as it happens: at its worst, it simply repackages our existing prejudices in an electronic pill that is easier to swallow.

Traditional news vs. new media

It hardly needs to be restated that news and journalism are global enterprises which form part of the backbone of capitalist enterprise worldwide. As Brian McNair states at the opening of his book, *News and Journalism in the UK*:

> The production of news, and journalism of all kinds, is today big business. The supply of information (whether as journalism or as rawer forms of data) occupies an industry of major economic importance, employing huge human and financial resources, and enjoying high status. Across the world, top news-readers, anchor persons, and newspaper columnists acquire the glamour of movie stars and exert the influence of politicians. Broadcasting companies judge themselves, and are judged, by the perceived quality of their news services.
>
> (McNair 1996: 3)

There is something faintly nostalgic about such a statement in the early twenty-first century. After decades of unprecedented growth, the world's media have been hit hard by the decline of advertising revenues; indeed, the Internet itself, which barely registered on McNair's radar in 1996, has done much to undermine the movie-star anchors and newsreaders who held sway over much of the media (particularly in the USA) during the 1990s.

News and the data business

None the less, many of McNair's comments are – and remain – true. News production is big business, and this is unlikely to change in the near future. Indeed, as Habermas and others drawing on Habermas' notion of the origins of a public sphere point out, the beginnings of news provision in the seventeenth century were intimately connected to the data business, providing merchants and insurers with information on their investments that could make or break such organisations and individuals. It is hardly surprising that those news providers online who have been most successful at converting their news into hard cash are publications most closely associated with the stock markets, such as WSJ.com, the electronic version of *The Wall Street Journal*.

The usefulness of cyberspace to news and the data business pre-dates the Web. As Tunstall and Palmer (1991: 45–6) indicate in their enlightening case study of Reuters in the 1980s, the news provider had become 'the indispensable tool of the foreign exchange or currency markets' (45–6). Within two decades, following Nixon's decision to float the US dollar in 1971, Reuters had become the biggest distributor of news-based information, with a reported $640 billion tapped out on its 200,000 terminals in thirty-five countries per day.

Companies such as Reuters, founded in 1851, a few years after Havas (1835), to provide information from the colonies using the new technologies centred on the telegraph, were suffering in the twentieth century with the decline of European colonialism and the expansion of American news agencies. Its answer was to return to some first principles: financial information had been important to Reuters (because of its links to the City of London) from the start, so in the late twentieth century it combined general news and financial information on computerised platforms for a global market. By 1989, the media represented only 7 per cent of its revenue, but as General Manager Gerald Long pointed out, 'if someone assassinates the American President is that general or market news?' (cited in Tunstall and Palmer 1991: 57). Behind many of the technological changes to the production of news lies this financial imperative: knowing the news as it happens can make or break the markets, and the provider who is first to scoop a story can often charge dividends.

The Daily Me

As part of the general enthusiasm for all things digital in the mid-1990s, Negroponte, in his book *Being Digital* (1995), outlined the following scenario, whereby John Markoff, writing for the *New York Times*, would be paid the proverbial 2 cents for his stories:

> If one two-hundredth of the 1995 Internet population were to subscribe to this idea and John were to write a hundred stories a year (he actually writes between one-hundred-twenty and one-hundred-forty), he would earn $1,000,000 per year, which I am prepared to guess is more than *The New York Times* pays him. If you think one two-hundredth is too big a proportion, then wait a short while. The numbers really do work. Once somebody is established, the added value of a distributor is less and less in a digital world.
>
> (Negroponte 1995: 84)

Unfortunately for Negroponte, the numbers have failed to add up: less than a millionth of the Internet population appear willing to pay their 2 cents for each story or, more to the point, there is no system yet in place that can deal effectively with such micro-payments.

If webenomics suck for the news media, however, another concept pushed by Negroponte has had better success. As he observes, newspapers are read differently on different days and at different times, and when we begin to conceive of newspapers as an interface to the news, more interesting things can be done with them:

> What if a newspaper company were willing to put its entire staff at your beck and call for one edition? It would mix headline news with 'less important' stories relating to acquaintances, people you will see tomorrow, and places you are about to go or have just come from. It would report on companies you know. In fact, under these conditions, you might be willing to pay the Boston *Globe* a lot more for ten pages than for a hundred pages, if you could be

confident that it was delivering you the right subset of information. You would consume every bit (so to speak). Call it *The Daily Me*.

(Negroponte 1995: 153)

As Hall (2001) points out, *The Daily Me* (derived from a model first developed by MIT and Apple in the 1980s, called *Fishwrap* – 'Today's news wraps tomorrow's fish') has provided the mode for consumption for a wide range of online news services, such as Pointcast and My Yahoo. Again, however, while the provision of such news filters (sometimes referred to as pointcasting; that is, targeting the individual consumer with specifically relevant material) is undoubtedly useful, it is not without its problems. How can one be sure that such filters are effective, that information I am interested in is not being wrongly sorted out of my *Daily Me*? It is foolish to assume that editors and reporters know more about my tastes and interests than I do, but part of the pleasure of watching the evening news or reading a newspaper is obviously to encounter that news we do not already know and, more to the point, may not realise until we encounter it that it is of interest.

One criticism made by Doull (1997) is that such pointcasting results in a solipsistic relationship with the media. By carefully screening out information that may not be to our taste, we casually close down large parts of the world and engage increasingly with only like-minded people. This is true, but cyberspace is often cast in the role of arch-fiend in this matter, something it may not deserve insofar as such selection often takes place, and is encouraged, by other media: once people depend on a particular news channel or daily newspaper, they are often less promiscuous (that is, likely to change allegiance) than with other media such as magazines.

Multimedia news: multi-tasking or deskilling?

Digital technology, as Boczkowski observes, had been influential in the production of the news for two decades before the advent of the World Wide Web, at a time when 'the "information society" rhetoric was popular in both the press and scholarly works' (2002: 271). Yet the popularisation of the web, coupled with substantial decreases in the costs of computer hardware and software after 1990, disseminated such technology much more widely. As such, a claim that was often repeated throughout the 1990s was that the digital revolution would make everyone a publisher (just as, of course, it would make nearly everyone millionaires). While the Web in particular has revolutionised certain elements of self-presentation via what Charles Cheung (2000) calls the 'sign vehicles' of personal homepages, this should not be translated into a perception that the millions of participants in cyberspace who create their own homepages have suddenly become publishers.

Even in the early stages of the digital revolution, there were dissenting voices regarding the future role of publishing online. Robert Reid, in his *Architects of the Web*, outlines an argument that took place between Louis Rosetto, founding editor of *Wired*, and Howard Rheingold. While Rheingold believed that *Hotwired*, the companion website to the magazine, would provide a radical forum for bottom-up media, Rosetto disagreed that this was a legitimate form of media:

> [Dave Winer] said, 'a billion publishers,' and I think that's ahistorical bullshit. It's just not real. Typewriters have made everybody a publisher, or desktop publishing made everybody a publisher, or whatever. It's not true. People don't want to sit down and create their own entertainment. They can. Anyone in America, in the world, can come home from work at the end of the day and sit down and write a novel. They don't. They don't for good reason. They don't because . . . they don't have the smarts to do it, or the inclination, or they prefer to let somebody else carry them out of their normal day-to-day life and give them what they can't provide for themselves. That's the function of the media.
>
> (Reid 1997: 303)

Even those professionals whose function it is to provide entertainment or information have found the digital revolution a two-edged sword. As Matthew Doull points out, the early days of radio were entirely dominated by users, who gradually gave way to professionals as more and more consumers tired of amateurs proficient in Morse code. Likewise, for Doull, software will never be able to create a *Daily Me* because 'it cannot yet seek out and then elegantly speak the truth' (1997: 276).

And yet, increasingly, this is what software (or rather, journalists using such software) is being asked to do – if not to find the truth, exactly, then at least a modicum of information that can be repackaged ('repurposed' is the preferred term) for consumption. Michael Bromley (1997) has indicated the ways in which changes in workplace practices in the press and broadcasting during the 1990s have resulted in a downgrading of journalism: while the 'one-journalism' model that emerged after the war deserved critical scrutiny, Bromley observes that multi-tasking practices such as 'video journalists', who are both camera operators and journalists, is fragmenting journalism too rapidly, 'enskilling some as "entrepreneurial editors", but deskilling others to the status of machine hands and extensions of the computer' (1997: 346).

Global news and information futures

The process begun in the 1980s, by which production and ownership of news was concentrated increasingly into corporations that extended across different media, extended at a pace during the 1990s following the fall of the former Soviet bloc. Globalisation, which we have encountered several times already in the pages of this book, has affected the news as thoroughly as any other activity linked to cyberspace and the network society of which it is part. Curran and Seaton (1997) have remarked, with specific reference to broadcasting, on the absurdity of how the apparently indisputable 'iron law' of globalisation emerged just at that historical moment when overarching theories such as Marxism and Keynesianism were being swept away.

Post 11 September 2001, some of the certainties of globalisation have not always seemed so secure, or rather the consensus that supported it has – at least in some parts of the world – been revealed as an imposition of a Western (and specifically US) vision of economic development. Yet, as subsequent events in Afghanistan demonstrated, while truly multinational – indeed, transnational – companies tend to be based in America and Europe (with a few scattered elsewhere, particularly in Japan), we not only expect activities worldwide to influence us indirectly through their impact on local markets or politics, but also directly as they are reported immediately.

Controlling the news

As Küng-Shankleman points out, 'large conglomerates of uncertain nationality, whose activities span many continents, pose problems for regulators. . . . These groups are skilled at fashioning and interpreting regulations and finding loopholes by which to advance their interests. The national perspective of domestic policy-makers and Europe's mosaic-like structure means that regulation processes are complicated and slow' (2000: 64). The activities of transnational networks such as AOL Time Warner, Canal+, Silvio Berlusconi's Fininvest and Rupert Murdoch's News International lead critics to suggest that Europe's system of regulated public monopoly is being replaced by an unregulated private monopoly. At the same time, European news and media companies complain that they are hampered by inconsistent cross-border legislation that prevents them from developing into players capable of taking on US companies.

If one considers the communications networks of cable, satellite and mass media provision developed by such companies, it is clear how fundamentally they have contributed to the network of cyberspace. Information technologies also have practical effects on the delivery of news. Tunstall and Palmer (1991) observe that the requirement to produce news for a potentially worldwide audience leads to an integrated audio-visual global industry, whereby such AV material is decon-textualised so that it can be quickly repurposed elsewhere. Other effects of new technologies, as Curran and Seaton point out, is the increasing contradiction of a growing rhetoric of 'immensity and opportunity', with more and more choice from twenty-four-hour news channels and websites, at the same time that less space is devoted to delivering the news:

> News has always been a commodity, but recently newsgathering capacity has been savagely cut. Now, fewer journalists produce more stories more frequently. Increasingly, they have little time to understand the complex background of developing affairs. Understanding requires time, time costs, and reporters everywhere may be becoming more, not less, vulnerable to the well packaged official lines produced not only by governments, but by the

armies of lobbyists employed by every conceivable interest to promote – and kill – stories.

(Curran and Seaton 1997: 258–9)

Control of the information space of online news may take place in much more direct ways, as was demonstrated in the 2003 war in Iraq. In the early stages of the war, the Arabic news site Al-Jazeera was forced down by a denial of service and its homepage taken over by a group calling itself 'Freedom Cyber Force Militia'. The Qatar-based service had drawn a number of more conventional attacks from parts of the Western media during the conflict because of its 'bias' towards Iraqi citizens and for publishing images of captured and dead US soldiers, and anonymous hackers patriotic to the US cause responded accordingly.

New world information orders

The moment when the Internet fulfilled its potential as a vehicle for the accelerated spectacle of news was the publication of the Starr Report on Bill Clinton and Monica Lewinsky to the Web in 1998, which within days was read by fifty-five million people and rapidly translated into other languages. As Hall (2001: 128) observes, the 'dissemination of this political document, largely bypassing the press, seemed to presage a new set of relationships between politics and the public', something already started by the initial report of the Clinton–Lewinsky relationship on Matt Drudge's website, the *Drudge Report*.

This, then, is the central paradox of the news in cyberspace: at the same time that transnational media organisations such as AOL Time-Warner or News International extend their reach across information networks, so it also becomes easier to bypass them. The increasing use of amateurs has its downsides: as Hall points out, Drudge was more than willing to publish unverified material (although Drudge's questionable ethics also led him to a remarkable scoop).

Indymedia

Perhaps the most extensive example of alternative news sources in cyberspace is Indymedia (www.indymedia.org), which describes itself as 'a collective of independent media organizations and hundreds of journalists offering grassroots, non-corporate coverage', and with outlets in some sixty countries. Growing out of the Independent Media Center, a number of alternative news agencies joined to form Indymedia to cover the Seattle riots against the WTO in 1999. The site received immediate attention, as a large number of volunteer journalists and technical assistants documented activities of rioters and police before releasing news stories and video footage on the Web.

The claim made by Indymedia was that it could reach a global audience without going through a 'corporate filter' and, according to Gene Hyde (2002), was an almost natural development of an American alternative press tradition that has sought ways to exchange information outside the control of media-owners for more than two centuries, using new media as a means of connecting with new and established communities. The loosely federal nature of Indymedia meant that by the beginning of 2000 reporting centres had sprung up in other cities and states in the USA and Canada, and by the end of the year there were thirty Indymedias across the globe.

The technical infrastructure provided by Indymedia on its website is one way in which very diverse networks of volunteers can provide some form of common purpose. Indymedia provides server space, templates, support and affiliation with the larger Indymedia network. Alongside this technical provision is an organisational programme or 'process', offering mailing lists and advice on editorial reporting, as well as guidance on grassroots reporting. This operated initially by encouraging open postings from anyone, but the value of such postings could vary greatly. As such, stories were ranked by readers, with the most significant being allocated as newsworthy, before more standard newsroom practices were set in place. As Fisher (2000) observes, this shift led to conflicts between notions of free speech and how to report effectively.

Some of the successes of Indymedia as an alternative source of news reporting have been dramatic. It has often offered some of the most vivid sources of

Figure 9.1 Indymedia represents one of the innovative ways in which cyberspace can reshape news and communication.

information on events such as the protests at the Genoa Summit in 2001, information that was then picked up by more traditional media (Rosner 2001), as well as virtually the only reports to have come out of Palestine during the most recent crises. The committed (indeed, aggressive) nature of such reportage can bring its own problems, as noted on the Global Indymedia Site (global.indymedia.org.au) with regard to the Indymedia Centre in Palestine which drew accusations of attracting white supremacist hate postings. Such material indicates some of the problems encountered by any radical alternative media involved in what Jackie Smith (2001: 50) has referred to as the 'dialectic between cyber subversion and the growing concentration of power that shape the politics of the new millennium', in that the alliance that has often formed around anti-capitalism is much more amorphous following the collapse of the Soviet bloc. At the same time, various Indymedia centres around the world indicate a successful and growing means of covering stories that are not dealt with by the consensus of established journalism.

10 Internet forms and e-zines

Jayne Armstrong

....

Internet formats
....

The ability to publish (or self-publish) a huge amount of information online has resulted not surprisingly in a wide variety of formats, ranging from those which have their origins in professional modes of publishing that pre-date the Internet to those that are resolutely amateur and experimental. While it is theoretically possible to publish information in any number of formations, what is significant is that a few tried-and-tested genres or forms have begun to emerge: many of these, such as the inevitable homepage, are understandably very wide and loose categories, but it is also the case that with genres such as portals and web logs (blogs) even casual cyberspace readers will have some idea what to expect.

This chapter will not be an exhaustive account of the variety of formats that can be encountered on the Web, but rather will outline some of the defining features of selected genres before going on to discuss in detail perhaps the most innovative and experimental format: the electronic magazine, or e-zine.

Homepages

Anyone who has tried his or her hand at web design will have constructed a homepage at some point. At its simplest, the homepage functions as a sort of contents page or index to a site, attempting to encapsulate a site's essential features for a visitor, perhaps to guide how they should approach or use that site. It is because of such information, as well as the use of such starting pages to brand sites, that commercial companies are often hostile to so-called 'deep linking', whereby another site links to pages buried deep within the architecture of a site, circumventing the metaphorical top level represented by a homepage.

Strictly speaking, then, the homepage is the starting point for a site; if we stop to consider for a moment, for a distributed networked entity such as the Web the notion of a starting page is logically implausible, just like the home button included in nearly every browser. Psychologically, however, such pages (and buttons) make perfect sense: it is common practice to define a browser's home button to a useful site, such as a search engine, so that with one click the user can return to a helpful page away from the morass of information he or she may have been browsing through for hours. Likewise, the existence of a homepage provides a sense of organisation that is often more virtual than real, but still often indicates some form of hierarchical direction for even the most extensive sites.

More than this simple use as an organisational key, however, the term 'home-page' has come to represent something much more to the many users and designers who create their own, *personal* homepages. As Charles Cheung remarks, 'regard-less of their content, and the motivations behind their production, all personal homepages inevitably involve self-presentation' (2000: 45). As a genre, then, personal homepages may share few similarities in terms of content – indeed, perhaps a key feature of a truly personal page is that it should reflect the interests and aspirations of its producer, no matter how idiosyncratic – but in terms of self-presentation homepages offer an opportunity for creative cultural identification and production that is perhaps unparalleled in terms of its range. Certainly self-publication has not been impossible for readers (as well as writers) of previous generations, but the extent of homepage production on the Web indicates much wider opportunities for self-presentation than ever before.

Newsgroups and bulletin boards

If personal homepages are intended primarily as expressions of individual interests and tastes, perhaps the defining feature of newsgroups and bulletin boards is that they are communal sites. While an individual may make newsgroup-style postings to a blog (considered below), those to an online bulletin board typically expect a more active response from readers – that is, readers do not simply consume mes-sages but are expected to post their own responses, whether as answers to questions or requests for help, or a public statement in reply to other (equally public) statements posted online.

While the content of a homepage – like e-zines – may be extremely varied and experimental, newsgroups still tend to be primarily textual. The main reason for this is the series of rules or protocols that govern Usenet, protocols that had their origin in maintaining as wide a user-base as possible for what was originally 'the poor man's Arpanet'. It is possible to post images, and even multimedia clips, to Usenet, but these must first be converted, or encoded, as text, and for this reason most online newsgroups still depend on text as the primary means of communication.

One effect of this has been that newsgroups have constituted a particularly rich area for linguistic research on the Net. Their communal nature, which for suc-cessful groups means that there is a steady stream of postings and replies, also offers opportunities to develop rhetorical strategies that are not encountered so frequently online. Two examples will suffice: as Connery (1997) observes, the practice of acronyms such as IMHO ('in my humble opinion'), so common on

Usenet newsgroups, is indicative of a potentially very rich rhetorical process, however economically expressed. The give and take of newsgroups means that authority is not something that can be taken for granted online, and deferring claims to self-authority (for example, by use of IMHO) is, ironically, one of the most effective means of gaining authority from the group. Likewise, as Tepper (1997) points out, the practice of 'trolling', or posting obviously stupid messages in order to catch out self-important respondees, is one of the ways in which cyber-subcultures police their own boundaries, playing subtle verbal games to establish a pecking order online.

Portals

The types of communities represented by newsgroups and online bulletin boards (to which may be added web rings, or sites linked by common interests) tend to be of a grassroots or even ad hoc nature. Once commercial interest was aroused in cyberspace during the 1990s, however, particularly following the advent of the Web, many companies began to push the notion of a portal as another type of communal service for users. The most ambitious of these, such as MSN, Lycos or Yahoo!, do indeed make claims that they provide opportunities for the development of communities (as, to a lesser extent, do ISP homepages such as those for Freeserve or BT Internet); at the very least, all portals – as the name suggests – seek to provide a starting point for locating news and information online, as well as other services such as shopping and commerce. A key feature of many portals is that the information offered to visitors may be selected and personalised, preventing data from overloading users and thus encouraging them to return more frequently.

Hall (2001: 23) summarises the role of portals as follows:

> Portals, or gateways to the Internet, might be the front pages of global (Yahoo!, AOL), national (*newsUnlimited*, *Liberation*) or regional (*ThisisCornwall*) news provider websites. They provide links to news services, e-shopping, entertainment schedules and information from weather and tides to financial advice. Globally branded portals attract millions of visitors every day and, naturally, the advertising that goes with such volumes of traffic. . . . Portals might look like simple indexes in the case of news aggregates such as UK provider Metaplus (*metaplus.com*) or can take quite complex magazine formats providing a large range of services.

In addition, as Vincent Miller notes, portals demonstrate that claims regarding the decentralised nature of the Web are overly optimistic: 'The history and pattern of portal investment suggests that the World Wide Web is centralizing and adopting an oligopolistic structure which is very much influenced by multinational "old media" firms as well as future "new media" giants' (2000: 119).

During the 1990s, advertising was held up by portals as the main means by which they would attract revenue streams: to be successful, a portal must attract as many

..... as possible – making subscription models less helpful (though this has not prevented companies such as Microsoft from recently mooting the idea, at least for more extensive services). The problem, particularly for global portals, is that while the original model may have been a literal gateway to the Web, providing no more than the launching pad for other sites that would deliver content to users, portals have had increasingly to provide content themselves to ensure that visitors remain on their sites (and so subject to advertising) for as long as possible: such content costs, and as with many other dotcom ventures of recent years, this has meant that portals – important as they frequently are to large media corporations – are not quite the gold-mines that they at first appeared.

Blogging

One phenomenon that has taken off in recent years is the practice of web logging, or blogging, an update on the mania for homepages that gripped the Web in its early years. At its simplest, a blog consists of a regularly updated diary or log of a person's interests or activities, though such sites can quickly develop into miniature virtual communities where more people contribute their own ideas and opinions. So widespread have blogs become in a very short time that they even now attract their own awards, the Bloggies (www.bloggies.com).

Unlike a homepage, where designers may wish to demonstrate their technological proficiency among other things, the technical side of blogs tends to be handled by software on a server, leaving the user to concentrate on content. As such, companies such as Webloggers (www.jish.nu/webloggers), Live Journal (www. livejournal.com) and the eponymous Blogger (www.blogger.com) provide the online tools for novice users to provide daily updates. As with personal homepages, blogs provide a variety of interests that range from the truly banal to the mind-boggling, such as Will Wheaton's board at www.willwheaton.net, which proposes to show the real man behind the former *Star Trek* ensign. Wheaton won six Bloggies for his site in 2002, including that for best tagline: '50,000 monkeys at 50,000 typewriters can't be wrong.'

Internet archives

One of the best ways of examining the changing face of cyberspace is to explore the Internet Archive (www.archive.org). Many of the comparisons made in this chapter depend on the pages stored at the Archive, which was founded in 1996 by Brewster Kahle, who in 1989 invented the WAIS (wide area information servers) system that enabled users to find documents from online databases. By the time the Wayback Machine, a free search engine to the Archive, was launched in October 2001, over ten billion web pages had been archived in a database comprising 100 Terabytes (Aiken 2002).

According to Kahle, the average lifespan of a web page is 75 to 100 days, and the Internet Archive's attempt to preserve this often ephemeral information has made it the largest known database. The Wayback Machine is used by simply accessing the website and entering a URL for the website that you wish to explore: you will then be provided with a number of dates corresponding to times when the Internet Archive has made a copy of that site.

Of course, despite the relative youth of the Internet, its history extends back some twenty years before such archival work began, and even the Web had come into existence some five years previously. As such, the Internet Archive is necessarily limited, particularly as it cannot cover every updated web page produced every day, but as a tool for research or – as here – for comparing the development and progress of Internet forms it remains invaluable.

E-zines

Consult one of the many e-zine directories on the Web (for example, e-zineuniverse. com, freezineweb.com, meer.net/john/e-zine-list, bestezines.com, zinos.com), and you will encounter an abundance of web texts that may be independently or commercially produced, addressing a range of topics, interests, issues, identities and lifestyles from a multitude of perspectives.

Prior to the Internet, the media environment in the West was dominated by corporately financed, industrially produced, professionalised and profit-driven journalisms, collectively understood as the mass media. The prohibitive costs entailed in the production of print magazines and periodicals and the constraints of advertising have been key factors in determining a media environment where alternative and radical publications either struggle for survival or are banished into the imperceptible – if not invisible – networks of zines and newsletters.

The nature of the Internet as a decentralised network of networks, its ubiquity, interactivity and connectivity, creates the potential for the transformation of our media environment. Relative to print, web publication costs are low and the opportunity exists for anyone with access to publish. In short, the Internet and the World Wide Web create the space for previously marginalized or silenced voices and expressions and for the production of new radical and alternative media forms. The promise of the Internet is of a more heterogeneous, dialogical and democratic media culture.

Yet we should be circumspect about these utopian claims. The promise of a 'new' media culture relies on a common-sense binarism (i.e. mass medium vs. new medium) that is underpinned by a set of elitist assumptions about the nature of the mass media (as monologic transmitters of dominant ideology) and mass media audiences (as manipulated and passive). The Internet does create space for the production of alternative and radical journalisms, but there is a danger of falling into an uncritical celebration of radical and alternative media as inherently liberated, progressive and free from the constraints of the market while consumers of mass media remain trapped within the prison house of dominant ideology.

Recent work in media and cultural studies has shown that consumers of mass media are critical and discriminating cultural *producers*. Far from producing a passive, homogenous culture, mass media provides its audiences with the resources to work out the contradictions of their everyday lives, construct resistant meanings and produce their own media forms (see Fiske, Radway, Jenkins and others). If we agree that this is the case (and there is a wealth of evidence to support this argument), the boundary between mass media audiences and independent media producers becomes less clearly defined.

We should also be wary of the claims implied in the utopian rhetoric of interactivity, connectivity and heterogeneity. Questions of connectivity and heterogeneity must lead us to questions of access and accessibility (discussed elsewhere in this book). There is also a need to address critically the nature and potential of interactivity and the ways in which interactivity is defined. As will become clear in this chapter, interactivity has very different meanings in the context of different e-zines, whether commercial, radical or alternative.

What is an e-zine?

In simple terms, an e-zine or electronic magazine is a zine or magazine that is produced as a hypertext and exists in cyberspace. As indicated above, the range of e-zines is vast and indeterminable, and the rapid pace of technological change renders the form relatively unstable.

Few studies of online journalism have addressed e-zines as a new web form. This may be an indication of the ways in which e-zines, like print magazines, are perceived as having relatively low cultural value compared to the more prestigious world of hard news. As McKay indicates, 'Hard news is seen as exciting, frontline and edgy, largely about war or crime or affairs of state. Magazines, with their less frequent deadlines, are thought to be light, less important and soft, largely about things that don't matter so much' (McKay 2000: 4). I would argue that the differences between magazine and newspaper journalism are less than clear, as 'soft' and opinion-led content comprises a substantial portion of the contemporary mainstream press. As we shall see, the Web further blurs the boundaries between the two.

This chapter aims to examine a small range of commercial, radical and alternative e-zines, and will consider their form, particularly the use of the hypertext link and opportunities for reader participation; content, that is, the kinds of knowledge and pleasure they offer their readers; and their various purposes.

Early e-zines

The history of the commercial e-zine is characterised by failure. Huge investment has been rewarded with little or no return and few publications survive in an increasingly competitive market and concentrated industry. In print media, a magazine's survival and profitability will depend on two key factors: advertising and circulation. As the Web grows and matures, it is the increasingly powerful portals and search engines and not e-zines which are controlling the biggest share of the diminishing advertising pot and few e-zines have developed a profitable model for selling content. Those that have survived have either developed targeted content for which consumers are willing to pay or are supported and funded by the global media giants, for whom a loss of revenue is easily absorbed.

Commercial e-zines exist in a number of forms as composite sites, subscriber sites or as e-zines proper. Composite sites are largely secondary to their print counterparts, containing part original content and part content drawn from their print version (commonly referred to by the derogatory term 'shovelware'). Subscriber sites exist purely to advertise and secure orders for their print magazine and may include limited content, but that content will be drawn from the print magazine. For example, the site for The London Review of Books publishes three articles from its print publication and some readers' letters, yet it exists primarily to promote and encourage subscription to its print version.

E-zines proper, however, have been developed entirely with the medium in mind and will typically include a number of themed sites or channels, comprising news, features, forums, an archive and search capabilities. Despite the opportunities for interactivity, most e-zines retain full editorial control over their content and limit opportunities for reader contributions to bulletin boards and forums. Commercial e-zines are also characterised by their lack of connectivity to other sites, the extent and nature of connectivity being determined by the need to retain a distinctive identity on the Web and to limit opportunities for readers to leave the site.

In print media, access to distribution networks is crucial to the success of a print magazine, but for commercial e-zines the key issues are visibility and connectivity. An e-zine's success is dependent largely upon obtaining a high ranking by search engines. The Web has grown to vast proportions, and recent research has shown that access to the Web has become increasingly concentrated around a handful of key portals and search engines. Being connected, and having the right connections is vital to survival on the Web as search engines typically rank sites according to the quantity and quality of links. At the centre of this strategy is the hypertext link. For search engines such as Google, quality is also defined by connectivity; that is, a site's quality is determined by the quality of the sites to which it is connected. The importance of being connected and having the right connections is also central to the construction and definition of a site's identity.

Hotwired

In web mythology, the pioneers and celebrated heroes of the electronic magazine are HotWired (hotwired.com) and Suck (suck.com). Developed by the Wired magazine team, HotWired became one of the first e-zines to take advantage of the Web's unique opportunities during a time when other publications were simply 'shovelling' their print content online.

> HotWired debuted in October of 1994 as the Web's most ambitiously-funded and staffed original content publication. It pioneered and soon popularised

notions like site membership and weekly member E-mailings. Its Wired-inspired look and *attitude* meanwhile informed the content and presentation of countless Web publications that came after it . . . HotWired helped set new standards for professionalism in a medium that was dominated by part-time pioneers with day jobs, it also *broke the Web* as an advertising medium. The banner advertisement that underpins the revenue hopes of almost every commercial content company on the Web today was a HotWired creation. Using its banners as a wedge, HotWired also set an important early precedent by recruiting real world companies to use the Web to promote their goods and services.

(Reid 1997: 282)

Combining travel, arts, entertainment and digital culture, HotWired offered its readers a distinctive repertoire of cultural knowledge that focused on travel, digital arts, entertainment, new technology and the emerging cultures that comprised the Internet and the World Wide Web. Its five channels or sites – World Beats, Renaissance, Kino, Signal and the Piazza – combined a sense of the new, the cool and the exotic. World Beats covered world travel accounts and events for a generation of 'post-tourists' (Urry 1990) or in HotWired's terms 'digital nomads', who sought out places 'off the beaten track', and traversed the boundaries between high and low culture, authenticity and inauthenticity. Renaissance focused on arts and entertainment, Kino and Signal celebrated digital arts and cultures, and the Piazza, with its combination of interactive forums, live events and discussion spaces, gave readers opportunities to participate. HotWired's irreverent, knowing and frequently ironic tone addressed an 'imagined community' (Anderson 1983) of educated, web- and media-literate young men who comprised the Web's early users.

Celebratory and self-congratulatory in tone and style, HotWired represented a utopian promise of digital possibilities. Writing in July 1995 for HotWired, Joshua Quittner coined the term the 'Way New Journalism', a direct reference to Tom Wolfe's essay 'The Birth of New Journalism' in the 1970s, to describe the future of journalism on the Web (hotwired.lycos.com/I-agent/95/29/waynew/waynew.html). Way New Journalism should be 'irreproducible in another medium' and 'must take proper advantage of the computer as a storytelling tool' incorporating interactivity, hypertext, instantaneous publishing and multimedia. The 'Way New' rallying cry was typical of HotWired's hyperbolic, self-important voice. During a period when many print titles were 'shovelling' their content on-line, 'Way New' with its central edict of 'no shovelware' was key to the construction of HotWired's distinctive identity as the voice of the digital generation.

So 'Way New Journalism' for the digital generation was born in the form of HotWired, with all its attendant promises for the transformation of journalism. But the early Hotwired team were divided as to what 'Way New' might become and primarily about the degree of editorial control that should be retained. This division was articulated in terms of 'content' and 'community': the 'community' camp envisaged HotWired as a 'heteroglossic' text with content developed 'from below' through the inclusion of other sites and readers' contributions within the main site. The 'content' camp, however, wanted to retain full editorial control. The 'content' camp eventually won out, and thus 'Way New Journalism', which could have become more radical in terms of organisation and content, remained strictly hierarchically organised (Reid 1997).

Hyperlinks to other sites enabled readers to access alternative viewpoints, but these stories were framed within HotWired's authorial voice. HotWired's journalism remained resolutely within a hierarchical model of mass communication, retaining the 'fundamental break between the producer and receiver in such a way that recipients have relatively little capacity to contribute to the course and content of the communicative process' (Thompson 1990: 218–19).

HotWired's membership system gave members a weekly emailed newsletter, HotFlash, and enabled readers to choose user names and to participate in the many forums. The combination of site membership and reader participation provided a new model for integrating marketing into the site, and enabled the HotWired team to collate information about their readership to ensure the content of the site remained relevant to its readers; but more importantly, that knowledge could be used to construct an audience profile which could be sold to advertisers. The development of the banner advertisement – one of the earliest forms of advertising on the Web – completed the model. Here interactivity and participation – far from radicalising journalism – are key strategies for integrating marketing, community and content.

HotWired became the blueprint for the many commercial e-zines that followed in its path, and has been copied by many, transforming the nature of magazines in the process. Articles became shorter, providing less in-depth information, more opinion-led comment and information grew as databases were developed. As Hall notes, 'The web simultaneously reduces the size of communications . . . and increases it in the huge amounts of information contained in distributed databases' (2001: 93).

The boundaries between news sites and e-zines are blurred as the most recognised business model for web publishing became one of targeting niche markets and building communities around a combination of news, opinion and features. In the context of the Web, news becomes a prime commodity, and daily updates are imperative for a site's survival. E-zines thus carry more news than their print counterparts and update sites daily, and the boundaries between web news sites and e-zines become less easy to identify.

Suck and Salon

HotWired's fairly conservative (although successful) use of the medium provided the impetus for the development of more experimental endeavours. Suck became popular for their Net moguls' trading cards, and for their use of the hypertext link. Unlike other e-zines at the time, Suck did not use links as an information resource, a means of connecting to alternative viewpoints or to enable site navigation, but as a 'rhetorical device'.

> The rest of the Web saw hypertext as an electrified table of contents, or a supply of steroid-addled footnotes. The Sucksters saw it as a way of phrasing a thought. They stitched links into the fabric of their sentence, like an adjective vamping up a noun, or a parenthetical clause that conveys a sense of unease with the main premise of the sentence. They didn't bother with the usual conventions of 'further reading'; they weren't linking to the interactive discussions among their readers; and they certainly weren't building hypertext 'environments.' (Each Suck article took the resolutely one-dimensional form of a thin column snaking down an austere white page.) Instead, they used links like modifiers, like punctuation – something hardwired into the sentence itself.
> (Johnson 1997: 133)

Suck used hyperlinks as a tool to undercut or subvert their narrative, but they also served another purpose. Sponsored in part by the booksellers Barnes and Noble, Suck was required to promote new books and provide links to their site each time a book was mentioned in the editorial. This prefigured a new moment in the blurring of editorial and advertising.

The hypertext link and the overt intertextuality it represents is regarded by many as the defining characteristic of the Web. However, the hypertext link has a liminal status. It is janus-faced, both sacred and profane, and its meaning is entirely dependent on the relationships it constructs between pages, blocks of text and sites. All e-zines use links as an intra-site navigational tool, but few commercial e-zines link to other e-zines or information sources. As with the example of HotWired, e-zines that link to alternative viewpoints attempt to contain and frame those viewpoints within their own authorial voice.

Salon (salon.com) is one of the few remaining consumer e-zines and continues to be a significant presence on the Web. Despite the combination ten content sites (Arts and Entertainment, Salon Audio, Books, Comics, Life, News, People, Politics, Sex, and Technology and Business), two communities (Table Talk and The Well bought by Salon in 1999), a personal service and a weblog service, constructed for an audience high in cultural and economic capital, Salon has risked closure on many occasions.

The bulk of Salon's news is supplied by the news agency Associated Press and is freely available, but Salon's original news stories, features, political journalism and gallery of erotic photography are accessible only via subscription to Salon Premium. The premium on news, politics and erotic photography is designed to appeal to an audience for whom this kind of entertainment and information is defined as of high cultural value, whereas the bulk of its free content focuses on celebrity, scandal, gossip and entertainment.

In a medium where visibility is vital to success, e-zines are reliant not only on connectivity, but also on the broader media environment for the construction and definition of its cultural status. Drawing on and extending the work of Pierre Bourdieu, Thornton argues that the media

> are not simply another symbolic good or marker of distinction (which is the way Bourdieu describes films and newspapers vis-à-vis cultural capital) but a network crucial to the definition and distribution of cultural knowledge. In other words, the difference between being in or out of fashion, high or low in cultural capital, correlates in complex ways with degrees of media coverage, creation and exposure.
>
> (Thornton 1995: 13)

Good reviews in the 'quality' print and broadcast media and the achievement of prestigious web awards are important to the construction of Salon's status, and Salon has managed to secure a range of web awards and reviews in, for example, *Time* and the *New York Times*. Salon also relies heavily on the perceived cultural status of its writers, and tends to draw upon a pool of respected academics and journalists.

Commercial e-zines have developed strategies that are fundamentally similar to those found in mass media forms, but the Web further enables the integration

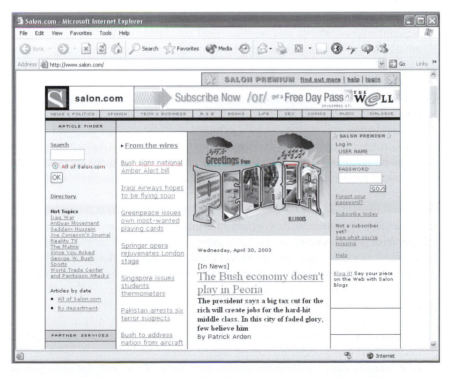

Figure 10.1 The Salon website – one of the few e-zines to turn a profit in 2003.

of marketing and content. As we have seen, an e-zine's success is dependent upon building a distinctive identity around content for an imagined community of readers, knowledge of whom is used to attract advertising. Use of hypertext links is limited primarily to intra-site navigation or to connect to sponsors and advertisers. Commercial e-zines thus adopt a *strategy of containment* in an attempt to retain their readers within their site. The potential of hypertext to enable readers to follow a centrifugal path that carries them outward from a text remains unrealised, as readers are guided ever inward, following a centripetal path.

Radical and alternative e-zines

If commercial e-zines adopt a strategy of containment, radical and alternative movements work to exploit the characteristics of the Internet as a 'foundation for self-directed networking as a tool for organization, collective action, and the construction of meaning' (Castells 2001: 55). Prior to the birth of cyberspace, alternative voices, movements, countercultures and subcultures used self-published zines and newsletters to communicate, construct alternative identities and build networks (Atton 2002; Duncombe 1997), but the Web provides opportunities to extend those networks across time and space and to connect readers with forms of 'useful' information.

The birth of the Web coincided with the development and growth of a number of new social movements and marginalized social groups that have taken the Internet and the Web as a key means of communicating and networking and for the construction of oppositional meanings and identities. As Castells (2001: 22) points out,

> The distinctive social and political trend of the 1990s is the construction of social action and politics around primary identities, either ascribed, rooted in history and geography, or newly built in an anxious search for meaning and spirituality. The first historical steps of informational societies seem to characterise them by the pre-eminence of identity as their organising principle.

Anti-capitalist organisations, environmental groups and animal rights groups and a plethora of grrrl, feminist, queer, fat lesbian and ethnic sites provide a snapshot of our particular historical moment and of the increasing popularity of the Web as a means to circumvent the restrictions of mainstream communications media.

Urban75

Urban75 (urban75.com) is an independent e-zine edited and maintained by Mike Slocombe. Like many enduring independent e-zines, Urban75 has its roots in zine culture, starting out as a football fanzine for Cardiff City with the intention of tackling issues such as racism, violence and homophobia in the game.

The fanzine entitled 'Bluebird Jones' gained huge popularity when it ran a comic strip about the impact of the Criminal Justice Bill on football fans which was reproduced in hundreds of UK football fanzines. Mike created an e-zine entitled 'Football Fans Against the Criminal Justice Act' that later became Urban75.

Urban75 retains many of the features of zine culture including an emphasis on DIY, autonomy and independence. The DIY ethic is 'at once a critique of the dominant mode of passive consumer culture and something far more important: the active creation of an alternative culture' (Duncombe 1997: 117). DIY in Urban75 is evidenced in the range of information and resources on 'culture jamming' and self-publishing, and in the implied call to resist and act.

Organised into nine linked sites (action, mag, photos, rave, drugs, punch, football, useless and boards), Urban75 provides a mixture of photography, features, drug and rave information, football, games, comics and a number of bulletin boards. Relevant information on the Criminal Justice and Public Order Act 1994 remains central to the site alongside 'useless' games including 'Instant Tabloid Writer', 'Shut Up Blair', 'Clinton's Underpants' and 'Slippery Bill Gates'. Information on 'issues' including the 'War on Terror', 'ID Cards' and 'Censored News' and listings of protests, talks and festivals and an extensive directory of links completes the site. Urban75's combination of entertainment, 'useful' information and links and issue-based features is both popular and radical. Its 'imagined community' is built around content that is characterised by the opposition of dominant cultural values, and depends upon an understanding of mainstream and consumer culture as an inauthentic 'other'.

Many zine cultures regard advertising 'with suspicion and scepticism, believing it to be the mechanism for the compromise, dilution and "recuperation" of the radical' (Atton 2002: 73). For this reason, Urban75 remains resolutely independent, and declares it is 'strictly non-commercial and carries no money-making banners, adverts or sponsorship deals, despite many offers'.

Urban75's relationship to contemporary popular culture and mainstream politics is best exemplified in the games 'Slap a Celebrity' and 'Punch a Politician'. The popularity of the 'Slap a Spice Girl' game is indicative of the kinds of pleasures Urban75 offers, pleasures that rely on a form of ironic distancing from the perceived inauthenticity and banality of popular cultural forms and culture.

Urban75 is characterised by content that opposes the norms and values of mainstream culture, but, unlike SchNEWS (schnews.org.uk), it remains hierarchically organised, refuses requests for links to sites and retains copyright over the content of the site.

SchNEWS, to which it promotes and is linked, maintains a philosophy that is anti-copyright, promotes open distribution and even encourages others to establish their own version of SchNEWS, using as much content as they wish. SchNEWS produces a weekly newsletter in portable document format (PDF) that can be downloaded and distributed, and is thus more interested in encouraging the participative production and dissemination of alternative news and perspectives than Urban75.

As much a news site as an information resource, SchNEWS cultivates an alternative value system based on an ideal of co-operation. If mainstream news providers typically report the news as a series of isolated events, disconnected from history, SchNEWS news and features are intended to expose the nature of power, and the inequalities that are characteristic of capitalism.

SchNEWS and Urban75 were both developed in response to the Criminal Justice and Public Order Act, address a similar audience and can be understood as radical e-zines in that they are both interested in promoting social change. Yet SchNEWS has developed a more radical use of the Internet that extends beyond radical content and links to resources. By encouraging participation at the level of production and dissemination, SchNEWS creates a culture of inclusion and co-operation, and one which is rooted in a belief that ideas should not be restricted by copyright law, but are freely available for all.

Grrrl e-zines

Women's and grrrls' e-zines are a new genre of web text that have emerged over the past ten years. E-zines such as Saucy Chicks (saucychicks.com), Heartless Bitches International (heartlessbitches.com), Disgruntled Housewife (disgruntled housewife.com), Planetgrrl (planetgrrl.com), Wench (wench.com), The F-word (thefword.org.uk) and Cuntzilla (cuntzilla.org) exemplify the ways in which young women and grrrls are appropriating the derogatory and stereotypical labels applied to women and girls and using the Web to express their views, articulate their interests, document aspects of their lives and create alternative representations of femininity.

Often cited as primary examples of Third Wave Feminism (Garrison 2000), grrrl e-zines combine personal and autobiographical writing with feminist critique, news, features, humour and fun. Like Urban75 and other alternative e-zines, many grrrl e-zines draw on notions of DIY to encourage young women to reclaim feminism with the rallying cry 'Your feminism is what you want it to be and what you make of it. Define your agenda. Claim and reclaim your F-word' (thefword. org.uk).

As with other independently produced websites, the hyperlink plays a key role. In the context of grrrl e-zines, hyperlinks are used primarily to create networks and webs of grrrl spaces, but also to connect readers with 'useful' information and resources.

Many grrrl e-zines have been developed to critique conventional notions of femininity. These e-zines will often draw upon the codes and conventions of women's and girls' magazines and other popular women's genres, using them as a resource to create alternative representations of femininity. This form of critique uses a range of textual and aesthetic strategies including irony, camp and parody. E-zines such as Saucy Chicks and Planetgrrl parody the conventions of women's magazines to subvert and critique conventional notions of femininity; Disgruntled Housewife employs camp as a device to subvert the meanings commonly associated with the housewife, and particularly the housewife that was represented in the popular culture of the 1950s; and Heartless Bitches International employs irony as a strategy to offer humorous explorations of contemporary gender relations.

Contrary to those forms of cultural criticism that understand women and girls to be passive consumers of the 'cult of femininity' created in the pages of women's and girls' magazines (Ferguson 1983), grrrl e-zines such as Planetgrrl, Disgruntled Housewife and Heartless Bitches testify to a highly media-literate and intensely critical reader. As Ballaster has noted, 'When talking about magazines, women endlessly, and delightedly, parody and mimic them, displaying their own literacy and mastery of its generic conventions' (Ballaster 1991: 35). The Web provides opportunities for young women and girls to take the next step; that is, to produce and articulate their own representations and expressions of femininity.

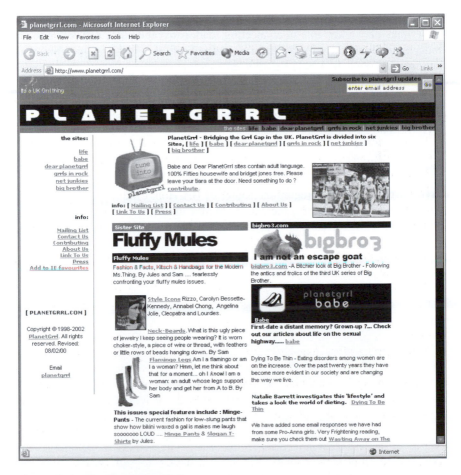

Figure 10.2 The Planetgrrl website.

For many young women and grrrls, the opportunity to document and publish their experiences in their own voice is an important first step. These forms of cultural production expand discursive space and create opportunities for the articulation of new feminine/feminist identities.

And finally . . .

This chapter has touched briefly on a handful of e-zines that may be found on the Web and there are many more that tackle an infinite range of topics and issues. Fan e-zines and sites, for example, are ubiquitous in cyberspace covering interests ranging from cult cinema to music, popular television genres and hobbies, and there are numerous others including scene e-zines, political e-zines, religious e-zines, travel e-zines, and literary and art e-zines.

What has emerged however from this consideration of e-zines is that while hyperlinks play a key role in connecting readers to other sites and resources in independently produced websites (i.e. connectivity is a key issue), commercial sites need to maintain a balance between enabling readers to have access to relevant information and resources and the need to retain readers within the site. Independently produced sites also place a much greater emphasis (to varying degrees) on ideals of co-operation and collaboration, and openly encourage and include multiple voices and perspectives.

Note

Jayne Armstrong is co-programme leader of BA(Hons) Journalism at Falmouth College of Arts. Her interests include alternative media, cyberfeminisms and grrrl culture, and she is currently studying for her Ph.D. on women's and grrrl's e-zines.

11 Writing for the Web

Online writing

Professional writing in cyberspace virtually did not exist before the 1990s. While there were a few services such as Prodigy, Quantum Computer Services (later AOL) and CompuServe that did employ journalists and editors to compile copy by the beginning of the 1990s, substantial activity in this area had to wait for the advent of the Web. This is not to say that writing began with the Web – far from it: newsgroups, email and bulletin boards flourished for decades before the invention of HTML, each of these a hotbed for electronic scribbling. The visual appeal of the Web, however, soon brought with it the anticipation that this was a new medium that could be used for commercial communication.

During the late 1990s, for reasons examined elsewhere in this book, it was widely assumed that any aspect of online activity would inevitably bring its own rewards and the Web in particular was widely hyped as the greatest innovation since Gutenberg. Dotcom frenzy was followed by fallout, with the marketplace for online writers and journalists having contracted.

Cyberspace was particularly susceptible to the economic downturn that occurred in the early twenty-first century because, more so than print and even broadcasting, it was almost entirely reliant on advertising for revenue. Throughout the 1990s, online publications such as Salon and the *Wall Street Journal* experimented with subscription with mixed results. Salon (www.salon.com) discovered that critical praise did not prevent subscribers from staying away: WSJ.com, on the other hand, has managed to generate substantial revenues (although not enough for a profit at the time of writing), although even this indicates that subscription is generally suitable only for specialised interests (Dyer 2001).

For other sites, any hope of income depended almost entirely on chasing a decreasing pool of advertisers after the boom of the late 1990s. The online market was, until recently, much bigger in the USA than in Europe, and the American new media explosion had made some companies rather bullish in their pronouncements.

Jupiter Communications (www.jup.com), for example, predicted a growth in online advertising revenues from $5.3 billion in 2000 to $16.5 billion by 2005: advertising revenue actually fell in 2001. Extreme scepticism regarding online markets, however, is probably misplaced. While the gold-rush is over, writing for the Web remains a potential career move, with some publishing companies having targeted the Net very actively, including Future Publishing (www.futurenet.co.uk), IPC Media (www.ipcmedia.com), EMAP (www.emap.com) and IDG (www.idg.co.uk). Although some of these, most notably EMAP and IPC, were forced to scale back their operations in 2001, writers and editors will continue to find work in a medium that did not exist a decade previously, let alone pay its contributors. As Owen Gibson (2001: 60) has remarked: 'Just as it was folly to take seriously the vast unsustainable investments promised in digital projects during the web's salad days, so there is a danger of swinging too far the other way.'

The market for online publications has been criticised for other reasons. Sam Ladner (2001), for example, has observed that many online journalists are alienated from their work to a much higher degree than other journalists and so tend to rely on money rather than professional pride for job satisfaction. During the mid-1990s, it was common for writers (Bromley 1997; Hammond 1995) to attack the demands of the multimedia newsroom as contributing to a decline in journalistic standards.

While journalistic standards have almost certainly changed in the past three decades, and much of this change is due to technological developments, it is not intrinsically the case that such technological innovation has caused a decline in standards (as opposed, for example, to concentration of ownership stifling competition). Indeed, it is possible to argue that the Internet has prompted greater diversity in the media and renewal of interest in different types of publication, and certainly sites such as Guardian Unlimited and Salon regularly produce material of an extremely high standard.

The practicalities of Webonomics

The bottom line is frequently the most important factor in determining the success or failure of particular sites. A fundamental problem affecting the commercial success of websites was the early assumption that the Internet was a free medium, both in terms of speech and easy access to information. As the Net came to be dominated by business concerns during the second half of the 1990s, however, so the bursting of the dotcom bubble early in the new millennium led to a more hard-headed attitude to generating revenue.

Advertising has been the most obvious revenue stream, but even before the attack on the World Trade Center in September 2001 this had begun to dry up, leaving too many competitors chasing too little advertising. Despite this, content sites remained popular, with 85 per cent of respondents to an AOL Europe/Roper Starch survey claiming this was their main use for the Net (cited in Dyer 2001).

The alternative, then, remains subscription, which not only generates revenue but may also be used to demonstrate reader demographics to potential advertisers.

We have already seen how subscription can have mixed results (fairly successful for WSJ.com, less so for Salon), but other alternatives include payment for particular articles or reports, as with *Science* magazine. The problem with 'pay-per-view' models for the Web is that credit card payments under £5 are not viable for the retailer: Stephen King, when he began to serialise his novel *The Plant* on-line, had readers send cheques or postal orders, but more sophisticated methods of micropayments are required to make this kind of subscription a success.

ISPs and telecoms-related companies such as mobile phone operators have probably provided the most accessible form of micropayment systems, where very small purchases may be added to a phone bill or monthly payment. Another alternative has been offered as electronic wallets, or ewallets, that will store secure bank and credit details, probably via a third party: when goods or services are purchased online, ewallet software will contact the bank account on behalf of the customer and add the appropriate amount to a bill. Such an approach, however, will depend greatly on consumers' willingness to trust in ewallet security.

Online style

While the online market will endure for the foreseeable future, even grow at a more realistic rate over the next decade or so, more writers, journalists, editors and publishers are concerned to establish a suitable style for this medium. We are not concerned here with outlining restrictive parameters – to prescribe how to write for the Web – but rather to examine whether there are any particular factors that influence online style.

The most important difference between writing for online media and print obviously relates to differences in technology: reading from a screen is very different to reading from a page. Usability research by Jakob Nielsen (2000) suggests that reading onscreen is about 25 per cent slower than reading print, and Nielsen's advice is not merely to be succinct but to aim for approximately half the word count of a paper version. Certainly much of the best writing online is succinct, but this is not the only way to consume information from the Internet. Text-only pages, while fairly dull to look at, may be perfect for reading when printed out. Probably more difficult are the ways in which a reader may come to a particular page: while he or she would have to plough through a book or magazine to arrive at the middle of an article (and thus have some understanding of the context of the publication), this is not necessarily the case with a web page, which can be accessed via a search engine. As such, readers may easily misunderstand online texts, and writers should work to establish context on every page and not simply at the beginning of an article.

Regarding style more generally, good writing is good writing whether in print, a television script or when produced for a web page. There are some differences between the web and other media (as between a script and a short story), but the pointers that exist for effective communication online are often similar to those for other forms of writing.

Most importantly, writing can be inclusive or exclusive. In a few cases, sites are most effective when exclusive; after all, not all writers wish to communicate with any passing visitor, but rather use jargon and culturally specific language to mark boundaries between groups. Most sites, however, will be more successful if they employ inclusive language. As Susan Ross (2001: 37) points out, in the competitive environment of the Internet 'poor writing may simply mean the end of communication. The user gives up and goes elsewhere'. Similarly, most writing for the Web tends to be a more polished version of conversation; write as you speak, but more precisely, paying attention to rules of grammar and avoiding irrelevant colloquialisms. In the words of Matthew Arnold, 'Have something to say, and say it as clearly as you can. That is the only secret of style.'

Injunctions for an effective style include several important maxims. George Orwell (1981: 130) described clichés as 'less of words chosen for the sake of their meaning, and more . . . tacked together like the sections of a pre-fabricated henhouse'. When an original phrase is overused, it ceases to create a vivid impression in the reader, and instead becomes the stuffing for tired sentences. Jargon is likewise to be avoided, primarily because although it may have a useful function for members of an institution or profession it excludes other readers. Finally, grammatical and syntactical errors will create a very poor impression for readers.

There are numerous texts, such as *Writing for Journalists* (Hicks *et al.* 1999), that are extremely useful for writers who wish to convey their thoughts as lucidly as possible. On a very personal level, however, while such books are helpful in developing a clear style, I would offer a note of caution against accepting all advice on plain writing as an eternal injunction. Henry James would not have satisfied most editors who want to avoid verbose sentences, but every once in a while *Washington Square* is a pleasant change from reading a newspaper.

Writing news

News has been particularly successful in cyberspace: while there have been some examples of ongoing news channels in other media, such as CNN cable television and Radio 5 Live, the Internet seems especially well suited for constant news updates that users can log on to whenever they wish.

As Wynford Hicks (1999: 11) observes, news is easy to define: 'To be news, something must be factual, new and interesting.' To determine what is of interest when creating your own news stories, it is a good idea to look at what is being published elsewhere; this does, however, bring its own dangers – after all, the news is not new if it simply regurgitates other publications, and you are unlikely ever to scoop a story this way.

News becomes a story when it is crafted and provides an unusual angle – according to the famous adage, 'dog bites man' is not a story, but 'man bites dog' is. Such stories have to be short and to the point – as Keeble (1998) observes, students who are used to writing 2,000-word academic essays frequently encounter difficulties when made to write a 300-word story. As such, introductions need to be short, punchy and contain relevant information in the first twenty or thirty words. This leads to a constructive technique known as the 'news pyramid' with the most important information given at the beginning of the story. Traditionally, this enabled editors to chop a story to fit space: while this appears less relevant for the Net, it is still useful insofar as it enables readers to determine the value of a story quickly in case they click on another link (Whittaker 2002b). It is worth noting that stories with dramatic endings are common exceptions to such pyramids.

A common technique when building a story is to provide a short introduction, then to retell this in the next paragraph, elaborating with further detail. This is not the only way to tell a story, but it can be useful. Typically, news writers are advised to include the famous five Ws: who, what, where, when and why (sometimes with the honorary sixth member, 'how'). Why, the causal factors of a story, tend to be the most complex and, as Keeble observes, this is what is often left out of a story or handled superficially.

There are different types of news stories. Running stories are returned to on a regular basis: regular readers will be irritated to be given all contextual information, but it is important to provide background material for new readers. Phrases such as 'a second death' or 'questions were asked again' are typically used to indicate the fact that a story is ongoing. Follow-up stories also typically rely on the memory of the reader. In this section, we have treated news stories as short, factual pieces that need to convey information quickly to the reader, but other styles of reporting, such as investigative journalism, covered in the next section also apply to effective news writing.

Writing features

While historically the roots of journalism lie in reporting the news, from the earliest days of newspapers writers and readers have looked to more diverse types of copy to provide information, opinion and entertainment. The *Courier* of the seventeenth century, dealing with news of the court and commerce, was quickly followed by the *Spectator* of the eighteenth century, concentrating more on issues of taste and style.

Features offer much greater variety and, as Sally Adams (in Hicks *et al.* 1999) observes, the sole constraint on writing features is to produce copy relevant to a publication and its readers. Feature writing may be more difficult to specify than news, but all good features demonstrate forethought, a focus and a flow that takes the reader along a logical progression of ideas. Most importantly of all, a feature writer should have something to say, even if the aim of what is said consists purely of entertainment.

Features are commonly associated with magazine writing (although newspapers also contain many feature articles, typically past the first few pages of breaking news as well as in magazine-style supplements). As we have seen in Chapter 10, e-zines are another format that has flourished online and writers can expect to produce magazine-style features for such sites.

Many of the comments that apply to news writing are relevant when discussing features: accuracy, for example, is important – a writer or publisher may be as easily sued for a feature or review as for a news story. At the same time, feature writing offers much greater scope for creativity and experimentalism than news writing. As John Morrish (1996) points out, objectivity and distance are not necessarily required, the word 'I' may be used and the writer sometimes features as a participant in the story. Features are also more likely to use the narrative techniques employed by fiction writers.

Different types of introduction may include narratives and anecdotes, descriptive scene-setting, a provocative statement or a quotation or question. The flow of content is important to features that are nearly always longer than news stories, particularly if they are heavy on facts; it is also worth bearing in mind that such facts may be much more important to 'trade' rather than 'consumer' publications; that is, sites aimed at readers with a higher common level of expertise in a particular area.

Of the various types of feature, common styles or components include: the interview or profile (the former based on information gained from the subject of the story, the latter more typically compiled from other background material); instructional features, such as recipes or workshops; picture features, where the main focus of the article is visual material; scheduled features, typically aimed at a specific market that may draw in certain types of advertisers (for example, a special lifestyle section on furnishings or new gadgets), and even advertorial, an article produced by or for an advertiser that is designed to appear as close as possible to other editorial copy. Features are also a good place to expand on the outcome of investigative journalism, where ongoing research and enquiries may be outlined and analysed in detail.

Finally, when preparing copy for a feature, bear in mind that there are many ways to break up a story, including the use of boxouts, panels, bullet points and captions. The precise layout of these will be left to a designer for a site, but it is useful to mark out elements of a feature that may be used in this way: readers do not always begin at the beginning and progress to the end of a story, but flit over snippets of quotes or captions that summarise elements of the main copy.

Writing reviews

As with other media, another staple of online writing to complement news and features is the review. From film sites such as the Internet Movie Database (www.imdb.com) to sites that express a personal grudge, the Internet has become a lively medium in terms of expressing critical opinions. Part of the reason for this has much to do with a suspicion that some professional publishing is driven more by the requirements of PR than in terms of offering an honest opinion – though cyberspace enjoys more than its fair share of hype, and amateur bias is not of itself preferable to professional spin.

While the Internet has provided a useful counterblast to reviews that rely on a cosy relationship between publisher and producer, a good review – of food, creative products such as books or films, more utilitarian items such as white goods, holiday destinations or a vast range of other goods and services – comprises several features. First of these, and probably most important, is expertise: by this is not meant necessarily some form of formal qualification, but rather a knowledge of the area under review that has built up over time and can draw on comparisons with similar objects. Nor is an expert necessarily a practitioner: this can sometimes help, but the best reviewer of an artwork, for example, is not necessarily someone who can paint but someone who can write.

For the reader, an honest – and correct – opinion is also important. We shall deal with some of the practical implications of libel later in this chapter, but be prepared to research and get your facts right. You may only have one chance to listen to a CD or watch a film, but be sure that the facts are correctly noted: if you get the name of an actor wrong, at worst this could mean a libel suit (and no, amateur reviews for which you do not get paid do not protect you from this threat, though the injured party may judge it not worth their while if few people read your review), at best that your opinions will be considered as less valuable. The best reviews will also indicate background contexts, such as other works undertaken by an artist or similar productions, drawn from research or personal knowledge.

Finally, a suitable style for the target audience is also important: detailed reviews of complex products (with lots of charts and figures) may be perfectly adequate for enthusiasts, but casual readers will probably require something more compact. Savage reviews can be entertaining to read but be prepared for the results: if a work in the public domain is truly bad, then be prepared to say so and remember that while many writers fear libel their words are also protected insofar as they are fair comment. At the same time, writers who always trounce any work they survey are always in danger of becoming cultural boors. Be generous towards the best, fearless with regard to the worst.

Editing and editorial teams

The way in which content is produced for the Internet, particularly the Web, has changed considerably over the past few years. While the tendency has been to emphasise the individual working alone, almost heroically, to produce a site almost permanently under construction (to match the permanent revolution that the Internet was meant to herald), successful sites are increasingly the product of larger scale teams and enterprises. At the same time, the Net has contributed to an extension of freelancing, or rather a looser conglomeration of teleworking writers, designers and managers who may carry out their tasks in a more decentralised way, contributing material via email or uploaded on to servers.

Thus far in this chapter we have explored some of the different styles and formats of writing online; we will now turn to some of the roles and issues affecting writers, their place in creating content and in particular how legal issues such as copyright and libel affect their work. While we are still concerned primarily with writing, it is best to speak of editorial rather than simply writing per se; that is, the production of content, including graphics or multimedia, that is not simply advertising or marketing material, although editorial teams may frequently be involved with both, for example, in 'advertorials'.

This potential for blurring is significant: editorial independence is often upheld as an important contribution to the operation of a democratic media (see e.g. Curran and Seaton 1997; Hartley 1982; McNair 1996). This is probably most vital in terms of press and news broadcasting, but the same is true for any magazine, broadcast or web site that is concerned to develop a relationship with its readers. At its simplest, editorial should develop a pact with the reader: at the same time, success for commercial publications depends on profits that come not simply from circulation but also from advertising, and there are probably not a few editors who consider the reader to be a necessary evil. Any editorial, however, that simply becomes a sop to advertisers is unlikely to develop a critical reputation.

The issue of editorial independence (which, for the moment, we are treating as synonymous with quality, although this is not necessarily the case) is a pertinent point with regard to cyberspace. The traditions of editorial integrity and independence that have built up over decades, even centuries, in print and broadcasting are an important ideology of a free press, for all that they may be more observed in the omission. Websites, however, may be much more vulnerable in that it is much easier to attack an ISP, which often has little if any interest in the quality of content stored on servers, rather than a figure corresponding to a more traditional publisher or proprietor.

The editorial team

All but the smallest enterprises are likely to consist of some sort of editorial team: the following is intended as a guide to a typical magazine-style setup (of which I have most experience) rather than a definitive blueprint for all types of organisations.

The editor

We shall consider the role of the editor in more detail below, and on the Internet, particularly for small operations, the editor and publisher are liable to merge roles. Traditionally, however, editors are responsible for organising material, developing a relationship with readers and managing staff, if not the distribution of product online or through other means (typically the role of the publisher). The distinction between editor and publisher is neatly summed up by Morrish (1996: 18): 'A journalist who is only interested in making money, either personally or for his or her publication, is not to be trusted. Equally, any publisher who is not interested in making money should be treated with caution.'

Section editors

Once a publication extends beyond a certain size, an editor is likely to be supported by deputies and section editors: it is sensible to devolve responsibility for particular elements to individuals who become responsible for organising, commissioning and authenticating that material. These types of editorial role may be accounted for 'thematically' (technology, fashion, food) or according to clearly defined sections in a publication (features, reviews), more often by a combination of both. Section editors serve as middle management, responsible for writers and other staff and answering to the editor, but one way in which new technology has affected editorial departments as elsewhere has been in the levelling out of organisational structures, with considerable pruning of grades of responsibility between editor and assistants at the bottom of the scale.

Production and design

A production (sometimes managing) editor is essentially the person responsible for making the trains run on time, implementing deadlines and undertaking day-to-day project management. Such editors provide an important link between writers and editors responsible for producing content, and subs and layout artists who transform text into a finished product. Production for the Web includes multimedia and programming as well as more traditional forms of art direction (such as photography, layout and graphics).

Staff writers, subs and assistants

It would be too easy to dismiss staff who are not editors as relatively unimportant in the production process, but I have known from experience that sometimes section editors have been easily available while a good sub-editor was difficult to hire. Staff writers and sub-editors have an essential role to play in not merely producing copy for a site but ensuring that it is as fresh and accurate as possible: any editorial team, for the Web as elsewhere, is also recommended to invest in assistants who can develop contacts, handle queries and organise such things as meetings and deliveries. Again, the role of editorial assistant is one that is frequently overlooked and can be surprisingly difficult to fill effectively: a good writer (or, perhaps more accurately, a person who considers him or herself a good writer) may lack the necessary organisational and personable skills to be a helpful assistant.

The role of editor

The role of editor is important but, particularly in the light of a levelling out of organisational structure that is in part being brought into effect by new technologies, the role should not necessarily be fetishised. None the less, editors serve as important focal points for readers and the organisation of editorial. Key areas that fall under the remit of the editor include the following.

Editorial strategy

This involves identifying readers and what they want, the focus of a publication. It is common for every editor to invoke the maxim that he or she wishes to provide the 'best' for his or her readers, but the 'best' is always something that must be carefully evaluated. The best information on new developments in technology for a professional and technically qualified audience, for example, will be very different to that provided for a more casual consumer audience. Formal research may be too costly for most titles, but reader feedback and even focus groups are helpful in identifying what an audience may want from a title.

Team management

In all but the smallest publications (with a staff of one), an editor will be responsible for hiring and firing, implementing a team structure, staff morale and leadership. Personnel management is an important skill yet one that is not necessarily the main concern of many individuals who consider themselves potential editors.

Legal obligations

Managing a team brings with it an obligation to understand at least the basics of employment law: many, but not all, companies will have fixed, written procedures to deal with a variety of potential incidents, and any editor should be familiar with these. In addition, editors (and publishers) are responsible for other legal issues that arise from publication, particularly with regard to intellectual property rights and defamation or libel, both of which are dealt with in more detail elsewhere in this chapter.

Financial considerations

While we began this section on editors with a quote from Morrish that distinguishes the editor from the publisher with regard to their view of money, an editor who considers finance to be no more than filthy lucre is unlikely to survive long as an editor. Editorial requires budgets, for staff wages, commissions and other expenses, and while most editors will not be responsible for publication costs it is in their interests to be aware of these insofar as a publication's income – whether from subscription, advertising or other sources – is likely to determine how far that budget will stretch.

Freelancing

So far, we have been concerned with permanent or semi-permanent teams involved in content production, but many publications, online as elsewhere, depend on freelance staff to provide a considerable amount of material.

The 'golden age' for online freelancing was remarkably brief, lasting from about 1997 to 1999. Sites such as Mr Showbiz and MSNBC that had paid generous rates for articles and news stories had disappeared or drastically cut budgets as advertising dried up. As J.D. Lasica remarked for the *Online Journalism Review* (2001), many of the stars of the late twentieth century had turned into the turkeys of the twenty-first.

Websites are, however, still seeking content, and opportunities exist for writers, editors and publishers. At present, there are few freelancers who work exclusively online, but many sites require content for such things as corporate newsletters and background context. In order to find and locate work, the Internet itself offers some useful opportunities. Sites such as Guru (www.guru.com), iwantmedia (iwantmedia.com/jobs/) and eLance (www.elance.com) provide opportunities for freelancers to advertise their services as well as listings of jobs. Useful sites for UK writers include the freelance database at Journalism.co.uk (www.journalism. co.uk/searchf.html) and the WebProNews Newsletter (www.webpronews.com). One downside of the ease with which information (including rates of pay) can be published online is that many freelancers find themselves engaged in furious wars of attrition as they attempt to undercut the competition, but such sites are also a useful starting point for freelancers looking for a break.

Copyright issues for writers

One area that is of particular concern for freelancers but affects other writers is copyright. While high-profile cases have thus far tended to concentrate on the music industry (notably with regard to Napster), intellectual property rights are becoming increasingly important in other industries.

Traditionally, contracts have either assumed that a publisher will purchase national serial rights only, or have explicitly staked out publication rights in other media. Twenty years ago, when very few people had even heard of the Internet, electronic rights were rarely stipulated, with the effect that many publishers must now renegotiate fees with previous contributors. Today, as websites are treated as extensions to other publishing formats, the expectation is that material produced for one medium can easily be moved online. This is not necessarily the case: the case of New York Times Co Inc vs. Tasini established in June 2001 that freelance writers retain control over the use in electronic form of material sold for print publication, and there is no implicit agreement that a contract aimed at print guarantees rights for electronic publication. In the EU, in the meantime, directives on copyright issued in April 2001 will confirm an author's general exclusive right to authorise or prohibit any form of distribution of his or her material in any medium, including the Internet, when they are passed into national law by the end of 2003.

In practice, however, writers and journalists who look to develop a relationship with a publisher or editor will accept electronic publication of their work. The important point for a writer who is concerned to control where his or her material is published is to check any contract before agreeing to its terms.

Writers and libel

While copyright and intellectual property rights in the age of digital media have become more problematic than ever, still one of the most important causes of concern for any writer is the threat of libel. Although conflicts between potential defamation and the right to free speech have long been a feature of the US legal landscape, in recent years the European Convention on Human Rights has begun to provide some belated constitutional support in the EU. At the same time, as Morrish (1996: 209) observes, journalists operate increasingly 'in a world in which freedom of the press is seen as a sectional interest rather than a general human right, and in which the activities of journalists are viewed with public scepticism and hostility'. One such area of hostility is towards writers who are seen to abuse their access to public media and use it to defame the character of another individual in order to drive up sales.

As such, while the advantages of free speech versus other rights, such as protection from defamation and the right to privacy, are being re-evaluated in the courts, journalists and writers should still be aware of libel laws. Recent cases in the UK such as those involving Jeffrey Archer indicate that judges and juries will not always rule against a publisher, and that libel should no longer be seen as a meal ticket, but British libel rules remain very strict. The 1996 Defamation Act implemented a number of changes aimed at bringing the law up to date in terms of the technology it covers, as well as some new approaches to what had become a very complex law.

As such, the new law provides a defence of 'innocent dissemination', protecting those such as ISPs who do not necessarily know what material they are distributing. This defence does not, however, help when defamatory material is called to the distributor's attention, as in the 1999 lawsuit brought by Dr Laurence Godfrey against Demon, which left posts on a Usenet server after he had informed them of the nature of such postings (Whittaker 2002a). The new law also sought to reduce complications in libel cases, reducing the time limit for beginning a defamation action from three years to one and allowing a new 'summary' procedure, whereby judges could sit without juries in less serious cases.

Harriett Gilbert (in Hicks *et al.* 1999: 115–16) points out that there is a defence against the charge of libel in the form of fair comment, and outlines four simple tests that help to determine whether anything written is libellous. First of all, while anyone may express an honest opinion, opinion is not the same as facts, which should always be checked. Second, opinions should not be completely over the top, nor, third, should they be motivated by malice. Finally, the defence of fair comment requires that the subject be of interest to public opinion.

Practical exercises

While there are a few pointers listed in this chapter to bear in mind when writing for an online audience, the secrets of good writing are generally the same as for other branches of journalism or copyediting.

Write visually

Throughout the print world, as well as online, designers and art editors are becoming more important as the ratio of text to image changes in favour of the latter. Indeed, there is a new form of information graphic journalism often used by newspapers and the like which researches information (of a disaster, war reporting or foreign affairs, for example) to provide it in a graphic form with captions and headings. Even without going this far, however, it is important as Keeble (1998) observes to write with a visual sense, considering how the story will be presented on the page (print or screen), how it may be represented visually, and how the writer can portray scenes for readers so that they are able to 'see' what he or she describes.

The art of interviewing

While there is not the space in this book to consider interviewing in depth (Jim Beaman's *Interviewing for Radio* contains good advice for all writers), a good interview can be as important to online writing as interviews for print or broadcast media. Of course, the interview is a journalistic convention, but at best it appears unforced and natural. Interviews take several forms, of which we shall consider only three here: the extended interview or profile, which ideally should be adopted face to face and will typically dominate a piece; the short interview, which can improve a relatively featureless article with expert 'comment'; and the vox pop interview – asking members of the public to offer their opinions.

If you do not have a chance to interview a person face to face – conducting the interview by phone or email, for example – you should still strive to make the process as personal as possible. Phone or email is best used for follow-up (if possible) after a face-to-face interview for a profile. For all interviews, the golden rule is prepare, prepare, prepare. Discover as much as you can about your interviewee (vox pop comments aside), through press cuttings or a press/publicity officer if applicable, and be clear what questions you wish to ask. Finally, although this is obvious it is worth stating: A good interview does not consist of the interviewer doing all the talking – be prepared to listen actively.

Write economically

What is true for newspaper journalism is even more so for online writing: boil down your message to the essentials. Do not use three words where one will do and, for more vivid effect, use short words wherever possible and the active tense. 'Angry TUC members consider strikes' sounds more forceful than 'Industrial action was considered by cantankerous members of the TUC'.

Jargon

In a text such as this, dealing with new technology, jargon is sure to abound. Wherever possible, however, remove any excessively obscure terminology or argot from your writing.

12 Web design

Many times throughout this book we have pointed out that cyberspace should not and cannot be reduced to the Web. For many users, however, the World Wide Web, invented at the beginning of the 1990s and a technology that flourished throughout that decade, remains central to our notions of cyberspace. While most one-to-one communication continues to take place through email or, increasingly, instant messaging, websites and web pages are the first point of contact for general information or activities such as ecommerce.

Web design was, for a couple of years before the dotcom crash, a cool new technology that almost served as an excuse to print money. While this is no longer the case (a sign of the increasing maturity of the Web as well as the ongoing depression of new technology stocks), it remains an important medium for students who may need to produce a website as part of their course work, or individuals who may need to promote commercial information or publicise personal interests and hobbies.

Throughout this chapter, then, you will find an introduction to the principles and practice of web design. Readers who are interested in taking web design further are recommended to read my *Web Production for Writers and Journalists* (Whittaker 2002b), or Thomas Powell's *Web Design: The Complete Reference* (2000).

Principles of web design

Before demonstrating the practice of creating a basic website, it is worth revising the basics of what constitutes web pages and websites, the reason being that some knowledge of these underlying principles will enable you to create better pages. Good design practice consists of not only the look and feel of a site, but also its usability, how easy it is to navigate through a site and find the information that you are looking for. There is a tendency to consider new technology as something intrinsically valuable and, as a consequence, many sites overload their pages with animated 'features' which apparently add value but actually slow down and hinder the end-user. Usability expert Jakob Nielsen has described many Flash sites, for example, as '99 per cent bad': while I do not agree with Nielsen, it is true that many pages overloaded with graphics or interactive technologies such as Flash become slow to load and thus almost unusable.

The alternative – and fundamental to good practice in terms of web design as in other areas – is what is often referred to as 'user-centred design'. Such design factors in the end-user's experience of using a site and is important for several reasons: first of all, experienced web designers, as with other people who rely on computers for a living, tend to be more expert when it comes to using a computer than the average user, and so take for granted certain ideas; second, a good designer will always consider the workflow or throughput of information on a site, testing how people will use such a site when seeking out data or products; finally, because the end-user's browser cannot be guaranteed, a good web designer always considers the alternatives in order to prevent a nasty shock when viewing pages.

User-centred design, in my experience, does have certain limits that a web page creator should be aware of. First of all, while the customer may, in principle, always be right, he or she may not always know what he or she wants. It is the task of a good web designer to provide examples of what is possible and desirable: just because someone wants a movie and/or animation on every page does not mean that this is the shape a good site will take. In addition, and again through experience, while users should be involved in testing throughout development, it is also advisable to restrict their involvement in terms of input to key stages: the easiest way for projects to become bogged down is when multiple individuals return to that project with an ever-expanding wish list. Of course, it is not always possible to manage a customer's expectations – particularly if they are paying – but with confidence and practice a good web designer will actually fulfil the end-user's requirements more fully by making them aware of the Web's proper capabilities.

On this point, it is still important for web designers to be aware of the constraints of technology that most users employ to connect to the Web. While broadband is on the increase, particularly for student users, most people for the meantime still connect via slow 56 kilobits per second modems. There are more websites than ever before that target broadband users with video-, animation- and music-intensive pages, but if you are creating a site that needs to appeal as widely as possible to users, overloading pages with such multimedia is the quickest way to make a website non-functional. I am not suggesting for a moment that such multimedia should never be used – and I disagree very strongly with a rather purist and (it must be said) dreary approach to web design that eschews multimedia; none the less, if you are going to build such a site, be aware of restrictions that will operate for many visitors using slower modems to download pages, and either offer alternatives or accept that your potential audience will be, for the time being, somewhat lower.

Text and image

Almost since its inception, web design has been in a state of flux as the technologies associated with creating pages for the World Wide Web have developed rapidly. At present, this means that professional designers have to take into account broadband media, including audio-visual footage, and a transition across many sites from static web pages to dynamic, database-driven web *applications*.

Despite these changes, it is worth considering the fundamentals of most web pages: that is, they provide information primarily through text and image. This has, at least for text, been the case since the invention of the Web by Tim Berners-Lee at the beginning of the 1990s. Berners-Lee envisaged the Web as a medium that would be capable of linking scientific documents simply and easily regardless of the location and operating system of the servers on which they were stored. The significant feature of text for the Web, therefore, is that it has been designed from the very beginning to be hypertextual. Shortly after the introduction of the first graphical web browser (Mosaic, created by the National Center for Supercomputer Applications (NCSA)), the formatting language for text on the Web, HTML, was modified to enable it to display images, and this combination of words and pictures is still the primary way by means of which sites convey information.

Text is probably the most important part of most pages, but is also that to which least attention is often given. One of the key features of web browsers is that they allow visitors to customise how web pages appear, including setting the size of text – something that many web designers seek to curtail via the use of style sheets. As we shall see later in this chapter, encouraging as wide as possible access to sites (including increased font sizes for partially sighted viewers, for example) is extremely important.

When incorporating text into a page, there are a couple of other factors worth considering. You will often encounter references to typefaces and fonts, terms that are used interchangeably, although (strictly speaking) a typeface is a style of text while the font is its size (usually measured in points). Typefaces are divided into several main styles: serif and non-serif (sanserif), indicating whether letters have short strokes at their ends or not; proportional, where the space given over to each letter varies according to its size; or monotype, where the space for each letter is the same. For example:

Arial is a proportional, sanserif typeface
Times is a proportional, serif typeface
```
Courier is a monotype, serif typeface
```

We shall consider how to prepare and best use images later in this chapter, but it is worth considering image basics at this point. When preparing images for print, the resolution of an image (usually measured in dots per inch, or dpi) needs to be high for the image to print clearly, typically between 150 or 300 dpi, but sometimes as high as 600 dpi. On screen, images can be displayed at much lower resolutions, typically 72 or 96 dpi.

Most of the images encountered on the Web fall into two main types: JPEG (named after the Joint Photographic Experts Group) and GIF (graphic interchange format). JPEG seems to be, on first acquaintance, the more useful of the two: it can display true colour images (that is, selecting colours from a range of over sixteen million different hues) and also compresses photographic images much more efficiently. GIFs, by contrast, can only display images using a palette of 256 colours at a time. However, the reason why JPEG compression is much more efficient is because it is 'lossy'; that is, extraneous information is simply discarded from the image. GIFs, by contrast, use 'lossless' compression. The difference between the two becomes evident when creating an image with large areas of a single colour, such as a logo. The JPEG will appear speckled and inferior (and, surprisingly, be a larger file size) to the GIF. In addition, GIF images can be animated, meaning that they continue to be useful on the Web.

Other image formats have been developed in recent years, including the portable networks graphic (PNG) format that combines high compression rates with lossless compression and animation. PNG, GIF and JPEG are all bitmap formats – that is, each coloured pixel is mapped out on the image. Vector graphics, or line art,

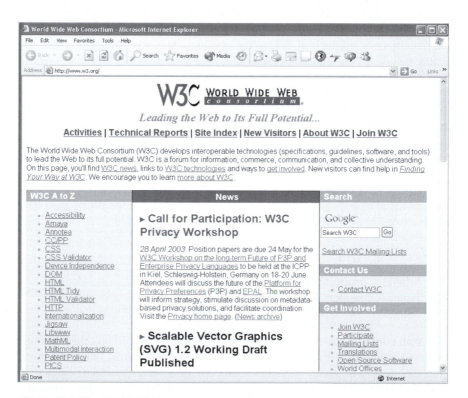

Figure 12.1 The World Wide Web Consortium (www.w3c.org) provides a wealth of information on all aspects of web design.

mathematically define each line or curve and can provide high-quality images in small file sizes. Macromedia's Flash format is the most commonly encountered vector format on the Web, but an alternative version is scalable vector graphics (SVG).

Colour

Simple but effective web pages are those which not only deploy text and image to good effect but take care with the use of colour. In general, the best web pages do not employ too many colours (typically no more than three) and are aware that certain colours which clash – such as red and green – may not be visible to colour-blind users.

HTML defines colours as a series of red, green and blue (RGB) variables in hexadecimal code; that is, numbers from 0 to 15 where the numbers 10 to 15 are represented by the letters A to F. Two digits are used for red, green and blue, so that black is 000000 and white is FFFFFF, while full red with no green or blue would be FF0000.

The number of colours that may be displayed at one time is referred to as the colour depth of an image. At its simplest, an image is 1-bit colour with a single reference to whether a pixel is on or off. More common are 8-bit images, capable of displaying 256 colours at one time, or 24-bit images that can display more than sixteen million colours.

Finally, although this is much less of a consideration with modern web pages, it is worth being aware that not all monitors can display all colours. If a (very old) monitor and graphics card are restricted to an 8-bit display, the colours that can be shown will vary depending on whether the monitor is for a PC or a Mac. As such, many graphics programs have developed a 'web-safe' palette that displays 216 colours; that is, those system colours used by both PCs *and* Macs.

Navigation

Fundamental to hypertext markup language is the ability to create hypertext, links that enable users to move from document to document. The value of electronic documents on the Web is not simply that the protocols for displaying and for-matting information are handled by the server regardless of the operating system that is used by the visitor to a website, but also that they can connect easily to other documents. At its simplest, this consists of a link attached to a word, but hyperlinks may also be attached to images and other, multimedia elements on a page.

Good design is concerned not simply with the look and feel of a web page, therefore, but also the ease with which a site can be navigated. Are hyperlinks clear and easy to find? Is it obvious where a link will lead? As such, good design is concerned with the interface to a site as well as such things as use of typeface, colour and images.

Ideally, navigation tools should be consistent in terms of position and look: changing colours of hypertext links, for example, will simply confuse visitors, as will shifting navigation bars from the top to the side of pages. Providing feedback to users can be helpful – typically in the form of rollover buttons or hypertext links that change colour when the mouse rolls over them, telling the user that something will happen when that button or link is clicked.

Navigation, finally, is concerned with the overall structure of a site: it is typical to include a homepage – a set of links, instructions and text that indicates the nature of the site and provides a convenient starting point. Next there will follow a series of top-level pages, which again provide a nodal point for various items contained in the whole site, for example, a page of links to reviews or news items: a navigation bar of some sort – a collection of links or buttons that connects to top-level pages – is a common and useful navigation tool for websites. Beneath this top level, then, are the pages that contain the vast majority of information, but which do not usually have a link to them from every other page on the site.

Multimedia and interactivity

Although originally designed for text and image, audio-visual (AV) elements have quickly become important to a number of websites, particularly those aimed at a broadband audience. As the Internet grows and develops, and as more and more users connect to it via technologies such as ADSL, the Web will converge increasingly with media such as television and radio, though with its own, particular forms of interactivity.

Internet sites such as web radio stations or video channels typically employ one or more forms of *streaming* media (which we encountered in Chapter 6). The most common streaming AV formats are as follows:

- **ASF**: Advanced streaming format – a Microsoft format for video that enables high compression rates for streaming AV material across the Internet.
- **AVI**: Windows native video format, though this is slowly being replaced by WMV and ASF.
- **MP3**: A highly compressed format for music that strips out information that the listener cannot hear.
- **MPEG**: The Motion Pictures Expert Group is responsible for formalising various codecs for music and video: MPEG-2 is the level of video compression used on DVDs, but later versions with higher compression rates are often encountered on the Internet.
- **Quicktime**: Apple's native video format which, in its latest version, uses MPEG compression to achieve very small file sizes.
- **Real Video/Audio**: A streaming format developed specifically for the Web, Real is particularly popular for web radio.
- **SWF**: Shockwave for Flash, the proprietary but popular format employed by Macromedia's Flash software.
- **WMV/WMA**: Windows media video/audio, the latest incarnations of Microsoft's streaming technologies that offer high compression rates for music and video.

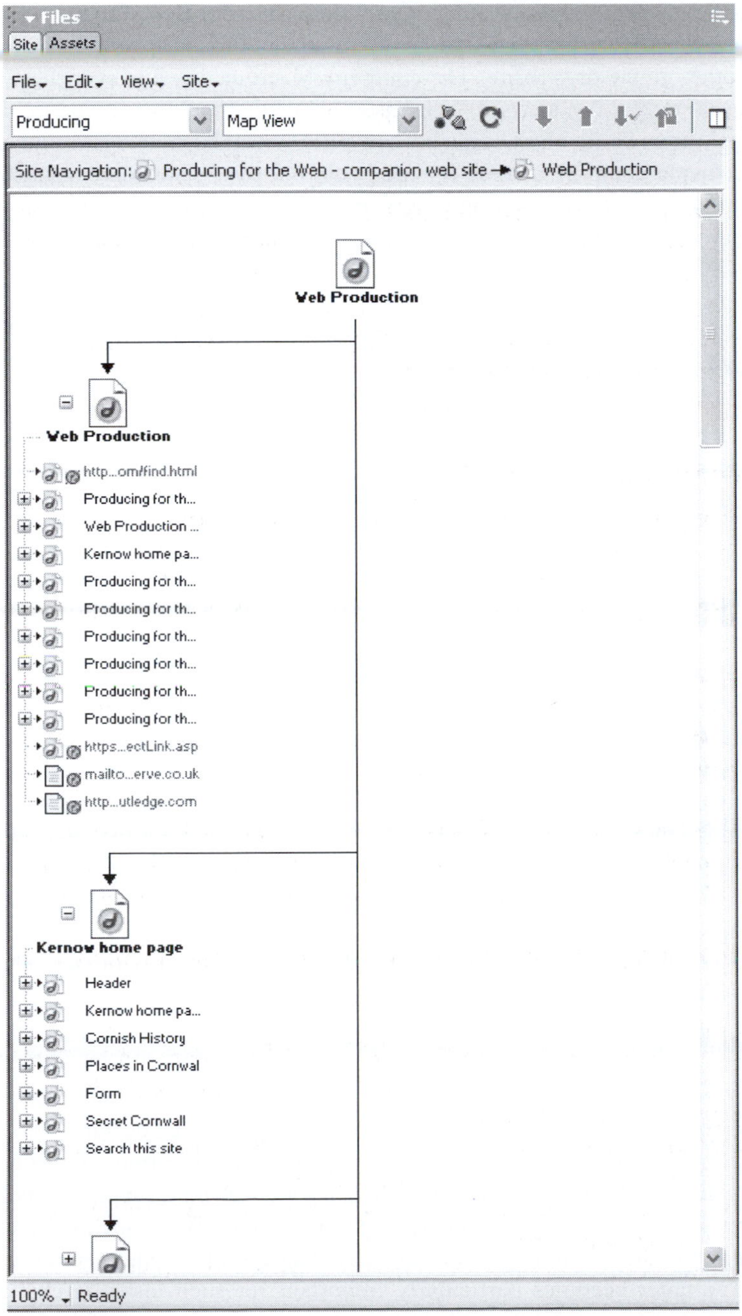

Figure 12.2 A map of the structure of a site as shown in the web editor Dreamweaver MX.

Multimedia formats such as Apple's Quicktime have developed to allow basic interactivity, particularly in the form of providing hot links that can be clicked to open another movie or website. The company Macromedia, however, has been instrumental in pushing forward Web-based interactive multimedia, particularly via its application Flash. Flash began life as a basic vector illustration and animation tool to provide compact images for the Web, but over successive versions it has grown into a fully functioning programming tool, capable of delivering fully functional applications for the Web that can collect and process information from visitors to a site.

The web designer's toolkit

While it is possible to create a website with little more than a text editor, designing all but the simplest of sites will be extremely time-consuming if you hand code every page. In addition, while most sites include (at the very least) pictures, you will also require some sort of image editor to photos and logos.

Web editors

A typical web editor offers a range of tools for laying out web pages and managing sites – very important once they begin to expand past a handful of pages. Unlike print DTP, which, at least until recently, was dominated by one software package, Quark XPress, web design has enjoyed considerably more competition; this said, Macromedia's Dreamweaver is perhaps the most widely used application, and will be referred to throughout this chapter.

The simplest task of creating a web page – organising text, images and multi-media elements in a layout – is offered by most web editors in WYSIWYG format (what you see is what you get). This is not true of every editor, however: some, such as HomeSite (formerly owned by Allaire, but now part of Dreamweaver), are code editors that display HTML code line by line. While this may be difficult to grasp, particularly for new designers, there are very good reasons for this: first of all, because different browsers render web pages slightly differently, no web editor can offer true WYSIWYG views for every browser; second, it is often easier to troubleshoot difficulties on a web page in code than on a visual design.

As well as common tools for inserting images, rollover buttons, multimedia elements such as Flash items or movies, then, a good web editor will also include a window for viewing HTML code (as well as for modifying such devices as cascading style sheets), and a site manager that displays all the pages contained in a site. The latter becomes particularly important for such tasks as changing components across a site: if the address to a top-level page changes, for example, modifying links on every page will become very laborious if you cannot perform a simple find and replace.

Some of the best web editors available are:

- **Adobe GoLive**: Originally designed for the Mac, GoLive has a slightly quirky interface but offers excellent support for advanced web design features, such as connecting to databases.
- **Macromedia Dreamweaver**: Probably the best all-rounder, the latest version of Dreamweaver, MX, also combines a range of tools for creating database-driven web applications. It incorporates excellent site management and reference tools, as well as a top code editor, HomeSite.
- **Microsoft FrontPage**: Popular with corporate users (it is bundled with certain versions of Office), FrontPage has lost some ground with professional web designers in recent years. None the less, it remains a decent editor and includes some advanced features that are supported by most ISPs.
- **NetObjects Fusion**: A good choice for the web design novice, Fusion hides most of the coding from the end-user and is extremely good in terms of offering template designs to create a website rapidly and easily.

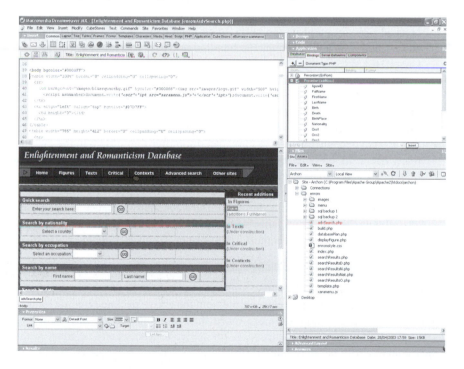

Figure 12.3 Dreamweaver MX has quickly become the favourite editor for web design professionals. This screenshot shows the main work areas in design and layout view on the left, with the properties panel where formatting is applied in the bottom left. To the right, the program displays a series of panels that cover a range of site management and coding tasks.

Image editors

Alongside a web editor, the next crucial item in a designer's toolkit is a good image editor. In this category, PhotoShop has long dominated the field – but its expense and exceptional print tools mean that other applications have now become popular. If you will be using an image editor simply to create and prepare graphics for the screen, PhotoShop may very well be overkill.

At its simplest, an image editor is used to crop and resize graphics so that they are suitable for web use; 300 dpi scans will simply slow down load times for pages, so image editors are often used to scale down photos and reduce file sizes as much as possible. In addition to this, image editors typically offer a wide range of tools for enhancing photos, not simply in terms of dramatic filters but also masking and repairing tools. Finally, web designers often need image editors to create graphics, such as logos or animated banners.

The most suitable image editors include:

- **Adobe PhotoShop**: Despite its expense, PhotoShop still remains the industry standard (for print as well as the Web) and is worth learning if you wish to practise web design professionally. It can handle any task required of a web editor, including animation via the bundled program ImageReady.
- **CorelDRAW!**: CorelDRAW! itself is a vector drawing program, but the package incorporates a suite of programs including a good photo editor and even an application for creating Flash compatible animations. While no single program is a market leader, CorelDRAW! is extremely good value for money.
- **Jasc Paint Shop Pro**: Another budget buy, Paint Shop Pro has developed over the years to become the next best image editor after PhotoShop in the eyes of many users. In general, it offers some 90 per cent of the tools available in PhotoShop's flagship program for less than one-fifth of the price.
- **Macromedia Fireworks**: Not quite in the same league as Dreamweaver and Flash, Fireworks is still the first choice for many because it integrates so well with these two programs. Although dedicated to Web, rather than print, use, it covers all web designers' requirements and is bundled as part of Macromedia's Studio MX package.

This list is by no means exhaustive: alternatives such as Illustrator or Freehand offer vector drawing tools that can complement the above packages, while budget applications such as PhotoSuite are more than suitable for the undemanding user; indeed, they may offer better tools for someone who wishes to create web-ready graphics with the minimum of fuss.

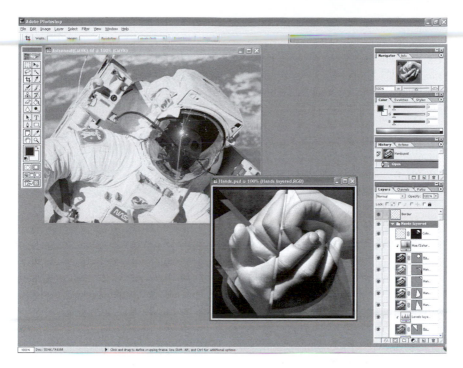

Figure 12.4 Adobe PhotoShop (here shown as version 6) has long been the chosen application for those working with print and, with recent versions, has also become a mainstay for web designers.

Multimedia tools

Image editing and layout cover most web designers' requirements, but there are still some other software packages that a user may wish to consider.

- **Flash and Shockwave**: Although interactive media are not restricted to Flash, this is the most popular application on the Web. Macromedia's flagship program, Flash MX, is more than a simple animator and may be used to develop online applications, but it is difficult for the new user to learn. Because of this, alternative animation programs such as Adobe LiveMotion or CorelRAVE have become popular. Another program from Macromedia, Director, was originally developed for CD applications but has been adapted to provide Internet-ready software in the form of Shockwave files: although difficult to learn, Director is probably the most fully functional multimedia program available and is also useful if you wish to provide 3D on your website.

- **Video editing**: Although broadband is slowly increasing in terms of usage, most sites still do not employ much video. This is likely to change in the future, and professional web designers need to be aware of the requirements of online video, particularly in terms of the codecs available to most users and how to compress video for the best effect. Premiere, from Adobe, is the most widely used semi-professional editor, while Cleaner from Discreet enables users to prepare video for a wide range of uses (including DVD).

- **Sound editing**: Related to the above, preparing audio for the Web is another task sometimes required of designers. Helix, from Real, is a useful tool for creating web radio, while Cleaner again provides codecs for converting wave files into highly compressed but usable sound files for online use.

Browsers and servers

Concerning browsers, most users will probably only ever use one: after the browser wars of attrition in the late 1990s, Microsoft's Internet Explorer has emerged as the lead player. This does not mean, however, that every visitor to a website will use the same browser and, although it is less important today than it was several years ago (not least because Microsoft has generally become more concerned with HTML and other web standards), part of a designer's toolkit will include multiple browsers to ensure that pages display as well as possible. Although it lags far behind IE, Netscape and its open source alternative Mozilla are the most important browsers still used by millions, with Opera becoming a favourite due to its quick render times. Alternatives, such as the Linux-based Konqueror or Apple's new browser Safari, are probably of little concern for most designers, though they do raise an important point: Windows is not the only operating system used to browse the Web, so wherever possible check how pages display on alternative systems such as Linux or MacOS.

Finally, when preparing sites it is often worth investing time if not money in a good web server: many advanced features of websites require server software to power them. For Windows users, Microsoft's Internet Information Server (IIS) is a respectable piece of software, but expensive if you need to purchase the Microsoft server operating system to power it. Most websites use the popular Apache server, which also has the advantage of being free (available from www.apache.org). Finally, a complex but powerful server application is Coldfusion, which has its own scripting language and is available as part of the Macromedia Studio MX package: the server version is expensive, but a single-machine developer release is available at no cost.

Designing a website

Over the following pages we will cover the basics of creating a simple site, outlining the fundamentals for designing pages in HTML as well as using a professional web editor, Dreamweaver MX, for more complex elements of page layout.

Preparation and planning

Planning your site and page design before laying out elements in HTML or an editor such as Dreamweaver can save you considerable time later on. First of all, sketch out the overall structure of your site, particularly which pages you expect to form a top level for your site (and, as such, will have links to them throughout the site). Second, draw a basic template for your page design – I would recommend doing this on paper: even if you are no artist, sketching out a layout using paper and pencil allows for considerably greater freedom when experimenting with ideas. When you are happy with this layout, and if you are using a web editor such as Dreamweaver, you can convert it into electronic format (either by scanning it into your computer or re-creating it in a drawing package) to use as a background drawing when designing your pages.

For more complex sites, you may wish to establish some sort of timetable to manage the project. Define your project into a series of tasks, each of which can be assigned deadlines and put in order. Breaking down a large project enables you to see what is required, and also allows you to plan for contingencies – for example, if you do not have time to complete one section as intended.

An important part of preparing your website is to take into account the work-flow of the project. You should be prepared to test your ideas at each stage: thus, for example, after outlining what you wish your website to consist of you should analyse what this will require in terms of pages; if the number of pages quickly grows, you may need to return to and simplify your original idea. When you move on to the stage of building the actual site, think in terms of building a prototype first, a set of pages that you will check for consistency and usability. If you think of your initial site as a prototype, you will be more prepared to test it at every step.

Creating a simple website in HTML

We will begin by creating the simplest type of web page in HTML. When learning to program, a typical convention is to create a 'Hello World' file, a simple example of the language or application. You can create the following in the code editor of Dreamweaver (go to View, Code in the menu if this editor is not visible), or by typing the instructions in a text editor such as Notepad. Once you have completed this first, simple Web page, save it as hello.htm and open it in your web browser. Opening this file in a web browser shows a page with a bold heading, separated by a horizontal line from a smaller bold heading and a short paragraph of text. The HTML that comprises this page may be divided into four parts. First of all, the line <!DOCTYPE HTML PUBLIC "-//W3C//DTD HTML 4.01 Transitional//EN"> provides some important information to the browser about how to render this page – its document type (indicated by the word DOCTYPE). While you do not need to include this line in a simple web page such as this, the World Wide Web Consortium has indicated a number of document types that may become important,

```
<!DOCTYPE HTML PUBLIC "-//W3C//DTD HTML 4.01
Transitional//EN">
<html>
<head>
        <title>Hello World</title>
</head>

<body>


              <center><h1>Hello World!</h1></center>
              <hr>
              <p><h2>Your first Web page</h2></p>
              <p>At its simplest, HTML works with text, formatting that
              text to emphasise certain features by <em>italicising</em>,
              <u>underlining</u> or making certain words
              <strong>bolder</strong>.</p>
</body>
</html>
```

as very different browsers (such as those for mobile phones) display documents in different ways. As such, it is worth adopting the habit of defining the document type of your pages, in this case the transitional HTML standard 4.01, which works in most current browsers. For more information on document types, see www. alistapart.com/stories/doctype/.

The next part of our page consists of the tags <html></html>. HTML works with pairs of tags, the final tag always using a forward slash (/) to indicate the end of any formatting. As you would expect, these two tags indicate that everything between them should be formatted by a browser as HTML.

Immediately following on from the first <html> tag is the <head></head> item, which typically includes information that is not displayed in the main browser window but which may, for example, be used to format web pages or house scripts that can be called upon by the main web page. Our simple page lists only one item in the <title></title> tag; as its name suggests, this is a title for the page that is displayed in the blue border at the very top of the web browser.

Beneath the <head></head> item is the most substantial part of our page: <body></body> is used to indicate the contents of a web page that will be displayed in the main window of the browser. Of the elements we have included here, <h1> and <h2> refer to different styles of headings, while the command <hr> inserts a 'horizontal rule' (a line) across the page. The tags <p></p> indicate paragraph breaks, and we have included some basic text formatting: <em></em> for emphasis (typically italics), <u></u> for underline and <strong></strong> to embolden text.

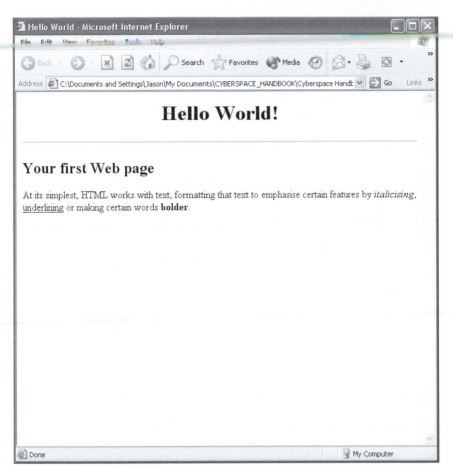

Figure 12.5 How your first web page should appear in a browser.

Preparing images

While we have created our first web page, pages that consist entirely of text tend to look very dull. The easiest way to liven them up is to make use of images.

Inserting an image into your web page requires the <img> element, with the tag src to indicate where the image will be found. For example, if you have an image of a car called Ferrari.jpg saved in a folder called 'images', the HTML to add your picture will look something like this: <img src='../images/Ferrari.jpg' width=56 height=32>. If you insert your image in an editor such as Dreamweaver, it will automatically add width and height tags to the img element, but even if you are hand coding it is a good idea to add the width and height of your image in pixels as this saves a little time when rendering a web page, the browser not having to work out the dimensions for an image before it is displayed.

In Dreamweaver, to add images, click on the Image button in the Insert panel, or go to Insert, Image. You will then need to navigate to the correct image on your hard drive before clicking OK in the dialog box that appears. Once you have added your image, either into its own layer or alongside text, take a look at the Properties palette (usually near the bottom of the screen). This provides you with important information about an element on the page, in this case your image: at the bottom of the Properties palette you will see an Align menu box, which aligns text to your image (right and left are the most useful).

Finally, bear in mind that text which runs too close to an image appears ugly, so enter a number for pixels (10 is usually a good number) to create an invisible border around the image.

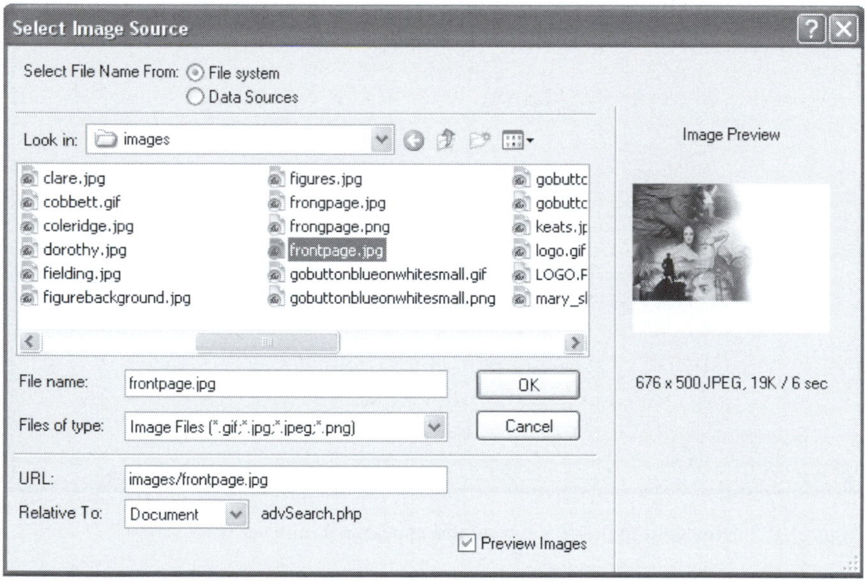

Figure 12.6 The Insert Image dialog box in Dreamweaver MX.

Layout using tables

Tables began as a means of showing information in a spreadsheet format, but quickly developed as a way of laying out more complex pages that did not simply run from top to bottom as in simple HTML. Tables are gradually being replaced by CSS as a way to format a page, but for the time being they remain a useful adjunct for web design.

For all but the simplest layouts, you will be best preparing your pages in a web editor: part of the advantage of tables is that they can be nested, one inside another, and this is what enables a designer to use them to create complex effects. The downside of this is that, for the hand coder, HTML code for tables becomes very complicated very quickly.

Tables are contained between the <table></table> tags and consist of rows and columns defined by the <tr></tr> (table row) and <td></td> (table data) elements. The table elements can be modified by tags for width (defined in pixels or percentage of the browser window), align, valign, border, cellspace and cellpadding. Alignment can be left, centre or right, valign (or vertical alignment) as top, middle or bottom, and border defines the width of line around the table: when using tables for page layout, this is usually set to 0. Cellspace and cellpadding determine the number of pixels between table cells and the extent to which content within those cells will be pushed into the centre.

The <tr> and <td> elements share many of the tags from their parent <table> elements, including width, align and valign. Another useful feature is the ability to set colspan and rowspan tags, defining whether a cell spans more than one column or row.

A simple table, then, would resemble the following:

```
<table>
        <tr>
                <td>Row 1, Column 1</td>
                <td>Row 1, Column 2</td>
        </tr>
        <tr>
                <td>Row 2, Column 1</td>
                <td>Row 2, Column 2</td>
        </tr>
</table>
```

When using an editor such as Dreamweaver, inserting a table is as simple as clicking on the Insert Table button or going to Insert, Table from the menu bar. This displays a dialog box where you can set such things as the width of the table, the number of rows and columns and cellspacing/padding. Once a table is added to your page, it can be modified further by changing its properties in the Property palette.

Adding links

One of the important features of web pages is the ability to link to other documents. Hyperlinks are added to pages by means of the <a></a> element, which surrounds the word or image that you wish to hotlink: in addition to the anchor element, links make use of a src tag (similar to that used for the img element, but in this case providing the address for the hyperlink to connect to) and other components such as a target, which tells the page where to load.

Hyperlinks work in two ways: absolute links include all information about an address – such as http://www.routledge.com – while relative links define a file in relation to the current page (for example, ../images/topbar.jpg). In general, you should use relative links for pages on your site and absolute links for external addresses.

Adding hyperlinks in an editor such as Dreamweaver is extremely easy: either click on the Hyperlink button in the Insert panel, or select the text or image you wish to use as a link and enter a valid address in the Properties palette.

Setting styles

In its earliest form, all information about the style and layout of a web page would be contained in an HTML file. Thus, for example, when you formatted a heading as style 1 or style 2, this would be represented by the tag <h1> or <h2> and then interpreted according to browser presets set by a visitor.

This poses a number of problems for web designers: first of all, it means that it is difficult to control the overall look and feel of a site (though one advantage of web pages is that users with eyesight difficulties, for example, can set different font sizes); second, designers who decide to change the layout of a site must go through each page making changes.

This is where style sheets are a huge bonus to working with text. While styles can still be set within an HTML document, if you create a style sheet in a text editor or using an editor such as Dreamweaver, it is possible to link to it from all your files: if you don't like the look of a particular heading – you wish it to be a different colour, for example – simply change the style sheet and your whole site will reflect those changes.

To create a style sheet in Dreamweaver, go to File, New and under the General tab select CSS Style Sheets (CSS stands for cascading style sheets, meaning that sheets can be placed one inside another, or 'cascaded'). Dreamweaver offers a number of template designs, and selecting one of these will show something resembling the following in the main code window:

```
body {
        background-color: blue;
        font-family: Arial, Helvetica, sanserif;
        font-size: 12px;
        line-height: 24px;
        color: yellow;
}
```

Alternatively, you can enter these items into a text editor. The body element indicates that this style sheet will affect text and colours contained in the main body of the HTML document, and the elements between the curly brackets indicate what components are to be set, in this case background and font colour (note American-English spellings), as well as font style (sanserif) and size, and the spacing between lines.

Style sheets control such things as text and background colour, positions of paragraphs and font or line sizes and are usually saved with the .css extension. To use a style sheet you must link to it, typically by inserting the following line of code into the <head> section of your HTML document: <link rel="stylesheet" href="style1.css" type="text/css">, replacing style1.css with the appropriate link to your style sheet. In Dreamweaver, create a web page as normal then go to Text, CSS Styles, Attach Style Sheet. In the dialog box that appears, navigate to the appropriate style sheet on your hard drive, and make sure that Link is selected in the Add As section. While you can import style sheets into HTML documents, editing a single style sheet will change the layout of an entire site if you link to a CSS file instead.

Adding complex features with Dreamweaver

For the remainder of this chapter, we will concentrate on Dreamweaver as an editor that provides additional powerful tools for managing sites, setting templates and creating database-driven web applications. In general, these functions are available in other professional level editors such as Adobe GoLive; indeed, it is possible to hand code most of these features, though the complexity of such coding lies beyond the remit of this book.

The Dreamweaver interface

Dreamweaver 4 made use of panels within the main interface to access important features, something that has been extended in MX. In the default view, panels for design, coding, creating applications and file management will be found on the right-hand side. To add Behaviors (DHTML or Javascript functions) to pages, for example, click on the Design panel and then the tab for Behaviors, then click the plus button to choose your Behavior. Go to Show Events For to select Behaviors to certain browsers, for example, all releases above 3 or only Netscape or Internet Explorer.

One of the most important panels in Dreamweaver is the one for File management, which includes tools for organising your site. Click on the Site tab and go to Site, New Site to define a root folder: this will hold all the pages you create and is important if you wish to use templates or site-wide features such as search and replace. After clicking New Site, Dreamweaver provides a series of dialog boxes that define where the local folder will be stored, whether you require a remote host, and what dynamic server technologies (if any) will be used.

Site management

In addition to these basics such as adding text and other media, Dreamweaver provides a highly customisable environment, only part of which we can cover here. We have already touched on the different code and design views, but the various panels on the right-hand side of the main work area also provide you with one-button access to a number of advanced features. In the Design section, for example, you can apply styles and behaviours (Javascript or Dynamic HTML functions) to your pages, while the Code panel allows you to change individual tags, add snippets of Javascript or HTML code, and browse through Dreamweaver's extensive reference library.

In the Files panel you will see a tab for the Site manager. To define a site, go to Site, New Site in this panel and enter relevant details such as where local files are stored and your server address. Once you have defined a site, you can use other features in Dreamweaver, such as the ability to create templates or change links site-wide.

To make a template, create a normal page, then go to File, Save as Template. Once a template is created, the basic components of a page are locked in place: to add new content you will need to define certain areas (such as a table or layer) as editable. Select the section you wish to update and click on Modify, Templates, Make Attribute Editable. With templates in place, if you wish to change the overall look and feel of a site you only need to edit one file.

Snippets, tags and extensions

If you have some experience of working with HTML, Dreamweaver simplifies the process by providing a range of tools under the Code panel. The Tag Inspector lists relevant attributes for each tag on your page, allowing you to fine-tune it by hand. Snippets are pieces of code that may be added to your page, and you can create new snippets by selecting code in Code view, right clicking and going to Create New Snippet. Dreamweaver 4 had introduced reference texts, and MX has extended these to include detailed books on web technologies such as HTML, Javascript and cascading style sheets.

Dreamweaver also allows you to use plug-ins, or extensions, to expand the program's capabilities. If you launch the Macromedia Extensions Manager and connect to Macromedia Exchange (www.macromedia.com/go/dreamweaver_exchange), you can download mini-applets designed to perform a range of tasks such as creating menus or adding random images. Once you have downloaded the extension you require, you use it by importing it into the Extensions Manager (File, Import Extensions). Click on the name of your new extension to see how it is accessed from within Dreamweaver, for example, by adding a line to the Commands menu or by creating a new tab in the Insert panel.

Dynamic features

Text and image still remain fundamental to web design, but Dreamweaver also supports a wide range of more dynamic features. Javascript and dynamic HTML components may be added with a few mouse clicks, while designers who work with applications such as Flash or Director can import Shockwave and Flash files quickly and easily.

The most commonly used dynamic features are rollover images, and these are added by clicking on the Rollover Image button in the Insert panel under the

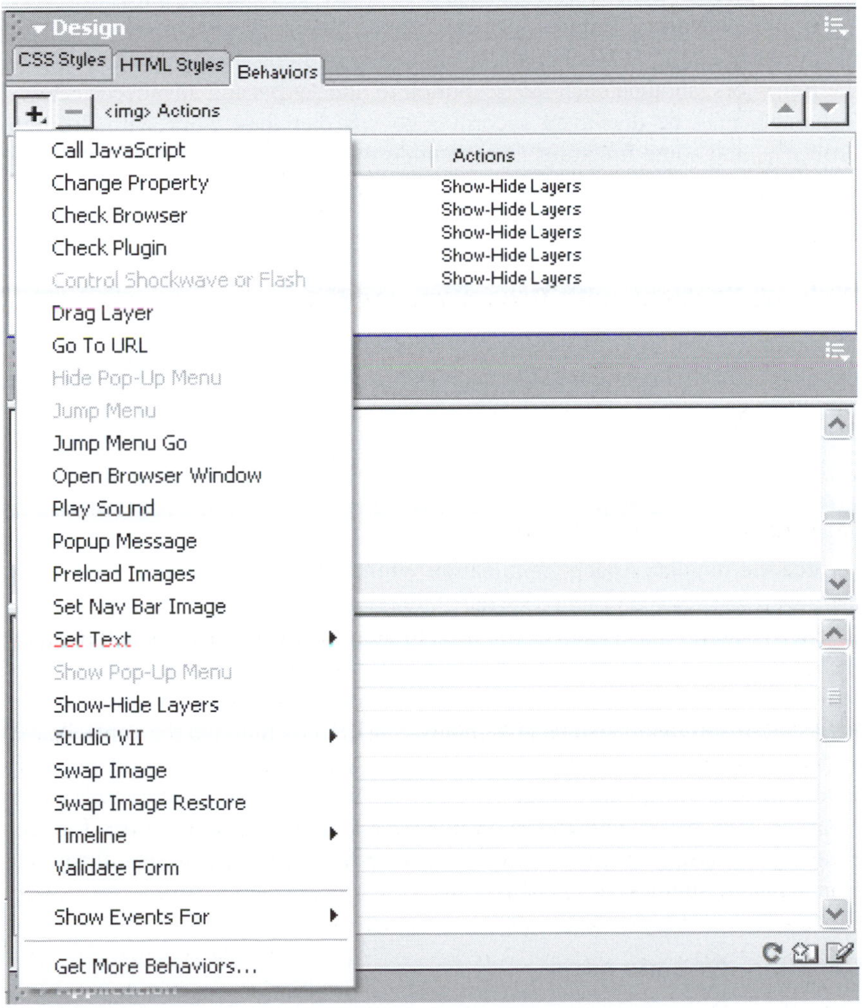

Figure 12.7 The Behaviors tag in the Design panel is where you add complex Javascript and DHTML features to your web pages using Dreamweaver.

Common tab. In the dialog box that appears, select two images for your rollover, provide a link and name, then click OK. Other components may be found under other tabs on the Insert panel. The Media tab, for example, is where you will find buttons to add Java, Shockwave or Flash applets: click each button and navigate to the appropriate file on your system.

A good way to add interactivity to a site is to include a form to collect information from visitors. Not surprisingly, commonly used form elements are found under the Forms tab. To define which part of a page will collect information from users, click the Form button and then add elements such as text fields, menus and different styles of buttons (radio, check box, submit or reset) to your form.

For more advanced features, you can take advantage of Dreamweaver's built-in Javascript and DHTML functions, or behaviors. In the Design panel, click on the Behaviors tab, then click the '+' button to add scripts and advanced features. Behaviors may be displayed according to whether they work with different browsers, and some functions are available only with certain HTML tags (for example, images or forms). If you no longer require a behavior, click on the '–' button to remove it.

Web applications with Dreamweaver MX

The latest version of Dreamweaver, MX, integrates the active data features that were previously part of UltraDev, such as the ability to create a database-driven web. If you wish to use Dreamweaver to create active sites, a web server is fundamental to the process: pages cannot simply be stored in a folder on a hard drive as with static sites, but instead requests from the browser must be interpreted by server software and HTML output accordingly. Windows NT, 2000 and XP Professional users will have Microsoft's Internet Information Server (IIS), but alternatives include the popular Apache application while Macromedia's MX Studio also includes a test version of its powerful Coldfusion server.

Once your server is installed, you need to define a site that uses an active server technology, such as Microsoft's Active Server Pages (ASP) or Coldfusion, and register a database using Microsoft's ODBC Administrator (the location of this varies under different versions of Windows: in XP, it is found in the control panel under Administrative Tools). The final step once your page is laid out is to bind your registered data source to the page. While this is more complex than creating static pages, Dreamweaver does most of the important work for you, creating database (SQL) queries that can search and organise your information from dynamic sources.

Creating dynamic sites

If you have the Studio version of MX, you will also have a copy of the personal version of ColdFusion, a powerful server that allows you to create dynamic websites. To make a database-driven site, first of all you must register a data source

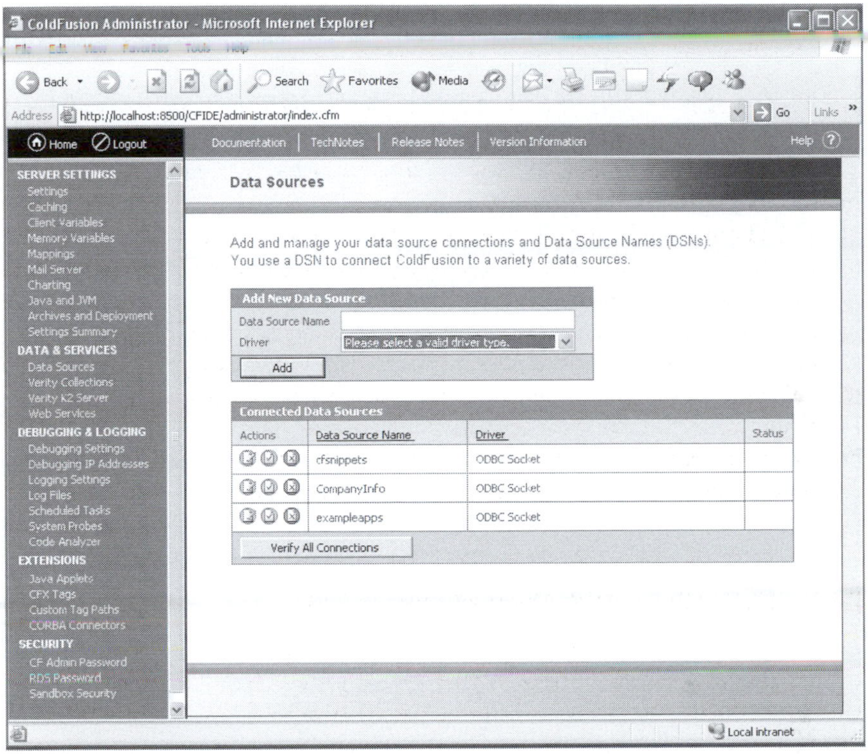

Figure 12.8 The Studio MX release of Dreamweaver includes a powerful server application, ColdFusion, as well as copies of Fireworks and Flash.

using Microsoft's ODBC Data Source Administrator (which you will find in the control panel). Open the Administrator and click on the DSN tab: installing ColdFusion adds a couple of sample DSN sources, but you can include more by clicking the Add button and selecting a data source and type.

Once you have registered a data source, you need to make sure that it is available to ColdFusion. To do this, open ColdFusion, enter your administrator password, and click on the menu entry for Data Sources under Data and Services. This lists databases that will be available to your site: if your database is not listed, enter the name of the data source you created in the ODBC Administrator, select the appropriate data type and click Add. You will now be able to use that database to create a dynamic site.

Once your database is registered and a site with dynamic server technology has been set up in Dreamweaver, you are ready to begin adding data sources to your page. The structure of a page is laid out as normal, but its content is drawn from the data source. To do this, click on the Application panel and, under the Databases tab, select the database you wish to use by clicking on the Plus tab. This will display sample ColdFusion databases as well as any others that you will have added.

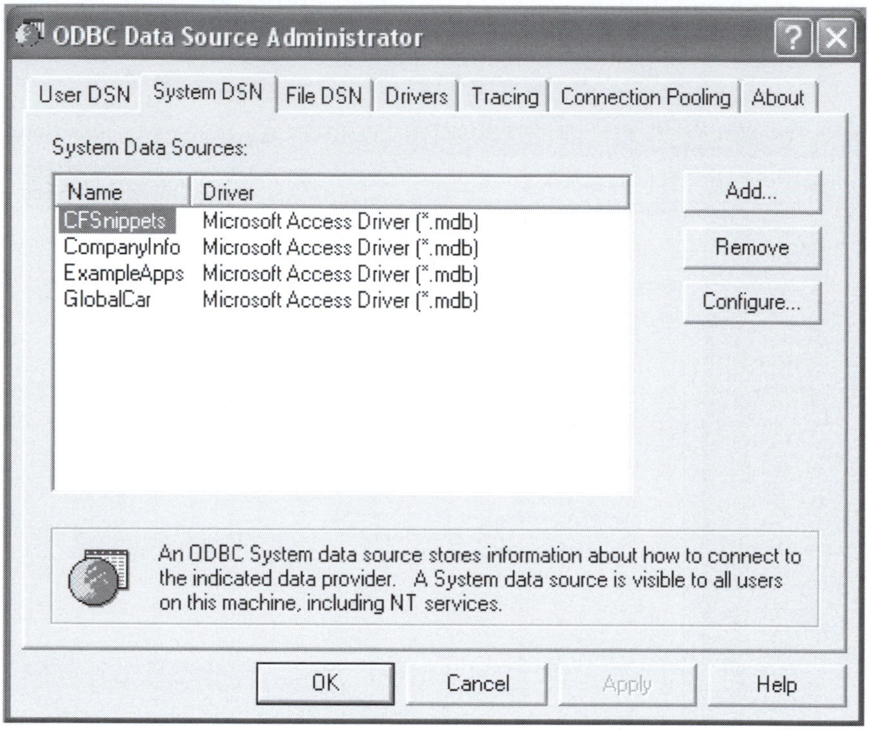

Figure 12.9 To use a database with ColdFusion and Dreamweaver, you must register it as an ODBC source.

After you have selected the database you wish to use, the next step is to add a Recordset. From the Bindings tab in the Applications panel, click on the Plus button and select Recordset. In the dialog box that appears, you select a database, a table from that database, and the relevant columns you wish to use, as well as any filters or passwords. Once your Recordset is defined, you add fields to your web page from the Application tab in the Insert panel, beginning with a Master/Detail Page Set that will output the results of your records. For more information, look under the Developing Applications Rapidly section of Dreamweaver's online help.

Publishing your site

Unless your site is to remain private, you will wish to publish it to a web server using file transfer protocol (FTP) software. FTP, unlike email, is used to transfer files to a public server rather than between individuals. FTP clients may be stand-alone programs such as WS_FTP for Windows or Fetch for Macs, or are incorporated into the browser with Navigator and Internet Explorer 5 and above.

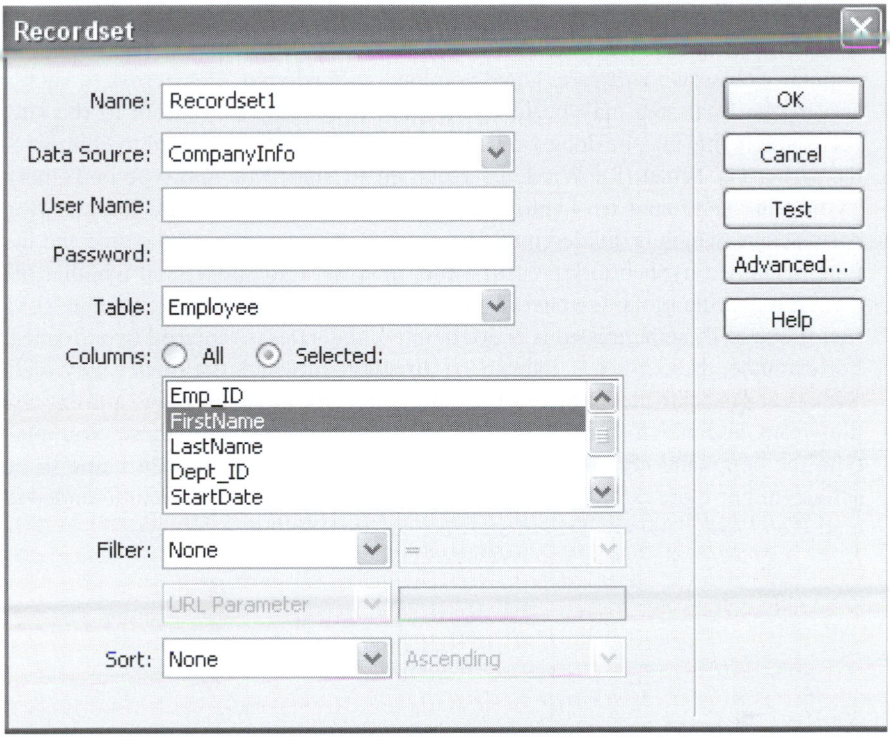

Figure 12.10 Once your database has been registered, you can add it as a Recordset to your pages in Dreamweaver to create a dynamic website.

It should be noted that the FTP capabilities in these browsers are fairly basic, and may be used to transfer files to and from a server as long as it is set up without any peculiarities (such as using a different port to the standard FTP port). More complex programs include WS_FTP (www.ipswich.com). To connect to an FTP server, enter the address in the browser which usually begins with ftp:// rather than http://; for a private directory on an ISP's server, this will usually be in the format ftp://userID:password@servername.

Once files are placed on to a site, directories and folders must be established to contain files, permissions set for files that need to be read or executed, and any old files deleted and cleared away. Windows NT, 2000 and .Net servers enable users to set permissions on different files down to the level of individual files as well as directories. In most cases, executable files (that is, applications that must run on the server as well as be read by the browser) will be contained in a folder in which the permissions are set accordingly; it is highly unlikely, unless you have administrator privileges to the site, that you will be able to set a folder as executable. However, other files can be hidden by right clicking on the file and changing the file properties.

While Windows is gaining ground as a web server, most servers on the Internet run the UNIX or Linux operating systems to host sites, with Apache being the most popular web server software. Once you have copied your files across to such a server, the final step may be to make them accessible to visitors to the site. Increasingly this may be done via FTP programs, but you may need to connect to the server via Telnet (for Windows users, go to Start, Run and type in Telnet). Typing the command ls –l into the Telnet client provides a file list showing permissions, which is divided into four fields, – rwx rwx rwx, indicating the file type (usually a hyphen to represent a file, or d for a directory) and whether the owner, a specific group or other users can read (r), write to (w) or execute (x) a file: if one of these permissions is not granted, the letter is replaced by a hyphen. For example, d rwx r-x r – indicates a directory in which the owner may read, write to and execute files as he or she wishes, a specific group may read and execute files from, and which all other users may only read. To change these, you must type the command chmod followed by +r, +w or +x and the file name to be activated. For more information on using Unix servers, you are recommended to read *Web Production for Writers and Journalists* (Whittaker 2002b).

Part IV

Regulations, institutions and ethics

13 Regulation and cybercrime

Cyberspace has brought into sharp focus some of the issues facing national law: although other media (satellite broadcasting, for example) share some of the features of the Net as a potentially global medium, the ease with which online production may be decentralised and shifted around the world means that governments and legislators face a much more difficult task when seeking to fit the Internet into existing legislative frameworks.

Should one country be able to influence what appears online in another nation state, or at least how that information is transmitted, as appeared to happen in the recent case involving Yahoo!, which was accused of making available Nazi memorabilia to French citizens? In addition, while crossing international boundaries poses a set of issues that will be explored in this chapter, a new medium also raises difficulties for current legislation in itself, for example, the ease with which digital copying, combined with the distributive network of the Internet, enabled Napster to become an infamous phenomenon.

Key areas of policy development with regard to new media have been around intellectual property, privacy and freedom of expression, as well as the concern of how best to deal with criminal activity such as fraud, exchanges of illegal material such as images of child abuse, and even terrorism. During the late 1980s and early 1990s, it was common to hear cyberspace described as the new Wild West, a frontier society that would not – even could not – be regulated. This is patently no longer true: while the international nature of the Internet makes some issues of regulation difficult to deal with, the 1990s were merely a period of time when the law was catching up with new technology.

Whether cyberspace *should* be regulated, however, or how it should be governed, is a very different question. Many of those involved with the development of cyberspace, particularly in its early years, have taken a largely libertarian stance, most notably in the case of organisations promoting freedom of speech, such as the Electronic Frontier Foundation (www.eff.org), or businesses interested in ecommerce who did not want government interference. At the same time, governments and other socio-political groups have become increasingly concerned about the effect of information and communication technologies on society. As Stein and Sinha (2002: 410) observe:

> ICTs are enmeshed in the social and cultural fabric of nations. Information and communication are part of the shared national symbolic environment, as well as the environment of other social or communal formations. Consequently, many nations are concerned with how ICTs may impact their social and cultural life. For example, many nations fear that the availability of obscene, racist or blasphemous speech on the Internet will have a corrupting influence on their societies.

Cybercrime

The rapid development of cyberspace has seen growth in crime online. Some activities, such as breaking into networks or exploiting weaknesses in systems using applications designed to take advantage of such networks, could not exist before the invention of computers. Others, however, such as fraud, spying or even terrorism, are simply the extension of actions that existed long before information technologies broke into the realms of cyberspace.

In this section, we shall explore some of the different aspects of cybercrime, from hacking and cracking to online fraud and various forms of espionage. It is worth bearing in mind however that with an international medium such as the Internet it is not always clear what constitutes a crime: obviously international law has become increasingly important throughout the twentieth century, but not all laws are signed up to by all nations across the world and, in any case, many states that still regard themselves as sovereign do not always agree about where the limits of their jurisdiction end and those of other bodies begin.

It is fairly easy to point to examples of states with a strongly authoritarian stance towards cyberspace, such as China and Iran, countries that seek to impose restrictions on what can be accessed by their citizens. Conflicts can also rise, however, between countries which have more liberal regimes with regard to cyberspace, as, for example, in 2000 when French authorities prosecuted the portal Yahoo! for permitting the sale of Nazi-related memorabilia on its auction site. In addition, especially as we shall see with regard to cyberspying and sabotage, such actions are often committed in the covert interests of democratic governments, further greying the edges of cybercrime.

Donn Parker (1998) distinguishes between computer crimes, in which the perpetrator makes use of special knowledge about computer technologies, from cybercrime, in which the crime is committed using the Internet or requires specific knowledge about networked cyberspace in order to proceed. Probably a more useful distinction, made by Steven Furnell in his book *Cybercrime* (2002), is between those crimes where computers are used in a supporting capacity, but the crime itself pre-dates the emergence of such technologies (for example, fraud and misuse of personal data), and those crimes where the action is a direct outcome of information technologies (for example, viruses or hacking). This second example, namely, computer-focused crime rather than computer-assisted crime, is more important to this chapter.

The extent of cybercrime

Computer-related crimes have increased dramatically since the 1980s, as statistics in Table 13.1 from the UK Audit Commission demonstrate, rising nearly sevenfold in the decade from 1984 to 1994 (although there was a slight decrease in reported incidents from 1994 to 1998). The estimated cost of such abuse was £1.1 million in 1984, but nearly £3.3 million in 1998, while a report by the National High Tech Crime Unit (www.nhtcu.org) estimated that worldwide cybercrime cost $1.6 trillion in 2001.

Table 13.1 Reported computer crime incidents in the UK

	Fraud	*Theft*	*Hacking*	*Viruses*	*Other*	*Total*
1984	60	17	–	–	–	77
1987	61	22	35	–	–	118
1990	73	27	26	54	–	180
1994	108	121	47	261	–	537
1998	67	88	56	247	52	510

Source: UK Audit Commission

Statistics from the Computer Security Institute and FBI show a similar growing trend, with reported incidents of computer crime up by 50 per cent in the five years from 1996 to 2001. At the same time, these statistics probably underestimate the real extent of cybercrime, as many companies that are affected by hackers or potential fraudsters do not always report such incidents because they believe it will affect public perception of their sites. None the less, it is clear that computer crime is growing: according to detective sergeant Clive Blake from the Metropolitan Police Computer Crime Unit in London, 'Computers are the future of crime. . . . They will become as crucial to the criminal as a gun or getaway vehicle' (cited in Furnell 2002: 26).

Cybercrime covers the following areas: hacking into a system, theft of information or espionage, fraud, sabotage of data, denial of service, virus writing and spoofing (pretending to be at a different IP address). Furnell distinguishes three types of abuser that are important to bear in mind when dealing with cybercrime: the first type, and the one usually concentrated on by the media, is the external perpetrator, the archetypal myth of the hacker breaking into a system; the second type are internal perpetrators, either those who masquerade as other users or evade any form of auditing or control over their actions on a network; finally, there are malfeasors who are authorised to use a system but abuse their privileges. The latter two are more likely to be perpetrators, sometimes even unwilling abetters, of cybercrime.

Security consultants often explain that, when performing a security audit, one of the first tasks is to pretend to be the IT manager: having forgotten a password, they ask a member of staff for a user name and password in order to log on – almost without fail their 'authority' is never questioned and they are provided with the details they (or a would-be hacker) required to enter the system. Indeed, as The Human Firewall Council reported at the 2002 London Infosec Conference, human management issues remained a much worse threat than hardware and software flaws, with 90 per cent of employees willing to run unknown executable files or documents with unsafe macros. As Sarah Gordon, an adviser at the IBM Thomas Watson Research Center, remarks with regard to corporate security, 'stereotyping [cybercriminals] can be dangerous' (cited in Power 2000: 10).

Hacking and cracking

Probably most people who think of cybercrime immediately associate such activities with hackers. This is an extremely emotive word that tends to be poorly defined: the earliest hackers had no interest in criminal activities, seeking rather to understand computer systems as fully as possible. Certainly in this book we will devote more attention to hackers as pursuing a particular ethic; that is, a relationship with new technologies.

None the less, despite attempts to distinguish such computer enthusiasts from criminals, for example, by using the term 'crackers' for the latter, there are large swathes of computer crime for which the best word still seems to be 'hacker'. This probably reflects the ambiguity at root in the process of hacking, where it is potentially a very small distance from understanding a system fully to exploiting it for personal, possibly criminal, ends. David Tetzlaff (2000) provides useful distinctions between computer users in this grey area, for example, hackers who were originally computer improvisers, seeking to push the best performance they could get from a system, crackers (specialising in breaking copy protection), pirates (anyone who obtains software illegally on a regular basis) and warez traders. The latter, the real subject of Tetzlaff's paper, can be distinguished from pirates in that while pirates will generally attempt to make commercial gain from illegally distributed software, warez are often collected as trophies of technical expertise. As David Pogue remarked, 'Warez are like baseball cards; their value is the prestige of ownership' (cited in Tetzlaff 2000: 108). Illegal activities based on any of these groups are sometimes grouped together under the term 'Black Hat'.

Typical criminal hacker activity includes financial and credit card fraud, writing malware (such as viruses), breaking copy protection on commercial software or entertainment goods (such as DVDs), and spying/sabotage. Many of these will be dealt with in more detail later in this chapter, but it is worth looking at a couple of examples of hackers that demonstrate something of criminal hacker activity. In 2001, the Federal Computer Incident Response Center (www.fedcirc.gov) reported 6,000 attacks on federal agency networks, ranging from website graffiti to root server hacks, up from 586 in 2000 and 580 in 1999 (Winder 2002).

According to the 1999 *Guinness Book of Records*, Kevin Mitnick was the world's most notorious hacker. Throughout the 1980s and early 1990s, Mitnick engaged in a hacking spree that involved breaking into computers belonging to major software companies, phone companies and even the Pentagon. Having gained a large number of credit card numbers, trade secrets and proprietary software, Mitnick made the mistake of targeting the home computer of a security expert, Tsutomu Shinomura, who was a research fellow at the San Diego Super-computer Center. Shinomura's personal interest in the case led to Mitnick's arrest in 1995, and he was eventually sentenced to more than four years' imprisonment in 1999, most of which time had already been spent in jail following his arrest (Furnell 2002; Power 2000).

Mitnick was a hacker with a long record of activity, but a more surprising instance occurred early in 2000 when large online companies such as Yahoo!, Buy.com, Amazon and eBay reported significant downtime. The surprise was not so much the attack itself: Distributed Denials of Service (DDoS), where hundreds, or even thousands, of computers attached to the Internet are used to make false requests to a server slowing traffic to a crawl, were becoming more common by 2000; rather, it was the identity of the perpetrator, known online as Mafiaboy, a Montreal teenager, the name of whom could not be revealed under Canadian law when he was arrested as he was only fourteen years old. Ironically, as Verton (2002) observes, despite the differences in their ages there are a considerable number of similarities between Mitnick and Mafiaboy, not least that neither was especially good at the technical process of hacking itself (one of the reasons they were caught), but much better at marketing themselves as computer experts. The most significant difference was the way the authorities responded to each activity: the Mafiaboy investigation involved more than a hundred agents in Canada and the USA, compared to the three agents working full-time on the Mitnick case (Verton 2002: 88).

Cyberterrorism

In the months following 11 September 2001, when members of Al Qaida hijacked planes that were then flown into the World Trade Center and the Pentagon, the focus on cybercrime has shifted from concentrating on perceived threats from hackers to terrorism. The use of video by Osama bin Laden indicated his own perception of how the media could be effective as a tool for propaganda (having taken on board at least some lessons from the West), and experts quickly began to warn that the Internet was vulnerable to cyberterrorists.

Thus, warned Karl Auerbach, a board member of ICANN, the thirteen root-name servers vital for routing Internet traffic worldwide represented a clear line of attack:

if all thirteen were out of action simultaneously, remote servers could only be accessed directly by using numerical addresses. Likewise, in late 2001, Gartner took the almost unprecedented step of warning businesses to move from Microsoft's Internet Information Server (IIS) to rivals such as Apache or iPlanet due to perceived security threats. The immediate cause of the warning was a virus attack, Nimda, which affected the servers of several major organisations. The worm was unrelated to events of 11 September, but indicated the ways in which future terrorists could target commerce and communication.

Reaction was, not surprisingly, most severe in the USA – which saw President Bush sign the USA Patriot Act into law in October 2001, easing many restrictions on electronic surveillance and wiretapping. In the EU, however, governments also moved to counter increased terrorist activity. The Council of Europe rushed through its Convention on Cybercrime in response to the attack, and the UK Parliament passed the Anti-terrorism, Crime and Security Act 2001 (ACSA), broadening the definition of terrorist organisations to include cyberterrorists for the first time, defining these as a person who interferes with or disrupts electronic systems (Winder 2002).

Even before 11 September, security experts had begun to worry about the potential for cyberterrorist activity across the Internet, the perfect environment, according to Simson Garfinkel, for the 'irrational terrorist' (2000: 211). By irrational terrorists, Garfinkel means individuals often acting alone and not to further a common cause: such terrorists are not interested in negotiation, and one example (though an ironic one with regard to cybercrime) is the Unabomber, a former maths professor named Theodore Kaczynski, who targeted technological organisations between 1978 and 1995. At the same time that it is difficult to monitor individuals, observes Garfinkel, it is possible to monitor the movement of materials such as explosives and nuclear resources that could be used in terrorist activities. Likewise, Neil Barrett, of Information Risk Management, argues that cyberterrorist claims in the wake of 11 September have been alarmist, and that while hacking into a water system was possible it would also be extremely difficult to make disastrous changes without being noticed: 'Hacking into utilities networks is harder than putting a bomb somewhere. Terrorists will go for tried and tested methods' (cited in Akass and Middleton 2002: 16).

Cyberwar

One of the most popular visions of hacking (for example, in the 1983 film *War Games*) is of the individual hacker infiltrating military systems, causing mayhem that his (and, as with most hacker myths, it is usually 'he') wits manage to prevent from falling into disaster. While there is undoubtedly a strong link between hacking and espionage, the direct relationship between military activity and infiltration of networks, particularly across the Internet, is a much murkier area, more likely to be sponsored by government bodies than lone operators. None the less, such operators do exist: in 2001, for example, Ehud Tenenbaum, also known as 'The

Analyser', was fined $18,000 and given a two-year suspended prison sentence after admitting to breaking into US Department of Defense networks. Tenenbaum was said to have almost started a cyberwar alarm in 1988 after exploiting weaknesses in the network.

One of the first cases of cyberwar to come to the attention of the wider world occurred in 1995, when fifty-four Serbian sympathisers attacked network installations in Croatia, and Internet conflicts between Palestinian and Israeli hackers have resulted in events such as the theft of a database containing personal information on 700 members of the American Israeli Public Affairs Commission. Similarly, after the Chinese/US split following the capture of an America P-3 spy plane in 2001, pro-Chinese supporters attacked at least six US government sites, releasing a worm that defaced 8,500 servers (Kidner 2001); in return, a northern Californian company SafeWeb, funded with money from the CIA via its technology company In-Q-Tel, provided information on human rights concerns in China as well as software for users to cover their tracks. Technology has always been a part of warfare: indeed, argues Manuel de Landa in his book *War in the Age of Intelligent Machines* (1991), tactics and strategy, offence and defence could be the principal agents in the technological, political, economic and even social developments of society. What is new is the way in which cyberwar is becoming an increasingly important component.

As Hall (2001: 119) remarks, the 1999 Kosovan conflict was probably the most comprehensively reported war in history, but one where NATO appeared to lose control of the information war online:

> While the Serbs were unable to compete on equal terms with NATO in the local propaganda war, with leaflet drops, airborne TV and radio transmitters disrupting terrestrial programming and, when all else failed, the bombing of RTS headquarters along with the country's civilian telephone and computer networks, they were able to conduct an alarmingly effective Netwar which left NATO looking outdated, out of touch and even vulnerable.

As Taylor (2000) remarks, while only one in ten Serbs used the Internet during the war, it was more highly placed than NATO TV (though less effective than the 104 million leaflets dropped during the conflict). Certainly the USA appears to have learnt that the information war must be continued online as well as in the field and traditional media: as Defense Secretary Donald Rumsfeld told the *New York Times*, 'When we "invade the enemy's territory," we may well be invading his cyberspace' (cited in Rawlinson 2002: 36).

Fraud and computer misuse

Throughout the 1980s, it was increasingly clear that legislation was required to deal with computer crime, which in turn led to the Computer Misuse Act (CMA) 1990. The CMA covers three types of offence, from simple unauthorised access to information, to illegal modification of such material or use of it to commit further offences, carrying up to five years' imprisonment or an unlimited fine.

One of the most common examples of computer misuse is online fraud, particularly via credit cards. Worldwide credit fraud was estimated to be worth around $6 billion in 2001 according to the FBI, and although only 2 per cent of credit card transactions were carried out online in that year about half of those losses came from online business.

Credit card fraud is the most common type of financial computer crime, but by no means the only kind. Online thefts, particularly from banks, have understandably been a cause of concern to authorities (one convicted hacker, Shi Biao, was even executed in 1993 for the theft of £122,000 from the Agricultural Bank of China), and more sophisticated crimes include using the Internet to manipulate information. Posting financial misinformation in cyberspace typically takes place for reasons of fraudulent profiteering, which is very different from insider dealing where someone uses valuable and confidential information to trade in company shares before that information becomes more widely available. Misinformation, on the other hand, is aimed at falsely inflating or decreasing share values in order to sell at profit or buy more cheaply. One highly publicised example of this took place in 2000 when a securities trader based in Houston, Fred Moldofsky, issued nineteen false press releases claiming that Lucent Technologies, the world's largest phone equipment manufacturer, expected its earnings to fall short of market expectations, causing Lucent's share price to drop by 3.6 per cent in March that year. Moldofsky was found guilty of securities fraud a year later.

While fraud targeted at large banks and financial houses attracts most attention, however, the most common types of online fraud are very small scale, involving credit card misuse and auction sites such as eBay, which estimated in early 2002 that one in 40,000 auctions was fraudulent (out of a potential 1.5 million transactions a day). Initially, auction sites had tended to take a *laissez-faire* attitude to activities on their sites, but a number of well-publicised cases of fraud in 2001, where buyers did not receive goods, prompted many of them, such as QXL, to remove fraudulent sellers. Nor are all auction scams particularly small: one of the most celebrated was the sale of a fake Richard Diebenkorn painting on eBay in 2000 for $135,000, with fraudsters placing false bids to drive up the price.

Fighting cybercrime

While technologies are frequently used to perpetrate offences, they are also increasingly employed to solve crime both online and off. Equally important is the legislative and regulatory infrastructure to deal with crimes that, by taking place in cyberspace, fall outside the remit of traditionally national legal bodies. In 2002, twenty-six members of the Council of Europe and four non-member states (including the USA) signed a Convention on Cybercrime, aimed at creating cross-border cybercrime laws. The Convention covered four main areas: fraud, viruses, child pornography and copyright violation. None the less, despite this agreement, effective international agreement is not likely to arrive soon: individual states would then need to ratify the Convention, implementing it into national law, and some countries disagree with certain protocols such as those governing racism and xenophobia.

The year 2002 saw the introduction of the National High Tech Crime Unit (NHTCU), a national body that supplements traditional county or metropolitan units, representing a step towards recognition of the national and international nature of much cybercrime. Principal targets of the NHTCU, which received £25 million funding in 2001, include fraudsters, paedophiles and hackers.

Information technologies are not necessarily used just to fight crimes committed in cyberspace. Other techiques available to police include software profiling, as with the system called Rigel, developed in Vancouver, which creates a graphical display of the scene of a crime and surrounding areas to construct a 3D surface map of potential areas where a suspect may live. A similar application, PowerCase, produced by Harlequin Inc in Cambridge, Massachusetts, was used effectively in Toronto in 1999 to catch a suspect, Eli Stewart Nicholas, who had been dubbed the Bedroom Rapist.

There have been a few high-profile success stories in the prosecution of various types of cybercrime, but there have also been more than a few problems with law enforcement. It has already been remarked that many businesses are unwilling to report attacks on their systems lest these be seen as evidence of insecurities. What is more, as Furnell (2002: 215) remarks, since

> the likelihood of even being prosecuted for hacking in the U.S. is 1 in 10,000 (and the odds of being imprisoned are even less), it can be questioned whether the sentences of hackers such as Mitnick . . . are genuinely fair, or whether they are effectively part of a 'show trial' approach, resulting from the hacker's own celebrity.

Copyright and intellectual property

Copyright refers to limitations on copying certain types of intellectual property (such as text, images and music) without the explicit permission of the person who produced that property, put in place for a certain length of time. For different types of artists, copyright has been an important issue since at least the eighteenth century, when booksellers argued that their trade had to be protected to prevent competitors from pirating their goods without providing a return both to the writer who produced a text and the merchant selling that product. Throughout the twentieth century, and despite protections such as the Berne Convention and Unesco Universal Copyright Convention, technologies (for example, audio- and videotape) have sparked off copyright crises because producers have seen the ability to copy easily as detracting from their markets. These analog technologies, however, have barely attracted the opprobrium and invective heaped on cyberspace because digital techniques are capable of copying without any degradation of quality compared to the original.

If digital media provide the main villains for mass piracy, however, they also supply new techniques for enforcing much more rigorous control over who views and uses certain items, where and for how long. Lawrence Lessig (2001) has argued that the current copyright law is balanced, providing authors with the right to take unauthorised copiers to court but also providing users with some rights, preventing the author from dictating what a purchaser does once they have purchased a piece of intellectual property. This, however, could alter due to changes that have been in progress during the past decade, which is aimed at wrapping data in software – something not protected by the balances of current copyright law. As Lessig points out, 'software gets 95 years of copyright protection. By the time the Mac OS finally falls into the public domain, no machine will be able to run it' (2001: 80).

Furthermore, changes to intellectual property rights reflect an attempt to transform public notions of ownership, away from outright possession of material goods to a model closer to renting, whereby consumers buy only the right to use information. Not surprisingly, the public has frequently been resistant to such a transformation, although the ease with which digital information can be copied (and the eagerness with which many people copy that data) has forced a crisis that is only slowly being worked through.

Digital Millennium Copyright Act

The most dramatic changes to copyright law may be seen in the 1998 Digital Millennium Copyright Act (DMCA), although this was the result of lobbying by the World Trade Organisation (WTO) that began in the early 1990s. The WTO and the UN body the World Intellectual Property Organisation (WIPO) set up a working committee to establish a global standard for copyrights and patents. The 1996 Copyright Treaty they set up, as well as other treaties such as that for database copyright, extended certain areas of copyright protection and tended to neglect fair use. As a result of these treaties, the Database Investment and Intellectual Property Antipiracy Act (DIIPAA) and Digital Millennium Copyright Act were passed: one reason for the latter act was that Disney did not wish to release copyright on important brands such as Mickey Mouse, which were nearing the end of their period of copyright protection.

The DMCA explicitly forbids reverse-engineering or circumventing copy-protection mechanisms, in addition to specifying what constitutes fair use in a digital environment. Fritz Hollings, one of the Congress sponsors of the DMCA, also pushed for a new Security Systems Standards and Certification Act (SSSCA) in 2001, which would require anti-copying features to be built into all digital electronics and software. The SSSCA was also followed up by the Consumer Broadband and Digital Television Promotion Act (CBDTPA), although the latter act was defeated. In part, this defeat indicated the ambivalence with which recent developments in intellectual property law were being greeted by the computer industry: while most ICT companies will aggressively protect intellectual property (particularly via patenting laws), many digital products are marketed precisely on their ability to copy. This has led companies such as Disney (who, alongside other media groups, supported Senator Hollings) and the Recording Industry Association of America (RIAA) to indicate their concern about the direction being taken by digital technologies, but has also led them into direct conflict with many computer companies, an estimated $600-billion industry in the USA.

According to Lessig and others, one of the main consequences of acts such as the DMCA is that it indicates a potentially draconian shift away from balancing the rights of producers and consumers towards the former. Technologies protecting copyright are not as subtle as copyright law. Large companies like Disney are able to lobby organisations such as the WTO or WIPO, an option not open to private citizens. In the USA, the DMCA could come into conflict with the First Amendment, but equivalent protections of free speech are less clearly embedded in European legislation. As such, the European Union Copyright Declaration (www.eurorights.org/eudmca/index.html) has been a cause of concern for organisations such as the Campaign for Digital Rights (uk.eurorights.org), the Foundation for Information Policy Research (www.fipr.org) and Privacy International (www.privacyinternational.org). As Herman and McChesney (1997) remark, the issue of intellectual property rights is often pursued assiduously by Western governments as a means of economic hegemony, so that they are at their keenest when preserving that hegemony regardless of citizens' rights.

Patents and patenting

Software patents in the USA have attracted a great deal of attention as companies attempt to protect their investments or monopolise the market by excluding competitors. A patent is a property right that gives the holder exclusive rights to profit from the manufacture, use and sale of an invention. As such, patent holders may file a suit against others who try to make use of an invention and, under GATT regulations, patents are in place for twenty years.

While US companies may pursue patents aggressively against other nations, they are also equally likely to fight each other. Adobe and Macromedia, who had built up competitive markets throughout the 1990s as producers of creative software (Adobe largely print-based, Macromedia aimed more at multimedia), realised they could gain a great deal more by supplying first-class tools for web design and management. Adobe's PhotoShop is still market leader when it comes to image editing, but its LiveMotion encroached on the animated visuals associated with Flash, Macromedia also producing the renowned Dreamweaver and Shockwave.

In 2000, Adobe filed a suit against Macromedia for infringement of a US patent (5,546,528) covering Adobe's tabbed palettes. The company claimed that Macromedia copied these palettes in products such as Flash and Dreamweaver and had failed to comply with requests to desist first made in 1996. Although other companies introduced similar 'innovations', Macromedia remained Adobe's fiercest competitor with a number of products. The case was similar to the 'look and feel' suit brought by Apple against Microsoft in the early 1990s (which Apple, having developed its GUI along the lines of original designs at Xerox Parc, lost). Macromedia counter-sued, and in 2002 both companies were successful, Adobe having to pay Macromedia $4.9 million and Macromedia in return handing over nearly $3 million. According to Rob Burgess, Macromedia's Chairman, this was 'Adobe one, Macromedia one, customers zero' (Berger 2002).

Perhaps one of the strangest examples of a patent lawsuit (amidst ones for popular graphic formats such as gifs and jpegs) was that taken out in June 2000 by BT, which announced that it owned the rights to hyperlinks on web pages, much to the astonishment of the telecommunications industry. An audit had uncovered an old patent (due to expire in 2006) that, BT argued, covered the core technology, and it approached the largest American ISPs asking for royalties, with a test hearing against Prodigy in early 2002 that was, however, thrown out of court in September of that year.

Copy protection and digital rights management

Thus far, we have concentrated on the legal response to the commercial threat posed by digital copying, but another response has been to use technology to protect intellectual property and control who uses it under what circumstances. Digital rights management (DRM) software encrypts media files, allowing only rightful licence holders to decrypt such files. DRM is a growing business: Napster demonstrated widespread interest in online music, and now media content producers are hoping that they will be able to convert this interest into capital. The aggressive attack on piracy conducted against Napster has, however, created concern among some users that DRM will completely remove any notions of fair use: in theory, a song could only be downloaded and played for a certain number of times and only on a particular machine. To play it again, or in the car, for example, would require payment for another copy. At the same time, a realistic model to pay producers and distributors could result in media being more widely available in cyberspace. 'In its best implementation, it would offer untethered access to a vast universe of creative works . . . [it is] an opportunity to rewrite business rules as information rules, to make information more, rather than less readily available' (Howe 2001: 147).

A common means of establishing copyright ownership of electronic versions of images, movies and music is to use digital watermarking. To be fully effective, digital watermarking has to fulfil two conditions: it is invisible under normal usage, and is fully integrated into content. The kind of watermark that is found in a banknote, for example, can only be removed by destroying the banknote. Digital watermarks are encrypted by using redundant data bits in a file: a greyscale image, for example, represents each pixel by one of 256 shades of grey, using values from 00000000 to 11111111. The difference between insignificant parts of an image (such as 10101010 and 10101011) will be barely perceptible to the human eye, so slight variations can be introduced in a relatively random sequence to store watermark information. This, and similar techniques, are used by companies such as Digimarc (www.digimarc.com) and the Copy Protection Working Group (www.cptwg.org) to provide copy protection for images and movies. IBM uses a watermarking technique to distribute images: when downloaded from its website, these display a logo that renders them useless for commercial purposes, but paying for a key renders the logo invisible.

Piracy and counterfeiting

The problem of digital piracy has not surprisingly grown as more and more people have access to computers. Ironically, however, the involvement of organised crime has probably decreased: according to Laurence Westwood of the Federation Against Software Theft (FAST), 'the profits from organised piracy have fallen in the last few years because now everyone has a CD-writer' (cited in Charlesworth 2001: 160). Organisations such as FAST and the Business Software Alliance (BSA) estimate, however, that 26 per cent of software used in the UK is not legally licensed, including many large corporate businesses that may use thousands of licenses; for small businesses in Britain, the rate may be as high as 50 per cent.

Even this, however, is minor compared to the counterfeiting culture that has grown in countries such as China and parts of the former Soviet bloc. One of the most popular areas for software and media piracy is the Ukraine, where as many as seventy million unauthorised discs for music, software and movies may be produced each year (Boulware 2002). The US government has attempted to stem the flow of such illicit copying, ordering trade sanctions worth $75 million against the Ukraine at the end of 2001: such actions have had some effect in countries such as China and Bulgaria, but is a long and difficult process in countries that have a low awareness of intellectual property.

Moves to foil the counterfeiters in the UK have included the establishment of the Federation Against Copyright Theft (FACT) and the Anti-Counterfeiting Group (ACG). The latter, claiming to represent more than 200 major UK brand owners, was involved in the organisation of the first World Anti-Counterfeiting Day on 27 June 2002, an event that sought to highlight the growing menace of piracy, particularly online. Ironically, the effect of ACG's early efforts seems to have been merely to increase anxiety over online shopping at a time when ecommerce needed all the help it could get. While organisations behind counterfeiting may indeed be connected to other forms of crime such as drug trafficking and extortion, and while the problems represented by counterfeiting and piracy may not be trivial, the sensationalist message from supposedly responsible companies represented by the ACG is probably just as likely to have a detrimental effect on cyberspace as the activities it opposes.

Music and entertainment

The most high-profile case of digital copyright infringement or piracy thus far has involved the ill-fated Napster. Launched in July 1999 by Shawn Fanning, who had realised the popularity of file sharing while a student at Northwestern University, Napster (Fanning's high school nickname) connected users in a peer-to-peer network where they could share music, but also provided a centralised server containing file details that could be more easily searched. By 27 July 2000, a US district judge had ruled that users of the service were guilty of infringing copyright laws by obtaining music for free that they would probably have paid for after a case was brought by the Recording Industry Association of America (Alderman 2001). Initially, Napster attempted to filter files, but the RIAA claimed that such filters could be easily circumvented: despite attempts to renovate the service by Bertelsmann, Napster was eventually closed in 2002.

Similar cases with sites such as MP3.com had previously been resolved: EMI and MP3.com, for example, came to an agreement whereby the website was able to provide music to which EMI held rights after paying approximately $20 million in fees and damages. Shortly afterwards, three major record companies (Time-Warner, Bertelsmann and EMI) announced plans to provide their own subscription-based service online called MusicNet and set up by RealNetworks. Many commentators were divided on the overall impact of sites such as Napster: certainly it offered a radical new model for delivering music, particularly as consumers would not necessarily be compelled to purchase entire albums for single tracks, but it threw media producers into turmoil over the potential loss of revenue that would be caused by mass pirating online.

In a bizarre volte-face in 2001, however, the music industry found itself being sued by the Electronic Frontier Foundation (EFF) over allegations that research was being suppressed. The EFF represented scientists from Princeton and Rice Universities who had sought to publish a paper on weaknesses in new digital distribution technology that made use of electronic watermarks to prevent illegal copying. The researchers had found flaws in the system, but had withdrawn the report following pressure from the SDMI (Secure Digital Music Initiative) and the RIAA. According to Edward Felton, the principal author of the report, a letter from these groups claimed the work would violate the Digital Millennium Copyright Act, but Felton and the EFF argued that this interpretation would make scientific progress illegal in the area of electronic rights. The SDMI denied that it had ever planned to take legal action, remarking instead that it was merely attempting to protect the rights of watermark licensees who had submitted materials for testing.

Cybersquatting and domain names

A novel way to make fast money that emerged in the 1990s was the practice of 'cybersquatting', namely, buying up domain names with the aim of selling them at a profit. As many major corporations were slow to catch on to the Internet, some entrepreneurs were able to cash in before those companies (and the law) caught up with their practices. An alternative form of cybersquatting was used by John Zuccarini, who was taken to court by trade officials in 2001. Rather than registering trademarked sites, Zuccarini employed addresses consisting of common mis-spellings of popular sites, filling these with ads for gambling and pornography and earning an estimated $1 million per year.

Attempts to regulate and resolve domain name disputes have become increasingly important. ICANN established a Uniform Domain Name Dispute Resolution Policy (UDRP) that came into force at the beginning of 2000, alongside which run other policies such as STOP (Start-Up Trademark Opposition Policy) and the Sunrise Registration Policy, all of which are monitored by the World Intellectual Property Organisation (WIPO). In disputed cases between registrants and third parties, WIPO and ICANN attempt to establish who has best rights to a domain name: in the case of a registered trademark, these organisations may intervene to force a domain name owner who does not hold the trademark to relinquish that domain; alternatively, new domains such as the .biz top-level domain may be 'randomised', chosen at random for the successful applicant.

While cybersquatting has been a problem for businesses, how best to regulate it has not always been clear (Adediran 2002: 33–4). Thus, for example, non-US bodies expressed concern that the 1999 US Anticybersquatting Consumer Protection Act would lead to fines for foreign companies that registered domains sharing a name with US businesses which had American registered trademarks. Courts in the USA had previously ruled against companies that insisted web addresses should not have names similar to someone else's trademark, but some lawyers at the time argued that the Act reversed this position, with potentially huge fines for offending site owners.

Despite such difficulties, however, it is also possible that the high watermark for cybersquatting has already passed. In the early months of 2002, Web-tracking firm Netcraft (www.netcraft.com) released a report in which it suggested that domain name speculators were abandoning the Web. The number of domain names allowed to expire exceeded new registrations for the first time.

Quick and dirty links

Most issues around copyright online have focused on the content of material transferred, but the fundamental nature of HTML as a hypertext medium (that is, one where the ability to link between documents is built into the formatting language) has raised other problems. Linking between documents is often transparent to visitors, so that they may not always be aware when they are being transferred between different domains, which in turn has led to several court battles over the use of links.

In December 2000, for example, Keljob, a French-based employment search engine, was taken to court by Cadres Online: Keljob, it was claimed, enabled users to access job vacancies on other sites, bypassing homepages and changing the source code of those links to replace Cadres Online's logos and titles with Keljob's. The courts held that the nature of the Web was such that links were permissible without the authority of an original website owner, but that it was an infringement to provide links which changed the nature of original content or misled visitors. A similar outcome was reached in a court case in Cologne, again between two recruitment companies where one, OFIR, provided links to other agencies including StepStone, which brought the court action.

Cases in the USA that also involve deep linking have not been resolved in quite the same way. One, initiated by Ticketmaster Corp against Tickets.com in 2000, involved the latter company linking to pages on the Ticketmaster site for tickets which Ticketmaster had been granted sole rights to sell. The Tickets.com links would bypass the Ticketmaster homepage, but always displayed that company's logo. At a preliminary hearing, most of Ticketmaster's claims were dismissed, and its attempts to gain an interim injunction failed because it was held that the information being disputed – ticket prices, dates and locations of events – was factual information in the public domain that could not be copyrighted. Similarly, another US case that was also brought in 2000, by eBay against rival Bidder's Edge, led to an injunction being granted but only under a series of strict conditions.

The sex industry online

Since the mid-1990s at least, adult sexual material has been the most widely represented category in cyberspace. As JoAnn di Filippo (2000) remarks in her survey of online pornography, such sites range across a number of tastes and fetishes, as well as styles and types of business, from amateur homepages to increasingly sophisticated, multimedia corporate sites.

The rapid boom of such adult sites has also been a major concern for regulators and those concerned with the moral status of the Internet. The banal adage that sex sells is particularly true of many types of technology, having contributed, for example, to the success of VHS video systems over technically superior Betamax in the 1980s (adult movies were more easily available on VHS than its competitor).

Adult business

Attempts to quantify the online sex trade have often been beset by similar problems that affect estimates elsewhere, particularly the furtive nature of many online transactions. Best guesses for adult entertainment as a whole provide figures for $8 billion (or more than the value of Hollywood movies); the research company Forrester estimated as far back as 1998 that online porn was worth $1 billion a year, but has since stopped reporting figures which it believes cannot be accurate.

Online pornography has been flaunted as one of the few examples of cyberspace activity where practitioners can make money. As di Filippo remarks, for example, 'Mechanisms for online shopping, credit card processing, banner advertising, chatrooms, video-streaming and general web marketing were often pioneered by adult site developers' (2000: 125). At the same time, even cybersex suffered from the dotcom downturn: while well-established operators such as Cybererotica and Sex.com were still able to generate millions of dollars each month, small operators were finding it increasingly hard to make money: as Edward Cone has remarked, Internet pornography is 'a market where the easy money has long since been pocketed – and where even the established players aren't enjoying work the way they once did' (2002: 101). As Cone observes, while sex sites may make more money than other dotcoms, the market is competitive, reducing the number of sites that can make more than $10,000 a year, and the industry faces its own particular difficulties, such as a keen interest from regulators, and consumers who frequently refuse to pay.

The adult sex trade has itself long been a source of scams, and online sex sites do not necessarily buck the trend. In 2001, for example, two Canadian firms Virtualynx Internet and 583 665 BC were ordered to repay $26,000 to visitors to their sites, which had duped users into downloading software that offered free pornography but actually connected them to premium rate numbers in Africa and South America at $7 per minute. Indeed, such cases – as well as the frequency with which consumers deny that they purchased pornography online – has led credit card companies such as American Express to stop processing online transactions with adult websites, which are liable if the customer claims that fraud has taken place (Mitchell 2002).

Criminal activities

Of the various ways in which a sex site operator may find him or herself in jail, Cone (2002) lists posting images of under-age models, providing copyright pictures that are unlicensed, and legislation aimed at protecting children, such as the US Child Online Protection Act (COPA), passed in 1999 and currently going through appeal courts. In addition, because of the international nature of cyberspace, pornographic sites find themselves constantly breaking obscenity laws around the globe.

Where online pornography typically extends furthest into criminal activity is in terms of paedophile material, with several cases since the mid-1990s having demonstrated that the distribution of indecent images, stories and videos of sexual activity with minors takes place in the murkier corners of cyberspace. Policing of such activities has increasingly taken place on an international scale, for example in the Landmark operation in 2001 where 400 people were arrested in nineteen countries. One of the most high-profile cases in recent years was the sentencing of Gary Glitter (real name Paul Gadd) to four months' imprisonment for the possession of indecent images on his computer, discovered by staff at a computer store where he had delivered his PC to be repaired.

The UK Protection of Children Act 1978, as well as amendments to the Criminal Justice Act 1988, make it illegal to create or distribute indecent images of minors, as well as to possess such images or – indeed – pseudo-images, created with applications such as PhotoShop. Significantly, Gary Glitter did not merely plead guilty to possessing such images, but also to making them, because downloading or printing such images can also constitute making a new copy of an image. The apparent harshness of this interpretation (possession alone is a lesser offence) is due to the fact that the law is as concerned with the dissemination of online child pornography as it is with its creation in the first place.

Privacy

The growth of computer-mediated communication has made it easier than ever before to track what users look at and do. While detailed logs can demonstrate how long a browser stays on a particular site, email contacts and a mass of statistical information, mobile technology is increasingly capable of physically pinpointing the location of a person.

User privacy has increasingly become a contentious issue on two points: the responsibilities of governments to monitor activities by their citizens and the rights of those citizens to protection from undue interference; and the collection of personal information by businesses for commercial purposes. The state may frequently pursue a double role in relation to privacy, offering protection against the growing trade in personal information while also implementing legislation that extends its power over the individual. The issue of privacy, particularly follow-ing the terrorist attacks on the USA in 2001, has become ever more difficult to reconcile, with different voices arguing that regulation of privacy may be bad for business, technologically unenforceable, or an intrusion into the rights of the individual in the case of surveillance, while proponents see it as a social value that governments must protect or even deny to protect other rights (Stein and Sinha 2002).

Behind these arguments, particularly where surveillance by the state is involved, lie different conceptions of the role of government, whether as a separate (and potentially hostile) body to 'the people', who have power insofar as they are able to limit government, or as their agent established to protect their rights (Raab 1997). Such positions are rarely encountered in any 'pure' form in cyberspace, with legislation frequently serving to both protect the individual's rights (as, for example, in the case of the UK Data Protection Act) and encroach upon them (in elements of the RIP Act dealt with below).

Cyberspace surveillance

While discussions of cybercrime concentrate most frequently on antisocial groups or individuals breaking national or international laws, technology is probably more often used by governments and official organisations to gather information about their citizens and employees surreptitiously. As became clear after the fall of the

Berlin Wall, large proportions of the populations of the former Eastern bloc were employed by their governments to spy on neighbours and colleagues, while organisations such as the CIA and GCHQ routinely collect information on targets in the West.

For European and North American governments, surveillance can be legitimated as part of a fight against crime, particularly terrorism, but recent regulations have become more draconian, even before 11 September. It is comparatively easy to understand the passing of the US Patriot Act in the wake of the attack on the Twin Towers, regardless of whether one agrees with it or not, but the UK Regulation of Investigatory Powers (RIP) Act 2000, ostensibly aimed at regulating complicated procedures governing what can and cannot be viewed by government and business, included extremely strong measures. By issuing an s22 notice, various government bodies would be able to demand complete records of incoming and outgoing email and telephone calls without a judicial warrant, and even informing others that this order has been placed is a criminal offence. In the summer of 2002, an amendment to the original RIP Act was to be passed enabling health authorities, local government bodies, postal services, fire departments and many other organisations to access records without a warrant: the changes were publicised by stand, the campaign for Internet users' rights (www.stand.org.uk) and taken up by *The Guardian*, forcing a rather humiliating climb-down for the government.

A potentially much more sinister world of surveillance in cyberspace than RIP became clearer in 2001, when a report by the European Parliament's Temporary Committee on the Echelon Interception System reported its findings. Such is the secrecy surrounding Echelon, a global system run by the US, Canadian, British, Australian and New Zealand governments and capable of intercepting email and telephone communications between these countries, that a major revelation of the Committee's report was simply to state that its existence is 'no longer in doubt'. Established after the Second World War to gather military intelligence, MEPs suggested that its main use until their report in mid-2001 was to intercept commercial and personal telecommunications. Since 11 September 2001, its use in counter-terrorism is likely to have increased, but suggestions had also been made by member states of the EU that the system gave the countries running Echelon privileged access to commercial secrets.

Significantly, systems such as Echelon are not covered by European human rights and privacy laws because activities of police, secret services and the army in issues of security are excluded. In addition, laws for privacy and security are typically set at a national level that, again, does not cover an international operation such as Echelon. Cyberspace libertarians also expressed concerns in 2001 and 2002 over a rumoured Trojan called 'Magic Lantern', a small application that could be used to track a user's every keystroke. The reason for the concern was that Magic Lantern was devised by the FBI to provide electronic surveillance as part of the US government's war on terror, although the FBI refused to comment on such rumours.

Data protection

While government and military surveillance represents the sharp end of an Orwellian invasion of privacy, the vast majority of data produced by us throughout our lives tends to find its way into commercial and organisational databases that have a less sinister interest in us but also tend to influence us much more. The proliferation of personal information, stored in increasingly large databases, led to the implementation of the Data Protection Act (DPA) 1998 to protect the rights of individuals. Put simply, the DPA stipulates that data should be fairly and law-fully processed for limited purposes, must be accurate and securely kept, not excessive nor kept longer than necessary, and finally that data should not be trans-ferred to countries without adequate protection. The DPA also gives individuals the right to access data held on them under section 7(1) of the Act, with more information available from the Data Protection Register (www.dpr.gov.uk; see also Adediran 2002: 78–99).

Companies that hold data on customers must now register with the Data Protection Register, and those that do not comply with the Act can be fined and there is no exemption for small businesses, although, as we have already seen, information on security matters is excluded as are data held for the detection or prevention of crime. None the less, the imperative to protect citizens' rights to privacy may conflict with other legislation carried out by the government in the UK. Indeed, a year and a half after the RIP Act gave companies the right to inves-tigate workers' electronic traffic, the Information Commission questioned the validity of such conduct and warned that covert monitoring without clear suspicion could lead to prosecutions. However, it is still not clear, particularly in the light of anti-terrorist legislation following 11 September, how conflicting sets of regulation will co-exist.

Online advertising and user profiling

While the legitimate business of advertising will be dealt with in more detail in the following chapter as part of ecommerce, online advertising has raised concerns among privacy groups due to the ways in which it can be used surreptitiously to track users' movements across the Internet. In the early stages of the dotcom boom, claims were made for the efficacy of online advertising (targeting users more accu-rately by means of profiling, for example) many of which could not subsequently be justified. As customers began to question the value of such advertising, so the process of building profiles and tracking users' tastes and interests online began to heat up.

Online profiling can work in a number of ways: in its most obvious form, visitors to a site may be asked to provide information. Sometimes this may be in return for a free service, but often consumers purchasing an item may be asked to provide information (such as age, occupation and income bracket) that is irrelevant to the sale. Indeed, this has prompted the Data Protection Commissioner to issue warnings several times to online businesses. Information gathered in this way may be stored as part of a database and even sold to third parties.

Providing this sort of information is relatively clear compared to the other ways in which user profiling takes place. The most common surreptitious form consists of using cookies, small text files that are sent to the browser: these serve a useful purpose, storing information between sessions (such as preferences for a site, or a logon password), but they can also be used to monitor when and how often a visitor returns to a site. Later versions of Internet Explorer provide control over cookie usage, and so some advertisers have adopted other tactics, such as sending images from a third-party server: as this may be called from very different sites, it becomes possible to some degree to track a user's movements across the Web.

The potential for abuse led the Center for Democracy and Technology (www. cdt.org) to launch a campaign against a major online advertiser, DoubleClick, in 2000. According to the CDT, DoubleClick could link personal information to cookies that could then be passed to third parties, a charge denied by DoubleClick. Users could opt out of the scheme, but online profiling is still a cause of concern for users who may find themselves subject to unwanted 'tailored' advertising. The EU also attempted to restrict the use of cookies, insisting that users be notified before such files were placed on their system, but after criticism from the Union of Industrial and Employers' Confederations Europe (UNICE), among others, that such a proposal would devastate ecommerce, the plans were watered down.

Spam

One of the most common nuisances that can arise from online profiling is spam. Spam (so-called after the repetitive Monty Python song – 'Spam and chips, egg and spam, spam and spam, spam, spam') is the electronic equivalent of junk mail, sent out to bulk email addresses. Such email addresses may be garnered from websites or Usenet postings, but automated systems are also likely to generate potential addresses (which is one reason why certain email accounts, such as those attached to Hotmail or AOL, are high-profile targets for spammers).

There is no global legal definition of spam, but the key factors are that it is unsolicited, non-personal email sent in bulk, usually with the aim of selling something, and this has become a major nuisance for many users and indeed for service providers. As Tynan (2002) points out, however, many bulk emailers define themselves as 'permission based emailing organisations', although it is not clear where such permission comes from: when ISP PaeTec Communications attempted to cut off the account of one such organisation, MonsterHut, after receiving more than 40,000 complaints, MonsterHut sued, initially gaining an injunction against its ISP until PaeTec won an appeal and closed the site.

Whereas junk mailers have to pay for postage when sending snail mail overland, the costs for email spam are borne by recipients and ISPs that carry those messages. For those involved in direct marketing, sending messages electronically provides a cheap solution to reaching potential audiences, and similar services are frequently offered by commercial sites that can inform customers of new products or releases. At the same time, it is easy for so-called 'emarketers' to misuse this tool and send out emails indiscriminately, which is where direct marketing becomes spam.

A 2001 report by Jupiter Media Metrix predicted that a typical consumer may expect to receive nearly 1,500 spam messages, double the current average, at an estimated cost of $8 to $10 billion per year in bandwidth charges alone. Spam abuse has led to a number of initiatives by regulatory bodies. In early 2000, for example, the Direct Marketing Association (DMA) in the UK set up its E-mail Preference Service (e-MPS, www.e-mps.org), a directory of users who could register to have their names removed from lists used by emarketers: the scheme has been a voluntary one, however, requiring companies to request the directory, and the EuroISPA has been sceptical about its ability to curb determined junk mailers.

Even some high-profile ISPs have been affected (rather embarrassingly) by accusations of spamming, such as BTOpenworld: because some anti-spam organisations block blacklisted IP addresses, junk mailers exploiting BT's Internet services had caused some addresses (which would then be used by other customers) to be blocked. BT's response was to filter outgoing spam to block culprits at source. At the same time, some bulk emailers have reported ISPs as more than willing to do business in return for hiring leased lines: as a self-described spammer Ronnie Scelson remarks, 'If you were getting $40,000 a month . . . would you want to shut me down?' (cited in Tynan 2002: 109).

Blocking spam

While universal laws against spam do not exist, it is unlikely that it is legal anywhere, and most ISPs have contracts that specifically prohibit such bulk emailing. Because of this, spammers tend to use open relays, mail servers that (usually because of ignorance on the administrator's part) anyone can use to send email.

Software, such as SpamCop and SpamKiller, is available from spam.abuse.net, and you can report spammers to blackhole lists for rejecting spam such as the Open Relay Blackhole Zones (www.orbz.org) and Spamhaus (www.spamhaus.org). Replying to a spam message asking to be removed from a list is unlikely to have any other effect than to confirm that the address is active (and thus amenable to future spamming), unless it is from a genuine emarketer and you previously asked to subscribe to a service.

The EU announced in 2002 that it would clamp down on spam, the European Parliament's Citizens' Rights and Freedoms, Justice and Home Affairs Committee also having announced that SMS (short message service) messages would be included in legislation against unsolicited commercial email. Significantly, however, not all member states welcomed the move and some, including France and the UK, said that they preferred an opt-out approach, whereby users would have to state that they did not wish to receive such messages, rather than the EU's opt-in plan, already adopted by countries such as Germany and Italy. The US Congress was also considering anti-spam legislation – not to ban it, which would be difficult in the light of constitutionally guaranteed right to free speech, but to improve powers of enforcement against spammers who behaved badly, such as by concealing identities or using misleading subject lines. One test case was initiated by the US law firm Morrison & Foerster LLP against Etracks.com: after it received 6,500 unsolicited emails during a six-month period, Morrison & Foerster asked for damages of $50 for each email, or up to $25,000 per day.

Encryption

One way to keep private information private is to perform some form of encryption. Cryptography (from *kruptos*, 'secret', and *graphia*, 'writing') has been practised in some form or another for at least 3,000 years and, as its name suggests, originated as ciphers that would obscure the meanings of texts.

The practice of encryption entails a number of stages: codes involve substitutions, such as the common phrase 'paging Mr Sands' to indicate a fire alert without alarming members of the public, and ciphers typically involve the substitution of characters; the creation of these ciphers constitutes cryptography. One of the earliest forms of cryptography, the transposition cipher, simply required a piece of cloth to be wrapped in a spiral around a rod of a particular circumference, with the message then being written line by line: to read the message, the recipient would need to know the circumference of the rod, reading every seventh character, for example. The most famous ancient cipher, attributed to Julius Caesar, consisted of replacing each letter of a text with a letter three steps along the alphabet: this is still used today as ROT-13, where each letter is shifted (or rotated) thirteen places.

One problem with cryptography is that it is often very obvious: hence the development of steganography where one type of data is disguised as another. Probably the best known form of steganography is the fabled lemon juice that becomes visible only when heated over a fire, but it is commonly used in digital techniques to obscure information, hiding text in graphics files, for example.

Computing brought radical changes to cryptography, and the standard developed in the 1970s was the Data Encryption Standard: by 1997, however, it was clear that the 56-bit key insisted upon by the US National Security Agency (NSA), which provides some 72,000,000,000,000,000,000 keys, could be cracked by computers in a few hours. One attempt to provide a more secure method of encryption, Pretty Good Privacy (PGP), released by Phil Zimmerman in 1991, led to an investigation by US Customs that claimed Zimmerman had broken the International Traffic in Arms Regulation by exporting a 'munition' which could be used by those hostile to the USA (Nott 2002). Encryption has long been held up as necessary to helping ecommerce by encouraging trust in cyberspace, but it has also remained a potential sore point for governments who fear its use by criminals or subversive elements.

Signatures and security

A fundamental feature of many transactions is the ability to verify the identity of one or more participants. Traditionally, signatures have been taken as valid when it is the author's intention to sign a particular document, validating not only the author's identity but also his or her willingness to be bound by the contents of a document.

Digital signatures are not simply digitised versions of manuscript signatures, scanned on to a hard drive, for example, and converted into an image, but rather a 160-bit number created as part of a private encryption key: as with a manuscript signature, the ID created is intended to be linked irrevocably to a particular document. Although the Electronic Communications Act 2000 implemented European directives governing the creation and use of electronic signatures, enabling them to be legally effective and admissible before the law, there remains some doubt in the UK as to the precise status of digital signatures: although technically valid, the processes governing their creation and issue by a Certification Authority have still not been entirely worked out.

Digital signatures have not caught on particularly well thus far, especially among ordinary consumers who prefer to sign a piece of paper, and this has not necessarily been helped by the difficult process of gaining a verifiable signature: for government transactions, for example, an individual must visit the local Chamber of Commerce. At the same time, there are certain pieces of legislation that still require an auditable paper trail. None the less, the hope is that digital signature systems will help prevent online fraud and ultimately eliminate many of the costs of paperwork.

Viruses and malware

The first virus to be identified was Brain, which emerged in 1986. By the end of the 1980s, the number of known viruses had increased to just seven, but rose more rapidly the following year, numbering eighty. This exponential growth showed no sign of abating by the end of the 1990s when, according to the Symantec Antivirus Research Centre (SARC), the number of viruses more than doubled between 1998 and 1999 from 20,500 to 42,000. By the beginning of 2002, estimated growth of viruses was 1,200 a month.

At the same time, the threat from such viruses must be kept in perspective. Figures such as the above from SARC and other virus research centres represent the total number of known viruses, many of which are confined to the laboratory or a single computer. The actual number of viruses in the 'wild' rarely amounts to more than 200 active ones, and the electronic security firm mi2g (www.mi2g.com) observed in 2002 that henceforth exploitation of software vulnerabilities would be a bigger issue than viruses. None the less, with the development of the Internet and increasing numbers of users online, more computers than ever before are affected by malware that has the potential to damage data or have other destructive effects.

The growth of viruses in the 1990s is due to a number of factors: probably the most important is the spread of the Internet and email, but close behind this is the fact that computing systems are now less diverse than ever before, particularly with the success of Microsoft products such as Windows and Office. In addition, whereas early viruses would be programmed in a complex language such as C++ or binary code, more common viruses today depend on common Office macros or products such as the VBS Worm generator, which requires little or no programming skills. According to Graham Cluley, a consultant with the anti-virus firm Sophos, the Internet means that 'the speed of infection has gone from 33 to 78 rpm' (cited in Gann 2001: 130). What is more, the Net provides a forum for virus writers to share skills and information.

Defining a virus

Viruses tend to come in a variety of shapes and forms: while the common appellation of 'virus' covers a number of malware programs (that is, applications that are destructive or have deleterious effects), strictly speaking it is simply a piece of code that reproduces itself without user intervention. It is perfectly possible, therefore, to produce a utilitarian virus that duplicates itself across systems to perform a serviceable task. Examples include the Cheese worm, which was designed to close security back doors in Linux systems, and the Noped email worm, which was designed to hunt down child porn images, although police confirmed that they would not respond to the worm alerts (Gann 2001).

Most viruses take the form of a worm; that is, they do not simply operate on an isolated system but take advantage of network communications to spread to other computers. An increasing number of viruses, particularly those targeted at common Microsoft products such as Outlook, Outlook Express or Office, are written in simple visual basic script (.vbs), such as the HomePage Virus that spread across email systems in mid-2001 and the earlier Anna Virus, so named because it promised the recipient a picture of tennis player Anna Kournikova. Probably the most damaging virus, which also struck in 2001, was the Nimda worm ('admin' spelt backwards), that infected systems running Microsoft's Internet Information Server (IIS), installing itself as a file that would grant the worm full administrator rights. Worms such as Nimda and the earlier Code Red caused considerable havoc on networks around the world, bringing down servers and infecting PCs accessing those systems but, in mid-2001, Crimelabs Security Unit researcher Jose Nazario also warned attendees at the DefCon Conference in Las Vegas that future 'superworms' would be capable of updating automatically on the fly, transforming into a different virus. To combat the next generation of super-viruses, researchers at the University of New Mexico, Albuquerque, have taken a new approach that imitates the human auto-immune system: autonomous programs will work in a fashion similar to lymphocytes (white blood cells) in the human body, looking for unexpected code in memory which can then be eliminated (www.cs.unm.edu/~forrest).

Thus far, we have been concerned largely with worms that replicate themselves across systems. Another common malware threat is a Trojan horse, which, like the wooden horse of classical mythology, disguises itself as an innocuous file or attachment. One famous example is the BackOrifice Trojan that acts as a server application on infected systems, enabling hackers to access and control the computer. A common use of such PCs is for a Distributed Denial of Services (DDoS), where multiple infected machines – Zombie PCs – bombard a website with requests for information, the aim being to cripple the site. Such DDoS attacks are becoming more common, particularly after an onslaught against commercial sites such as Amazon and MSN in February 2000 (Verton 2002).

14 Cyberspace and the public sphere

Governing cyberspace

It has become common in recent years, when discussing the political impacts of cyberspace, to note that the rise of cyberspace has coincided with the extension of globalisation and the fall of the nation state. Undoubtedly that would be news to those various nation states involved in conflicts during the 1990s, in Europe, Asia and Africa, and indeed to the sense of patriotism engendered in the USA following terrorist attacks on 11 September 2001.

With this proviso in mind, however, it remains true that the political situation supporting cyberspace is still very different to that which saw the development of the telegraph or television. As Brian Loader (1997: 9) observes:

> Governance in the postmodern world is further characterised by the weakening of the nation-state through the accentuation of the local and global dimensions of human interaction. ICT networks such as the Internet facilitate the deconstruction of national financial and cultural boundaries which are an intrinsic attribute of modernism. Instead, it is maintained that power is decentralised as the traditional functions of the modern state – external defence, internal surveillance and the maintenance of citizenship rights – have been challenged.

Castells (1996–98) argues that the network society results from the convergence of three strands: the IT revolution itself, the restructuring of global capitalism that took place in the 1980s and 1990s, and cultural and social movements such as civil rights and women's rights that began in the 1960s and 1970s. The impact of these can be exaggerated – external defence in particular has demonstrated that the nation state is very much alive and well.

As we saw in the previous chapter, the issue of cybercrime and contested areas such as intellectual property rights have led to a steady stream of legislation in the past five to ten years aimed at regulating the activities of participants in cyberspace. It is commonly assumed that cyberspace is an entirely unregulated sphere, partly from the assumption that a lack of face-to-face communication provides simple anonymity, as well as the fact that in its early years legal bodies struggled to keep pace with emerging technologies, particularly when they were less public (and less important) than other media arenas such as television and print publishing. Cyberspace as another wild frontier, however, is rapidly being tamed as another sphere of social, political and economic life, which although it presents special problems due to its international nature and more open access in terms of publishing, can none the less be regulated and even policed. Certain areas remain lawless – may even always remain so – but just as areas of the world offline may be outside the law, this itself does not invalidate the requirement for public policy and legislation elsewhere.

In this chapter, we will explore issues that arise from legislation to counter crime, and more on policies and activities that seek to define the role played by cyberspace in public life. Sometimes this crucial interaction between cyberspace and society is directed from the top down, via government strategies, guidelines and statutes, but often the direction taken by the Internet stems from the grassroots activities of its users. To cover the wide area indicated by both these directions, it is worthwhile considering the relationships that emerge in cyberspace as a public sphere.

Theories of the public sphere

Although they originate much earlier (particularly as notions of a 'public forum' or 'fourth estate'), theories of the public sphere have become particularly important in media studies since the 1989 translation of Jürgen Habermas' *The Structural Transformation of the Public Sphere*. For Habermas, notions of a public sphere (which translates from the German *Öffentlichkeit*) originated in classical antiquity, centred on the Greek city (or *polis*, hence our 'politics') in which discussions that affected the well-being of the city could be discussed in the open marketplace, or agora. As traders sold goods or bought commodities from the city, so they also brought with them information that could affect life within the city.

For Habermas, the public sphere was moribund during the Middle Ages, which did not recognise a distinction we take for granted between private and public lives. During the sixteenth and seventeenth centuries, however, particularly in countries that would contribute greatly to the early stages of capitalist revolution such as Britain, the increasing importance of a domestic space led many private individuals to seek out actively a public agora where they could discuss and debate their views. In the latter half of the seventeenth century, the combination of private trade and public discussion led to the formation of the classic bourgeois public sphere, where merchants, journalists and other members of the middle classes would gather in coffee houses and salons to read newspapers and discuss literature, religion and politics. As the confidence of this middle class grew, so its demands for formal involvement in politics increased, using the new organs of communication – the journal and newspaper – to organise opinion and support.

At its most simplistic, the theory of the public sphere has been criticised as offering too formulaic a view of society as an aggregate of individuals and government as the seat of power: as Curran remarks, this tends to lead to envisaging media 'primarily as vertical channels of communication between private citizens and government' (1998: 31). More radical approaches to the public sphere are concerned, as Curran points out, to broaden the public domain, to widen access for it that may require collective action on behalf of people who are too weak as individuals. Despite its flaws, however, theories of the public sphere (or public forum) remain useful for examining the ways in which groups of individuals or communities interact in online spaces. Brian Connery (1997), for example, has drawn explicit parallels between the coffee houses where merchants and journalists gathered in the seventeenth century and online chat rooms where gossip and information circulate freely. Similarly, Howard Rheingold (2000: 175) argues that the Internet has the potential to counter 'the sophisticated and wholesale manufacture of public opinion, and the domination of popular media by electronic spectacles' that has damaged the public sphere – though it could equally well contribute to further harmful spectacles.

Organising cyberspace

As Graham remarks, one idiom common to popular thinking about the Internet is that it represents a state of anarchy due to its internationalism and populism: 'In this respect, the Internet is to be contrasted sharply with what philosophers call "civil society", whose characteristic is that it connects strangers by unifying them within one political rule or realm' (1999: 86). The common mistake of such thinking (although not made by Graham) is to associate such potential anarchy with chaos and incoherence. Yet, from its earliest days, cyberspace has demonstrated a remarkable capacity for self-organisation, with (often voluntary) bodies forming to help maintain the open standards governing technical protocols necessary for it to run.

Bradner (1996: 2), in a guide to Internet standards, defines the Internet as:

> a loosely-organized international collaboration of autonomous, interconnected networks [that] supports host-to-host communication through voluntary adherence to open protocols and procedures defined by Internet Standards. . . . In general, an Internet Standard is a specification that is stable and well-understood, is technically competent, has multiple, independent, and inter-operable implementations with substantial operational experience, enjoys significant public support, and is recognizably useful in some or all parts of the Internet.

The important points here are that such standards are open – they may be scrutinised and contributed to by all – and voluntary. There is nothing to prevent a commercial organisation from establishing its own proprietary network, but for such a network to operate as part of the international Internet, users must agree to participate by the standards process.

This process is maintained by a number of organisations, many of which are gathered together under the umbrella organisation of the Internet Society (ISOC, www.isoc.org). This is a professional membership society, formed in 1990, with more than 150 organisations and 11,000 individual members in over 182 countries, and is the home for the groups responsible for Internet infrastructure standards, including the Internet Engineering Task Force (IETF) and the Internet Architecture Board (IAB). Of these subsidiary organisations, the IETF (www.ietf.org) represents an international community of network designers, operators, vendors and researchers concerned with the architecture and operation of the Internet, and is in turn responsible for the Internet Engineering Steering Group (IESG), which guides the standards process. The IAB (www.iab.org), which in turn stemmed from the Internet Configuration Control Board founded by Vince Cerf in 1981, now serves as the technical advisory board to the Internet Society.

These groups, then, are concerned with the nuts and bolts of Internet operation and architecture, and are in turn joined by a number of other groups, of which the most important are the Internet Assigned Numbers Authority (www.iana.org), governing Internet address systems, and the World Wide Web Consortium (W3C, www.w3c.org), which was created in October 1994 in order to develop common protocols for the Web that would promote its evolution and ensure its interoperability. In the words of the Web's founder, Tim Berners-Lee (1999: 82), splintering factions 'would defeat the very purpose of the Web: to be a single, universal, accessible hypertext medium for sharing information'.

One example of the unwillingness of governments and organisations to contribute to an internationally open system of Internet regulation (particularly one so easily dominated by the USA) came to light in early 2002, when it was revealed in the press that the French registrar allowed only French companies or those with a trademark recognised in France to register .fr domains. This was in contrast to Nominet, the UK equivalent, which allows customers anywhere in the world to register a .uk address.

Cyberspace and democracy

Gordon Graham, in *The Internet:// A Philosophical Inquiry* (1999), begins not by asking whether cyberspace will be effective in furthering democracy, but whether democracy is itself the preferred mode of government. Since the introduction, or extension, of the franchise to wider areas of the population in the nineteenth century, the potential for direct democracy (of the kind, for example, practised by free men in classical Athens) in most political systems in the West has receded, being replaced by different forms of representative democracy. As Graham observes, there are a number of deficiencies within democracy as a form of government, deficiencies that have led a number of Internet commentators to assume (often unconsciously) a more libertarian or anarchistic position. However, while technology cannot address one of the deficiencies of democracy, according to Graham, 'its preference for equality over rationality', it can play at least one useful role:

> democracy can recover some ground by focussing once more on the impor-
> tance of influence as well as power. In a free society the role of the citizen
> extends beyond the ballot-box or referendum into the realms where political
> opinions are formed and particular causes are advanced. Access to this sphere
> of influence is just as important a part of democracy as the direct exercise of
> the power to vote, and it is a sphere to which the technology of the Internet
> gives increased access for ordinary citizens as more immediate and effective
> means of communication and expression become more widely available.
>
> (Graham 1999: 82–3)

As Graham observes, platitudes such as 'information is power' often remain just platitudes, and the ability of the Internet to effect faster and more efficient communication will not make cyberspace more democratic, nor democracy itself necessarily more valuable per se. None the less, a wide range of communal and civic projects involving the Internet, such as Network Pericles in Greece and Berlin's City Information System (see Tsagarousianou *et al.* 1998), have been put in place worldwide, both to share information with citizens and help them exercise democratic power. At its most ambitious, this consists of online voting systems, but on a daily basis civic networks attempt to place people in contact with appro-priate organisations and figures or provide them with the sort of information that helps them make decisions in their daily life. Elsewhere, as Lax (2000) points out, the main tendency of ICT is to make it easier to push single-issue campaigns and pressure politics, rather than the complex and messy business of government.

The question of access is crucial to the development of effective democracy in cyberspace. As writers such as Dave Carter have noted, inequalities in access to information result less in digital democracy than the creation of an information aristocracy. As such, 'developments in advanced communications need to be accompanied by a strategy for development from below' (Carter 1997: 138).

eGovernment

In 1997, *Wired* magazine, with the aid of Merrill Lynch, undertook a survey of 1,444 Americans in which it claimed to discover a new peer group: the 'Digital Citizen'. According to the results of this survey, those who were most likely to be connected to cyberspace were also more likely to value democracy and place most confidence in the free market. For Jon Katz, the results of the *Wired*/Merrill Lynch survey indicated that this group was highly engaged in mainstream politics:

> In fact, Digital Citizens love their political system more than the system loves
> them. Almost all conventional wisdom about digital culture – especially as
> conveyed in recent years by journalists, politicians, intellectuals, and other

fearful guardians of the existing order – is dead wrong. The Internet, it turns out, is not a breeding ground for disconnection, fragmentation, paranoia and apathy. Digital Citizens are not alienated, either from other people or from civic institutions. Nor are they ignorant of our system's inner workings, or indifferent to the social and political issues our society must confront. Instead, the online world encompasses many of the most informed and participatory citizens we have ever had or are likely to have.

(Katz 1997: 71)

More accurately, Katz was responding to the misinformation he had (as he admitted) disseminated regarding a superconnected elite that was arrogant and alienated from mainstream politics. If anything, the reverse has been true in the decade since the fall of the Berlin Wall, with middle-class voters more likely than ever to engage politically while other sectors of society gradually become more and more disillusioned. Katz's vision of the disconnected, apathetic and paranoid member of cyberspace is, for the moment, very much a straw target. In the UK, by contrast, the Labour government has, like the Conservative administrations that preceded it, theoretically favoured the use of ICT to extend democratic access to all areas of society – though certain areas where technology can empower citizens, such as extending rights to information, are often glossed over by all governments when that information interferes with the power of the state.

As Lax (2000) observes, the Internet can serve as a one-way and a two-way network. A common daily use of cyberspace by governments (such as at www. gov.uk and www.firstgov.gov) is to deliver information to individuals and organisations, an extension of the use of channels such as print (newspapers, mailshots) and broadcasting that has long been in place. However, 'more information of itself does not mean more democracy' (Lax 2000: 161), but instead must also consider the involvement of citizens in making decisions that will affect them.

Following the disappointing turnout for the 2001 UK election, where only 59 per cent of voters cast their vote, the British government began 2002 by promoting the notion of electronic voting. While unlikely to be in place by the 2006 election, the leader of the House of Commons, Robin Cook, believed that such voting could be in place by 2011, making the UK the first country to vote online. Networks, however, are more than hardware and software, but also rely on national, regional and local organisations that enable people to view themselves as more than individuals, as part of political communities. As Carter observes, 'there is no technological "short-cut" to the establishment of such networks but rather the long, hard slog of alliance building, experimentation, negotiation, campaigning and self-organisation' (1997: 151).

Cyberauthoritarianism

So far, we have concentrated on the ways in which cyberspace has been seen as possibly effecting greater interaction with a democratic public. And yet, as Castells (1997) observes, one of the defining features of the network society has been its distinct lack of engagement with mass politics as defined from the late nineteenth century onward. More than this, however, Kroker and Weinstein (1994: 117) suggest that the end of the twentieth century has been witness to 'the growth of cyberauthoritarianism, a stridently protechnotopia movement, particularly in the mass media'. Technology, as Philip Bereano (1984) observes, has always been the servant of powerful elites, and commentators such as Dorothy Nelkin (1994) note that the steady accumulation of increasingly larger databases poses a real threat to individual liberties.

It is, perhaps, easiest to caricature the Internet as a threat to countries outside North America and Europe, yet the threat of cultural imperialism can be felt in a technophile country such as France as well as in a more suspicious country such as Iran or North Korea. None the less, it is the case that there are hotspots around the world where cyberspace is more likely to be considered politically intrusive. In China, for example, the government introduced new legislation in 2000, demanding that the country's security forces approve Internet content in order to prevent state secrets from being leaked online. While it has been impossible for the government to vet every web page produced in China, it has clearly indicated the willingness of officials to monitor the Internet. Constraints were also placed on businesses, that were required to register encryption keys, again ostensibly to prevent confidential information flowing out of the country but also to make intelligence work more easily. In practice, the laws have been rather vague, their primary purpose apparently to serve as a warning to Chinese citizens that those seen as troublesome would be watched.

And yet the example of restraint and coercion that is evident in a country such as China frequently arouses our anger only because it is overt. The much more liberal approach to cyberspace that was typical of many Western countries in the 1990s could, as we have already seen, co-exist quite happily with massive surveillance operations such as Echelon. What is more, since the events of 11 September it is quite clear that one of the effects of the war on terrorism will be to pay much closer attention to the previously libertarian sphere of cyberspace. A rash of anti-terrorist and other criminal legislation (some of it, such as the RIP Act, already in place before 11 September) provides a two-edged sword: the Internet cannot be a free-for-all, and certain activities that are not tolerated nationally should not be allowed to flourish unregulated simply because they occur in an international medium. Yet the key note in many of these governmental interventions seems to be one of cyberauthoritarianism – not merely the active promotion of technology suggested by Kroker and Weinstein, but the use of such technology to implement mass surveillance of supposedly democratic societies as a matter of course.

Access and civic networks

One particular contribution of cyberspace to this network society can be extended from the rhetoric of the information society that was prevalent in the 1970s and 1980s: if information is important to informed decisions in modern democracies, then it is especially significant to consider who has access to that information, and this has become a significant factor in many discussions of the social and political aspects of cyberspace. For Castells (2001: 144), perhaps the most important social function of information technologies has been to foster these 'civic networks'.

Who has use of new technologies, then, is a major concern for those who see the Internet as a potentially universal service that can influence economic and political outcomes. Commentators such as Cooper (2000) and McConnaughey and Lader (1998) speak of a 'digital divide' to refer to the differences between the information rich and poor, with such discrepancies often based on race, gender and location, as well as income. Pessimistic views of the problems of information access indicate that this can easily become a vicious cycle: labour markets prefer those with experience, skills and information that can be gained by participation in new technologies, and such participation brings with it more opportunities to develop such skills – making the gap between information rich and poor more likely to increase without intervention. Results of surveys such as the 2000 *UCLA Internet Report* are generally not surprising: of 2,096 households questioned in the survey, 86.3 per cent of respondents with a college degree used the Internet, but only 31.2 per cent of those who had not graduated from high school (cited in Rice 2002). Lack of participation can also have less obvious disadvantages: as well as lower wages, individuals without access to email and electronic data will be less well informed about their employers and less likely to be involved in corporate decisions (Carrier 1998).

Access to cyberspace, however, has not been left completely to the free market. Since the beginning of the 1990s in particular, work has been ongoing in terms of extending the use of ICT outside the workplace. Many of the case studies discussed in Tsagarousianou *et al.* (1998), for example, deal with access to informational or civic networks. The Digital City project begun in Amsterdam in 1994, Network Pericles in Greece and Berlin's City Information System are all aimed at improving the participation of citizens in daily civic life. It is significant that those projects which are most likely to be successful occur on a regional (or, more accurately, a metropolitan) than national level. On the one hand, such projects rely on technologies that should effectively remove the *polis* from its sense of a specific geographical location, but they also interact with the urban reality of particular cities. What they have tended to do less well is to extend notions of 'cyber-democracy', inviting citizens to participate in the political life of their city.

Furthermore, access may not be the only key to solving the problem of the digital divide. As Castells (2001) argues, drawing on surveys conducted by the US Commerce Department's National Telecommunications and Information Administration (NTIA) between 1995 and 2000, divisions in access may be slowly closing, only to be replaced by more fundamental divisions in terms of income and education. Most significantly, suggests Castells, while the digital divide between genders is closing, cyberspace is by no means colour-blind.

Disintermediation and interactivity

Participation in political processes is one of the key claims made for the democratic potential of the Internet. The assumption is that interactivity enables a citizen to assume a more 'active' status. As Graham (1999) observes, however, this assumption about the status of democracy, the direct participation and exercise of power by the people, is generally very different to the actual practices of parliamentary democracies in the West which function more as representative rather than direct democracies. None the less, as Hacker (1996) points out, new technologies theoretically allow citizens the ability to engage with governments directly, on the basis that representatives will work best when there is continual interaction between governors and the governed.

Key to this direct interaction is the notion of 'disintermediation'. Disintermediation, as its name suggests, is supposed to clear lines of communication, and politically and socially it is important as an idea that indicates a reduction of intermediaries to shape and transform the flow of information between producer and recipient. As Porter (1997) and Bentivegna (2002) observe, the very practice of surfing the Web makes many of the features of newspaper, magazine and television production irrelevant, insofar as links to original documents, background material and other information previously restricted to journalists and professionals is increasingly available to more and more people.

Virtual communities

Events such as elections or the role of governments in surveillance of cyberspace may focus attention on the political uses of cyberspace, but the daily practice of participation in a public sphere is more likely to arise from being part of a virtual community.

With the emergence of the Internet into popular consciousness in the early to mid-1990s following the invention of the World Wide Web, commentators such as Howard Rheingold in *The Virtual Community* (1995) made grand claims for the potential of online or virtual communities. No longer would individuals be restricted to accidents of geography, social status, biology or ethnic identity when forming connections in cyberspace, but would instead pursue their own interests and desires. This virtual world was entirely virtuous, and Rheingold defined such communities as 'social aggregations that emerge from the net when enough people carry on those public discussions [that interest them] long enough, with sufficient human feeling, to form webs of personal relationships in cyberspace' (1995: 5). Slevin (2000: 98) sees virtual communities as part of an attempt to revitalise a sense of community in the face of 'problems of solidarity' at the end of the twentieth century.

By the end of the 1990s, opinion was becoming much more sceptical about the possibilities of online communities. Michele Wilson (1997), for example, has argued that much thinking on these groups tends to confuse community merely with communication, and that the complete withdrawal from an embodied, political and social reality results in an abstract notion of community that favours nostalgic simulacra over the messy reality of engaging with a social environment that does not conform to one's every desire. Similarly, Shawn Wilbur (1997) points out that the much-abused phrase 'virtual community' disguises the fact that we operate within not one but several notions of community, that as well as communication it involves 'immersion', usually geographical (indeed, it is notable that Rheingold's example of a transcendental online collective, The Well, was populated largely by people living near the San Francisco Bay area). At the same time, we had become used to notions of virtual community long before the arrival of the Internet, relying on communal experiences shared by letter or phone and, particularly with the advent of television, a sense of shared experience in major events such as the Olympics or World Cup. For Wilbur, then, virtual communities are not impossible but the attempt to reduce them to a single, elegant definition is less preferable to the multiple, even contradictory accounts that one encounters online and elsewhere.

The practice of virtual communities has been investigated by a number of writers, such as Susan Clerc's (1996) examination of electronic fan culture, Randal Woodland's (1995) and Nina Wakeford's (1997) discussions of the gay community online, and the work of Ananda Mitra (1997), Madhavi Mallapragada (2000) and Ellen Arnold and Darcy Plymire (2000) on different ethnic groups on the Web and in discussion groups. Such writers have uncovered a number of concerns – ethical, social and discursive – that such communities engage with. It is very difficult, therefore, if not impossible, to offer a comprehensive and elegant solution to how such virtual communities should operate.

While Rheingold's vision of a virtual community is naive, he is right to point out that for any claim to community there must be an element of persistence and group endeavour: this is not the same as permanence, for all communities eventually perish, but individual efforts, while they may participate in a wider collective, do not alone constitute evidence of a vibrant co-operative venture. As Slevin (2000: 109–10) remarks:

> I take the view that when individuals use the Internet to establish and sustain communal relationships, they do so as intelligent agents. As such, they know a great deal about the properties of the technical medium and about the constraints and capabilities afforded by the institutional contexts in which they deploy it.

Early communities

Communities in the early days of the Internet were restricted largely to academics and government bodies, particularly those involved in technical research, but as the Net expanded, particularly following the introduction of the Web in the 1990s, there was an eruption of interpersonal communication and even community online. Such expansion has often been viewed ambivalently: some early participants felt that the introduction of a third C – commerce – to the previous online ingredients of content and community has diminished the latter, but others, such as Scott Kumit, CEO of About.com, an umbrella site for hundreds of small communities, have argued the opposite, namely, that the Internet has been democratised by the expansion of the web (cited in Matthews 2001).

Beyond academia, early communities were often encouraged by commercial enterprises as a forum to encourage user participation online that could (with luck) be transformed into profitable activities. This was true, for example, of chat rooms and forums on AOL, Prodigy and CompuServe, as well as perhaps the most impressive early online environment, Habitat, developed by Lucasfilm and Quantum Computer Services (later to become AOL) in 1986. Up to 20,000 computers could access the central mainframe that stored Habitat simultaneously, making it the first electronic environment in which users would assume the role of interactive avatars (Oswald 1997).

Although the graphical environment of Habitat was extremely simple compared to today's massive multiplayer games – crude even – the possibilities of avatars, their ability to organise virtual 'houses' and engage in online elections to govern the way Habitat was run, indicated the real attraction for those taking part – the ability to participate in a virtual community. Indeed, it is frequently text-based environments, such as Usenet newsgroups and later web forums or chat rooms, that have often provided the liveliest forms of such communities. Immediacy and interactivity are more important than slick graphics. This was extremely true of one of the most important communities ever, established in 1985: The Well. The subject of Howard Rheingold's 1995 book, *Virtual Communities*, and the model for some of that author's more utopian pronouncements, The Well has been described by Katie Hafner as 'synonymous with online communication in its best, worst, and, above all, most vital forms' (1997: 100). For Hafner, the key ingredients of The Well, those which fostered a sense of 'intense connectedness', were principles of free speech, privacy and anonymity where required, these also being helped by the ability of Well members to meet (irregularly) in the Bay Area. Indeed, it is a feature of many subsequent communities which flourish that they often overlap with a physical and geographical space: some users want to connect with like minds regardless of their actual location – but, just occasionally, it helps to press the flesh.

Community and commerce

While old hands on the Net may be critical of the changes in cyberspace initiated by commercial involvement, at the same time many larger portals have been instrumental in encouraging some sense of communal engagement between users. Tripod, for example, was established in 1992 (and bought by Lycos in 1998) as a simple means of constructing homepages that is used by individuals with a common interest, as well as by business users. Similarly, companies such as AOL and Yahoo! are keen to create a community spirit among subscribers, particularly through media such as chat rooms and shared sites.

There is, as Matthews (2001) points out, an ulterior motive for community content: it is one means of encouraging 'stickiness' that will return users to a site (and advertisers on that site). For Hagel and Armstrong (1997), online communities would be the next 'killer applications' on the Web, an estimate that led Yahoo! to pay $4.5 billion for GeoCities in 1999. As Andy Greenman of The Yankee Group has pointed out, however, the community spirit of such ventures may be dubious: 'A lot of their community talk is hype. Sometimes they are just bundling together a few tools and proclaiming a new community. In fact, the most successful communities tend to emerge organically and unofficially' (Cited in Matthews 2001: 121).

The conflict between communal interests and commercial will became clear following the Yahoo! takeover of GeoCities, when Yahoo! had to climb down over an implicit claim that it owned copyright over any material hosted on its community sites. Another insight into such potential conflicts has been offered by Theresa Senft (2000), who was hired by Prodigy in 1997 to be a community leader for Prodigy Internet. While Senft admitted that there were some problems with the idea of a commercial virtual community, not least of which were that The Well was a 'notorious money-loser' and the difficulties around whether computer-mediated communication constituted a community, she agreed to a proposal to host a 'Baud Behavior' community.

For Prodigy, suggests Senft, the branding of specific communities was merely a form of fetishistic commodity 'magic', whereby loyal customers would identify themselves with the brand, and expenditure on the brand provided 'the sacrifices large American corporations make to grow richer' (Senft 2000: 190). To work, the brand must not only bring together like minds (imitation) but also a desire to communicate on similar subjects (contact). Unfortunately for both her and Prodigy, Baud Behavior never gelled as a community. Senft's own analysis, however, is not that communities cannot be engineered, but that in order to be successful they must combine imitation with the much more elusive contact.

Ecommerce and consumerism

A chapter on the public sphere is certainly not the only place to consider the role of ecommerce, but it does represent an important way of considering theoretically how such buying and selling online affects that sphere: Habermas' agora, it must be remembered, was the marketplace for the city, or *polis*. It has long been established in other areas of media studies that the impact of such things as advertising and consumerism has been immense on the publishing and broadcasting industries, and the same is very true of the Internet. In the words of John Phelan (1998), for many media organisations the public sphere has merely become that place where they can 'sell consent'.

While the similarities between the Internet and other media are extremely obvious, there have also been some important differences at the end of the twentieth century. First of all, the explosion of dotcom mania (and greed) and its subsequent collapse happened in an extremely compressed period, barely five years after the first stirrings of interest in Netscape's initial stock floatation to the initial signs of collapse. The rapidity of this eruption of hugely inflated stock valuations has tended to obscure an alternative argument that had gained ground during the 1980s and early 1990s, namely, that a value of the Net as a medium was that if not exactly free of the consumerism of other media it was at least not controlled by the large commercial organisations that dominated other areas of mass communication.

Utopian visions of cyberspace as a non-capitalist environment have been foolish since the Internet was transferred from academic and governmental to commercial hands, an event that was required to fund the extension of the Internet to more than a handful of privileged users. As we shall see in the next chapter, however, cyberspace has played an important role in the organisation of anti-capital protest, as well as the extension of global capitalist economics. It is also important to recognise that cyberspace as a commercial environment is not the result of an automatic evolution, but emerged very clearly from decisions made in the early and mid-1990s that have had important repercussions on its development.

From academy to industry

When Bolt Beranek and Newman (BBN) began work on the infrastructure of ARPANET in 1968, the prototype of what was to become the Internet was conceived of as a purely governmental and academic network. Indeed, even as late as 1980 BBN was dependent on government contracts for nearly 80 per cent of its revenues – which resulted in trouble for the company when the US federal government accused it of conspiring to overcharge (Hafner and Lyon 1996: 259). Throughout the 1980s, the Internet remained a largely academic system, providing (expensive) connections for researchers and scientists in universities and government departments around the world, but, particularly following the introduction of the Web, more and more users wished to connect, and it was unlikely that this would happen with the levels of investment provided by the federal government.

In 1991, the National Science Foundation, responsible at that time for maintaining the infrastructure of the Internet, lifted restrictions on the commercial use of the Net. Throughout the 1980s, a number of companies had grown rich supplying the Internet with the software and hardware required to run it, but now other entrepreneurs would be able to capitalise on new technologies by taking their business online. With the burden of responsibility for maintaining the Net transferred from the NSF to a mixture of governmental and commercial bodies in 1993, commerce in cyberspace became less of an opportunity and more of an imperative for those companies such as IBM, WorldCom and MCI involved in extending the Net to the masses.

In its current form, ecommerce is largely a high-tech version of mail order: a purchase is made online and then goods are shipped to the consumer. A more radical variation is what is known as edistribution, where those goods are delivered electronically. Obviously, edistribution only works with certain items that can be digitised, such as software, videos or music (clothes and food in bits are unlikely to be appealing). Companies such as the Tornado Group (part of Cable & Wireless), Sony and Microsoft are currently working on edistribution systems, for example, the Tornado system, using virtual 'tickets' to release items from electronic vaults for third parties.

The international nature of ecommerce, however, creates its own problems. For example, an EC Electronic Commerce Directive (2000) backs the principle of 'country of origin'; that is, customers are bound by the trading laws of the country where the selling country resides. However, a conflicting Brussels Regulation says that legal disputes should be dealt with according to legislation in the country where the customer resides. MEPs are concerned to balance the needs of businesses with the rights of consumers, although many businesses are concerned that they could be sued in every country where they do business.

Another problem for the dotcom economy has come in the form of payment: while most transactions take place via credit card, these are insufficient for very small, or micro, payments, or for purchases from individuals or small companies that may not have a merchant agreement in place with a credit card company. Several alternatives sprang up in the late 1990s to provide alternative forms of currency, such as beenz, but these failed because consumers did not require alternative currencies, simply ways of exchanging the dollars, pounds or euros they had in their pockets and bank accounts. As a result, systems such as PayPal (www.paypal.com) and a smaller, UK version, Nochex (www.nochex.com), have developed as means of transferring money online.

Dotcom mania

The seeds for ecommerce were sown in 1991, when the NSF allowed companies to use the Internet for business, but this lifting of restrictions did not result in a sudden flurry of activity. While cyberspace was slowly moving from being an academic to a commercial medium, its primary participants were still likely to be researchers, students and engineers. Until the mid-1990s, there simply were not enough consumers online to make ecommerce viable. Quantum Computer Services, later to become AOL, had been established in 1985, but its virtual malls were still proprietary (and thus restricted) spaces.

An important change was announced with the launch of Amazon.com, which went live in July 1995. Founded by Jeff Bezos, Amazon was not the first company to start trading online, but Bezos agreed a series of important decisions that were to make ecommerce an important reality. First of all, Bezos decided to sell books because the inventory was huge – hundreds of thousands of titles, only a few of which could be carried in a typical store. This meant that Amazon.com attempted to provide many more titles from its warehouses – combining bits with atoms – in a move that meant it could match most orders, but which also resulted in almost crippling debts for the company (Bayers 1999).

None the less, Amazon.com trail-blazed key features of the subsequent dotcom economy, such as personalisation (recommendations and mass customisation), the move to one-stop, all-in-one portals, and just-in-time inventories or, as with 'etailers' such as Buy.com, zero inventory, reselling goods from other distributors.

Within five years, the dotcom phenomenon had exploded: by the beginning of 1999, Amazon.com which had been floated with a market cap of $503 million was valued at more than $22 billion – and this a company with losses of $85 million. Indeed, Amazon was only able to post a small profit in 2002, and this only by using pro forma practices that allowed certain expenses to be deferred. None the less, thousands of companies and individuals jumped aboard the gravy train, spurred on by analysts' predictions of stratospheric and long-lived growth. In the words of Peter Schwartz, co-founder of the Global Business Editor, and Peter Leyden, a features editor at *Wired*:

> We are watching the beginnings of a global economic boom on a scale never experienced before. We have entered a period of sustained growth that could eventually double the world's economy every dozen years and bring prosperity for – quite literally – billions of people on the planet. We are riding the early waves of a 25-year run of a greatly expanding economy that will do much to solve seemingly intractable problems like poverty and to ease tensions throughout the world. And we'll do it without blowing the lid off the environment.
>
> (Schwartz and Leyden 1997: 116)

Schwartz and Leyden's twenty-five year boom barely lasted for five, and with the benefit of hindsight it is extremely easy to mock bitterly the view that global capitalism would ease tensions, poverty and environmental disaster while making more billionaires than ever. The 'New Economy', much vaunted by *Wired* and similar publications during the late 1990s, would harness technology to exploit and promote rapid growth as part of open, global integration. A new economy required new rules, such as the importance of branding over revenue, the idea being that – as with Microsoft's dominance of the desktop – the company that became a household name would be able to reclaim vast revenues in the future.

In fact, the new economy was obeying some very old economy laws. The success of the US markets during the 1980s and, after a slump in the early 1990s, throughout the rest of that decade, meant that investors were unlikely to receive a particularly good return on investment in traditional companies: rates of profitability were slowly decreasing, a phenomenon of capitalism that had been recognised since the mid-nineteenth century at least (Heller 2001). Furthermore, the increased tendency to value a company by its share price, rather than by revenue, could not be sustained indefinitely – as indeed it was not. After a five-year boom, helped in large part by technology companies, Wall Street witnessed a $2.1 trillion loss in August 2000.

Ebusiness and the new economy

Some commentators have argued that the failures of the dotcom boom at the end of the 1990s have less to do with intrinsic failures of the new economy than simple greed on the part of investors. Indeed, in *The Internet Galaxy* (2001), Castells outlines what he sees as the fundamental ways in which a networked economy has transformed national and international economies fundamentally, while accepting that such transformations will not take place in a single leap forward.

Traditionally, observes Castells, networks may have been more flexible but have been very poor at achieving set goals, something that advances in computer technology have revolutionised. One effect of ebusiness, then, has been to implement new organisational models, based around flexible, *ad hoc* networks, which were slowly coming into effect following deregulation during the 1980s. Such network organisations are not restricted to IT and new media companies, Castells providing examples of more traditional businesses such as Valeo (a French automobile parts manufacturer) and Webcor (a US construction firm) that have consciously reorganised themselves in this way.

Castells sees five elements as essential to the success of such networked businesses, particularly those trading in the ever more important commodity of information: *scalability*, or the ability to achieve set aims with as little or as much (and no less nor more) than the network requires; *interactivity*, which for Castells means the ability to make decisions and transactions directly, without recourse to a traditional, vertically integrated management structure, without such transactions becoming lost; *management of flexibility*, best achieved by decentralising power down throughout the network; *branding*, essential as a recognised sign of value; and *customisation*, the ability to diversify on a mass scale.

The final key to the success of network business consists of its labour force, and Castells believes that labour will not disappear but become even more important as more and more information must be collated, produced and processed. The requirements from such a labour force, however, mean that it must be highly educated and self-organising – 'self-programming', is Castells' term (2001: 91). While this represents the optimistic end of the spectrum, it is probably also true that most of the jobs which require simple data entry will be much less self-programmable than Castells envisages.

Virtual stocks and shares

One feature of the dotcom boom in the late 1990s that has survived has been the proliferation of online brokers: throughout the 1980s and 1990s as a whole, particularly in the USA, more individuals than ever before began to invest money in the stock market and to take a personal interest in the performance of their shares. The quarterly APCIMS/ComPeer Survey for the end of 2001 estimated that there were 346,000 online broker accounts in the UK – a small percentage of the estimated twelve million people holding shares (many through privatisations of companies such as BT), but the practice of online trade sharing had grown by a huge degree to 30 per cent of all deals in that year.

While online brokering is a very young business, it contributed to the bullish tech market in the late 1990s as those more willing to trade online tended to be more excited about technology stocks. Such investment is riskier than investing in traditional stock markets as new products emerge and disappear very quickly, and one company tends to dominate its chosen area very quickly, as in the case of Microsoft, Intel, or Nvidia, the graphics chipset manufacturer: those backing a winner take all – but can also lose everything if they make the wrong choice.

The hyperinflation of the dotcom boom could not last in such intense conditions, and in April 2000 Internet shares dived in value: henceforth, many high-profile companies such as boo.com and boxman closed on a weekly, even daily, basis. The online research company Webmergers (www.webmergers.com) reported that 225 US dotcoms folded in 2000, doubling to 537 in 2001. Of those companies that remained trading, an increasing number such as Lastminute.com and QXL joined the '99 club', a disparaging term used to refer to those businesses that had lost 99 per cent or more of their floatation share value. As Ernst Malmsten (2002), co-founder of boo.com explained, the extremely quick growth of the business meant that although the company was valued at $390 million at its launch, spending could not be controlled as staff enjoyed lavish salaries and parties (its payroll for one month was $1.4 million).

J. David Kuo, initially an investor in and then Vice-president of Value America, an online store selling a wide range of products, explains in his book *Dot.bomb* (2002) how many people saw dotcoms as a quick and easy way to make huge amounts of money. Value America was intended as a huge cyberportal for all forms of shopping, but its unbridled optimism (and greed) covered unnecessary expenses and luxuries:

> By mid-1997, the Internet gold rush was under way, rapidly rejiggering the entire U.S. economy. Suddenly the business world was being divided into the old (people who manufactured tangible products or offered traditional services) and the new (anything that used the Internet for any part of its business). It was becoming a winner-take-all search for alchemy, as young and old, rich and poor, educated and uneducated raced to turn sand into gold. The

growing conventional wisdom was that anything Internet gave huge payouts and was therefore worth huge risks.

(Kuo 2002: 25)

Superbrands and viral marketing

One notion that emerged very early on during the craze for dotcom investments was that market share was more important than sustainable growth and revenue: even though many companies suffered an amazing burn rate, venture capitalists were – for a time at least – willing to pour good money after bad in the hope that ecommerce sites would establish themselves as 'superbrands'. The thinking was very simple: ubiquity was all. As Marc Andriessen remarked of Microsoft, 'market share now equals revenues later, and if you don't have market share now, you are not going to have revenue later. Another fundamental lesson is that whoever gets the volume does win in the end' (cited in Reid 1997: 31). Even if a company had to give its product away, or sell it at a loss, the more people using it meant that that company would be able to charge higher prices in the future. Companies such as Amazon.com and eBay pioneered this approach to superbranding, becoming what Moon and Millison (2000) refer to as 'firebrands'.

The notion behind such superbranding is that modern commerce relies not so much on the exploitation of natural resources and industrial production for a mass market that was important during the nineteenth and most of the twentieth centuries, as on what Moon and Millision, after Peter Drucker, call 'trust networks'. In contemporary networked and distributed economies, brands 'become collaborative expressions, with customers and other stakeholders . . . [delivering] new satisfactions, principally through self-service satisfactions initiated by customers and other stakeholders' (Moon and Millison 2000: 8). As consumers are faced with a proliferation of often bewildering choices, so – the argument goes – they will rely on the trust networks provided by superbrands to simplify that choice in a fast-paced electronic marketplace.

Viral marketing is another buzz-word that emerged at the turn of the millennium – a high-tech version of word of mouth, although one that typically occurs with some prompting on the part of organisations attempting to build up their brands. At its simplest, viral marketing means encouraging people to pass on a marketing message to others, usually in the form of forwarding an email and its contents to people whom they know. Marketing of this type relies on a number of incentives, whether simply the interest and entertainment built into a message, or providing prizes and rewards, for example, to the person who passes on the most contacts.

Mass customisation

One of the main promises made during the height of dotcom mania was the potential for mass customisation. While this phenomenon is not dependent purely on the Internet, the explosion of the Web at the end of the twentieth century appeared to be the perfect environment for the extension of such customisation. For the two main commentators on mass customisation, James Gilmore and Joseph Pine, companies such as Levi's and Dell had already begun working on the principle that mass-produced goods could be adapted to suit the individual requirements of personal customers, rather than insisting on selling products aimed at the average (and non-existent) customer (Gilmore and Pine 2000; Pine *et al*. 1999).

There were many sites launched in the late 1990s that paid lip-service to mass customisation, simply profiling users before suggesting pre-packaged goods for purchase. Such sites failed to offer anything more substantial than conventional ways of doing business and disappeared in the subsequent cull. Others, however, particularly in areas such as music, offered genuine customisation and innovation (for example, iPrint (www.102iprint.com), offered personalised stationery, clothing and other items). As Gilmore and Pine observe, anything that can be digitised can be customised.

Mass customisation has not fulfilled the wilder predictions that were being made in 1999 and 2000, but has brought some benefits to areas such as print on demand, for example, via the book retailer, Borders. Print on demand is not a panacea for all publishing woes, but does offer the possibility for removing some of the guesswork involved in publishing as well as keeping more titles in print.

Wider implications

Commentaries on the impact of the dotcom bubble have tended to concentrate on Internet stocks, but the wider IT market also suffered the fallout from the recession in 2001. As the Internet gold rush led to outlandish speculation rather than sound investments, the collapse of technology stocks was probably inevitable, and this collapse was not helped by the additional spend that had occurred at the end of the twentieth century as companies invested in equipment and software to avoid potential Y2K problems.

Yet short-term assessments of the damage caused by dotcom mania could be as damaging as the over-optimistic evaluations in the late 1990s, a point made by the CEO of Sun Microsystems and respected venture capitalist, Vinod Khosla, in a 2001 speech entitled 'Tech Wreck or Tech Trend'. Arguing that as companies seek to become 'realtime' enterprises, so network investments will become more important than ever before: indeed, predicted Khosla, the amount of money invested in IT will rise from 3.5 per cent to 10 per cent of sales by the end of the decade. Ultimately, according to pundits such as Khosla and others working in Silicon Valley, 'we are still in the early stages of the Internet Revolution' (Bajarin 2001: 28).

15 Ethics in cyberspace

Computer ethics and ethical theories

Many people hold a common-sense view of technology that is contradictory: that the development (if not actual progress) of information and computing technology will proceed according to its own, internal and inevitable logic, and that at the same time technology is often 'neutral' in human affairs, that it is not machines that influence our lives for better or for worse but rather the people who control them.

While ethics often overlap with morals, they are not always the same (as when we speak of professional ethics that, while they can be and often are concerned with doing good, focus more on expert and specialist practices). The question of the relation of ethics and morality is far beyond the scope of this book, but as we have seen in the previous chapter it is not uncommon for ICT to be used for bad ends. What those ends are, however, and how we determine them as bad is not necessarily always clear. As such, those concerned with the professional, technical skills involved in using cyberspace to the best of their abilities may also require a more developed sense of ethical skills. The fact, for example, that a proficient programmer can code software that circumvents the privacy of users does not automatically mean that he or she should, and while the ICT industry has more than its fair share of practitioners motivated almost entirely by money, the history of cyberspace and the Internet, as well as associated productions such as Richard Stallman's Free Software Foundation, indicate that it also attracts its share of idealists.

This chapter begins with more abstract formulations of ethical theory, which can be helpful when deciding how to proceed in cyberspace, before continuing to take a different look at hacking than in the previous chapter (which concentrated on it as a criminal activity); hacking has, in one form or another, been very important in providing a distinctive flavour to cyberspace, and has, indeed, progressed to such a stage that we may talk of a 'hacker ethic'. Finally, throughout this chapter we will consider some wider social and political issues that affect the development of cyberspace today, such as questions around who has access to new technologies, and what their impact is on society and the environment.

Ethical frameworks

A common ethical theory, one that was formulated rigorously by Jeremy Bentham in the late eighteenth and early nineteenth centuries, but which has long formed a part of 'common sense' in Western thinking, is what is known as utilitarianism. At its simplest, this consists of the maxim of 'the most good for the most people', although the application of this deceptively straightforward principle has often proved extremely difficult. In the words of John Hospers (1972), 'the main tenet of utilitarianism is the maximization of intrinsic good' (34).

Right or wrong acts, under utilitarianism, are first of all voluntary: involuntary reactions, where they cannot be controlled, are generally considered beyond the province of such an ethic. A voluntary act is one where a person could have acted differently if he or she chose to do so. Defining what good is, however, can prove to be complicated: early forms of the greatest good for the greatest number tended to define the good as happiness, yet this has generally been refined as more than the balance of happiness against unhappiness – the pleasure of ten sadists in one victim's pain does not constitute a balance for the good. Rather, utilitarian thought is neither egotistic (what is usually referred to as 'enlightened self interest') or altruistic, rather it seeks to measure potential consequences against a rational and universal principle of maximising intrinsic good. It may, indeed, be morally good for an individual to sacrifice him or herself for the sake of a community, but only if that provides the highest possible good for the greatest number of people. While utilitarians will probably consider most moral prescriptions to be good in general, none are sacrosanct and all possible routes should be considered, for example, whether murder may be sanctioned if it will prevent further mass slaughter.

In contrast to utilitarianism, many people would probably consider themselves to operate according to a certain set of rules, whether prescribed by a cultural frame of reference (usually, but not always, religious) or according to what they believe to be rational laws or instructions. To simplify, utilitarianism considers voluntary actions as a means to an end (the maximisation of intrinsic good), but the attitude known as deontological ethics, that is, an ethics of duty best espoused by Immanuel Kant in his *Lecture on Ethics* (1772) and *Groundwork of the Metaphysics of Morals* (1785), takes a very different approach. In short, certain actions and attitudes have an intrinsic or universal value which means that they should not be treated as means to other ends: for example, if it is wrong intrinsically to murder, then no amount of public happiness can justify such an act. For Kant, such universals constituted a 'categorical imperative', that one should act only according to maxims that one believes should be universal. Treating people as ends in their own right did not, for Kant, preclude punishment – we can, after all, hold them as responsible for their own conduct – but we should always treat them as agents rather than instruments of our own desires.

The distinction between a deontological ethic, the duty to obey a categorical imperative that we believe should be universal, and a utilitarian ethic, that seeks to measure and increase the amount of good in the world, is not necessarily as clear-cut as outlined above. There are also other approaches, such as existentialism or situation ethics, that share similarities with these two broad frameworks. A good introduction to the subject in relation to ICT is Ermann *et al.*'s *Computers, Ethics, and Society* (1997).

Personal and professional ethics in cyberspace

Since many activities and occupations such as publishing and medicine sought to professionalise themselves from the early nineteenth century on, we have gradually become used to the idea of professional codes of conduct for specialists such as doctors and journalists. As a much younger industry, ICT may be expected to be less mature in this respect; as was noted in the last chapter, the 'winner-takes-all' approach to the business of capturing new media markets has frequently resulted in an image of extremely aggressive capitalism. While it dealt rather crassly in thinly veiled allusions to the case of Microsoft, *Antitrust* (2001) did capture a popular caricature of the IT billionaire as antisocial monomaniac, the obverse side of the coin to the shy geek or even cool nerd that had slowly been gaining fashion throughout the 1990s. Whether or not the fictional Gary Winston or the real Bill Gates devote large sums of their wealth to philanthropic causes – as, indeed, is the case with the Bill and Melinda Gates Foundation – entrepreneurs who have accrued fantastic amounts of wealth in the past two to three decades are often perceived as demonstrating excessive levels of greed. A common (and eventually rather tiring) joke in Robert X. Cringeley's television adaptation of his book *Accidental Empires* consisted of the author listening to yet another multimillionaire's list of houses, cars and planes and telling us that he didn't feel jealous at all.

Such attitudes are by no means restricted to the computer industry, nor do they sum up that industry. *Antitrust* itself (again, crudely) posits the open source movement as a positive alternative to corporate greed: outside such black and white oppositions, professionals involved in the computing practice have sought to espouse some form of ethical conduct. Professional ethics are often concerned with best practice, ensuring that a process is conducted as effectively as possible. Tim Berners-Lee, for example, the inventor of the World Wide Web, was keen to promote open recommendations so that HTML and HTTP would be adopted as widely as possible as standards for simplifying communication and, as he recounts in *Weaving the Web* (1999), was often frustrated by the actions of companies and organisations such as the National Center for Supercomputer Applications and, later, Netscape and Microsoft when they promoted proprietary or restricted versions.

As well as individual expressions of ethical behaviour with regard to ICT, organisations such as the Association for Computing Machinery have sought to clarify professional conduct, as when the ACM drew up a Code of Ethics and

Professional Conduct in 1992. The Code (reprinted with ten not dissimilar, though slightly more tongue-in-cheek 'Commandments' from the Computer Ethics Institute in Ermann *et al.* (1997)) includes personal considerations, such as being honest and trustworthy, as well as professional considerations over such things as respecting intellectual property and adhering to competent and legal work practices (which it also notes may come into conflict with ethical considerations). Anderson *et al.* (1993: 331) observed a year after its publication that the ACM Code provided clearer guidance to the role of ICT professionals: 'While the ACM Code does not precisely prescribe what an individual must do in the situations described, it does identify some decisions as unacceptable. Often in ethical decision making many factors have to be balanced. In such situations computer professionals have to choose among conflicting principles adhering to the *spirit* of the Code as much as to the *letter*.'

Ethics, work and society

Ethical decisions are rarely (if ever) issues affecting the individual alone; indeed, the very notion of a professional code is based on the notion that the professional will have to interact with others, that his or her occupation affects the activities undertaken by others. Although Arthur and Marilouise Kroker (1996) have suggested that the tendency of ICT is to isolate individuals tapping away at their keyboards and staring into computer monitors, creating a 'bunkered self', like television (which has attracted sometimes similar criticism), everyday relationships are somewhat more complex. As Gergen suggests:

> The technology of the age both expands the variety of human relationships and modifies the older ones. When relationships move from the face-to-face to the electronic mode, they are often altered. Relationships that were confined to specific situations – to offices, living rooms, bedrooms – become 'unglued.' They are no longer confined, but can take place anywhere.
>
> (Gergen 1991: 64)

Such 'ungluing' has occurred across many media, of course: relationships confined to work and the bedroom account for a vast quantity of novels, newspaper articles, films and television soaps. Of the world of work, one of the justifications for the extension of ICT was that it would free our time from labour for other things (usually leisure, itself a major industry by the end of the twentieth century). After two decades of such promises, the increasing hours worked by those who had not been downsized during the 1980s led Tom Forester to observe: 'Computers have infiltrated many areas of our social life, but they have not transformed it. Computers have proved to be useful tools – no more, no less' (1991: 198). In addition, the extension of cyberspace has revealed how much economic propaganda some of these promises were: although research into US and German labour markets (DiNardo and Pischke 1997; Kreuger 1993) demonstrated that ICT skills could increase wages, the vast majority of such work is conducted at a much lower level, as data entry or, indeed, factory work that can be farmed out to a global 'flexible' workforce (Pearson and Mitter 1993).

The movements of global capital do not necessarily lend themselves to the worst accusations of capital: as Gloria Liu (2001) suggests, factories in Taiwan may be valued by the women who work in them because they enable them to defer other, not necessarily welcome, decisions, such as early marriage and childbirth. None the less, one of the main accusations of those critical of globalisation, particularly those who may take a lead from theorists such as Noam Chomsky or George Monbiot, ethical issues concerning the use of new technologies are necessarily concerned with a just society, particularly the role of protecting the weak.

Such issues, of course, long pre-date the technologies that contribute to cyberspace, and in terms of the global relations of labour began to assume greater importance during the eighteenth and nineteenth centuries. As ICT contributes to globalisation and capitalism, it is important that its users share some responsibility for using such technology justly, but it is now time to turn to a very different ethical perspective, one which is more peculiar to cyberspace itself.

Hacking and hacktivism

We have encountered hacking already in Chapter 13, which dealt with the typical public perception of hacking as involved with criminal – or at least antisocial – activities. Yet the term 'hacking' has also been used in conjunction with the work of figures such as Richard Stallman and other technical innovators associated with the Open Source movement. Rather than being antisocial, the investment made by such people in terms of developing new software and systems has been crucial to the development of cyberspace itself. Castells (2001), following Steven Levy and Pekka Himanen, sees hacker culture as the 'informationalism' that incubates technological breakthrough, identifying hackers as 'the actors in the transition from an academically and institutionally constructed milieu of innovation to the emergence of self-organising networks transcending organisational control' (Castells 2001: 42).

It is clear – and this point has already been made but is worth reiterating – that hacking is an ambivalent term. The term 'hacking' is almost as old as computing itself, having derived from computer enthusiasts at MIT who borrowed the term from train buffs who 'hacked' trains for better performance (Levy 2001). At root, then, a hacker was originally a person who sought to understand computers as thoroughly as possible. Very quickly, however, hacking came to be associated with 'phreaking', namely breaking into phone networks to make free phone calls, and while accessing computer systems outside allotted times may have been commercially ambiguous rather than overtly criminal, there was little doubt about the illegal nature of phreaking.

This chapter, then, will concentrate on aspects of hacking that have often been portrayed in a more positive light, particularly in terms of a 'hacker ethic' that has become very important to many participants in cyberspace. At the same time, the very ideals espoused by such an ethic raise problems with the perception of hackers. I do not believe at all that hacking is automatically a criminal activity (though it is still a useful term to describe some elements of cybercrime), but at the same time a contested site of activity that by its very nature invites discussion of what constitute criminal, indeed, ethical, actions.

The hacker ethic

The notion of a hacker ethic stems back to the activities of the original hackers at MIT and Stanford in the 1950s and 1960s, and its main points may be summarised from Levy (2001; see also Furnell 2002) as follows:

1   Access to computers should be unlimited and total.
2   All information should be free.
3   Authority should be mistrusted and decentralisation promoted.
4   Hackers should be judged solely by their skills at hacking, rather than by race, class, age, gender or position.
5   Computers can be used to create art and beauty.
6   Computers can change your life for the better.

The hacker ethic, then, fulfils three main functions: central to it is the notion of individual activity over any form of corporate authority or system of ideals; it also espouses a completely free-market approach to the trade of information and access; finally, it promotes the notion that computers can have a beneficial – indeed, life-changing – effect. Documents based on this hacker ethic have been circulating the Internet since the 1980s. While it is probably going too far to suggest that the hacker ethic is a rigorous formulation (even that it would welcome such a claim), it is clear that it at least aspires to a deontological rather than utilitarian position: aphorisms such as 'all information should be free' (or, more commonly, 'all information wants to be free') are offered as universal maxims.

  Some of the questions raised by the notion of a hacker ethic are discussed in Ermann et al.'s Computers, Ethics and Society (1997), and commentators' positions tend to polarise strongly: those concerned with opposing cybercrime, such as Power (2000), tend to position hackers as purely juvenile and irresponsible at best, overtly dangerous at worst, while at the other end of the spectrum writers such as Steven Levy, whose book Hackers: Heroes of the Computer Revolution was originally published in 1984, are much more celebratory. Alternatives are available, such as the tendency to view hackers as a (largely youthful) sub-culture, as in Dan Verton's Confessions of Teenage Hackers (2002), attracting opprobrium and fascination in equal measure, all mixed up with a large dose of misunderstanding.

Hacker manifestos

Such differences immediately make it increasingly difficult to talk of one hacker ethic, and we should be willing to admit that there is no single code that anyone described as a hacker should automatically subscribe to. However, in various statements of hacker intent, such as a document known as the *Hacker Manifesto*, or other, lesser publications, such as the *Genocide2600 Manifesto*, there are similarities based on the list printed above. The following extract from the *Hacker Manifesto* is particularly revealing:

> Did you, in your three-piece psychology and 1950s technobrain, ever take a look behind the eyes of the hacker? Did you ever wonder what made him tick, what forces shaped him, what may have molded him? I am a hacker, enter my world. . . . Mine is a world that begins with school . . . I'm smarter than most of the other kids, this crap they teach us bores me. . . . Damn under-achiever. They're all alike.
>
> . . . This is our world now . . . the world of the electron and the switch, the beauty of the baud. We make use of a service already existing without paying for what could be dirt-cheap if it wasn't run by profiteering gluttons, and you call us criminals. We explore . . . and you call us criminals. We seek after knowledge . . . and you call us criminals. We exist without skin color, without nationality, without religious bias . . . and you call us criminals. You build atomic bombs, you wage wars, you murder, cheat, and lie to us and try to make us believe that it's for our own good, yet we're the criminals.
>
> (Cited in Furnell 2002: 59–60)

The rhetoric here deserves some analysis, principally because it replicates the type of simplistic binary thinking that the *Hacker Manifesto* claims to subvert: while it is more than correct to point out that plenty of non-hackers engage in criminal and antisocial behaviour, the implicit suggestion that hackers are above this sort of thing ('*you* build atomic bombs, *you* wage wars') is laughable considering the number of hackers or former hackers who are employed as part of the military-industrial complex. At its most infantile, this is the fantasy of such films as *Hackers* (1995), *The Matrix* (1999) and the execrable *Anti-Trust* (2001), fighting the power without regard for sex, creed or colour – despite the fact that many hackers duplicate a particularly exclusivist macho culture, for all that it wears its geekiness on its sleeve.

The hacker ethic is essentially a libertarian and individualist code, a particular brand of anarchy that, at its best, fulfils some of the promises made by corporate capitalist meritocracy that are rarely achieved outside cyberspace. Vivian Sobchack (1994) makes the cutting observation that many of these 'corporate anarchists' who fly the Jolly Roger in cyberspace are precisely the people coding for the system for their day jobs. At the same time the hacker ethic indicates that cyberspace is a contested territory, and that the discourse of free-market economics and liberal democracy which has provided the foundation for much online activity is taken more seriously than corporate oligarchies which pay lip-service to an open market that they seek to monopolise: information wants to be free.

Hacker groups

It is hardly surprising that hacking has resulted in the formation of a number of loose groups or associations, particularly when viewed as an extension of political or social activism. Hacker forums include the annual Def Con convention in Las Vegas and various chapters of the 2600 group. The following are some of the most well-known groups (see Furnell (2002) and Power (2000) for more details).

Legion of Doom

Based in Chicago and formed in 1984, the LOD has housed various figures who take their names from comic-book characters (most notably the founder of the group, Lex Luthor). Involved in the theft of a BellSouth document discussed below as part of the hacker crackdown, LOD eventually disbanded in 1990, but members subsequently formed a security firm called ComSec and, after that company went bankrupt, LOD Communications Inc. Legion of Doom was also responsible for providing technical information to the hacking community in the form of 'LOD/H Technical Journals'.

Chaos Computer Club

The most high-profile hacking group outside the USA, the Chaos Computer Club was founded in Hamburg in 1984 and distinguished itself by being politically active. The most notable example of this was when the KGB enlisted members to obtain military secrets from the USA, an incident described by Clifford Stoll in *The Cuckoo's Egg* (1989). In 1996, the group demonstrated weaknesses in ActiveX technology at a time when Microsoft was attempting to drum up support for Internet home banking, and in 1998 exposed how mobile subscriber identity module (SIM) cards could be cloned. The CCC may still be accessed at berlin. ccc.de.

Masters of Deception

After being kicked out of LOD, Mark Abene (also known as Phiber Optik) formed MOD which targeted organisations such as AT&T and the Bank of America – as well as LOD. As with the former group, MOD came to an end when several members were arrested as part of Operation Sundevil in 1990.

L0pht Heavy Industries

Formed after the crackdown on groups such as Masters of Deception and Legion of Doom, L0pht included members interested in ethical hacking. L0pht specialised in exposing security flaws and cracking, releasing tools such as L0phtCrack for breaking NT passwords, but it also contacted manufacturers before making their results more widely known. In 1998, L0pht announced that it could render the entire Internet unstable (but chose not to do so) during a testimony to the US Senate Committee on Governmental Affairs. L0pht became the security firm @Stake Inc in 2000 (www.atstake.com).

Cult of the Dead Cow

Probably the most famous of hacker groups in the 1990s, cDc was actually founded in the mid-1980s and has taken an approach to hacking that is more reminiscent of West Coast countercultures such as the Discordians or Church of the Sub Genius. While not being restricted to hacking and security (cDc releases include 'My Life as Santa's Rubber-Clad Love Slave' and 'cDc's Guide to Sexually Transmitted Diseases'), the Cult of the Dead Cow is most widely known for Back Orifice, a remote administration tool that allows users to take over and control computer systems running Windows software.

The hacker crackdown

Throughout the 1980s, nascent hacking groups were perceived increasingly as a threat, especially to business. Hacking could be a useful tool for espionage, but the main problem for government, particularly in the USA, was that the hacker ethic was often at odds with commercial interests. Thus, for example, in 1990, raids were carried out against a number of hackers accused of stealing information from Bell South and crashing AT&T's computer system, an action known as Operation Sun Devil (Sterling 1992).

A more recent example of a strong reaction to the perceived commercial threat posed by hacking was the action of software giant Adobe against a Russian programmer, Dmitry Sklyarov. Sklyarov, who was employed by the Moscow security firm ElcomSoft, was attending the DefCon Hacker Conference in Las Vegas in 2001, where he was giving a seminar on insecurities in Adobe's eBook software, and had taken along copies of ElcomSoft software that could apparently crack the eBook system.

A complaint from Adobe led to Sklyarov's arrest at DefCon by the FBI, which prompted protests by conference members and the Electronic Frontier Foundation, as well as the setting up of a site (www.boycottadobe.com). Adobe backed down shortly after the outcry, although the FBI charged Sklyarov with trafficking a product designed to circumvent copyright prevention measures. Sklyarov eventually escaped prosecution, although the US Department of Justice maintained that he would testify against his employer.

Hackers are not the sole means of thinking through an ethics of cyberspace, but they probably represent the most significant contribution made by cyberspace and new technologies to our daily lives and practices. The adage that information wants to be free, and the libertarianism that it represents, has often found itself at odds with (as well as supportive of, at other times) the capitalist libertarianism that has driven forward cyberspace since the end of the twentieth century.

Glossary

....

ADSL Asymmetric digital subscriber line, offers much faster connections across standard copper phone lines.

AI Artificial Intelligence, the theory and practice of programming (human and non-human) intelligence in machines.

AOL America Online, the largest commercial online service in the world that merged with Time Warner in 2000. AOL Time Warner has become the largest media corporation to dominate the Internet.

API Application program interface, any set of routines that can be called upon by programmers to perform basic tasks, such as displaying windows or buttons.

ARPANET Advanced Research Projects Administration Network, the prototype computer network established in 1969 that laid the foundations for the Internet.

ASCII American standard code for information interchange, a set of rules enabling the exchange of text between different hardware and software.

ATM Automatic teller machine, or cash machine.

AVI Audio-Video Interleaved, a video format developed by Microsoft.

Banner advertising First developed by the *Hotwired* site, banner ads quickly became a standard-sized format for web-based promotions.

BBS Bulletin board system, originally computer text message boards that could be dialled into via a modem, BBS now tends to be used to refer to a wide variety of forum or discussion formats on the Internet.

Berners-Lee, Tim (1955–) Inventor of the World Wide Web while working at CERN (European Nuclear Research Centre), Geneva, from 1990–91. Later established the World Wide Web Consortium (W3C),in 1994 to develop universal standards for the Web.

Bit depth The number of bits assigned to an image to determine the number of colours it can display.

Bitmap A type of graphic in which the image is described pixel by pixel. Bitmap graphics tend to produce better photographic images but with larger file sizes.

Browser Program for viewing web pages: the earliest of these were text-based applications such as Lynx, but since the release of Mosaic in 1993 have nearly all been capable of displaying graphics. The browser market is currently dominated by Microsoft's Internet Explorer followed by Netscape Navigator.

Bug Any computer glitch or malfunction. The term supposedly has its origins in the story that an early programmer, Grace Murray Hopper, found a moth in one of the first computers.

CD-ROM Compact disc, read only memory, similar to audio compact disc but capable of storing between 640 and 700Mb data that can be used by a computer.

CGI Common gateway interface, a standard used to pass data dynamically between servers and clients so that it can be processed on the server and sent back to the web browser as meaningful information. Also, computer generated imagery, still and animated images created in software and usually seen as movie or television special effects.

Chat Synchronous form of communication (as opposed to asynchronous forms, such as email),where the correspondent's messages appear instantly on the screens of all participants.

CMYK A subtractive colour model using the primary colours cyan, magenta, yellow and black (the K stands for 'key plate'). These colours absorb light waves (hence subtractive),and, when mixed, produce all other hues.

Codec COmpressor/DECompressor, an algorithm or equation used to encode video and audio, typically by using a frame of video and noting only where subsequent frames differ, or by discarding information not audible to the human ear.

Cookie A small text file sent from a web server and stored on a visitor's hard drive. Cookies provide pieces of information such as dates or reference numbers that can be recalled on later visits.

Cracker Often used to distinguish between 'good' and 'bad' hackers (in that crackers break into systems to perform illegal activities). Strictly speaking, a cracker is someone who breaks encryption codes, to distribute software as warez, for example, or to gain access to credit card information.

CSS Cascading style sheet, an extension to HTML that is used to control the style and position of elements of web pages such as text. Also, the content scrambling system used to encrypt DVDs.

Cyberpunk A subgenre of science fiction that originated with Bruce Bethke's 1982 story 'Cyberpunk' and which draws much of its inspiration from William Gibson's novel of 1984, *Neuromancer*. The term is also often used to refer to technological subcultures.

Cyberspace Term coined by William Gibson in *Neuromancer* referring to the conceptual space created by new technologies. Often used as another term for the Internet.

Cybersquatting The practice of buying domain names so that they may be resold to companies for a profit.

DCT Discrete cosine transform, a compression algorithm used by JPEGS and in video compression.

Digital The storage or transmission of data in a form of discrete symbols, usually translated from electronic or electromagnetic signals as binary 0s and 1s (from the simplest state of a switch as off or on).

Directory A database of websites, such as Yahoo!, that is indexed and maintained by individuals rather than by software.

DNS Domain name system, a hierarchical system of routing IP addresses: a server looks up an address to check whether it matches a computer on the local network and, if not, passes it up the ladder to a server holding more detailed domain listings. Before DNS, every server had to store a list of the IP addresses of every computer attached to the Internet.

Domain A website's location, with endings such as .com or .co.uk that specify commercial sites (the latter associated with a geographical location), government (.gov), educational (.edu), non-profit organisations (.org), and internet related (.net), among others. In 2001, ICANN released a new set of domain names including .pro for professional users and .museum for museums.

DSL Digital subscriber line, digital communication network that offers faster speeds than analog telephone wires. See also **ADSL**.

DVD Digital versatile disc, originally digital video disk, a high-density storage medium which, as its name suggests, was first developed for video but has since come to be used for other forms of data. Although approximately the same physical dimensions as CD-ROM, DVDs can store much more information.

Ecommerce The generic term given to using the Internet (and particularly the Web) for commercial purposes. Various commentators have predicted that e-commerce will change the way we do business in our daily lives – though this has yet to materialise for most people.

Email Electronic messages sent via the Internet, usually as text but increasingly incorporating more diverse elements such as images, sound and even video. The 'killer app' of the Internet.

E-zine An online-based magazine or newsletter, usually found on the Web, that may be produced by corporate organisations or share features with print-based fanzines.

FAQ Frequently asked questions, a list of the most common queries for a newsgroup, website, software program and so on. When using a new application or joining a new group, it is considered good practice to consult any FAQs before posting/emailing queries that may have been answered several times before.

Flame The practice of sending provocative (and usually abusive) messages, typically via email or newsgroup postings.

Flash A popular format for vector graphics, animation and interactive design.

FTP File transfer protocol, a method of transferring files between computers on the Internet.

Gates, Bill (1955–) Co-founder of Microsoft with Steve Allen, and its Chief Executive from 1975 to 2000; currently Chairman and Chief Software Architect, as well as usually the richest man in the world depending on the value of Microsoft shares.

GIF Graphic interchange format, a commonly used image format which uses a palette of limited colours to keep down file sizes and which can be used with transparency and animation.

GNU A recursive acronym for GNU's Not Unix, an alternative to Unix developed under the guidance of Richard Stallman in the 1980s and 1990s as part of a free software movement. Applications developed under the GNU project are usually found as part of the Linux/GNU operating system.

Google One of the most popular sites online, Google is a search engine for the Web and newsgroups at www.google.com.

Gopher Developed at the University of Minnesota, Gopher was a precursor to the Web designed to allow users to locate information on the Internet via a system of hierarchical menus.

GPL GNU Public Licence, the copyright notice (often called Copyleft) that enables users to change open source code so long as they do not transform such code into proprietary software. Unlike public domain material, which may be taken and incorporated into proprietary systems, code available under the GPL must also be made available for other programmers to make potential changes.

GSM Originally Groupe Speciale Mobile, now Global System for Mobile Communication Governing Mobile Phone Standards.

GUI Graphical user interface, a shell that uses visual tokens (typically Windows, icons and menus) to enable input and output to the operating system.

Hacker Originally derived from the activities of model train enthusiasts who would 'hack' their models to improve performance, a computer hacker was anyone who sought to understand a system as thoroughly as possible. Increasingly the term has come to be used to mean someone who gains access to computer systems without the owner's consent (or even knowledge).

Hits The number of requests made for files to a web server such as HTML files, images and Java applets. In the early days of the Web, hits were taken to indicate the amount of visitors, whereas in fact they are very different figures.

HTML Hypertext markup language, a simple tagging language used to format pages so that they can be displayed in a browser. HTML tags use angular brackets < > to indicate such formatting information.

HTTP Hypertext transfer protocol, the series of rules (protocol) devised to pass files across the Internet.

Hyperlink A graphical or textual link that connects one document to another on the Internet.

ICT Information and communication technology, a blanket term for a wide range of new technologies and applications.

Internet The worldwide network of networks that grew out of ARPANET and other systems during the 1970s, 1980s and 1990s. The Internet connects millions of computers and their users around the globe, comprising services such as email, the Web, newsgroups and chat.

Internet Explorer Web browser released by Microsoft in 1996 based on an earlier version of Spyglass Mosaic. Subsequent development saw IE overtake its main rival, Netscape, by the end of the 1990s which in turn led to a monopoly investigation by the Department of Justice due to its inclusion or 'bundling' with Microsoft's operating system, Windows.

ISDN Integrated services digital network, a series of communication standards that provides faster communication and more efficient links across a digital network than standard phone lines.

ISP Internet Service Provider, a company that provides access to the Internet by allocating IP addresses to users at home or work.

Java A programming language developed by Sun Microsystems (called Oak in its first incarnation). The main virtue of Java for application development is that it can be written for multiple operating systems.

JPEG Joint Photographic Experts Group, a compression standard for images that results in small file sizes for images containing up to 16.7 million colours.

LAN Local area network, any wired or wireless network connecting computers in the same vicinity.

Linux Linux, invented by Linus Torvalds in 1990, is often used to refer to an alternative and increasingly popular operating system to Windows. Linux is, strictly speaking, the kernel, the drivers that communicate between software and hardware, with the operating system consisting of this kernel and GNU applications. Linux is part of the Open Source movement, meaning that not only can it be downloaded and distributed for free, but its source code is fully available to anyone for modification.

Listserv Servers that maintain mailing lists for automated distribution of email topics.

LZW Lempel Ziv and Welch, a compression algorithm used in GIFs.

Metasearch A search engine that builds its results by scanning the indexes of other search engines.

Microsoft Founded by Bill Gates and Paul Allen in Albuquerque, New Mexico, in 1975, Microsoft has grown into the world's largest software company responsible for Windows, Internet Explorer and Office among other applications.

MIME Multipurpose Internet email extensions. Series of instructions enabling a browser to interpret different types of information.

Modem MODulator/DEModulator, a device that converts digital signals into analog signals (and vice versa) that may be communicated across a telephone line.

Mosaic The first widely available graphic web browser.

MP3 Or MPEG1 Audio Layer 3, an audio format that compresses sound between 4:1 and 12:1 by discarding information which is inaudible to the human ear. MP3s have become a popular format for distributing music across the Internet.

MPEG Moving Pictures Expert Group, the organisation responsible for international standards for compression of streaming video and data. MPEG is commonly used to refer to a type of highly compressed video used in DVDs and on the Internet.

MUD and MMORPG Multi-user domain, massively multiplayer online role-playing game. MUDs are online role-playing environments which, until recently, tended to be text-based but are becoming increasingly visual. MMORPGs are a recent innovation, allowing thousands of users to role-play online.

Netscape Navigator The browser developed by Marc Andriessen and the main product of the company he co-founded with Jim Clark, Netscape, which led the dotcom phenomenon before being bought by AOL. The main competitor to Microsoft's Internet Explorer.

Newsgroups Public form of bulletin board, typically found on Usenet, where users can post messages that are widely read and responded to.

ODBC Open database connectivity, a protocol established by Microsoft that enables databases to communicate with each other and other programs.

Opera An alternative browser to Internet Explorer and Netscape Navigator.

PBX Private branch exchange, standard for transferring telephone calls between local/national lines and a large organisation with its own telephone system.

PDA Personal digital assistant, also known as a handheld or mobile computer, which offers computing facilities in a small format.

Plug-in Software that is used to extend the functionality of an application, typically a browser, enabling it to view certain file types or communicate with other users.

PNG Portable network graphics, an image file format that supports transparency and higher colour depths than GIF, and has also been designed to reduce differences in appearance on PCs and Macs.

Portal A website that aims to be the starting point for all Internet-based activity such as email, web browsing and news. Typical portals are MSN and Yahoo!

QuickTime A video format and application developed by Apple.

RealAudio/RealVideo Audio and video standards developed by Real.com that provide streaming material as quickly as possible.

SAX Simple API for XML, a tool for parsing XML documents in order to read and reformat information in such documents.

Search engine A search facility that indexes websites using 'spiders' or 'robots', applications that scan pages to build databases of content.

Server A computer that provides client machines with shared resources such as printers, files or web pages.

SGML Standard generalized markup language, a meta-language that defines how other markup languages (such as HTML) format information.

Spam Junk email sent to multiple recipients simultaneously and which is usually unwanted and unsolicited mail.

SVG Scalable vector graphics, open standards competitor to Macromedia's flash format for displaying and distributing vector (line) images online.

UNIX An operating system developed in the late 1960s and early 1970s between General Electric, AT&T Bell Laboratories and MIT. Used to support telephony systems and networking systems, UNIX gradually became the backbone of the Internet, supported by its later imitator, Linux.

URL Uniform resource locator (occasionally Universal resource locator), the individual address that is used to locate files on the Web.

Usenet Established at Duke University in 1979, Usenet is the largest collection of newsgroups arranged into hierarchical groups such as rec., comp., alt. and misc. Although not strictly part of the Internet, Usenet is largely accessed via ISPs.

Vector graphics Unlike Bitmaps, vector graphics describe an image in terms of the positions of elements, their direction and shape. They usually produce smaller file sizes than bitmaps and, although they tend not to be useful for photographic reproduction they can be scaled to any size without pixellation.

VOIP Voice-over-IP, protocol for transferring telephone voice messages across an Internet-compatible network.

WAIS Wide area information servers, an older protocol for retrieving information from networks.

Web Or World Wide Web, the collection of sites that use HTML and HTTP to connect to each other and accessed via a browser.

Well Whole Earth 'Lectronic Link, an online community established in 1985 for the San Francisco area and which has since grown into an international forum.

WYSIWYG What you see is what you get, a phrase used to refer to visual editors that display what the page actually looks like as you work on it.

XML eXtensible markup language, an extension of SGML that enables web designers to define the logic of the content in their pages, which may then be passed to and analysed by other applications.

Yahoo! Directory founded by David Filo and Jerry Yang in 1994 and one of the first collections of links to useful sites on the web. Yahoo! has since grown into a major portal offering a range of services such as news, shopping and email.

Web resources

The following links may also be supplemented at *The Cyberspace Handbook* website (www.producing.routledge.com/cyberspace/resources.htm). Other links may also be found in Chapter 8.

Education and reference

Ask Jeeves – www.ask.com. A directory that responds quite well to natural language searches.

Babel – babelfish.altavista.com/tr. Web-based translation service.

BBC Learning Zone – www.bbc.co.uk/education/izone. Online resources aimed particularly at those wishing to learn new hobbies or skills.

BOOKNews – www.booknews.co.uk. Information on new publications.

Click2Learn –www.click2learn.com. Online training for companies requiring structured e-learning.

Dogpile – www.dogpile.com. One of the better meta-search engines that trawls through other sites.

Euractiv – www.euractiv.com. A database of events and information in the EU.

Fast – www.alltheweb.com. Quick search engine that is used by many other sites.

FreeTranslation – www.freetranslation.com. Web-based translation service.

Google – www.google.com. The best search engine on the Web, particularly as you can search images and newsgroups.

Infobel – www.infobel.com/uk/. Useful for finding names and addresses in the UK.

InterTran – www.tranexp.com:2000. Web-based translation service.

LearnDirect – www.learndirect.co.uk. Computer hardware and software training.

MedNet – www.mednets.com. Database of medical information.

National Grid for Learning – www.ngfl.gov.uk. Collection of education resources.

NETg – www.netg.com. Corporate online training provider.

Northern Light – www.northernlight.com. Particularly useful site for students as it links to reports and articles.

Premier IT – www.premierit.co.uk. Professional online training and certification provider.

Search Engine Colossus – www.searchenginecolossus.com. List of online search engines and databases.

Systran – www.systransoft.com. Web-based translation service.

Yahoo! – www.yahoo.com. The first directory and still one of the best for structured searches of information in a particular area.

Zetoc – zetoc.mimas.ac.uk. List of tables of contents from journals, based on the British Library's electronic data.

New media and web development

Adobe – www.adobe.com. Developer of PhotoShop, Premiere and other multimedia and web technologies.

Ben's Planet – www.bensplanet.com. A complete HTML reference guide.

Big Info – www.biginfo.net. A complete webmaster resource website.

DVD Forum – www.dvdforum.org. Official website for the DVD Forum.

ECTF – www.magnet.at/telework/ectf.htm. European Assembly on Teleworking.

Helpdesk – web.canlink.com/helpdesk. HTML support.

Home automation site – www.smarthome.com. Information on computerising the home.

IBM – www.ibm.com. One of the most important innovators in computing.

Internet Content Rating Association – www.icra.org. Information on rating sites for sex, violence and bad language.

Macromedia – www.macromedia.com. Developer of Flash and other Internet and multimedia technologies.

Microsoft – www.microsoft.com. Site of technologies and services provided by the most important software company in the world.

Netmechanic – www.netmechanic.com. NetMechanic monitors errors on your site with an HTML validator.

OpenDVD.org – www.opendvd.org. Resource for developers looking to make use of DVD technology independently of the DVD Forum.

Perl.org and Perl.com – www.perl.org and www.perl.com. Official sites for the Practical extraction and reporting language.

PHP.net – www.php.net. Official site for PHP: Hypertext preprocessor.

Python.org – www.python.org. Official site for the Python programming language.

The Register – www.theregister.co.uk. News and gossip site for new technologies.

Sun Microsystem's Java – java.sun.com. Official site for the cross-platform Java language.

Telework Association – www.tca.org.uk. Information on teleworking.

Web Developer – www.webdeveloper.com. Links to other sites providing information and guidance.

Web Monkey – hotwired.lycos.com/webmonkey. A good web developer's resource.

Web Reference – www.webreference.com. FAQs, articles and resources for web design.

Internet and Web

Association of Internet Professionals – www.association.org. Site for technical professionals working with the Internet.

Blogger – www.blogger.com. Host site for web logs (blogs).

The Bloggies – www.bloggies.com. Awards to best blogs of the year.

CAIDA – www.caida.org. Cooperative Association for Internet Data Analysis.

CIO.com – www.cio.com/metrics. Various online statistics from Cio.com.

Digital divide – www.digitaldivide.gov. US government initiatives to overcome 'digital poverty'.

Domain wars – www.domainwars.com. Information on administration and registration systems on the Net.

ECAUCE – www.euro.cauce.org. European campaign against unsolicited commercial email.

History of the Internet – www.netvalley.com/intval.html. A history of the Internet with links to other relevant sites.

How the Internet came to be – www.bell-labs.com/user/zhwang/vcerf.html. Contribution by Vince Cerf.

Internet Providers UK – alt.internet.providers.uk. Newsgroup that keeps track of British ISPs.

International Telecommunication Union – www.itu.net. Geneva-based organisation that agrees such things as modem standards.

Internet and web history – www.elsop.com/wrc/h_web.htm. Histories and biographies of important figures.

Internet Corporation for Assigned Names and Numbers – www.icann.org. Site of the body responsible for domain name registration.

Internet Engineering Task Force – www.ietf.org. Site of the organisation responsible for Internet standards.

The Internet Society – www.isoc.org. Promotes Internet development.

Live Journal – www.livejournal.com. Host site for web logs (blogs).

MAPS – www.mail-abuse.org. Blackhole listing for reporting spam sites.

Open Relay Blackhole Zones – www.orbz.org. Blackhole listing for reporting spam sites.

Open Relay Database – www.ordb.org/faq. List of mail servers used to forward spam.

Spamhaus – www.spamhaus.org. Blackhole listing for reporting spam sites.

SPEWS – www.spews.org. Blackhole listing for reporting spam sites.

WAP Forum – www.wapforum.org. Organisation responsible for development of wireless application protocols and wireless markup language (WML).

World Wide Web Consortium – www.w3c.org. Responsible for technical standards governing the Web.

News and entertainment

ABC Electronic – www.abce.org.uk. The online arm of the Audit Bureau of Circulation.

Advanced Television Enhancement Forum – www.atvef.com. A cross-industry alliance of companies representing broadcast and cable companies.

Advanced Television Systems Committee – www.atsc.org. An international organisation that develops voluntary standards for advanced television systems.

Always Independent Films – www.alwaysindependentfilms.com. Independent short movies, including early classic silent movies.

Atom Films – www.atomfilms.com. Film distributor and showcase for online short movies.

BBC Online – www.bbc.co.uk. Web and broadband services for the BBC, and the largest site in Europe.

Bijoucafe – www.bijoucafe.com. Independent and cult movie showcase.

CBS News.com – www.cbnews.com. Online site for CBS television network.

C-NET – www.cnet.com. American cable and online content provider.

DFilm – www.dfilm.com. Festival site for web movies.

Digital Spy – www.digitalspy.co.uk. Reference site for digital media and entertainment news.

Digital Television Group – www.dtg.org.uk. News and information on digital television worldwide.

Drew's Script-O-Rama – www.script-o-rama.com. Large collection of movie scripts and transcripts.

Exposure – www.exposure.co.uk. Advice and guidance on independent film-making.

Film Education – www.filmeducation.org. Resources for film studies.

Gamespot – gamespot.com. ZDNet's game site.

Heavy – www.heavy.com. Broadband content specialising in music videos.

Hypnotic – www.hypnotic.com. Showcase for experimental short movies.

iFilm – www.ifilm.com. One of the best-known sites for online movies.

International Film – www.internationalfilm.org. Critical articles on world cinema.

Movie Critic – www.moviecritic.com. Interactive site for rating and recommending movies.

Reelscreen – www.reelscreen.com. New and archive movies based on the work of British film-makers.

RESFEST – www.resfest.com. US-based online digital film festival.

Urban Entertainment – www.urbanentertainment.com. Black culture site for US filmmakers.

Variety – www.variety.com. Site for Hollywood news and gossip.

Wired.com – www.wired.com. Portal for *Wired* magazine, Wired technology newswire and *HotWired* online magazine.

Bibliography

Aarseth, Espen (1997), *Cybertext: Perspectives on Ergodic Literature*, Baltimore, MD, and London: Johns Hopkins University Press.

'ABC Electronic will begin auditing user numbers, which means that accurate audience numbers for streamed audio/video and live web casts soon will be available' (2001), *New Media Age*, 12 April.

Adediran, Peter (2002), *A Practical Guide to Business, Law and the Internet*, London: Kogan Page.

Aiken, Billy (2002), 'The Future of History?', *Personal Computer World*, 25.5, pp. 90–2.

Akass, Clive (2001), 'The Humbling of a Giant', *Personal Computer World*, 24.11, pp.22–3.

Akass, Clive (2002), 'Wan View of Multimedia Services', *Personal Computer World*, 25.2, p.23.

Akass, Clive (2003), 'Limits of CMOS – and the Alternatives', *Personal Computer World*, 26.3, p.27.

Akass, Clive and Middleton, John (2002), 'Cyber-war Fears are Alarmist, Say Experts', *Personal Computer World*, 25.1, p.16.

Alderman, John (2001), *Sonic Boom: Napster, P2P and the Battle for the Future of Music*, London: Fourth Estate.

Anderson, Benedict (1983), *Imagined Communities*, London: Verso.

Anderson, Ronald E., Johnson, Deborah G., Gotterbarn, Donald and Perrolle, Judith (1993), 'Using the New ACM Code of Ethics in Decision Making', *Communications of the ACM*, reprinted in M. David Ermann, Mary B. Williams and Michele S. Schauf (eds), *Computers, Ethics and Society*: 323–33.

Arnold, Ellen and Plymire, Darcy (2000), 'The Cherokee Indians and the Internet', in David Gauntlett (ed.), *Web.Studies*, London: Arnold, pp. 186–93.

Atton, Chris (2002), *Alternative Media*, London: Sage.

Bajarin, Tim (2001), 'Don't Jump Out of the Window Yet', *Personal Computer World*, 24.8, p.28.

Ballaster, Ros (ed.) (1991), *Women's Worlds: Ideology, Femininity and the Women's Magazine*, Basingstoke: Macmillan.

Barlow, John Perry (2000), 'The Next Economy of Ideas', *Wired*, 8.10, pp. 240–52.

Bayers, Chip (1999), 'The Inner Bezos', *Wired*, 7.3, pp. 114–21.

'BBC heralds new interactive era' (2001), www.bbc.co.uk/hi/english/entertainment/new_media/newsid_1643000/1643259.stm, 7 November.

Beer, Stafford (1994), *Decision and Control*, New York: John Wiley & Sons.

Bell, David (2001), *An Introduction to Cybercultures*, London: Routledge.

Bell, David and Kennedy, Barbara (eds) (2000), *The Cybercultures Reader*, London and New York: Routledge.

Bentivegna, Sara (2002), 'Politics and New Media', in Leah Lievrouw and Sonia Livingstone (eds), *The Handbook of New Media*, London: Sage, pp. 50–61.

Bereano, Philip (1984), 'Technology and Human Freedom', *Science for the People*, November/December, pp. 132–43.

Berger, Matt (2002), 'It's Macromedia 1, Adobe 1 in Patents Face-off', *Digit*, 49, p. 18.

Berners-Lee, Tim (1999), *Weaving the Web*, London: Orion.

Boczkowski, Pablo J. (2002), 'The Development and Use of Online Newspapers: What Research Tells us and What We Might Want to Know', in Leah Lievrouw and Sonia Livingstone (eds), *The Handbook of New Media*, London: Sage, pp. 270–86.

Bolter, Jay David (1991), *Writing Space: The Computer, Hypertext, and the History of Writing*, New York: Lawrence Erlbaum.

Bonchek, Mark (1997), 'From Broadcast to Netcast: the Internet and the Flow of Political Information'. www.ai.mit.edu/people/msb/thesis.

Boulware, Jack (2002), 'Pirates of Kiev', *Wired*, 10.3, pp. 113–15.

Bradner, S. (1996), Internet Standards Process, RFC 2026, October, www.ietf.org/rfc/rfc2026.txt.

Brewer, Wendy and Alveranga, Siman (2002), 'Next-generation PCs', *PC Advisor*, February, pp. 54–62.

Brice, Richard (2002), *Newnes Guide to Digital Television*, Oxford: Butterworth-Heinemann.

Briggs, A. (1985), *The BBC: The First 50 Years*, Oxford: Clarendon Press.

'Broadcasting: Past, Present and Future' (2001), news.bbc.co.uk/hi/english/in_depth/entertainment/2001/broadcasting/.

Bromley, Michael (1997), 'The End of Journalism? Changes in Workplace Practices in the Press and Broadcasting in the 1990s', in Michael Bromley and Tom O'Malley (eds), *A Journalism Reader*, London: Routledge, pp. 330–50.

Bulkeley, Kate (2002), 'Tune in, Turn on – Or Else', *Guardian*, 28 January.

Caldwell, John Thornton (ed.) (2000), *Theories of the New Media: A Historical Perspective*, London: Athlone Press.

Carrier, Rebecca (1998), 'Training the Information-poor in an Age of Unequal Access', in Bosah Ebo (ed.), *Cyberghetto or Cybertopia: Race, Class and Gender on the Internet*, New York: Praeger.

Carter, Dave (1997), '"Digital Democracy" or "Information Aristocracy"? Economic regeneration and the information economy', in Loader (ed.), *The Governance of Cyberspace*, pp. 136–52.

Cassy, John and Wells, Matt (2002), 'Death of a Dream, but Nightmare is Far From Over', *Guardian*, 28 March.

Castells, Manuel (1996–98), *The Information Age*, 3 vols, Oxford: Blackwell.

Castells, Manuel (2001), *The Internet Galaxy*, Oxford: Oxford University Press.

Chandler, Daniel (1997), *Writing Oneself in Cyberspace*, www.aber.ac.uk/~dgc/homepgid.html.

Chandler, Daniel (1998), *Personal Home Pages and the Construction of Identities on the Web*, www.aber.ac.uk/~dgc/webident.html.

Chapman, Gary (1994), 'Taming the Computer', in Dery (ed.), *Flame Wars*, pp. 297–319.

Charlesworth, Andrew (2001), 'Stop Faking It', *PC Advisor*, 69, pp. 160–5.

Cheung, Charles (2000), 'A Home on the Web: Presentations of Self on Personal Home Pages', in Gauntlett (ed.), *Web.Studies*, pp. 43–51.

Clerc, Susan (1996), 'Estrogen Brigades and the "Big Tits" Thread', in L. Cherny and E. Reba Wise (eds), *Wired Women: Gender and New Realities in Cyberspace*, Seattle: Seal Press. Reprinted in David Bell and Barbara Kennedy (eds), *The Cybercultures Reader*, London and New York: Routledge, pp. 216–29.

Collins, Richard and Murroni, Christina (1996), *New Media, New Policies*, Cambridge: Polity Press.

Cone, Edward (2002), 'The Naked Truth', *Wired*, 10.2, pp. 100–3.

Connery, Brian (1997), 'IMHO: Authority and Egalitarian Rhetoric in the Virtual Coffeehouse', in Porter (ed.), *Internet Culture*, pp. 161–80.

Cooper, Mark (2000), *Disconnected, Disadvantaged, and Disenfranchised: Explorations in the Digital Divide*, New York: Consumer Federation of America.

Cornford, J. and Robins, K. (1999), 'New Media', in Stokes, J. and Reading, A. (eds), *The Media in Britain: Current Debates and Developments*, London, Macmillan, pp. 108–25.

Cringeley, Robert X. (1996), *Accidental Empires*, London: Penguin.

Cubitt, Sean (1998) *Digital Aesthetics*, London: Sage.

Curran, James (1998), 'Rethinking the Media as a Public Sphere', in Peter Dahlgren and Colin Sparks (eds), *Communication and Citizenship*, London and New York: Routledge.

Curran, James and Seaton, Jean (1997), *Power Without Responsibility: The Press and Broadcasting in Britain*, London: Routledge.

Dahlgren, Peter and Sparks, Colin (eds) (1998), *Communication and Citizenship: Journalism and the Public Sphere*, London and New York: Routledge.

Davis, Erik (2001), 'The Fellowship of the Ring', *Wired*, 9.10, pp. 120–32.

Davis, Erik (2002), 'Songs in the key of F12', *Wired*, 10.5, pp. 96–101.

Deans, Jason (2001), 'A Date with Davina'. *Guardian*, 21 May.

De Landa, Manuel (1991), *War in the Age of Intelligent Machines*, New York: Zone Books.

Denzin, Norman (1997), *Interpretive Ethnography: Ethnographic Practices for the Twenty First Century*, London: Sage.

Dery, Mark (ed.) (1994), *Flame Wars: The Discourse of Cyberculture*, Durham, NC: Duke University Press.

Dery, Mark (1996), *Escape Velocity: Cyberculture at the End of the Century*, London: Hodder & Stoughton.

Deutsch, Peter (2000), 'Archie – A Darwinian Development Process', *IEEE Internet Computing*, 4.1, www.computer.org/internet/v4n1/deutsch.htm, 21 August.

di Filippo, JoAnn (2000), 'Pornography on the Web', in Gauntlett, *Web.Studies*, pp. 122–9.

DiNardo, John E. and Pischke, Jorn-Steffen (1997), 'The Returns to Computer Use Revisited: Have Pencils Changed the Wage Structure Too?', *Quarterly Journal of Economics*, 112.1, pp. 291–303.

Dodge, Martin and Kitchin, Rob (2001a), *Mapping Cyberspace*, London: Routledge.

Dodge, Martin and Kitchin, Rob (2001b), *Atlas of Cyberspace*, London and New York: Addison Wesley.

Doull, Matthew (1997), 'Journalism into the Twenty-First Century', in Michael Bromley and Tom O'Malley (eds), *A Journalism Reader*, London: Routledge, pp. 273–7.

Duncombe, Stephen (1997), *Notes from Underground: Zines and the Politics of Alternative Culture*, London: Verso.

Dunsire, Andrew (1993), 'Modes of Governance', in Jan Kooiman (ed.), *Modern Governance: New Government Society Interactions*, London: Sage.

Dyer, Adele (2001), 'No More Mr Nice Guy', *Personal Computer World*, 24.8, p.30.

Dyke, Greg (2000), 'A Healthy and Competitive Europe Depends on Strong Digital Public Service Broadcasters', www.bbc.co.uk/info/news/news218.htm, 31 January.

Edwards, Paul N. (1997), *The Closed World*, Cambridge, MA: MIT Press.

Ellis, Desmond (1984), 'Video Arcades, Youth, and Trouble', *Youth and Society*, 16.1, pp. 47–65.

English, Simon (2002), 'The Fat Lady Sings Napster's Swansong', *Daily Telegraph*, 5 September, p. 40.

Ermann, David, Williams, Mary and Schauf, Michelle (eds) (1997), *Computers, Ethics and Society*, Oxford: Oxford University Press.

Evans, Russell (2001), 'Making Web Movies', *Computer Arts*, 65, pp. 26–30.

Fearon, David (2002), 'PCW Expert: 3D Graphics', *Personal Computer World*, 25.6, pp. 133–44.

Ferguson, Marjorie (1983), *Forever Feminine: Women's Magazines and the Cult of Femininity*, London: Heinemann.

Fielding, N.G. and Lee, R.M. (1998), *Computer Analysis and Qualitative Research*, London: Sage.

Fisher, Marc (2000), 'Low Power to the People', *American Journalism Review*, October.

Flichy, Patrice (1995), *Dynamics of Modern Communication: The Shaping and Impact of New Communication Technologies*, London: Sage.

Flichy, Patrice (2002), 'New Media History', in Lievrouw and Livingstone, *The Handbook of New Media*, pp.36–50.

Frasca, Gonzalo (2001), *Videogames of the Oppressed*, MA thesis, www.jacaranda. org/frasca/thesis/

Freund, Jesse (1999), 'Listen Up', *Wired*, 7.03, pp. 138–9.

Furnell, Steven (2002), *Cybercrime: Vandalizing the Information Society*, Boston, MA, and London: Addison-Wesley.

Gann, Roger (2001), 'The Threat from Without', *Personal Computer World*, 24.10, pp. 128–32.

Gann, Roger (2002), 'The Officeless Office', *Personal Computer World*, 25.5, pp. 86–9.

Garfinkel, Simson (2000), *Database Nation: The Death of Privacy in the 21st Century*, Cambridge: O'Reilly.

Garrison, Ednie Kaeh (2000), 'U.S. Feminism-Grrrl Style! Youth (Sub)cultures and the Technologics of the Third Wave', *Feminist Studies*, 26, p. 1.

Garton, Laura, Haythornthwaite, Caroline and Wellman, Barry (1999), 'Studying On-Line Social Networks', in Jones (ed.), *Doing Internet Research*, pp. 75–105.

Gates, Bill (1995), *The Road Ahead*, London: Penguin.

Gauntlett, David (ed. 2000a), *Web.Studies*, London: Arnold.

Gauntlett, David (2000b), 'The Web goes to the Pictures', in Gauntlett, *Web.Studies*, pp. 82–7.

Gergen, Kenneth J. (1991), *The Saturated Self*, New York: Basic Books.

Gibson, Owen (2001), 'Growing Pains', *Media Guardian*, 3 September, p. 60.

Gibson, William (1984), *Neuromancer*, London: Victor Gollanz.

Gibson, William (1996), *Idoru*, London: Viking.

Gilmore, James and Pine, Joseph (2000), *Market of One: Creating Customer-Unique Value through Mass Customization*, Boston, MA: Harvard Business School Press.

Gleick, James (1987), *Chaos: Making a New Science*, London: Viking.

Graham, Gordon (1999), *The Internet:// A Philosophical Inquiry*, London and New York: Routledge.

Greenfield, Patricia (1984), *Media and the Mind of the Child: From Print to Television, Video Games and Computers*, Boston, MA: Harvard University Press.

Griffiths, Mark (1997), 'Video Games and Children's Behaviour', in Tony Charlton and Kenneth David (eds), *Elusive Links*, Cheltenham: Park Published Papers.

Gunther, Marc (2001), 'Sony's Boogie Knight', *Fortune*, 19 March.

Hacker, K.L. (1996), 'Missing Links: The Evolution of Electronic Democratization', *Media, Culture & Society*, 18, pp. 213–22.

Haddon, Leslie (1999), 'The Development of Interactive Games', in Hugh MacKay and Tim O'Sullivan, *The Media Reader*, London: Sage, pp. 305–27.

Hafner, Katie (1997), 'The Epic Saga of The Well', *Wired*, 5.05, pp. 98–142.

Hafner, Katie and Lyon, Matthew (1996), *Where Wizards Stay Up Late: The Origins of the Internet*, New York: Simon & Schuster.

Hagel, John and Armstrong, Arthur (1997), *Net Gain: Expanding Markets through Virtual Communities*, Boston, MA: Harvard Business School Press.

Hall, Jim (2001), *Online Journalism: A Critical Primer*, London: Pluto Press.

Hammond, R (1995), 'You Ain't Seen Nothing Yet', *UK Press Gazette*, 27 November, p. 37.

Hand, John (2000), 'Madonna Gig: Webcast Review', *BBC Online*, news.bbc.co.uk/hi/english/entertainment, 29 November.

Haraway, Donna (1991), *Simians, Cyborgs and Women: The Reinvention of Nature*, London: Free Association Press.

Hartley, John (1982), *Understanding News*, London: Routledge.

Hayles, Katherine (1996), 'Boundary Disputes: Homeostasis, Reflexivity and the Foundations of Cybernetics', in Robert Markley (ed.), *Virtual Realities and Their Discontents*, pp. 12–40.

Heim, Michael (1991), 'The Erotic Ontology of Cyberspace', in Benedikt (ed.), *Cyberspace: First Steps*, pp. 59–80.

Heller, Robert (2001), 'Return of the Silverback', *Business 2.0*, 9 February, pp. 109–14.

Herman, Andrew and Swiss, Thomas (eds) (2000), *The World Wide Web and Contemporary Cultural Theory*, London and New York: Routledge.

Herman, Edward and McChesney, Robert (1997), *Global Media: The New Missionaries of Corporate Capitalism*, Leicester: Continuum.

Herman, Leonard (1998), *Pheonix: The Fall and Rise of Videogames*, Union, NJ: Rolenta Press.

Hermes, Joke (1995), *Reading Women's Magazines*, Cambridge: Polity Press.

Herz, J.C. (1997), *Joystick Nation*, London: Abacus.

Hicks, Wynford, Adams, Sally and Gilbert, Harriett (1999), *Writing for Journalists*, London: Routledge.

Holt, Morgan (2000), 'The Whole World is Watching', *Guardian*, 10 July.

Hospers, John (1972), *Human Conduct: Problems of Ethics*, London: Harcourt Brace & Co. Extract reprinted in Ermann, Williams and Schauf (eds) (1997), *Computers, Ethics and Society*, pp. 33–41.

Howe, Jeff (2001), 'Licensed to Bill', *Wired*, 9.10, pp. 140–9.

Huizinga, Johannes (1930), *Homo Ludens: A Study of the Play Element in Culture*, New York: Roy Publishers.

Hyde, Gene (2002), 'Independent Media Centers Cyber-subversion and the Alternative Press', *First Monday*, www.firstmonday.DK/Issues/issue7_4/Hyde/.

Jackson, Tim (1997), *Inside Intel*, London: HarperCollins.

Jenkins, Henry (1992), *Textual Poachers: Television Fans and Participatory Culture*, London: Routledge.

Johnson, Bobbie (2002), 'We Can Provide For You', *Media Guardian*, 9 September, p. 50.

Johnson, Steven (1997), *Interface Culture: How New Technology Transforms the Way We Create and Communicate*, San Francisco: Harper Edge.

Jones, A.J. (2000), *Game Theory*, Chichester: Horwood Publishing.

Jones, Steve (ed.) (1999a), *Doing Internet Research: Critical Issues and Methods for Examining the Net*, London: Sage.

Jones, Steve (1999b), 'Studying the Net: Intricacies and Issues', in Jones (ed.), *Doing Internet Research*, pp. 1–27.

Katz, Jon (1997), 'The Digital Citizen', *Wired*, 5.12, pp. 68–82.

Keeble, Richard (1998), *The Newspapers Handbook* (2nd edn), London: Routledge.

Keighron, Peter (2002), 'Digital Strategy – Will C4 Stick to its Digital Guns?', *Guardian*, 11 January.

Keizer, Greg (2000), 'The Best and Worst ISPs', *PC World*, November, pp. 148–62.

Kellner, Douglas (2002), 'New Media and New Literacies: Reconstructing Education for the New Millennium', in Lievrouw and Livingstone (eds), *The Handbook of New Media*, pp. 90–104.

Kenner, Rob (1999), 'My Hollywood', *Wired*, 7.10, pp. 214–21.

Kidner, Sarah (2001), 'War of the Web', *PC Pro*, 82, p. 55.

Kinder, Marsha (1991), *Playing with Power in Movies, Television and Video Games from Muppet Babies to Teenage Mutant Ninja Turtles*, Berkeley: University of California Press.

Kreuger, Alan B. (1993), 'How Computers Have Changed the Wage Structure: Evidence from Microdata, 1984–89', *Quarterly Journal of Economics*, 108.1, pp. 33–60.

Kroker, Arthur and Kroker, Marilouise (1996), *Hacking the Future: Stories for the Flesh-eating 90s*, Montreal: New World Perspectives.

Kroker, Arthur and Weinstein, Michael (1994), 'The Theory of the Virtual Class', reprinted in Caldwell (ed.) (2000), *Theories of the New Media*, pp. 117–36.

Küng-Shankleman, Lucy (2000), *Inside the BBC and CNN: Managing Media Organisations*, London: Routledge.

Kuo, J. David (2002), *Dot.bomb: Inside an Internet Goliath – from Lunatic Optimism to Panic and Crash*, London: Random House Business Books.

Kuptz, Jerome (2000), 'Independence Array', *Wired*, 8.10, pp. 236–7.

Kurzweil, Ray (1999), *The Age of Spiritual Machines*, London: Orion.

Ladner, Sam (2001), Simon Fraser University's School of Communications in Canada, www.sfu.ca/~sladner/.

Laing, Gordon (2001), 'The State of the Art', *Personal Computer World*, 24.11, pp. 168–74.

Landauer, Thomas (1995), *The Trouble with Computers*, Cambridge, MA: MIT Press.

Landow, George (1992), *Hypertext: The Convergence of Contemporary Critical Theory and Technology*, Baltimore: Johns Hopkins University Press.

Landow, George (1997), *Hypertext 2.0*, Baltimore: Johns Hopkins University Press.

Lasica, J.D. (2001), 'Party's Over for Web Freelancers', *Online Journalism Review*, ojr.usc.edu, 27 April.

Laurel, Brenda (1993), *Computers as Theater*, London: Addison Wesley.

Lax, Stephen (2000), 'The Internet and Democracy', in Gauntlett (ed.), *Web.Studies*, pp. 158–69.

Le Diberder, Alain and Le Diberder, Frédéric (1996), *L'Univers des jeux video*, Paris: Editions.

Lessig, Lawrence (2001), 'May the Source be with You', *Wired*, 9.12, pp. 78–82.

Levy, Steven (2001), *Hackers: Heroes of the Computer Revolution* (2nd edn), London: Penguin.

Lievrouw, Leah and Livingstone, Sonia (eds) (2002), *The Handbook of New Media*, London: Sage.

Liu, Gloria Zhang (2001), *Chinese Culture And Disability: Information For U.S. Service Providers*, Center for International Rehabilitation Research Information and Exchange, cirrie.buffalo.edu/china.html.

Loader, Brian D. (ed.) (1997), *The Governance of Cyberspace*, London and New York: Routledge.

Lovelock, Peter and Ure, John (2002), 'The New Economy: Internet Telecommunications and Electronic Commerce?', in Lievrouw and Livingstone (eds), *The Handbook of New Media*, pp. 350–68.

McCarthy, Kieren (2000), 'M$ Pays Madonna $0m for Online Gig', *The Register*, www.theregister.co.uk/content/archive/14857.html, 20 November.

McCarthy, Kieren (2001), 'Madonna Webcast Company Hits the Wall', *The Register*, www.theregister.co.uk/content/7/23212.html, 5 December.

McConnaughey, James and Lader, Wendy (1998), *Falling Through the Net II: New Data on the Digital Divide*, Washington, DC: US Department of Commerce, www.ntia.doc.gov/ntiahome/net2/falling.html.

McIntosh, Neil and Schofield, Jack (2002), 'Tom's Toys', *G2*, 22 July, pp. 4–5.

McKay, Jenny (2000), *The Magazines Handbook*, London: Routledge.

MacKenzie, Donald and Wacjman, Judy (1999), *The Social Shaping of Technology* (2nd edn), Buckingham: Open University Press.

McLaughlin, Thomas (1996), *Street Smarts and Critical Theory: Listening to the Vernacular*, Madison: University of Wisconsin Press.

McLuhan, Marshall (1964), *Understanding Media: The Extensions of Man*, New York: McGraw Hill.

McNair, Brian (1996), *News and Journalism in the UK* (2nd edn), London: Routledge.

Machlup, Fritz (1962), *The Production and Distribution of Knowledge in the United States*, Princeton, NJ: Princeton University Press.

Magee, Mike (2001), 'Names Behind the Names', *Personal Computer World*, 24.10, p. 30.

Magee, Mike (2002), 'Down But Far From Out', *Personal Computer World*, 25.1, p. 32.

Mallapragada, Madhavi (2000), 'The Indian Diaspora in the USA and Around the Web', in Gauntlett (ed.), *Web.Studies*, pp. 179–85.

Malmsten, Ernst (2002), *Boo Hoo: A Dot.com Story from Creation to Catastrophe*, London: Random House Business Books.

Mariano, Gwendolyn (2000), 'Madonna Webcast shows Internet is not TV', *C-NET Tech News*, news.cnet.com/news/0-1005-200-3890055.html, 28 November.

Martin, Hugo (2001), 'An Autumn Chill', *Digital News*, p. 22.

Matthews, Guy (2001), 'Community Spirit', *Personal Computer World*, 24.10, pp. 118–22.

Miller, Vincent (2000), 'Search Engines, Portals and Global Capitalism', in Gauntlett (ed.), *Web.Studies*, pp. 113–21.

Mitchell, Stewart (2002), 'Porn Brokers', *PC Pro*, 91, pp. 173–7.

Mitchell, William J. (1992), *The Reconfigured Eye*, Cambridge, MA: MIT Press.

Mitra, Ananda (1997), 'Virtual Commonality: Looking for India on the Internet', in Steven Jones (ed.), *Virtual Culture*, London: Sage, pp. 55–79.

Moon, Michael and Millison, Doug (2000), *Firebr@nds: Building Brand Loyalty in the Internet Age*, Berkeley, CA: Osborne.

Morrish, Jon (1996), *Editing for Magazines*, London: Routledge.

Moschovitis, Christos, Poole, Hilary, Schuyler, Tami and Senft, Theresa (1999), *History of the Internet: A Chronology, 1843 to the Present*, Santa Barbara, CA: ABC Clio.

Munt, Sally R. (ed.), (2001), *Technospaces: Inside the New Media*, London and New York: Continuum.

Murray, Janet (1997), *Hamlet on the Holodeck*, New York: Free Press.

Nasaw, David (1993), *Going Out: The Rise and Fall of Public Amusements*, New York: Basic Books.

Naughton, John (1999), *A Brief History of the Future: The Origins of the Internet*, London: Weidenfeld & Nicolson.

Naylor, Richard, Driver, Stephen and Cornford, James (2000), 'The BBC Goes Online: Public Service Broadcasting in the New Media Age', in Gauntlett, (ed.), *Web.Studies*, pp. 137–48.

Negroponte, Nicholas (1995), *Being Digital*, London: Hodder & Stoughton.

Nelkin, Dorothy (1994), 'Information Technology Could Threaten Privacy, Freedom and Democracy', in Ermann *et al.* (eds), *Computers, Ethics and Society*, pp. 20–32.

Nielsen, Jakob (2000), *Designing Web Usability: The Practice of Simplicity*, New Riders.

Nott, Tim (2002), 'PCW Expert: Encryption', *Personal Computer World*, 25.9, pp. 123–35.

OECD (2000), *A New Economy? The Changing Role of Innovation and Information Technology in Growth*, Paris: OECD. electrade.gfi.fr.

Oleson, Virginia (1994), 'Feminisms and Models of Qualitative Research', in Norman Denzin and Yvonna Lincoln, *Handbook of Qualitative Research*, London: Sage.

O'Leary, T. (1993), 'Terrestrial Digital Audio Broadcasting in Europe', *EBU Technical Review*, spring, pp. 19–26.

Orwell, George (1981), *A Collection of Essays*, London: Harcourt and Brace.

Oswald, Michael (1997), 'Virtual Urban Futures', in David Holmes (ed.), *Virtual Politics*, London: Sage, pp. 37–45.

Packan, Paul (1999), *'Pushing the Limits'*, *Science*, 285, pp. 2079–81.

Parker, Donn (1998), *Fighting Computer Crime: A New Framework for Protecting Information*, New York: John Wiley & Sons.

Pearson, Ruth and Mitter, Swasti (1993), 'Employment and Working Conditions of Low-skilled Information-processing Workers in Less Developed Countries', *International Labour Review*, 132.1, pp. 49–64.

Phelan, John M. (1998), 'Selling Consent: The Public Sphere as a Televisual Market-Place', in Dahlgren and Sparks (eds), *Communication and Citizenship*, pp. 75–93.

Phillips, Patrick (2001), 'Global Media Hit by Attacks on US', *Europemedia.net*, www.europemedia.net/shownews.asp?ArticleID=9038.

Pilati, Antonio and Libbey, John (1993), *Media Industry in Europe (MIND)*, London, Paris, Rome: Institute of Media Economics.

Pine, B. Joseph, Davis, Stan and Pine II, B. Joseph (1999), *Mass Customization: The New Frontier in Business*, Boston, MA: Harvard Business School Press.

Poole, Steven (2000), *Trigger Happy: The Inner Life of Videogames*, London: Fourth Estate.

Poole, Steven (2001), 'Tooled Up, But Not Turned On', *Guardian*, online, 28 June.

Porter, David (ed.) (1997), *Internet Culture*, London and New York: Routledge.

Postman, Neil (1990), 'Informing Ourselves to Death', in Ermann, Williams and Schauff (eds), *Computers, Ethics and Society*, pp. 128–36.

Powell, Thomas (2000), *Web Design: The Complete Reference*, Indianapolis, IN: Que.

Powell, Thomas (2001), *The Complete Reference HTML*, Berkeley, CA: Osborne/McGraw Hill.

Power, Richard (2000), *Tangled Web: Tales of Digital Crime from the Shadows of Cyberspace*, Indianapolis, IN: Que.

Raab, Charles D. (1997), 'Privacy, Democracy, Information', in Loader (ed.), *The Governance of Cyberspace*, pp. 155–74.

Radway, Janice (1984), *Reading the Romance: Women, Patriarchy, and Popular Literature*, Chapel Hill: University of North Carolina Press.

Rawlinson, Nik (2002), 'Watching the Detectives', *Personal Computer World*, 25.3, p. 36.

Raymond, Eric (2001), *The Cathedral and the Bazaar*, Cambridge: O'Reilly.

Reid, Robert H. (1997), *Architects of the Web: 1,000 Days that Built the Future of Business*, New York: John Wiley & Sons.

Rheingold, Howard (1991), *Virtual Reality: Exploring the Brave New Technologies of Artificial Experience and Interactive Worlds from Cyberspace to Teledildonics*, London: Secker and Warburg.

Rheingold, Howard (1995), *The Virtual Community: Finding Connection in a Computerized World*, London: Minerva.

Rheingold, Howard (2000), 'Community Development in the Cyberspace of the Future', in Gauntlett (ed.), *Web.Studies*, pp. 170–7.

Rice, Ronald E. (2002), 'Primary Issues in Internet Use: Access, Civic and

Community Involvement, and Social Interaction and Expression', in Lievrouw and Livingstone (eds), *The Handbook of New Media*, pp. 105–29.

Roof, Judith (2001), 'Depth Technologies', in Munt (ed.), *Technospaces*, pp. 21–37.

Rosner, Hillary (2001), 'Network: A Very Different View of Genoa', *Guardian*, London, 30 July, p. 5.

Ross, Susan (2001), *Writing for your Website*, London: Pearson Education.

Rushkoff, Douglas (2002), 'Signs of the Times', *Guardian*, online, 25 July, p. 6.

Scannell, P. and Cardiff, D. (1982), 'Serving the Nation: Public Service Broadcasting Before the War', in B. Waites, T. Bennett and G. Martin (eds), *Popular Culture: Past and Present*, London: Croom Helm, pp. 161–88.

Schramm, Wilbur (1977), *Big Media, Little Media: Tools and Technologies for Instruction*, Beverly Hills, CA: Sage.

Schwartz, Peter and Leyden, Peter (1997), 'The Long Boom', *Wired*, 5.7, pp. 115–29.

SEL Network (2001), 'Sony's Gateway to Success', *Winter*, BSSC.sel.sony.com/news/network/index.html.

Senft, Theresa M. (2000), 'Baud Girls and Cargo Cults', in Andrew Herman and Thomas Swift (eds), *The Worldwide Web and Contemporary Cultural Theory*, London and New York: Routledge, pp. 183–206.

Sheff, David (1993), *Game Over: Nintendo's Battle to Dominate Videogames*, New York: Random House.

Sherman, Barrie and Judkins, Phil (1992), *Glimpses of Heaven, Glimpses of Hell: Virtual Reality and its Implications*, London: Hodder & Stoughton.

Sherman, Chris and Price, Gary (2001), *The Invisible Web: Uncovering Information Sources Search Engines Can't See*, Medford, NJ: Cyberage Books.

Silberman, Steve (1999), 'G-Force: George Lucas Fires up the Next Generation of Star Warriors', *Wired*, 7.5, pp. 126–35.

Silver, David (2000), 'Cyberculture Studies 1990–2000', in Gauntlett (ed.), *Web.Studies*, pp. 19–30.

Slack, Jennifer Daryl and Wise, J. MacGregor (2002), 'Cultural Studies and Technology', in Lievrouw and Livingstone (eds), *The Handbook of New Media*, pp. 485–501.

Slevin, James (2000), *The Internet and Society*, London: Polity Press.

Smith, Jackie (2001), 'Cyber Subversion in the Information Economy', *Dissent*, 48.2, pp. 48–52.

Sobchack, Vivian (1994), 'New Age Mutant Ninja Hackers: Reading *Mondo 2000*', in Dery (ed.), *Flame Wars*, pp. 11–28.

Sosnoski, James J. (1999), 'Configuring as a Mode of Rhetorical Analysis', in Jones (ed.), *Doing Internet Research*, pp. 127–43.

Stallman, Richard (1985), *The Gnu Manifesto*, reprinted in Ermann *et al.* (eds) (1997), *Computers, Ethics and Society*, pp. 229–39.

Standage, Tom (1998), *The Victorian Internet*, London: Weidenfeld and Nicolson.

Star, Leigh (1999), 'The Ethnography of Infrastructure', *American Behavioral Scientist*, 43.3, November/December, pp. 377–91.

Stein, Laura and Sinha, Nikhil (2002), 'New Global Media and Communication Policy: The Role of the State in the Twenty-First Century', in Lievrouw and Livingstone (eds), *The Handbook of New Media*, pp. 410–31.

Stephenson, Hugh and Bromley, Michael (eds) (1998), *Sex, Lies and Democracy*, London and New York: Longman.

Sterling, Bruce (1992), *The Hacker Crackdown: Law and Disorder on the Electronic Frontier*, London: Penguin.

Stoll, Clifford (1989), *The Cuckoo's Egg*, New York: Doubleday.

Sudweeks, Fay and Simoff, Simeon J. (1999), 'Complementary Explorative Data Analysis: The Reconciliation of Quantitative and Qualitative Principles', in Jones (ed.), *Doing Internet Research*, pp. 29–55.

Swift, Caroline (2000), 'Magnetic Chips Pack Super-PC Power', *Personal Computer World*, 23.5, p.58.

Taylor, Philip M. (2000), 'The World Wide Web Goes to War: Kosovo 1999', in Gauntlett (ed.), *Web.Studies*, pp. 194–201.

Tepper, Michele (1997), 'Usenet Communities and the Cultural Politics of Information', in Porter (ed.), *Internet Culture*, pp. 39–54: p.40.

Tetzlaff, David (2000), 'Yo-Ho-Ho and a Server of Warez', in Andrew Herman and Thomas Swiss (eds), *The World Wide Web and Contemporary Cultural Theory*, London and New York: Routledge, pp. 99–126.

Thompson, J.B. (1990), *Ideology and Modern Culture: Critical Theory in the Era of Mass Communication*, Cambridge: Polity Press.

Thornton, Sarah (1995), *Club Cultures: Music, Media and Subcultural Capital*, Oxford: Polity Press.

Tsagarousianou, Roza, Tambini, Damian and Bryan, Cathy (eds) (1998), *Cyber-democracy: Technology, Cities and Civic Networks*, London and New York: Routledge.

Tufte, Edward R. (1997), *Visual Explanations: Images and Quantities, Evidence and Narrative*, Cheshire, CT: Graphics Press.

Tunstall, Jeremy and Palmer, Michael (1991), *Media Moguls*, London: Routledge.

Tynan, Daniel (2002), 'Spam Inc.', *PC World*, August, pp. 107–11.

Umesao, Tadeo (1963), *Information Industry Theory: Dawn of the Coming Era of the Ectodermal Industry*, Tokyo: Asahi Hoso.

Urry, John (1990), *The Tourist Gaze: Leisure and Travel in Contemporary Societies*, London: Sage.

Verton, Dan (2002), *The Hacker Diaries: Confessions of Teenage Hackers*, New York: Osborne.

Wakeford, Nina (1997a), 'Cyberqueer', in Andrew Medhurst and Sally Munt (eds), *Lesbian and Gay Studies: A Critical Introduction*, London: Cassell. Reprinted in Bell and Kennedy (eds), *The Cybercultures Reader*, pp. 403–15.

Wakeford, Nina (1997b), 'Networking Women and Grrrls with Information/ Communication Technology', in Jennifer Terry and Melodie Calvert (eds), *Processed Lives: Gender and Technology in Everday Life*, London: Routledge, pp. 51–66.

Wakeford, Nina (2000), 'New Media, New Methodologies: Studying the Web', in Gauntlett (ed.), Web.Studies, pp. 31–41.

Wallace, James and Erikson, Jim (1994), Hard Drive: Bill Gates and the Making of Microsoft, New York: John Wiley.

Weber, Jack (2000), 'Profile: Harold Cohen', PC Pro, 65, pp. 220–7.

Wells, Matt (2002), 'BBC Pledges to Sharpen Focus on Arts', Guardian, 19 January.

Wertheim, Margaret (1999), The Pearly Gates of Cyberspace, London: Virago.

Whittaker, Jason (2002a), The Internet: The Basics, London: Routledge.

Whittaker, Jason (2002b), Web Production for Writers and Journalists, London: Routledge.

Wilbur, Shawn (1997), 'An Archaeology of Cyberspaces: Virtuality, Community, Identity', in Porter (ed.), Internet Culture, pp. 5–22.

Williams, Huw (2002), 'Two Can Play That Game', Guardian, 19 December.

Wilson, Michele (1997), 'Community in the Abstract: A Political and Ethical Dilemma', in Bell and Kennedy (eds), The Cybercultures Reader, London and New York: Routledge, pp. 644–57.

Winder, Davey (2001), 'Talking Technology', PC Pro, 77, pp. 214–21.

Winder, Davey (2002), 'War Games: The Truth', PC Pro, 96, pp.155–61.

Winston, Brian (1998), Media Technology and Society, A History: From the Telegraph to the Internet, London: Routledge.

Wise, Richard (2002), Multimedia: A Critical Introduction, London: Routledge.

Woodland, Randal (1995), 'Queer Spaces, Modem Boys and Pagan Statues', in Works and Days, 13.1–2, reprinted in Bell and Kennedy (eds), The Cybercultures Reader, pp. 416–31.

Wray, Richard (2002), 'Is This Lights Out for the Internet?', Guardian, online, 11 July, pp. 1–3.

Wyman, Bill (2000), 'Reality Flops: Who Screwed Up "Big Brother"? Everyone', Salon.com, www.salon.com/ent/tv/feature/2000/09/29/bb_final/index.html, 29 September.

Young, Margaret Levine (1999), The Complete Reference Internet, Millennium Edition, Berkeley, CA: Osborne/McGraw Hill.

Zickmund, Susan (1997), 'Approaching the Radical Other: The Discursive Culture of Cyberhate', in S. Jones, Virtual Culture, London: Sage, pp. 185–205.

Index

....